"How do 'we' move beyond the Eurocentric, hetrosexist and humanistic binds of international law? As much critical scholarship has demonstrated, it is not through more law. This wide-ranging collection, written by some of the most exciting thinkers of international law and posthumanism, provides readers with ways of thinking otherwise – ways out of the binds. This is critique as hope."

Maria Elander, *La Trobe University, Australia*

"The chapters of this book offer, each in their specific manner and through different angles, multi-directional answers, provide examples and illustrations of what is at stake. They share one, empowering belief, which I take as axiomatic, namely that posthuman legal thought aims to critique the humanistic, Eurocentric, normative and heterosexist core of legal theory and practice, in order to make it more inclusive and less discriminatory. In so doing, they make room for the non-human, more-than-human entities, agents and subjects of our posthuman times. The intertwined critiques of humanism and anthropocentrism serve to illuminate contemporary patterns of power, subjugation, injustice and exploitation. And to offer ways out."

Rosi Braidotti, *Utrecht University, the Netherlands*

INTERNATIONAL LAW AND POSTHUMAN THEORY

Assembling a series of voices from across the field, this book demonstrates how posthuman theory can be employed to better understand and tackle some of the challenges faced by contemporary international law.

With the vast environmental devastation being caused by climate change, the increasing use of artificial intelligence by international legal actors and the need for international law to face up to its colonial past, international law needs to change. But in regulating and preserving a stable global order in which states act as its main subjects, the traditional sources of international law – international legal statutes, customary international law, historical precedents and general principles of law – create a framework that slows down its capacity to act on contemporary challenges, and to imagine futures yet to come. In response, this collection maintains that posthuman theory can be used to better address the challenges faced by contemporary international law. Covering a wide array of contemporary topics – including environmental law, the law of the sea, colonialism, human rights, conflict and the impact of science and technology – it is the first book to bring new and emerging research on posthuman theory and international law together into one volume.

This book's posthuman engagement with central international legal debates, prefaced by the leading scholar in the field of posthuman theory, provides a perfect resource for students and scholars in international law, as well as critical and socio-legal theorists and others with interests in posthuman thought, technology, colonialism and ecology.

Matilda Arvidsson is Associate Professor in International Law and Assistant Senior Lecturer in Jurisprudence at the University of Gothenburg, Sweden.

Emily Jones is an NUAcT Fellow based at Newcastle Law School, Newcastle University, UK.

INTERNATIONAL LAW AND POSTHUMAN THEORY

Edited by Matilda Arvidsson and Emily Jones

Routledge
Taylor & Francis Group
a GlassHouse Book

Designed cover image: Eakarat Buanoi / © Getty Images

First published 2024
by Routledge
4 Park Square, Milton Park, Abingdon, Oxon OX14 4RN

and by Routledge
605 Third Avenue, New York, NY 10158

Routledge is an imprint of the Taylor & Francis Group, an informa business

A GlassHouse book

British Library Cataloguing-in-Publication Data
A catalogue record for this book is available from the British Library

Library of Congress Cataloging-in-Publication Data
Names: Arvidsson, Matilda, editor. | Jones, Emily, 1990– editor.
Title: International law and posthuman theory / edited by Matilda Arvidsson and Emily Jones.
Description: Abingdon, Oxon [UK] ; New York, NY : Routledge, 2024. | Includes bibliographical references and index.
Identifiers: LCCN 2023037334 (print) | LCCN 2023037335 (ebook) | ISBN 9781032658025 (hardback) | ISBN 9781032044040 (paperback) | ISBN 9781032658032 (ebook)
Subjects: LCSH: International law. | International law—Philosophy. | Posthumanism. | Humanism. | Agent (Philosophy)
Classification: LCC KZ3410 .I57825 2024 (print) | LCC KZ3410 (ebook) | DDC 341.01—dc23/eng/20231002
LC record available at https://lccn.loc.gov/2023037334
LC ebook record available at https://lccn.loc.gov/2023037335

ISBN: 978-1-032-65802-5 (hbk)
ISBN: 978-1-032-04404-0 (pbk)
ISBN: 978-1-032-65803-2 (ebk)

DOI: 10.4324/9781032658032

Typeset in Sabon
by Apex CoVantage, LLC

The Open Access version of chapter 9 was funded by London School of Economics.

The Open Access version of chapter 11 was funded by University of Victoria.

CONTENTS

CONTRIBUTORS

Matilda Arvidsson is Associate Professor in International Law and Assistant Senior Lecturer in Jurisprudence at the University of Gothenburg, Sweden. Her research is interdisciplinary and includes AI and law, international law, feminism, posthumanism and technology, as well as the embodiment of law in its various forms and in interspecies relations.

Rosi Braidotti is Distinguished University Professor Emerita at Utrecht University, the Netherlands. She received honorary degrees from Helsinki and Linköping. She is a Fellow of the Australian Academy of the Humanities and a member of the Academia Europaea. Her main publications include *Nomadic Subjects* (2011), *Nomadic Theory* (2011), *The Posthuman* (2013), *Posthuman Knowledge* (2019) and *Posthuman Feminism* (2022).

Maneesha Deckha is Professor and Lansdowne Chair in Law at the University of Victoria in British Columbia, Canada, where she directs the Animals & Society Research Initiative. Her research expertise includes critical animal law, ecofeminist theory and postcolonial theory. She is the author of *Animals as Legal Beings: Contesting Anthropocentric Legal Orders*.

Anna Grear is an Adjunct Professor of Law, University of Waikato, New Zealand. Her research is located within a combination of critical legal theory and jurisprudence, with a focus on the relationship between human rights and the environment, and on the theme of legal subjectivity, locating these in relation to contemporary globalization and to a central concern with the implications of the materiality of the living order – including the theme of lived embodiment.

Oscar Guardiola-Rivera is Professor of Political Philosophy and Human Rights at Birkbeck College, University of London, UK. He's working on an ethnographic chronicle titled *Diary of the Twenty-First Century Years of Plague* with Juan F. Garcia, and *Marx Club*, a mix of dance and a critique of finance. The second part of his fiction trilogy *Night of the World* is due early next year with The 87 Press.

Vanja Hamzić is Reader in Law, History and Anthropology at SOAS University of London, UK. His legal, anthropological and historical research addresses issues in human subjectivity formation – especially those related to gender, sexual, class, race, linguistic and religious difference.

Gina Heathcote is Professor of Public International Law at Newcastle Law School, UK. Gina's research focuses on collective security, the law on the use of force and the international law of the sea, developed with a queer feminist methodology that applies interdisciplinary, postcolonial, posthuman and intersectional frames in dialogue.

Jessie Hohmann is Associate Professor of Law at the University of Technology Sydney Faculty of Law, Sydney, Australia. Her research encompasses the objects and material culture of international law, Indigenous Peoples and international law, and housing as a human right.

Emily Jones is an NUAcT Fellow based at Newcastle Law School, Newcastle University, UK. Emily's work cuts across feminist and queer theory and international law; posthuman legal theory; international environmental law; the law of the sea; technology and international law; and political economy, colonialism and international law.

Kojo Koram is Senior Lecturer in Law at Birkbeck School of Law, University of London, UK. In 2022, he published his debut book *Uncommon Wealth: Britain and the Aftermath of Empire*.

Hedvig Lärka is a doctoral candidate in international law and tax law at the University of Gothenburg, Sweden.

Jasmijn Leeuwenkamp is a doctoral candidate in philosophy at the University of Amsterdam, the Netherlands. Her research focuses on anthropocentrism in human rights and explores the interrelations between political philosophy, ecology and rights-based environmental protection strategies. She has written on topics such as posthumanism, religion and ecology, and colonialism in ideas of nature.

Delaney Mitchell is a PhD student and Mellon-Chancellor Fellow in the Department of Anthropology at the University of California Berkeley, USA. She holds an MSc from the London School of Economics, UK, and LLM from SOAS University of London, UK. Delaney lives and works between Alaska and California, USA.

Marie Petersmann is Assistant Professorial Research Fellow at the LSE Law School (UK). Her project *Anthropocene Legalities: Reconfiguring Legal Relations within More-than-human Worlds* is funded by a Dutch NWO Veni grant (2022–2025). Her book *When Environmental Protection and Human Rights Collide* was published with Cambridge University Press in 2022.

Christine Schwöbel-Patel is Professor of Law at Warwick Law School, UK, and Alexander von Humboldt Fellow at the Humboldt University Berlin, Germany. Her most recent monograph is *Marketing Global Justice* (2021). Christine's research and teaching in international law is framed by a political economy and aesthetics critique.

Cristian van Eijk is a doctoral candidate and Northern Bridge Scholar at Newcastle University, UK. His research questions what it means to make space 'common', and how international law attempts to do so.

PREFACE

We do not know what a legal body can do, let alone a legal corpus. The speed with which the Law – more specifically critical legal thinking – intervenes in the world and flows across multiple dimensions and instances of lived experience is breathtaking. Flexible, yet rooted in canonical concepts and traditional procedures, legal discourse is a resourceful and dynamic field. While doctrinal international law, as outlined by Jones and Arvidsson in this volume's introduction, has not always been especially responsive to changing life conditions, because it relies so much on precedents, critical legal scholarship in international law has proven itself otherwise. As this remarkable volume demonstrates, there is an eagerness and sense of urgency in legal theory and critical legal scholarship that reflects the commitment of this field to find real solutions to problems in the world and to improve the life experiences and conditions of subjects whose well-being is of paramount importance. This is the pragmatic and collaborative side of the law: rejecting any form of cynical opportunism, it shows the potential to think lucidly and methodically about the issues at hand. At the core of the legal theory exemplified in this book, therefore, there is an ethical drive to operate for the common good – and that assumption already takes us halfway to the conclusion. It partly answers the simple question of what is at stake in posthuman law as an affirmative critical project.

Until recently we knew even less what posthuman legal bodies could do, let alone the growing bodies of work in this area. The chapters of this book offer, each in their specific manner and through different angles, multidirectional answers, provide examples and illustrations of what is at stake. They share one, empowering belief, which I take as axiomatic, namely that posthuman legal thought aims to critique the humanistic, Eurocentric, normative and heterosexist core of legal theory and practice, in order to make it more inclusive and less discriminatory. In so doing, they make room for the nonhuman, more-than-human entities, agents and subjects of our posthuman times. The intertwined critiques of humanism and anthropocentrism serve to illuminate contemporary patterns of power, subjugation, injustice and exploitation. And to offer ways out.

This is no easy challenge, as humanism carries not only a philosophy of the knowing subject but also a political ontology that has elevated the European Renaissance ideal of the human to a universal status. Man as 'the measure of all things' is endowed with the universalizing powers of a sovereign notion of reason, and self-regulating moral control. This humanistic vision of the human is also a marker of European culture and it highlights especially the scientific and technological aspects of its view of human progress. These humanist values are extended to European culture as a whole, designated as the motor of human evolution, and thus made responsible for the progress of human civilization.

This 'Man' is positioned at the peak of an evolutionary pyramid that organizes all other kinds of humans hierarchically, down the ranks and files. They are the 'others' defined as the negative opposites of the dominant human norm: they are not only 'other than' but rather 'different from' 'Man'. And, more importantly, they are perceived as being 'worth less than Man'. Exclusions on this scale are not abstract: they translate into concrete and material discriminations, marginalization and daily violence for the real-life people who happen to coincide with these categories of negative difference. They are the women and LGBTQ+ people (sexualized others), Black and Indigenous people (racialized others) and the animals, plants and earth-entities (naturalized others). Their social and symbolic existence is downgraded in the Humanistic hierarchy of human status and perfectibility, leaving them disposable and unprotected.

Colonialism is, in this respect, a clear offshoot of the power of European 'Man' as a hegemonic civilizational model that proved instrumental to the project of Western modernity and the ideology of European expansion. 'White Man's burden' as a tool of imperialist and patriarchal governance made it manifest that Europe is not just a geopolitical location but rather a universal attribute of human consciousness that can transfer its quality to any suitable subjects, provided they comply with the required discipline. Europe as a philosophical concept and a superior form of consciousness posits the power of reason as its distinctive characteristic, and humanistic universalism as its particularity. The humanistic idea of the human is therefore controlled by the paradigm of a white, European, heterosexual, property-owning, male, legal citizen, who upholds mainstream humanistic culture and selects who is best suited to represent it.

Posthuman critical theory argues that the hegemonic value attributed to this vision of the human makes it urgent to develop critiques of both humanism and anthropocentrism and to expose the power relations they uphold and transmit. The reason why this critical approach has acquired axiomatic value in this volume, as in much of posthuman scholarship, is that it resonates with revendications, claims, critiques and protests currently being voiced in the real world by a myriad of social subjects and movements. It responds actively to the problems issuing from the double imperative of the posthuman convergence: advanced technological developments on the one hand, and even faster environmental devastation on the other, with continuing patterns of social injustice flowing across them. Feminism and queer theory, critical race theory, decolonial thought and Indigenous philosophies, as well as environmental activism are especially relevant to this study and they frame this book's perception of the present, of the here and now.

In some ways the law has no choice but to resonate with present-day reality – that is where it has a head start over philosophy and other disciplines in the academic humanities, which tend toward the preservation of their past. Legal practice, on the other hand, is more actively embedded in the present. The present, however, is neither still nor monolithic, but rather in perpetual movement. It is both the record of what we are ceasing to be – our historical tracer – and the seed of what we are in the process of becoming – the pointer to a virtual future. Keeping track of such a multidimensional flow of effects is quite a challenge, especially on the methodological plane, where the calls and cries of the present meet the requirements of the legal discipline.

It is striking how many chapters in this book, while being based very much in the present, and actively engaged with it, also look to the past, as precedent and archival memory. This balancing act, one of the strengths of legal discourse, is admirable and in my eyes it can provide an example for the other academic humanities on how to find ways and means to remain faithful to their disciplinary histories, while becoming tuned to the inequalities of everyday life now. One of the approaches adopted in this book to strike this precarious balance is the systematic focus on colonialism. This makes sense in terms of the critique of humanistic principles outlined earlier, which comes through with particular relevance in the volume. But it is also partly due to the nature of international law itself, which was historically created as a tool for colonialism and colonial governance and continues to display a distinctly imperialist impulse. The specific history and conceptual structure of the discourse of international law makes it even more urgent to adopt and apply the posthuman critique of both humanism and anthropocentrism. The specificities of this discipline make the application of posthuman theory quite unique not only for the law but also for all the academic humanities. The lesson international law teaches us is that there is no more time to waste and that all the humanities today should increase the focus on the present, address the inequalities of the here now and pay special attention to the aftermath of racism and colonialism.

Beyond thematic additions and critical conceptual innovations, it is at the level of the methodology that this volume makes a most crucial and original contribution. The contributors are vowed to a meta-methodological approach. They take enormous care to trace the steps of the legal tools, the key concepts and innovative ideas, which they mobilize in their arguments. Most chapters have adopted a post–social constructivist method that borrows from multiple schools of contemporary neo-materialist philosophies. All of them are proudly interdisciplinary; they all engage with intersectional approaches that address gender, race, age and able-bodiedness, and many rely on artistic and media practice as a research method. None shirk their responsibilities for social justice and respect of the dignity of all.

Unsurprisingly, both natural and post-natural objects of knowledge are studied here, most of them not human. It is quite a kaleidoscope of themes and objects of study picked across a spreading spectrum of a zoe/geo/techno-mediated matter. The subtitle of the book may as well be 'what's the matter with matter?' Matter, as exemplified in the different chapters here, means elemental and elementary matter: air, including greenhouse gases; the earth, as soil, minerals and mines, Motherland and stolen land; fire, smoke; and a vast abundance of water as seas, oceans, rivers, floods and drinking fluids. This is a book about the atmosphere, the geosphere, the biosphere and the hydrosphere, and it discusses these elemental structures within the flows of capital, neocolonialism and human greed. Keeping the techno-sphere always close at hand.

As a matter of fact, the real second nature nowadays is designed by technology, and the volume comments extensively on the threats and opportunities created by the high degrees of technological mediation we have reached, notably digital but also neural and genetic. Contemporary 'naturecultures' are mediated through and through. It is uncertain what modes of political and legal governance can sustain and regulate such a complex general ecology, but this book takes important steps in the right direction.

It is no wonder, therefore, that so many of the contributions in this volume call for an urgent change in thinking about legal subjectivity and encourage us to learn to think otherwise even about the naturecultural continuum. Humans and nonhumans need to strike a new balance. The subject of posthuman law and legal knowledge is neither *homo universalis* nor *Anthropos* alone, but a more complex assemblage of zoe/geo/techno-related factors, collaboratively linked to a material web of human and nonhuman agents. Reading through the contributions, I felt more and more comforted by their shared belief that critical thinking in the law is not the prerogative of legal discourse alone but takes place in the world, which is defined by the coexistence of multiple organic species, technological artifacts and networks alongside each other. We are eco-sophically connected. For me, acknowledging this living continuum signals a becoming-world of posthuman critical theory.

One of the features of critical legal discourse that struck me as very compatible with posthuman critical theory is the high degree of attention it pays to situated or immanent perspectives. Each contributor practices the politics of locations and defines carefully the parameters of its intervention. Each contributor knows its place within and across a specific discourse and practice and deploys their skills in developing critical insights perfectly suited to the case at hand. The chapters are pragmatic, embedded and embodied, immanently situated and therefore both accountable and extremely effective. Maybe there is a lesson here for the rest of the humanities on how to draw cartographies that frame critiques of power in the world and in scholarship. Critical legal theory shows us how to take a broader critical movement like posthuman theory and anchor it in empirical realities, allowing us to think about it in more concrete ways.

But let us delve even deeper. We are all aware that there is a significant difference between accepting the structural interdependence of all species and actually treating nonhuman subjects as equal partners and collaborators. That difference is qualitative, not merely quantitative. In other words, it is not enough to turn our attention to nonhuman objects of inquiry in legal discourse, we also need to defamiliarize our mental habits. Such a radical shift is necessary, because we live in the age of computational, neural and genetic networks, of AI and synthetic biology on the one hand and climate change and the threat of extinction on the other, with recurrent patterns of social and economic injustices. As a result, we need to de-globalize, de-carbonize and de-colonize our thinking patterns and be demographically aware of their implications for future generations. Critical posthuman thinkers have to work toward becoming good ancestors, or 'kin' as Donna Haraway puts it.

Thus, granting equal status to natural and postnatural organisms, in an explicit and deliberately posthumanistic and post-anthropocentric move, is a far-reaching decision. But a focus on nonhuman objects or topics of research, however necessary, is not a sufficient condition for the production of posthuman legal theory in international law. This volume teaches us that in order to produce a credible qualitative shift, we also need conceptual and methodological transformations.

Key among them is the determination to retain and redefine our understanding of what it means to be a subject in the posthuman convergence. All the authors of this study agree that we need an enlarged, distributed and transversal concept of what a subject is, and of how it can deploy its relational capacities and ethical responsibilities. Mainstream posthuman scholarship, however, tends to be polarized between, on the one hand, vehement dismissals of the need for a theory of subjectivity at all (e.g. a tendency within some works within Actor Network Theory or Object Orientated Ontology) and, on the other, a tendency to reinscribe subjectivity into the humanistic tradition, albeit it with a few revisions and corrections (transhumanism). This volume skillfully avoids such a polarization and seeks for a series of alternative planes of encounter. Each chapter offers illuminating examples of subject positions worthy of our times. This 'supra' or even 'post'-disciplinary character is what makes the contributions to this volume so crucial. The driving force that sustains them, on top of loyalty to their discipline, is an even stronger love for the world, that is to say the modes of relation, resonance and hybridization they are able and willing to engage in.

What is at stake in posthuman legal theory is a variety of ways of moving beyond humanist exceptionalism, Eurocentrism and patriarchal heteronormativity. The transversality of feminist intersectionality and race theory is one of the operational forces that helps to reconceptualize the subject across all these multiple axes, as are concepts such as trans-sex and transgender, trans-species, trans-corporeality and trans-generational solidarity.

I felt energized by reading this book – it is a lively and dynamic piece of scholarship that practices what it preaches. It shows posthuman legal subjects as a work-in-progress, emerging as both a critical and creative experiment within the posthuman convergence along posthumanist and post-anthropocentric axes of interrogation. By assessing with vision and generosity the posthuman impact on the question of subjectivity, exploring its contradictions and highlighting potential, they never cease questioning what it means to be, become, remain, aspire to be human today. What does it mean to be a subject in an era that claims to be simultaneously more-than-human and less-than-human? More than human because of its multi-scalar transformations and technological advances, and less than human in its inhumane economic and social polarizations and irreversible environmental devastation. So the question is: who are 'we'?

One of the strengths of the volume is the passion and the rigor with which it interrogates the self-representations and conventional understandings of being human, which 'we' have inherited from the past. What this critical stance offers is the field of problems and questions themselves, that is to say the cartography of the power relations that are currently reshaping the formulation of the problem of subjectivity and call for new concepts.

In this respect, this volume about legal discourse and practices in international law also manages to fulfill a valuable cartographic function, by mapping the geopolitical terms that situate posthuman subjects across multiple fractures and strident power differences. These include different degrees of access to the benefits of technological advances. Global flows of migration and the displacement of populations, growing economic disparities, mass evictions, rising racism and xenophobia, extensive warfare and climate change, public health and access to vaccines and adequate medical care are the critical markers of our current condition.

The cartographic question therefore doubles up as both conceptual and ethical: what kind of subjects are 'we' – the human and inhuman inhabitants of this planet – positioned within a technologically driven 'second life', genetically modified food, robotics, synthetic biology, the acidification of the seas and the desertification of the earth? How can 'we' develop a posthuman theoretical legal framework that aspires to justice but is made within a neo-materialist order that does not reduce everything to social constructivism, encompassing instead what we used to call the natural?

The authors in this volume explore the multifaceted and differential nature of the collective posthuman 'we' in a grounded and accountable manner. The challenge then is how to redefine the subject of knowledge and power without reference to that unitary, humanistic, Eurocentric and masculinist subject. Firmly committed to ontological pacifism, I have always aspired to affirmative ethics as a collective praxis of co-construction of alternatives in a critical and creative manner.

The affirmative stance – a sense of care for the common good – is not the least of the virtues of this volume. The affirmative ethical aspiration aims to compose a transversal subject assemblage – 'we, posthuman legal subjects' – that actualizes the unrealized or virtual potential of what 'we' are capable of becoming. But this new collective subject, 'we', unfolds into a relational process ontology: 'we-are (all)-in-this-together-but-we-are-not-one-and-the-same' kind of subject.

'We' are both a vulnerable and an insurgent category.

Posthuman subjectivity is a practical project. It is a praxis. What matters is to negotiate collectively about *what* exactly we are in the process of becoming, and how much transformation, pain, dis-identification or enhancement our embodied and embrained selves can take. The posthuman is just the question. The answer is what 'we' are capable of becoming. The particular answer must and can only be a practical and pragmatic one, bound to time and space, to a continuous present that just flows. At this particular point in time, as the process unfolds, there is no knowing what the destination is, yet this book makes it absolutely clear that the methods and insights of legal discourse are indispensable navigational tools to steer a course between the 'no longer' and the 'not yet'.

Rosi Braidotti

INTRODUCTION TO INTERNATIONAL LAW AND POSTHUMAN THEORY

Emily Jones and Matilda Arvidsson

In *Posthuman Knowledge*, Rosi Braidotti (2019) formulates the predicament of the world in the following terms, defining the posthuman condition as that which 'we' – subjects and non-subjects of international law, humans and animals, robots and moths, oceans and minerals, pieces of plastic and artificially intelligent (AI) powered algorithms – are facing:

> We – the human and non-human inhabitants of this particular planet – are currently positioned between the Fourth Industrial Revolution and the Sixth Extinction. Yes, we are in this together: between the algorithmic devil and the blue sea (2) . . . At the core of our predicament – but not its sole cause – is the unprecedented degree of technological intervention we have reached, and the intimacy with which we have developed with technological devices. And yet, the posthuman condition cannot be reduced to an acute technological mediation. This convergence, with its distinctive combination of speedy transformations and persistent inequalities, is planetary and multi-scalar. It affects social and environmental ecologies as well as individual psychic and shared emotional landscapes. It is not a linear event. *(3)*

It is clear that 'we', in Braidotti's use of the term, are faced with multiple predicaments, from climate change to technological change and beyond. As Braidotti therefore continues, '[i]n such a context, neither universalistic notions of "Man" nor exceptional claims for "Anthropos", are sufficient to explain how we are supposed to cope with this challenge' (2019: 3).

While international lawyers instinctively seek to fix problems through either extending the scope of existing international law or through extending

DOI: 10.4324/9781032658032-1

the law via ever-more detailed and fragmented legal regulations, it becomes clear, in the face of Braidotti's insights, that in these times, and perhaps in all times, more of the same – more, or 'better', international law – is not necessarily the answer. International law is, after all, based upon a series of assumptions that work to reinforce 'universalistic' notions of 'Man' through exclusionary humanism (i.e. structural oppression based along the lines of race, gender, class and ableism: for an overview and references, see further on in the chapter) as well as anthropocentrism (see Jones 2023). What is consequently required are new epistemological or even onto-epistemological foundations. In light of this, this collection asks: Can posthuman theory provide methods and practices that may help restructure international legal knowledges, relations, preferences, hierarchizations and boundaries? What could international law and international lawyers learn about the world, a world that international law seeks to order, and indeed about international law itself, by adopting posthuman theory? Could this process of defamiliarization help international lawyers to reconsider and do international law differently, maybe even to less violent and destructive ends?

As noted, international law has a particular and often violent history underpinned by a series of underlying structures and assumptions (e.g. Koskenniemi 2006, 2009, 2021; Orford 2003, 2021; Parfitt 2019, 2014; Skouteris 2012). While these are commonly presented by the doctrinal canon of the discipline as intrinsic to international law's character, with international law being deemed to be a truth-driven and even scientific order that manages relations between formally equal states, critical international legal scholarship has long challenged this position (*inter alia* Anghie and Chimni 2003; Beard 2007; Charlesworth and Chinkin 1993; Kennedy 1985; Orford 2004; Otto 2010). However, and undeniably, assumptions that underpin international law have changed over time, driven primarily by the 'truths' of their own time before times and trends have changed by which international law is said to have 'overcome' its own past. The result, however, remains the same, that is, an unequal, violent and often unruly global order of the past and present.

Toward this end, international law has been widely critiqued for upholding exclusionary humanisms, whereby some subjects, particularly gendered, racialized, colonized and classed subjects, are systematically devalued, made invisible and oppressed by and through the operation of international law despite international law's claims to universality (ibid; *inter alia* Charlesworth 2022; Chimni 2017; Heathcote 2019; Jones 2023a; Knox 2022; Meiville 2006; Nesiah *et al* 2016). This criticism is not only directed toward the past – that which international law is conventionally said to have overcome through its 'modern' iterations in the era of the United Nations (UN) Charter, peaceful cooperation between states and the formal dismantling of colonialism. It is also, and importantly, directed against international law in the present in which 'The Old world', as Jennifer Beard puts it, 'has renamed itself variously as "modernity", "the West", "The First World", or "the developed world" ', leaving 'no freedom in the system of accounting for developing nations to "be something" other than a First World marketplace' (2007: 167). For example, Marxist international legal scholars have highlighted how capitalist and neoliberal values permeate international law, these ideologies often being presented as neutral and objective yet having very real, very unequal impacts on lived subjects (Baars 2019), with Tzouvala arguing that the 'standard of civilization' in international law, which has, of course, a very long history, has come to be defined, in part, through 'conformity with the basic tenets of capitalist modernity' (2020: 2).

However, exclusionary humanism is not the only assumption that underpins the international legal project; anthropocentrism is another such assumption. Critical international environmental law scholarship has highlighted how international law is set up so as to render the environment only ever as an object to be extracted and exploited for human consumption and pleasure (Natarajan and Dehm 2022; Jones 2021, 2023a; Grear 2017; Cusato 2021). Likewise, critical international and global animal law scholars have noted how nonhuman lives have been valued along the same anthropocentric lines (Arvidsson and Sjöstedt 2023; Deckha 2023; Jones 2023a; Offor 2022; Otomo 2013). Overall, these scholars expose the anthropocentric episteme of international law, with many arguing that international law is subsequently unable to address the environmental challenges of our times without an epistemic overhaul (Gilbert *et al* 2021; Jones 2021; Grear 2015, 2020).

In the meantime, international law is facing a series of core challenges in these posthuman times, particularly in relation to technological innovation, global inequalities and environmental degradation. From the use of ever-more complex technologies on the battlefield (Arvidsson 2018, 2020; Jones 2018, 2023a; Noll 2014), to the urgent need to address climate change (Dehm 2021), to the increasing complexities of frontier technologies in migration control (Van Den Meerssche 2022), to ongoing calls to address global inequalities (e.g. Anghie 2005; Jones 2023a; Heathcote 2019; Gathii 2021) and to challenge the capitalist global order (Baars 2019; Schwöbel-Patel 2021; Tzouvala 2020), to the use of big data as a tool for governance (Johns 2021, 2023), these challenges are vast. While some international lawyers are rising to these challenges – as exemplified by the aforementioned scholarship – these voices largely remain on the periphery. The assumptions that underpin international law operate to ensure that any attempts to address these challenges remain limited. International law is set up in a way that shores up the *status quo* as opposed to seeking or allowing for more radical solutions to the world's problems. International law conventionally aims to regulate and preserve a stable global order, one in which the underlying presumptions of that global order remain, for the most part, unchallenged.

The traditional international legal sources availed for this ordering exercise – as set out in Article 38(1) of the International Court of Justice (ICJ) Statute (the UN Charter): international legal statutes, customary international law, historical precedents and general principles of law – creates an *ex post facto* framework, reactive and conservative in character (Parfitt 2014; Arvidsson and Bak McKenna 2020). International law's perpetual turn toward its own past slows down its capacity to act on contemporary challenges and imagine futures yet to come – unless it is coupled with a theoretical framework worthy of that task. Yet this turn toward its own history also puts history at the center of its present, necessitating theories and analyses able to understand how the past conditions the present of law, as well as the present condition and challenges at large.

In the context of these challenges, this collection draws on critical posthuman theory (hereafter 'posthuman theory') to analyze and rethink international law. We define posthuman theory as sitting between the convergence, on the one hand, of critical posthumanism, that is, the critique of the white, heterosexual, able-bodied man as the central focus of Western thought (including legal thought) and post-anthropocentrism on the other, that is, the idea that the human sits in hierarchy over nature, matter, nonhuman animals and machines (Braidotti 2013, 2019, 2021).[1] Posthuman theory is drawn on in multiple ways throughout the collection, to analyze international law, to critique it, to rethink it and to reshape it. A variety of approaches are adopted and applied to multiple core topics in international law, including, for example, international human rights law, international humanitarian law (IHL), international legal method, international environmental law, the law of the sea, international tax law, decolonial international legal history and more, providing a holistic account of the ways posthuman theory can interact with and begin to shift thinking in international law (see, for example, Arvidsson 2018, 2021, 2020, 2023a; Jones *et al* 2018; Hohmann 2021; Jones 2018, 2021, 2023; Quiroga-Villamarín 2020; *Völkerrechtblog* 2023).

Posthuman theory is unique in how it brings together questions of inequality, the environment and techno-scientific innovation. Given that some of the core challenges being posed to international law in the contemporary moment relate to these three central issues, posthuman theory seems, on the face of it, to be an obvious starting point when it comes to critically analyzing and seeking to reconsider international law. This is not to say, however, that posthuman theory is the only framework that can be applied to tackle

1 The editors as well as the contributing authors all work within the framework of critical posthuman theory – in contrast to scholarship of, for example, transhuman inclinations. On the latter, see Ferrando 2018. When mentioned in this volume 'posthuman theory' denotes its critical variant, unless otherwise stated.

these issues. Rather, and as exemplified by this collection, posthuman theory can, and we argue should, be used to bring together a wide array of critical perspectives, allowing for conversations between these perspectives to come to the fore. The authors in this collection thereby draw on posthuman theory alongside feminist and queer theory, Marxism and critical environmental law scholarship, as well as historical, Third World Approaches to International Law (TWAIL) and Indigenous scholarship and beyond, bringing these various perspectives into play as part of each chapter's unique posthuman convergence (Braidotti *et al* 2023). This collection does not, therefore, seek to propose a *new* theory of international law per se, and is certainly not written in the aim of replacing or surpassing other important critical theories in international law. Rather, the collection poses posthuman theory as a way of bringing to the fore the multiple vectors of inequality that international law is complicit in upholding, including the inequalities between humans but also, importantly, the hierarchical position of humans over the nonhuman. In this sense, what is being proposed is a truly intersectional framework, one that allows for a focused lens to be applied to a particular issue of inequality or injustice without rendering other issues of inequality and injustice invisible (a critique that can be all too easily made of much critical scholarship). We are, therefore, in this collection, and as scholars, deeply indebted to intersectional feminism in this regard (Crenshaw 1989), with posthuman theory, as Braidotti reminds us, having its roots in feminist thought (2021).

Posthuman legal scholarship has grown exponentially as a field over the past decade (see, for example, Davis 2017; Deckha 2010; Grear 2015, 2020; Kang 2018; Kang and Kendall 2020; Käll 2022; Norman 2021; Philippopoulos-Mihalopoulos 2015). One of the strongest take-ups of posthuman theory in law has, however, and as we will outline in more detail in this introduction, been in international law. This field brings together the work of posthuman philosophers such as Karen Barad (2007), Donna Haraway (1991, 1997, 2016) and Rosi Braidotti (2013, 2019, 2021), alongside and into the work of critical international legal scholarship. The meeting of these two strands of scholarship, posthuman theory and international law, has resulted in the formation of a thriving, albeit still relatively new, field of scholarship. This current volume brings many of these emerging voices together into one collection. It therefore provides an example of both the richness of the field and its forms and of some of the new and emerging directions scholars in this field are beginning to take, with posthuman theory being applied to a wider array of international legal topics than has yet been seen elsewhere, including several fields that have, until now, not been subject to a posthuman analysis.

In this introduction, we outline how we, as editors, framed the volume from the outset and how we and the various contributors to this volume have defined and deployed posthuman theory. In doing so, we discuss how posthuman theory has come to enter into conversation with international law (and vice versa) thus far, outlining how this collection contributes to the wider field. When discussing posthuman theory, we emphasize feminist traditions and practices, this being core to the work and ethics of us both. Although not all the chapters in this collection explicitly draw on feminist traditions, each chapter is written from a critical and intersectional perspective and therefore each, in some way, can be read as speaking back to or alongside the feminist origins of the posthuman turn, as we outline it herein. We end by providing an overview of the sections and chapters of this collection, concluding by outlining the aims of the collection and how it speaks to international law, its scholarship and practice, and beyond.

Posthuman Theory

There are, by now, multiple strands of thinking within what is known as the 'posthumanities', from critical posthuman theory to new materialisms, to transhumanism, actor-network theory and beyond (for an overview, see Braidotti and Hlavajova 2018; Braidotti *et al* 2023). As noted earlier, in this volume, the various contributions each draw on critical posthuman theory, under the umbrella of which we include new materialism (more on this later). We define posthuman theory as being 'positioned between the convergence of posthumanism, based on post- and anti-humanist critiques of the subject on the one hand, and post-anthropocentrism on the other' (Braidotti *et al* 2023: 3). This definition brings forth the material and discursive emergence of subjects, the relations between humans, nonhumans, and the in-human and less-than-human subject, as well as bringing to the fore questions of power and knowledge-production. Critical posthuman theory is also deeply tied to interrogating the ways that technology, capitalism and anthropocentrism play a central role in the production of violence, inequality and planetary destruction (more on this later). Yet, whereas the posthuman condition in which 'this' takes place and in which 'we' are all together may seem nothing less than a catastrophe, posthuman feminism also brings hope, with affirmation being a core posthuman method (Braidotti 2013).

Our understanding of critical posthuman theory, as noted, contrasts strongly to other bodies of work that are, at times, likewise brought under the umbrella of the posthumanities. The differences between some strands of theory in the posthumanities and the critical posthuman theory we deploy in this volume can be examined by looking at transhumanism. Transhumanism broadly seeks to move humans beyond their current physical limitations by drawing on a mixture of human-machine and biomedical enhancements (Bostrom 2005). Transhumanism is thereby a broad label that includes ideas such as trying to prevent the aging process to creating more efficient human beings (ibid). Associated with philosophical traditions such as long-termism, futurism and fascism, transhumanism sits, in many ways, in opposition to the critical posthuman stance we and our authors take in this collection.

In *Posthuman Knowledge* Braidotti explains 'the posthuman' as a method through which the material and discursive elements can be analyzed:

> As a theoretical figuration, the posthuman is a navigational tool that enables us to survey the material and the discursive manifestations of the mutations that are engendered by advanced technological developments (am I a robot?), climate change (will I survive?), and capitalism (can I afford this?).
>
> *(Braidotti 2019: 2)*

This means that posthumanism's analytical framework consists of both discursive-linguistic and empirical methods, as outlined by Arvidsson in more detail in this volume (2023b) and as exemplified in various ways by each of the contributions in this book. Moreover, posthuman theory is dedicated to an ontological and epistemological critique that draws on feminist and other critical traditions (Braidotti 2021). As a theoretical and methodological framework it enables an analysis of how 'matter comes to matter' (Barad 2007) or, in Haraway's words:

> It matters what matters we use to think other matters with; it matters what stories we tell to tell other stories with; it matters what knots knot knots, what thoughts think thoughts, what ties tie ties. It matters what stories make worlds, what worlds make stories.
>
> *(2011: 6)*

To critically analyze the mattering, telling, knotting, thinking, and tying of international law, its scholarship and practice, thus, becomes a central aspect of posthuman international legal analysis, this being a core theme picked up by Jones *et al* in the volume (2023).

We have chosen posthuman theory as a theoretical and methodological framework through which to analyze international law in this collection for three main reasons. First, it brings scholarship on who is a subject and questions of matter together through both ontological and epistemological modes of questioning. Posthuman theory, in bringing together critiques of both humanism and anthropocentrism, ensures that matter can be thought through without risking the displacement of important epistemological turns that have come about through feminism, queer, critical race, postcolonial, crip and other areas of critical scholarship (Braidotti 2021; Jones 2023a). This, in contrast, is something that certain – although certainly not all – strands of new materialist theory and scholarship have been criticized of.

The concerns raised are that, in seeking to focus on and re-center ontology, epistemology is sidelined, working to create a theory of matter that thinks about matter alone, inadequately accounting for a world in which inequalities between humans remain (Jones 2023a) – this being a dilemma Anna Grear discusses in greater detail in her chapter in this volume (2023).

As noted, we view new materialism as part of as opposed to separate to our broader critical posthuman convergence, noting the often false distinctions made between these schools of thought, with both, in the end, bringing to the fore questions of the material world. In doing so, we seek to ensure that the pitfalls of the epistemological groundings of some strands of new materialism are avoided – with epistemic justice remaining a central theme throughout each of the contributions in this volume.

The second reason why we chose posthuman theory as our main theoretical framework for this volume as opposed to, for example, a slightly narrower focus on new materialism, is precisely because posthuman theory is broader, meaning it is able to encompass new materialist perspectives within the posthuman convergence at the same time as going beyond the narrower focus of new materialism. While new materialism(s), as noted, works to re-center the question of matter (*inter alia* Barad 2007; Bennett 2009) and while, in this collection, we have several contributions that focus more squarely on new materialism, in particular Grear (2023) and Hohmann and Schwöbel-Patel (2023), posthuman theory's broader remit also allows for a thinking through of the question of the agency of matter alongside other key issues – issues that are of vital importance for international law. These issues include, for example, human and legal interactions with technology – a theme Arvidsson discusses (2023b) – and also race and gender. Through focusing not only on the agency of matter but also actively making links between more and less-than-human subjects, posthuman theory allows and even ensures that the connections between human and nonhuman inequalities are brought to the fore. This is well exemplified by this collection, with several contributions strongly engaging with issues of race and coloniality (in particular see Hamzić 2023; Mitchell 2023; Koram and Guardiola-Rivera 2023; Leeuwenkamp 2023) and with others focusing on gender (in particular see Arvidsson 2023b; Heathcote 2023) or on Indigenous epistemologies (see Koram and Guardiola-Rivera 2023; Jones *et al* 2023; Heathcote 2023; Grear 2023). In international law, as we will expand on, staying with the trouble of its racist, colonial, anthropocentric and otherwise violent history – including its continuities and articulations in the present – is central to the critical strands of international legal scholarship and practice to which this volume seeks to add.

The third reason why we have chosen to focus on posthuman theory as opposed to the slightly narrower field of new materialism relates to debates around its relation to historical materialism. As Arvidsson (2023b) expands on in her chapter, as discussed by Hohmann and Schwöbel-Patel (2023), and as outlined by Jones in her recent monograph (2023), the terminology of 'new' inherently invokes a reaction in many who see the 'new' of new materialism as a challenge to historical materialism, that is, Marxist theory. Given the prominence and importance of new materialist approaches in international law and the vital insights such approaches have provided in uncovering how capitalist and neoliberal ideologies structure international law, resulting in real power inequalities that often map onto colonial power dimensions, we are wary of proposing that a 'new' materialism is needed in international law. The terminology of new materialism is in some way therefore unhelpful in that, while some new materialist theories do indeed engage with historical materialism, some do not. Rather, new materialism is a distinct body of work that has as much to do with historical materialism as does, say, feminism, or postcolonial theory – that is to say, it relates but it is not seeking to displace historical materialism or inherently, as a complete body of work, challenge it. Rather, the materialisms that new materialism(s) most often emerge from and seek to engage with are the materialist traditions of Spinoza, Nietzsche, and not the least Deleuze and Guattari (for more on this, in this volume, see: Arvidsson 2023b). Therefore, we contend that new and historical materialism must be read side by side and it is also for these reasons that we prefer the terminology of posthumanism, which, following the critical posthuman strand through the work of scholars such as Braidotti, can and does hold critiques of advanced capitalism alongside the need to re-center matter in our ways of thinking about the world.

Having positioned our collection in the context of ongoing scholarship and debates in posthuman theory, we next turn to outlining various key tenets of posthuman theory that we find to be important when it comes to understanding what posthuman theory is and does for the purpose of its interaction with and use to analyze international legal scholarship and practice. Taking heed of Braidotti's recent (2021) call to ensure that the feminist origins of the posthuman turn are not sidelined as the field expands, we outline the ways that the central questions of feminist theory likewise become, for us in this collection, some of the central questions of posthuman scholarship, focusing in particular on the question of who is or is not 'human' in international law, the necessity of an affirmative posthuman politics, presentism and critique as part of posthuman theory and international law, and the focus on capitalism and technology. While doing so, we will draw on – and briefly introduce – some of the central existing posthuman international legal work, situating the collection within the field.

Critical Posthuman Theory, Posthuman Feminism(s) and International Law

As noted, in creating and curating this volume, we took posthuman feminism as our starting point. In this section, we outline why we were specifically inspired by posthuman feminism, outlining the core tenets of that body of thought that have inspired and shaped the volume. At the same time, we highlight the ways some of these ideas have already been taken up in existing international legal scholarship that draws on posthuman theory, providing both a more detailed outline of how posthuman theory is engaged with in this volume alongside an overview of existing scholarship and the way the volume contributes to the wider field.

Who or What Is the 'Human' in International Law?

Not all posthumanisms are feminist. However, the form of critical posthuman theory used throughout this volume has strong links to feminism (Braidotti 2021), being an inherently intersectional framework that seeks to dismantle hierarchies both between differing humans and human and nonhuman subjects. One core element of feminist theory that therefore influences our understanding, as editors, of posthuman theory, and one which is drawn on throughout the contributions to this volume, is the question of who or what is the human subject.

Feminist theory has long questioned the human subject, challenging dominant modes of thinking in Western philosophy that pose the subject, either explicitly or implicitly, as the 'universal Man' (*inter alia* Beauvoir 1949; Cixous 1986; Irigaray 1985 [1974]; Harding 1986, 1991; McKinnon 2007). Yet, feminist scholarship has also been critical of the exclusion of non-white, non-middle class and queer and trans women in some strands of (earlier) feminist analysis (e.g. Braidotti 1991, 2021, 2019, 2013; Wynter 2015; Butler 1997). Moreover, feminist scholarship has been criticized for pursuing able-bodied, heteronormative, nuclear family oriented, colonial, ecocidal and Eurocentric visions of feminist futures (*inter alia* Crenshaw 1989; hooks 2000; Federici 2014; Gaard 1997; Spivak 1999; Wynter 2015). Drawing on this history of feminist critiques, the quest for posthuman feminism becomes a vision of intergenerational transversal alliance of feminist scholarship and critique (Braidotti 2021; Arvidsson 2023c; Arvidsson *et al* 2024 [Forthcoming]). The idea of posthuman feminism is thus *not* to transform or 'surpass' previous feminist scholarship, but rather to draw on previous feminist scholarship and action – building upon academic and political action and activism – and to transform it into actionable transversal and transgenerational alliances in the present. In Braidotti's words this means to 'reconnect with different feminist genealogies, archives and counter-memories across space and time' rather than to 'stay within the contemporary dominant theories' (2021: 9). Examples of such feminist genealogies and alliances, as well as the counter-memories, in international law include those of Dianne Otto and Emily Jones (Jones and Otto 2020), Vanja Hamzić (e.g. 2019; Hamzić and Mir-Hosseini 2010) and Gina Heathcote (e.g. Heathcote 2019; Berlotti *et al* 2021), just to mention a few.

Feminist legal scholarship has likewise shown how the legal subject is very much a 'he', being based upon a liberal male, heterosexual, able-bodied, middle class, Eurocentric model of subjectivity (Naffine 1997, 2011), with feminist and queer international legal scholars having uncovered the same to be true of the legal subject in international law (Charlesworth 1997; Ruskola 2009–2010; Jones 2023). What posthuman feminism then adds to this legal scholarship, however, is a focus also on the inequalities created between subjects through anthropocentric modes of thought. Unpacking the binary categorizations of the nature/culture divide, ecofeminists and posthuman feminists have questioned human-centric – anthropocentric – ontologies and epistemologies through which humans have come to access dominant positions of power and privilege at the cost of the environment (Alaimi 2016; Gaard 1997).

The focus on who or what the human subject of the law, is a central theme in much existing posthuman international legal scholarship, including scholarship that is explicitly labeled as feminist (e.g. Heathcote 2018; Arvidsson 2018; Jones 2018, 2023) – with Heathcote's chapter in this volume being one such example (2023), as well as in scholarship that is not explicitly labeled feminist but that draws on critical posthuman theory as formed and inspired by feminist theory (e.g. Boulot and Sterlin 2022; Jones 2021; Petersmann 2021). This mode of critique has perhaps, however, most strongly been taken up within critical environmental law scholarship, with scholars highlighting how international law operates to render the environment as an object to be exploited and extracted for the needs of elite humans (see, for example, Cirkovic 2021; Grear 2020; Jones 2021, 2023; Petersmann 2021). In this vein, many of the chapters in this volume likewise question who or what the legal subject of international law is, with Leeuwenkamp (2023) calling into question the anthropocentrism of the human subject of human rights while Deckha (2023) likewise makes a similar turn through a focus on global animal law and animal intensive farming. Likewise, Jones *et al* (2023) question the legal subject, arguing for the collective underlying the principle of the common heritage of humankind to be extended to include nonhuman subjects too, while Koram and Guardiola-Rivera (2023) call for nonhuman plant subjectivity to be better understood in international drug law. In the meantime, Hamzić (2023) outlines the role of capitalist colonialism in creating and reinforcing distinctions between gendered and racialized humans and nonhumans.

As already noted, 'transversal' alliances are central to posthuman feminist thought. These alliances provide, in Braidotti's words, a 'relational way of thinking by cross-referencing through categories and disciplines' to cultivate 'resonances among positions that may at first appear incompatible' (ibid). The emphasis on alliances is to respect that although allies stand together, we do so with different perspectives, positions and possibilities (see also Arvidsson 2023b, 2023c). Toward this end, posthuman feminist theory – in international legal scholarship and elsewhere – is substantially interdisciplinary. This volume exemplifies this interdisciplinarity. For example, Heathcote's chapter analyzes the international law of the sea drawing on posthuman and feminist theory alongside Indigenous epistemologies (2023), while Hamzić's chapter invokes international law and history (2023). Mitchell's chapter, on the other hand, draws on international law, art theory and colonial theory (2023).

In such alliances, all differences apart, there is an affirmative understanding that 'We-Are-All-In-This-Together-But-We-Are-Not-One-And-The-Same' (Braidotti 2009: 32). From such an intergenerational and transversal feminist stance, the posthuman feminist question opens several critical avenues: 'Can I, as a woman, Black, Indigenous, LGBTQ+ person, claim access to humanity? – *Am I human too*?' The question of 'inclusion' into categories of 'human' and 'humanity' is not a goal unto itself. Instead, the method of deconstructing binary categorization is done through questioning nominally 'value neutral' or 'universal' categories through which exclusion, subjugation, oppression and other forms of violence are performed: in other words, to 'cut' the world differently by which new possibilities of a less violent world and societies emerge. The result is a critical analysis of the relations and structures by which power and normative ordering come to act upon and in the world, as well as a political move through which affirmation of nonviolence is performed in the legal-political normative sphere. It is to these ends that the critical and feminist strands of posthuman thought emerge in this volume, which collectively imagines less violent, more equal worlds.

Affirmation, Presentism, Critique

Another core element of critical and posthuman feminist thought is affirmation and a persistent focus on the needs of the present. As Braidotti argues, posthuman approaches are thereby 'firmly grounded in the present (as actual and virtual), which means that they take real-life events seriously, and by extension, take power seriously' (Braidotti 2019: 39). This 'present' is the one in which posthumanism converges with post-anthropocentrism within an economy of advanced capitalism (Braidotti 2019: 2). While many posthuman scholars are concerned with issues that may seem futuristic and speculative – such as the 'posthuman', the 'cyborg' (Haraway 1991; Arvidsson 2018; Jones 2018) or the 'smart' city (Käll 2022) – and as many posthuman scholars are dedicated to visions of a more hopeful future yet to arrive, posthuman feminism has a fundamental connection to the 'now'.

The emphasis on affirmation in this body of posthuman thought can be seen in the focus on *potentia* – affirmative power – vitality and affect

(Braidotti 2013). However, another core tenet of posthuman affirmation is the focus on action and change. Toward this end, Braidotti states:

> I want to approach posthuman theory as both a genealogical and a navigational tool. I find it useful as a term to explore ways of engaging affirmatively with the present, accounting for some of its features in a manner that is empirically grounded without being reductive and remains critical while avoiding negativity.
>
> *(Braidotti 2013: 5)*

From this focus on affirmation follows a mode of hopefulness – even in the midst of the sixth extinction – that something *can* be done, and that it is on us to do something toward realizing a hopeful future – without nativity, but also without negativity (Arvidsson 2023b).

Affirmative and grounded thinking are both themes that permeate this volume. International law is, after all, a discipline of reality, with international law being a tool for governance, one that is deeply implicated in violence. The chapters in this volume, in analyzing various areas of international law, be it international tax law (as per Lärka 2023), international human rights law (as per Leeuwenkamp 2023) or international drugs law (as per Koram and Guardiola-Rivera 2023), to give a few examples, are inherently grounded in the fields they analyze. Each chapter is also deeply critical of the area of international law being evaluated, with critiques being made of international law's anthropocentrism (see, for example, Jones *et al* 2023; Heathcote 2023; Leeuwenkamp 2023; Deckha 2023; Koram and Guardiola-Rivera 2023; Petersmann 2023) with others, for example, focusing on the colonialism inherent in the structure of international law (e.g. Hohmann and Schwöbel-Patel 2023; Hamzić 2023; Mitchell 2023; Koram and Guardiola-Rivera 2023). However, yet another key focus that indeed comes through from the various contributions is a sense of hope, of the possibility of change, and of the ways that posthuman theory can be deployed to provide alternative models in the affirmative. That can be seen, again, throughout many of the contributions, but, to give a few examples, one can look at Petersmann's call for models of subjectivity and ownership to be challenged through commoning (2023) or Jones *et al*'s call for key principles in international law to be transformed to better account for human–nonhuman connections (2023). In this sense, the volume is not only written clearly in the vein of critical and posthuman feminist theory, but it likewise contributes to these bodies of thought, providing grounded, empirical examples of how posthuman theory can be deployed to foster more affirmative futures.

Capitalism and Technology

The final conceptual focus that critical and feminist posthumanism calls for attention to be paid to, and one that this volume heeds such calls for, is the understanding that capitalism, and its entanglement with technology, is a central part of the problem. This critique highlights the destructive violence of capitalism, its role in creating and sustaining economic inequalities in society, as well as how it is an intrinsic part of frontier technologies. An example of this latter is frontier technologies in warfare and its legal ordering through IHL (see *inter alia* Arvidsson 2018, 2020, 2021, 2023a; Arvidsson and Sjöstedt 2023; Jones 2018, 2023; Wilcox 2016, 2017. See also Arvidsson's contribution to this volume: 2023b). The material conditions of this violence, as expressed in international law, also include the 'resourcification' of the environment, rendering the environment and nonhuman animals as 'property' and thereby as tradable goods (Natarajan and Dehm 2019), including the rendering of oil into value through petro-capitalist extractivism (Grear 2017). Other examples include the extraction of nonhuman animal reproductive labor-value (Deckha 2020) under global animal and food law, and the intensification of global value-extraction through unpaid human labor in data harvesting (Käll 2022). Drawing on Marxist theory and traditions, posthuman feminism is concerned with economic relations as these are part of relations of violence and subjugation. Yet, in contrast to (more) traditional Marxist understandings, posthuman feminism analyzes economic relations as one of many ways in which violence and unequal power relations are formed and made to matter, materially and discursively speaking, with Hohmann and Schwöbel-Patel's chapter (2023) and Lärka's (2023) providing strong examples of this. In this context the agential understanding of matter (e.g. Barad 2007; Bennett 2009) as existing beyond capitalist and anthropocentric ideas of (monetary) value are central, with, as noted, many chapters in this volume focusing more squarely on the intrinsic value or the subjectivity of nature and of matter.

Posthuman feminism and critical posthuman theory embrace the fact that technology is part of our current posthuman condition, as is advanced capitalism (e.g. Braidotti 2021). This may seem similar to a 'technology optimist' or transhuman position – however, as already discussed, this is not the case. Under transhumanism, as discussed earlier, technology is employed toward human enhancement – or the enhancement of *parts of* mankind – without any regard for (or, indeed in contrast to) questions of equality, inclusion of all of humankind, and less so, nonhuman agents and entities. And, as previously pointed out, and as discussed by Arvidsson in this volume (2023b), posthumanism is neither technology optimist nor pessimist, yet it embraces *potentia*, affirmation and pursues a critique without resorting to negativity (Braidotti 2021).

Outline of the Themes and Chapters of This Collection

The 12 chapters of the present collection are divided into three interlinked parts. The first part focuses primarily on the methodological and conceptual implications of posthuman theory as deployed in international law. The second and third parts focus more on various issues in international law, focusing either on a particular subfield of international law or a particular time period or issue. Part 2 thereby centers on political economy, history and colonialism whereas Part 3 focuses on the environment and the nonhuman. Being scholarly interventions in their own right, however, each section and indeed each contribution also serves as an example of what posthuman theory can offer to international legal analysis and practice, as well as to the specific areas that each contribution engages with.

Part 1: Methodological and Theoretical Frontiers

Part 1 begins with Matilda Arvidsson's chapter, which is titled 'Posthuman Feminism as a Theoretical and Methodological Approach to International Law'. Arvidsson's chapter provides an overview of the field of international posthuman legal scholarship and practice with a focus on posthuman theory as both a linguistic-discursive and a material mode of analysis. Arvidsson takes on the question of how posthuman (legal) scholarship sits within a broader development of material and discursive ontological and epistemological approaches in philosophy, science and law. She contextualizes the emergence of posthuman theory and practice through the question of 'matter' and the 'real' of physics and philosophy and as part of a feminist, gender, postcolonial, Black studies, Indigenous and decolonial academic and political action. Drawing on posthuman international legal scholarship, with an emphasis on IHL and technology, Arvidsson argues that posthuman feminist theory offers new ways for reconsidering and reconfiguring international law in response to oppression, exclusion and predatory violence toward more inclusive and less violent ends.

In Chapter 2, 'Flat Ontology and Differentiation', Anna Grear likewise focuses on conceptual issues in posthuman theory and their implications for international legal scholarship. She does so through a critical examination of the politics of new materialism, whereby she discusses the claim that 'new materialisms' are insensitive to questions of structural power. Identifying the vital materialism of Jane Bennett as the archetypical target of such critiques, Grear defends Bennett's 'flattened' ontology from the charge that her work produces a 'systemic blindness to the inequalities, asymmetries and hierarchies enacted in vital materializations' (Lemke 2018: 33). The chapter also reflects on the promise of Bennett's imaginary as a potential bridge toward Indigenous scholarly and activist resistance to the closures and violence of the Eurocentric international legal order. A burning question for posthumanist and new materialist international legal theory is how to avoid replicating the logic of colonialism when pressing back against the Euro-modernist onto-epistemology of the current legal order. Grear positions

Bennett's work as a potentially promising contribution toward that vitally urgent critical project.

In the third chapter, Delaney Mitchell, in 'Aesthetics, New Materialism and Legal Matter: The "Art" of Anglo-American Colonialism', questions the ways in which aesthetic methodologies are making claims on international law through a detailed discussion of Cameron Rowland's *Depreciation*, a conceptual artwork that seeks to dis/locate colonial concepts of property and broader living legacies of Anglo-American colonialism. Mitchell argues that attention to the differentiation between matter, as that which is-not-yet but has the potential to take legal form, and material, as matter that possesses 'active' legal form vis-à-vis its attainment of meaning through legal interpretation, is needed to expand knowledge of the ways that law is actively being shaped by artists. She engages with more established international legal debates on reparation and other forms of reparative justice to demonstrate that paying attention to intra-actions – and the distinction between law's matter and material which they reveal – presents opportunities to address 'new' and historic injustices of Anglo-American colonialism. Insisting upon the potentiality of this approach, Mitchell joins the call for international legal theorists to 'queer' legal ethics through meaningful engagement with principles found in posthuman theory, to rethink how we conceive of 'responsibility' as an ethical and political stance in the context of settler societies and to always orient toward matter in our pursuits of justice.

In the final chapter in Part 1, Chapter 4, 'The Common Heritage of Kin-Kind', Emily Jones, Cristian van Eijk and Gina Heathcote 'reworld' the international legal principle of the common heritage of [hu]mankind (CHM). While the CHM, in its plain wording, invokes a sense of hope, suggesting both a disruption to models of property and sovereignty while fostering an environmental imaginary around a shared sense of responsibilities, Jones, van Eijk and Heathcote argue that, in reality, the principle is anthropocentric, being deeply implicated in capitalist extractivism. The chapter draws on posthuman theory, and primarily Haraway's use of speculative fabulation as method, to reworld the principle of the CHM through an ecological lens. Taking head of posthuman theory's call to dismantle hierarchies, not only between humans but also between humans and nonhuman subjects, alongside its focus on challenging dominant models of subjectivity, the authors reimagine the principle through the lens of the common heritage of kin-kind, seeking an international law that includes the interests of nonhumans in its core principles. The chapter concludes with some reflections on the use of speculative fabulation as a method, finding a promise in the use of this method of reworlding while noting several limitations, these limitations being primarily rooted in the constant focus in Eurocentric international law on the precedent and the past.

Part 2: Political Economy, History and Colonialism

In the fifth chapter, titled 'A Monument to E.G. Wakefield: New and Historical Materialist Dialogues for a Posthuman International Law', Jessie Hohmann and Christine Schwöbel-Patel examine the monument of Edward Gibbon Wakefield, the so-called founding father of the colony of South Australia. Centering the monument, they discuss two types of materialism – new materialism and historical materialism – arguing that an engagement with new and historical materialism, by bringing them together, may open up possibilities for critical engagements with posthumanism. Central to this critical engagement are themes of materiality, settler colonialism, agency and exploitation – themes that are key for understanding the operation of international law. By identifying where these two 'materialist' theories differ, and also where they converge, Hohmann and Schwöbel-Patel ultimately seek to identify the utility of a posthumanist critique for destabilizing international law's imperialist, capitalist, racialized and patriarchal structures.

In Chapter 6, titled 'Neither National nor International: A Posthumanist Retelling of Tax Sovereignty', Hedvig Lärka analyzes current developments in international tax law, through Karen Barad's notion of posthumanist agency. The chapter brings together posthuman, Marxist and TWAIL critiques of the OECD/G20 global minimum tax, bringing forth an argument on how sovereignty emerges through international taxation law and practices – rather than, as is commonly argued, the other way around. The chapter shows the analytical and explanatory power of posthuman theory, discussing the agency and motive of economically powerful states in bringing about a global legal infrastructure, enabling both tax competition and large-scale profit shifting by multinational enterprises. In addition, some previously underexplored, tentative implications of the OECD/G20 global minimum tax are brought to light within the context of international law.

Chapter 7 sees Vanja Hamzić read the history of international law through Sylvia Wynter's insurrectionary *homo narrans*, from within the wider Black radical tradition and decolonial trans/feminist critique in a chapter titled 'After *Homo Narrans*: Botany, International Law and Senegambia in Early Racial Capitalist Worldmaking'. The chapter calls for new, materialist figurations of posthuman *homo narrans* to be fostered, away from legal or lawlike biocentricity. Hamzić maintains that the challenge for posthuman critique in international law might be twofold: first, how to include material, localized, multiple senses of the past in any ongoing reworldings and re-imaginations of the present and the future, so as to rethink temporalities and recount anew, rather than 'recover', insurrectionary times; and second, how to retell critically international law's manyfold complicity in systemic world-destroying and worldmaking projects – such as that of racial capitalism – without succumbing to the false promise of international law's salvatory powers.

Part 3: The Environment and the Nonhuman

The third and last section of our volume opens with 'Terraqueous Feminisms and the International Law of the Sea', Chapter 8. In it, Gina Heathcote analyzes posthuman encounters in the ocean through three objects: a map, container ships and robots. In articulating a form of posthuman feminism, Heathcote's chapter pays attention to the articulation of human–nonhuman encounters and the prevalence of othering (knowledge, peoples and nature) within humanist traditions. Heathcote argues that knowledge, matter and justice frames require a theorizing of terraqueous, or land-sea encounters, to undo and move beyond the repetition of Anthropocene harm and humanist forms of othering. The legal jurisdictions imposed on the oceans via international law are exposed in the analysis as obscuring and maintaining a specific political and legal understanding of the ocean, while posthuman feminism is found to open an unmoored oceanic subjectivity.

In Chapter 9, Marie Petersmann reflects on international law and posthuman theory through a concrete example of 'posthumanist commoning', exploring the posthumanist and commoning dimensions of the legal and political collective actions around the 'Lago Bullicante' – 'insurgent lake' of Rome. The artificial-natural lake was accidentally created in 1992, when an underground parking lot was illegally constructed, and an aquifer was hit. The construction site and nearby area became flooded and a one-hectare large lake in the heart of the city of Rome was created. With the lake an insurgent political subjectivity emerged to resist and care for its preservation.

In her contribution, titled 'Becoming Common – Ecological Resistance, Refusal, Reparation', Petersmann argues that both the subjectivity and the political struggles around the lake are articulated and practiced in non-liberal, non-individualistic and in-human (or more and less than 'human') terms, revealing a particular mode of becoming common. This mode of posthuman commoning, Petersmann thereby argues, offers an example of a practice of ecological resistance, refusal and reparation as well as an example of the possibility of fostering transversal alliances forged within networks of transnational resisting collectives. This example, she thereby argues, enables us to (re)think how posthuman theory can inform international law. It does so by availing methods of reconfiguring the categories of the human, the land and its living ecology – while also revealing critical blind spots and methodological and conceptual limitations of both posthuman theory and international law.

Kojo Koram and Oscar Guardiola-Rivera, in 'The War on Drugs as the War on the Nonhuman', Chapter 10, analyze the so-called War on Drugs in international law and its material effects in implementation. Aerial fumigation and crop eradication programs, as regulated by international law, have exacerbated the climate crises through an organized policy of eviscerating some of the most biodiverse areas in the world. Underneath the paranoia surrounding drugs was a fear of the subjectivity of nonhuman plant life. Yet, as the War on Drugs slowly appears to be drifting to its tepid conclusion, its aftermath offers an opportunity, in international law and beyond, Koram and Guardiola-Rivera argue, to create a reformed relationship with drugs. Drawing on posthuman and Indigenous cosmologies, can, the authors argue, help address the crisis we see in relation to human relationships with our natural habitats.

The animal is at the center of the next chapter: 'Supplanting Anthropocentric Legalities: Can the Rule of Law Tolerate Intensive Animal Agriculture?', Chapter 11. In it, Maneesha Deckha explores how the rule of law, in international law and beyond, can support emergent legislative proposals around the world to curtail intensive animal farming. The chapter reviews the global emergence of legislative initiatives and identifies their common features and themes, as well as their limited success, and discusses the pliability of the rule of law to serve as an agent of social change. It explains how the rule of law can be a persuasive discursive legal tool in generating actual legal regulation to address social problems such as intensive farming and connects the analysis to broader questions regarding norm development in international law. Drawing on posthuman feminist theory, the chapter contributes to the growing field of global animal law that explores animal law issues through international law and transnational law frameworks, by highlighting the potential of the rule of law to challenge the legitimacy of at least some forms or portion of animal-based food systems. The chapter adds to the developing conversation as to how to supplant existing anthropocentric legal norms through innovative deployment of new legal arguments in favor of animals.

In the last chapter of the book, Chapter 12, 'Will Human Rights Save the "Anthropos" from the "Anthropocene"? Limitations of Human Rights Strategies in Responding to the Climate Crisis', Jasmijn Leeuwenkamp analyzes the claim that the climate crisis should be regarded as a human rights issue through a posthuman lens. Highlighting the 'Urgenda case', in which the Dutch Supreme Court ruled that the Dutch state had to increasingly reduce its carbon emissions to fulfill its human rights obligations under international law to its citizens, she argues that the reframing of the climate crisis as an international human rights issue has at least two important limitations. First, reference to anthropocentric human rights leads to the prioritizing of human over nonhuman life. Second, as posthuman and postcolonial theory shows, the anthropocentrism of human rights is conceptually and historically grounded on a hierarchical logic defining the 'human' in teleological terms, externalizing this human's 'Others'. The universal 'human' of human rights and the notion of a universal anthropos in 'Anthropocene' masks, Leeuwenkamp argues, exclusions and related inequalities in power, responsibility and vulnerability characterizing the climate crisis. The chapter proposes that a critical analysis of the genealogy of international human rights shows that pursuing a human rights strategy in responding to climate change limits a more critical re-evaluation of how humans threaten human and nonhuman life.

Conclusion

Building on previous critical scholarship in international law and posthuman theory, constructing intergenerational and transversal alliances with previous scholarship and practice, and invoking questions at the intersection of posthuman and post-anthropocentric critique, the authors of this volume interrogate central aspects of international law, drawing on examples from international human rights law, the international law of the sea, international legal history, international tax law, international and global animal law, the international law on drugs, international environmental law and international legal method, among other topics. In doing so, the collection gives tentative answers to the questions we set out to answer at the start of this project and this introduction, namely: of what posthuman theory may provide in terms of methods and practices in the aim of helping to restructure international legal knowledges, relations, preferences, hierarchizations and boundaries; what international law and international lawyers may learn about the world and about international law by adopting posthuman theory; and how processes of posthuman defamiliarization can help international lawyers to reconsider and do international law differently, maybe even to less violent and destructive ends.

Calling on international legal scholars, practitioners and activists – within and beyond the field of international law – this volume set out a path, one that is both rhizomic and transversal, toward a more sustained engagement with the most pressing concerns of our time. In doing so, methods and means for affirmative and grounded reconsiderations and actions are availed, building toward a more hopeful present and future.

References

Alaimi, S. (2016) *Exposed: Environmental Politics and Pleasures in Posthuman Times*, Minneapolis: University of Minnesota Press. DOI: https://doi.org/10.5749/minnesota/9780816621958.001.0001

Anghie, A. (2005) *Imperialism, Sovereignty and the Making of International Law*, Cambridge: Cambridge University Press.

Anghie, A. and B.S. Chimni (2003) 'Third World Approaches to International Law and Individual Responsibility in Internal Conflicts', *Chinese Journal of International Law*, 2(1): 77–103. DOI: https://doi-org.ezproxy.ub.gu.se/10.1093/oxfordjournals.cjilaw.a000480

Arvidsson, M. (2018) 'Targeting, Gender, and International Posthumanitarian Law and Practice: Framing the Question of the Human in International Humanitarian Law', *Australian Feminist Law Journal*, 44(1): 9–28. DOI: https://doi.org/10.1080/13200968.2018.1465331

Arvidsson, M. (2020) 'The Swarm That We Already Are: Artificially Intelligent (AI) Swarming "Insect Drones", Targeting and International Humanitarian Law in a Posthuman Ecology', *Journal of Human Rights and the Environment*, 11(1): 114–37. DOI: https://doi.org/10.4337/jhre.2020.01.05

Arvidsson, M. (2021) 'Who or What Is the Human of International Humanitarian Law?', in C. Chalmers and S. Pahuja (eds) *Routledge Handbook on International Law and the Humanities*, Abingdon: Routledge, 422–31. DOI: https://doi.org/10.4324/9781003201120-8

Arvidsson, M. (2023a) 'Post-Humanitarian International Law', in R. Braidotti, E. Jones and G. Klumbyte (eds) *More Posthuman Glossary*, London: Bloomsbury, 113–15.

Arvidsson, M. (2023b) 'Posthuman Feminism as a Theoretical and Methodological Approach to International Law', in M. Arvidsson and E. Jones (eds) *International Law and Posthuman Theory*, Abingdon: Routledge (this volume).

Arvidsson, M. (2023c [Forthcoming]) 'On Gardens of the Anthropocene: Gendered Violence, Colonial Legal Enclosures, and Feminist Posthuman Kinship', in A. Grear and D. Kwek (eds) *New Materialist Tangles in and for the Anthropocene*, Bristol: Bristol University Press.

Arvidsson, M. and M. Bak McKenna (2020) 'The Turn to History in International Law and the Sources Doctrine: Critical Approaches and Methodological Imaginaries', *Leiden Journal of International Law*, 33(1), 37–56. DOI: 10.1017/S0922156519000542

Arvidsson, M., D. Gandorfer and D. McQuillan (2024 [Forthcoming]) 'New Digital Technologies, Law, and a Non-Fascist Life? On Global Governance, Digital Networks, and the Molecular Unconscious', in F. Johns, G. Sullivan and D. Van Den Meerssche (eds) *Global Governance by Data: Infrastructures of Algorithmic Rule*, Oxford: Oxford University Press.

Arvidsson, M. and B. Sjöstedt (2023) 'Ordering Human-Other Relationships: International Humanitarian Law and Ecologies of Armed Conflicts in the Anthropocene', in V. Chapeaux, F. Mégret and U. Natarajan (eds) *International Law and Anthropocentrism*, Abingdon: Routledge, 122–41. DOI: https://doi.org/10.4324/9781003201120-8

Baars, G. (2019) *The Corporation, Law and Capitalism*, The Hague: Brill. DOI: https://doi.org/10.1163/9789004392861

Barad, K. (2007) *Meeting the Universe Halfway: Quantum Physics and the Entanglement of Matter and Meaning*, Durham: Duke University Press.

Beard, J. (2007) *The Political Economy of Desire: International Law, Development and the Nation State*, London: Routledge.

Beauvoir, S. (1949) *Le Deuxième Sexe*, Paris: Gallimard.

Bennett, (2009) *Vibrant Matter: A Political Ecology of Things*, Durham: Duke University Press. DOI: https://doi.org/10.1215/9780822391623

Berlotti, S., G. Heathcote, E. Jones and S. Labenski (2021) *The Law of War and Peace: A Gender Analysis*, London: Bloomsbury. DOI: https://doi.org/10.5040/9780755637836

Bostrom, N. (2011 [2005]) 'A History of Transhumanist Thought', in M. Rectenwald and L. Carl (eds) *Academic Writing Across Disciplines*, New York: Pearson Longman. https://nickbostrom.com/papers/history.pdf
Boulot, E. and J. Sterlin (2022) 'Steps Towards a Legal Ontological Turn: Proposals for Law's Place Beyond the Human', *Transnational Environmental Law*, 11(1): 13–38.
Braidotti, R. (1991) 'The Subject in Feminism', *Hypatia*, 6(2): 155–72.
Braidotti, R. (2009) 'Non-Fascist Ethics', in M. Hlavajova and W. Maas (eds) *Propositions For Non-Fascist Living: Tentative And Urgent*, Utrecht: BAK.
Braidotti, R. (2013) *The Posthuman*, Cambridge: Polity Press.
Braidotti, R. (2019) *Posthuman Knowledge*, Cambridge: Polity Press.
Braidotti, R. (2021) *Feminist Posthumanism*, Cambridge: Polity Press.
Braidotti, R. and M. Hlavajova (2018) *Posthuman Glossary*, London: Bloomsbury.
Braidotti, R., G. Klumbyte and E. Jones (2023) *More Posthuman Glossary*, London: Bloomsbury.
Butler, J. (1997) *The Psychic Life of Power: Theories in Subjection*, Stanford: Stanford University Press.
Charlesworth, H. (1997) 'The Sex of the State in International Law', in N. Naffine and R. Owens (eds) *Sexing the Subject of Law*, North Ryde, NSW: LBC Information Services, 251–68.
Charlesworth, H. (2022) *The Boundaries of International Law*, Manchester: Manchester University Press.
Charlesworth, H. and C. Chinkin (1993) 'The Gender of Jus Cogens', *Human Rights Quarterly*, 15(1): 63–76.
Chimni, B.S. (2017) *International Law and World Order: A Critique of Contemporary Approaches*, Cambridge: Cambridge University Press. DOI: https://doi.org/10.1017/9781107588196
Cirkovic, E. (2021) 'The Next Generation of International Law: Space, Ice, and the Cosmolegal Proposal', *German Law Review*, 22: 147–67. DOI: https://doi.org/10.1017/glj.2021.4
Cixous, H. (1986 [1975]) *The Newly Born Woman* [*La Jeune Née*]. Translated by Betsy Wing, Minneapolis: Minnesota University Press [Paris: Union Générale d'Éditions].
Crenshaw, K. (1989) 'Demarginalizing the Intersection of Race and Sex: A Black Feminist Critique of Antidiscrimination Doctrine, Feminist Theory and Antiracist Politics', *University of Chicago Legal Forum*, 1: 139–67.
Cusato, E. (2021) *The Ecology of War and Peace: Marginalising Slow and Structural Violence in International Law*, Cambridge: Cambridge University Press.
Davis, M. (2017) *Law Unlimited: Materialism, Pluralism and Legal Theory*, Abingdon: Routledge. DOI: https://doi.org/10.4324/9781315775913
Deckha, M. (2010) 'Teaching Posthumanist Ethics in Law School: The Race, Culture, and Gender Dimensions of Student Resistance', *Animal Law*, 16: 287–315.
Deckha, M. (2020) 'Unsettling Anthropocentric Legal Systems: Reconciliation, Indigenous Laws, and Animal Personhood', *Journal of Intercultural Studies*, 41(1): 77–97. DOI: https://doi.org/10.1080/07256868.2019.1704229
Deckha, M. (2023) 'Supplanting Anthropocentric Legalities: Can the Rule of Law Tolerate Intensive Animal Agriculture', in M. Arvidsson and E. Jones (eds) *International Law and Posthuman Theory*, Abingdon: Routledge (this volume).

Dehm, J. (2021) *Reconsidering REDD+: Authority, Power and Law in the Green Economy*, Cambridge: Cambridge University Press. DOI: https://doi.org/10.1017/9781108529341

Federici, S. (2014) 'Foreword', in M. Mies (ed) *Patriarchy and Accumulation on a World Scale*, London: Zed Books.

Ferrando, F. (2018) 'Transhumanism/Posthumanism', in R. Braidotti and M. Hlavajova (eds) *Posthuman Glossary*, London: Bloomsbury, 438–9.

Gaard, G. (1997) 'Toward a Queer Ecofeminism', *Hypatia*, 12(1): 114–37. DOI: https://doi.org/10.1111/j.1527-2001.1997.tb00174.x

Gathii, J. (2021) 'Writing Race and Identity in a Global Context: What CRT and TWAIL Can Learn from Each Other', *UCLA Law Review*, 67.

Gilbert, J., E. Macpherson, E. Jones and J. Dehm (2021) 'The Rights of Nature as a Legal Response to the Global Environmental Crisis? A Critical Review of International Law's "Greening" Agenda', *Netherlands Yearbook of International Law*, 52.

Grear, A. (2015) 'Deconstructing Anthropos: A Critical Legal Reflection on "Anthropocentric" Law and Anthropocene "Humanity"', *Law and Critique*, 26: 225–49. DOI: https://doi.org/10.1007/s10978-015-9161-0

Grear, A. (2017) 'Ecological Publics: Imagining Epistemic Openness', *global-e*, 10(44). https://globalejournal.org/global-e/june-2017/ecological-publics-imagining-epistemic-openness

Grear, A. (2020) 'Legal Imaginaries and the Anthropocene: "Of" and "For"', *Law and Critique*, 1: 351–66. DOI: https://doi.org/10.1007/s10978-020-09275-7

Grear, A. (2023) 'Flat Ontology and Differentiation: In Defence of Bennett's Vital Materialism, and Some Thoughts Towards Decolonial New Materialisms', in M. Arvidsson and E. Jones (eds) *International Law and Posthuman Theory*, Abingdon: Routledge (this volume).

Hamzić, V. (2019) *Sexual and Gender Diversity in the Muslim World: History, Law and Vernacular Knowledge*, updated, paperback ed., London: Bloomsbury. DOI: https://doi.org/10.5040/9780755609147

Hamzić, V. (2023) 'After *Homo Narrans*: Botany, International Law, and Senegambia in Early Racial Capitalist Worldmaking', in M. Arvidsson and E. Jones (eds) *International Law and Posthuman Theory*, Abingdon: Routledge.

Hamzić, V. and Z. Mir-Hosseini (2010) *Control and Sexuality: The Revival of Zina Laws in Muslim Contexts*, London: Women Living Under Muslim Laws.

Haraway, D. (1991) *Simians, Cyborgs, and Women: The Reinvention of Nature*, New York: Routledge. DOI: https://doi.org/10.4324/9780203873106

Haraway, D. (1997) *Modest-Witness@Second-Millennium.FemaleMan-Meets-OncoMouse: Feminism and Technoscience*, London: Routledge.

Haraway, D. (2011) 'Science Fiction, Speculative Fabulation, String Figures, so Far', Pilgrim Award Acceptance Comments, 7 July 7. https://people.ucsc.edu/~haraway/Files/PilgrimAcceptanceHaraway.pdf

Haraway, D. (2016) *Staying with the Trouble: Making Kin in the Chthulucene*, Durham: Duke University Press. DOI: https://doi.org/10.1215/9780822373780

Harding, S. (1986) *The Science Question in Feminism*, Ithaca: Cornell University Press. DOI: https://doi.org/10.1177/027046768600600048

Harding, S. (1991) *Whose Science? Whose Knowledge? Thinking from Women's Lives*, Ithaca: Cornell University Press. DOI: https://doi.org/10.7591/9781501712951

Heathcote, G. (2018) 'War's Perpetuity: Disabled Bodies of War and the Exoskeleton of Equality', *Australian Feminist Law Journal*, 44(1): 71–91. DOI: https://doi.org/10.1080/13200968.2018.1470447

Heathcote, G. (2019) *Feminist Dialogues on International Law: Successes, Tensions, Futures*, Oxford: Oxford University Press.

Heathcote, G. (2023) 'Terraqueous Feminisms and the International Law of the Sea', in M. Arvidsson and E. Jones (eds) *International Law and Posthuman Theory*, Abingdon: Routledge (this volume).

Hohmann, J. (2021) 'Diffuse Subjects and Dispersed Power: New Materialist Insights and Cautionary Lessons for International Law', *Leiden Journal of International Law*, 34(3): 585–606. DOI: https://doi.org/10.1017/S0922156521000157

Hohmann, J. and C. Schwöbel-Patel (2023) 'A Monument to E.G. Wakefield: New and Historical Materialist Dialogues for a Posthuman International Law', in M. Arvidsson and E. Jones (eds) *International Law and Posthuman Theory*, Abingdon: Routledge (this volume).

hooks, b. (2000) *Feminism Is for Everybody: Passionate Politics*, New York: Routledge. DOI: https://doi.org/10.4324/9781315743189

Irigaray, L. (1985 [1974]) *Speculum of the Other Woman* [*Speculum de l'Autre Femme*]. Translated by Gillian Gillm, Ithaca: Cornell University Press [Les Editions Minute].

Johns, F. (2021) 'Governance by Data', *Annual Review of Law and Social Science*, 17: 53–71.

Johns, F. (2023) *#Help: Digital Humanitarianism and the Remaking of International Order*, Oxford: Oxford University Press.

Jones, E. (2018) 'A Posthuman-Xenofeminist Analysis of the Discourse on Autonomous Weapons Systems and Other Killing Machine', *Australian Feminist Law Journal*, 44(1): 93–118. DOI: https://doi.org/10.1080/13200968.2018.1465333

Jones, E. (2021) 'Posthuman International Law and the Rights of Nature', *Journal of Human Rights and the Environment*, 12: 76–101. DOI: https://doi.org/10.4337/jhre.2021.00.04

Jones, E. (2023) *Feminist Theory and International Law*, Abingdon: Routledge.

Jones, E., S. Kendall and Y. Otomo (2018) 'Gender, War, and Technology: Peace and Armed Conflict in the Twenty-First Century', *Australian Feminist Law Journal*, 44(1), special issue.

Jones, E. and D. Otto (2020) 'Thinking Through Anthropocentrism in International Law: Queer Theory, Posthuman Feminism and the Postcolonial', *LSE Center for Women Peace and Security*. https://repository.essex.ac.uk/26574/

Jones, E., C. van Ejik and G. Heathcote (2023) 'The Common Heritage of Kin-Kind', in M. Arvidsson and E. Jones (eds) *International Law and Posthuman Theory*, Abingdon: Routledge (this volume).

Käll, J. (2022) *Posthuman Property and Law: Commodification and Control Through Information, Smart Spaces and Artificial Intelligence*, Abingdon: Routledge.

Kang, H.Y. (2018) 'Law's Materiality: Between Concrete Matters and Abstract Forms, or How Matter Becomes Material', in A. Philippopoulos-Mihalopoulos (ed) *Routledge Handbook of Law and Theory*, Abingdon: Routledge.

Kang, H.Y. and S. Kendall (2020) 'Legal Materialiality', in S. Stern (ed) *Oxford Handbook of Law and Humanities*, Oxford: Oxford University Press, 20–37.

Kennedy, D. (1985) 'Spring Break', *Texas Law Review*, 63(8): 1377–423.

Knox, R. (2022) 'Imperialism, Hypocrisy and the Politics of International Law', *TWAIL Review*, 3: 25–67.

Koram, K. and O. Guardiola-Rivera (2023) 'The War on Drugs as the War on the Non-Human', in M. Arvidsson and E. Jones (eds) *International Law and Posthuman Theory*, Abingdon: Routledge (this volume).

Koskenniemi, M. (2006) *From Apology to Utopia: The Structure of International Legal Argument*, Cambridge: Cambridge University Press. DOI: https://doi.org/10.1017/CBO9780511493713

Koskenniemi, M. (2009) *The Gentle Civilizer of Nations: The Rise and Fall of International Law 1870–1960*, Cambridge: Cambridge University Press. DOI: https://doi.org/10.1017/CBO9780511494222

Koskenniemi, M. (2021) *To the Uttermost Parts of the Earth: Legal Imagination and International Power 1300–1870*, Cambridge: Cambridge University Press. DOI: https://doi.org/10.1017/9781139019774

Lärka, H. (2023) 'Neither National nor International: A Posthumanist Retelling of Tax Sovereignty', in M. Arvidsson and E. Jones (eds) *International Law and Posthuman Theory*, Abingdon: Routledge (this volume).

Leeuwenkamp, J. (2023) 'Will Human Rights Save the "Anthropos" from the "Anthropocene"? Limitations of Human Rights Strategies in Responding to the Climate Crisis', in M. Arvidsson and E. Jones (eds) *International Law and Posthuman Theory*, Abingdon: Routledge (this volume).

Lemke, T. (2018) 'An Alternative Model of Politics? Prospects and Problems of Jane Bennett's Vital Materialism', *Theory, Culture & Society*, 35(6): 31–54.

McKinnon, K. (2007) *Women's Lives, Men's Laws*, Boston: Harvard University Press. DOI: https://doi.org/10.4159/9780674265684

Meiville, C. (2006) *Between Equal Rights: A Marxist Theory of International Law*, London: Haymarket Books.

Mitchell, D. (2023) 'Aesthetics, New Materialism and Legal Matter: The "Art" of Anglo-American Colonialism', in M. Arvidsson and E. Jones (eds) *International Law and Posthuman Theory*, Abingdon: Routledge.

Naffine, N. (1997) 'The Body Bag', in N. Naffine and R. Owens (eds) *Sexing the Subject of Law*, North Ryde, NSW: LBC Information Services, 73–93.

Naffine, N. (2011) 'Women and the Cast of Legal Persons', in J. Jones, A. Grear, R.A. Fenton and K. Stevenson (eds) *Gender, Sexualities and Law*, Abingdon: Routledge, 15–25.

Natarajan, U. and J. Dehm (2019) 'Where Is the Environment? Locating Nature in International Law', *TWAIL Law Review*, 30 August. https://twailr.com/where-is-the-environment-locating-nature-in-international-law/

Natarajan, U. and J. Dehm (eds) (2022) *Locating Nature: Making and Unmaking International Law*, Cambridge: Cambridge University Press.

Nesiah, V., L. Eslava and M. Fakhri (eds) (2016) *Bandung, Global History, and International Law: Critical Pasts and Pending Futures*, Cambridge: Cambridge University Press. DOI: https://doi.org/10.1017/9781316414880

Noll, G. (2014) 'Weaponising Neurotechnology: International Humanitarian Law and the Loss of Language', *London Review of International Law*, 2(2): 201–31. DOI: https://doi.org/10.1093/lril/lru009

Norman, J. (2021) *Posthuman Legal Subjectivity: Reimagining the Human in the Anthropocene*, Abingdon: Routledge.

Offor, I. (2022) 'Global Animal Law and the Problem of "Globable": Towards Decoloniality and Diversity in Global Animal Law Studies', *Asian Journal of International Law*, 12.

Orford, A. (2003) *Reading Humanitarian Intervention: Human Rights and the Use of Force in International Law*, Cambridge: Cambridge University Press. DOI: https://doi.org/10.1017/CBO9780511494277

Orford, A. (2004) 'The Gift of Formalism', *European Journal of International Law*, 15(1): 179–95.

Orford, A. (2021) *International Law and the Politics of History*, Cambridge: Cambridge University Press. DOI: https://doi.org/10.1017/9781108691765

Otomo, Y. (2013) 'Species, Scarcity and the Secular State', in Y. Otomo and E. Mussawir (eds) *Law and the Question of the Animal: A Critical Jurisprudence*, Abingdon: Routledge, 166–74.

Otto, D. (2010) 'Power and Danger: Feminist Engagement with International Law Through the UN Security Council', *Australian Feminist Law Journal*, 32: 97–121.

Parfitt, R. (2014) 'The Spectre of Sources', *The European Journal of International Law*, 25(1): 297–306. DOI: https://doi.org/10.1093/ejil/chu011

Parfitt, R. (2019) *The Process of International Legal Reproduction: Inequality, Historiography, Resistance*, Cambridge: Cambridge University Press. DOI: https://doi.org/10.1017/9781108655118

Petersmann, M. (2021) 'Response-abilities of Care in More-Than Human Worlds', *Journal of Human Rights and the Environment*, 12: 102–24. DOI: https://doi.org/10.4337/jhre.2021.00.05

Petersmann, M. (2023) 'Becoming Common – Ecological Resistance, Refusal, Reparation', in M. Arvidsson and E. Jones (eds) *International Law and Posthuman Theory*, Abingdon: Routledge (this volume).

Philippopoulos-Mihalopoulos, A. (2015) *Spatial Justice: Body, Lawscape, Atmosphere*, Abingdon: Routledge.

Quiroga-Villamarín, D.R. (2020) 'Domains of Objects, Rituals of Truth: Mapping Intersections Between International Legal History and the New Materialisms', *International Politics Review*, 8: 129–51. DOI: https://doi.org/10.1057/s41312-020-00083-w

Ruskola, T. (2009–2010) 'Raping Like a State', *UCLA Law Review*, 57: 1477–536.

Schwöbel-Patel, C. (2021) *Marketing Global Justice: The Political Economy of International Criminal Law*, Cambridge: Cambridge University Press. DOI: https://doi.org/10.1017/9781108697651

Skouteris, T. (2012) 'Engaging History in International Law', in D. Kennedy and J.M. Beneyto (eds) *New Approaches to International Law: The European and American Experiences*, The Hague: T.M. Asser Publishing, 99–211. DOI: https://doi.org/10.1007/978-90-6704-879-8

Spivak, G.C. (1999) *A Critique of Postcolonial Reason: Toward a History of the Vanishing Present*, Boston: Harvard University Press.

Tzouvala, N. (2020) *Capitalism as Civilization: A History of International Law*, Cambridge: Cambridge University Press. DOI: https://doi.org/10.1017/9781108684415

Van Den Meerssche, D. (2022) 'Virtual Borders: International Law and the Elusive Inequalities of Algorithmic Association', *The European Journal of International Law*, 33(1): 171–204. DOI: https://doi.org/10.1093/ejil/chac007

Völkerrechtblog (2023, 17 May) Book Review Symposium on 'Feminist Theory and International Law: Posthuman Perspectives'. *Völkerrechtblog*. https://voelkerrechtsblog.org/symposium/feminist-theory-and-international-law-posthuman-perspectives/

Wilcox, L. (2016) 'Embodying Algorithmic War: Gender, Race and the Posthuman in Warfare', *Security Dialogue*, 48(1): 11–28. DOI: https://doi.org/10.1177/0967010616657947

Wilcox, L. (2017) 'Drones, Swarms and Becoming-Insect: Feminist Utopias and Posthuman Politics', *Feminist Review*, 116: 25–45.

Wynter, S. (2015) 'The Ceremony Found: Towards the Autopoetic Turn/Overturn, Its Autonomy of Human Agency and Extraterritoriality of (Self-)Cognition', in J.R. Ambroise and S. Broeck (eds) *Black Knowledges/Black Struggles: Essays in Critical Epistemology*, Liverpool: Liverpool University Press, 184–252.

PART 1

Methodological and Theoretical Frontiers

1

POSTHUMAN FEMINISM AS A THEORETICAL AND METHODOLOGICAL APPROACH TO INTERNATIONAL LAW

Matilda Arvidsson

Introduction

This chapter takes on the question of how posthuman feminism may be helpful as a theoretical and methodological approach to international law. Its focus is on methodology. I will do two things, organized into three parts. *First*, I will set out some fundamentals about posthuman methodologies, with examples and emphases on posthuman feminism. In doing so, I will highlight Rosi Braidotti's method of posthuman figurations, and Karen Barad's diffractive method. Drawing on these examples, alongside the rich traditions of posthuman feminist scholarship, I will explain posthuman theory and methodology as necessarily both material and discursive-linguistic, setting out some theoretical and methodological context. Doing this I will show how posthuman feminist methodology combines methods to capture the figurative and the empirical dimensions of the posthuman condition. This means that an inter- and transdisciplinary mode of analysis is necessary. I will frame the discussion within existing international legal scholarship. *Second*, I will argue that posthuman feminism is useful for international lawyers when describing and analyzing international law in the historical and material context of the posthuman convergence – and argue that posthuman theory and, in particular, posthuman methodology are central to the doing of posthuman international legal scholarship and practice. In the vein of this second argument, I provide a step-by-step example, drawing primarily on my own experience in working with international humanitarian law (IHL), posthuman feminist theory and frontier technologies – including artificial intelligence (AI) – in contemporary warfare. The *third* and last part concludes the chapter. In it, I return to the two main arguments pointing to the need for further

DOI: 10.4324/9781032658032-3

theoretical and methodological attention to be paid to both material and discursive-linguistic aspects in posthuman international law analyses, while also arguing for the usefulness of posthuman feminism as a theoretical and methodological approach to international law for all international lawyers.

Posthuman Feminism and International Law: Why and How

Why should international lawyers use posthuman theory as a theoretical and methodological approach? And why posthuman *feminism*? Starting with the first question, the posthuman convergence that posthumanism and hence this chapter addresses lies, as Braidotti explains, at the conjunction of posthumanism and post-anthropocentricism, as defined by three related phenomena: the height of technological advancement, the intensification of advanced capitalism, and the catastrophic sixth extinction in the Anthropocene (Braidotti 2019). These are three areas that coincide with core contemporary challenges for international law: the rise of advanced technology – in particular AI (Arvidsson and Noll 2023; Korhonen *et al* 2023), capitalism as a failed international peace project (Baars 2019; Tzouvala 2019) and present and looming irreversible environmental and planetary degradation (Gilbert *et al* 2023; Jones 2023). These are all questions that international lawyers have engaged with – and critically so. Yet, many of international laws' responses are lacking in terms of an overarching theoretical and methodological framework capable of analyzing the complexity and interrelatedness of the problems altogether. Posthuman feminist theory, in contrast, has the tools needed to analyze and respond across these three core concerns simultaneously.

I follow Emily Jones in understanding posthuman theory in international law as 'broadly call[ing] for an account of subjectivity that includes non-human entities, including a better understanding of the agency of matter' (2021: 6). This means a possibility for international law and scholarship to reconsider fundamental categories of subjects and objects, and with that the rights, duties and international legal obligations that follow (Arvidsson and Sjöstedt 2023). Posthuman theory, Jones explains, 'sits at the convergence between post-humanism and post-anthropocentrism', with not only an aim to 'dismantle hierarchies of privilege' between humans in terms of, for example, gender, race and class (the central idea of posthumanism) but also to dismantle human hierarchical supremacy over other subjects – including the environment and nonhumans (the central idea of post-anthropocentrism) (Jones 2023: 9). Posthuman *feminist* theory, Jones continues,

> stretches in multiple, rhizomatic and tentacular directions, bringing critiques of humanism as found, for example, in intersectional feminist theory, postcolonial theory, queer theory and critical disability studies,

> together and alongside fields such as critical animal and environmental studies, and science and technology studies.
>
> *(ibid: 10, references omitted)*

So, why posthuman *feminism*? The feminist version of critical posthumanism to which both I and Jones ascribe (Jones and Arvidsson 2023) builds on feminist traditions and practices of critique: it distinguish itself from transhumanism and long-termism with its 'ethics' of 'human enhancement' (e.g. Bostrom and Savulescu 2009), and from the fascist eugenics that follow (Arvidsson *et al* 2024). Acknowledging differences among the many feminist and critical posthumanist traditions, the aim of the posthuman feminist jurisprudence I pursue is to build on feminist knowledge, politics and practice to pursue intergenerational and transversal posthuman and feminist alliances, encompassing intra- and infralegal, as well as cross-disciplinary relations (Arvidsson 2023a; Braidotti 2021; Jones 2023). I will return later and develop how this has already taken place in international law, scholarship and practice. Emphasizing that this is not a question of 'more' or 'better rights' (Harris 2022), more or better international law, or even a question of more and better 'inclusion' of the disenfranchised and de-selected, the posthuman feminist transversal alliance acknowledges that 'We-Are-All-In-This-Together-But-We-Are-Not-One-And-The-Same' (Braidotti 2009: 32, 2020). The 'we' is neither built around nor aims toward furthering the white, male, Western, heterosexual 'Man' – it is not even built on 'the human', regardless of gender, race or able-bodiedness. 'We' are in the posthuman condition together, and a posthuman feminist alliance, with 'the human' decentered from its previous and current privileges in our common ecology, can make a real difference in the world – also in international law.

The analytical force of posthuman feminism resides in its rich theoretical and methodological approaches toward describing and offering a 'navigational tool' to international law in the posthuman condition (Braidotti 2013: 3). Posthuman feminism concerns 'the human'– because of its historically hierarchical dominant position – and seeks to undo the continuation of oppression while building on feminist traditions of theory and practice. Just as feminism does not only or necessarily concern 'women', posthumanism does not only concern 'the human' for the sake of the human. Rather, the idea is to question how a dominant figure has come to direct international law's development, scholarship and practice. At the center of analysis are relations through which some subjects and objects emerge and become recognizable to international law, while others remain unrecognizable: inhuman, a-human, nonhuman, less-than-human, more-than-human, non-subjects.

Posthuman feminism is, moreover, helpful to international law as it tends to manifestations of both material and discursive relations. Its methods are empirical: to actively engage – physically, in minute and collaborative ways – with the problems, sites and entitles that international law seeks to address is vital. Yet, posthuman feminist methods tend to discursive elements too: the linguistic and psychic registers in the analysis focus on subjectivity, power, relations and the potentials for a more hopeful future. To 'reworld', as Donna Haraway notes, one must act with the power of language (Haraway 2011, 2016a; Jones *et al* 2023). I will return, later in the chapter, to set out in more detail how the discursive-linguistic aspect of posthuman theory has been overlooked in parts of the scholarly field, as well as why it forms an intrinsic and necessary part of posthuman analysis in international law and elsewhere. Here it suffices to note that the combined methodological approach enables an analysis that captures, on the one hand, the discursive-linguistic, normative and performative powers of international law, especially elements of binary categorization and knowledge-production in international law and beyond (e.g. an entity is *either* a weapons system under IHL regulation *or* not – and if it is a *new* weapons system it must pass the tests of Article 36 of *Additional Protocol I* of 1977, or else it is illegal under international law. See further: Jones 2023). On the other hand, posthuman feminism enables an analysis of the material effects and power by which international law moves and changes things. In addition, it enables analyses of the material effects of economic, technological and discursive hierarchical power-relations such as they emerge in international law and practice. This must occur while keeping a focus on the conjunction of technological advancement, the intensification of advanced capitalism and the sixth extinction in the Anthropocene.

Like Jones, I am dedicated to applying posthuman feminism to legal practice, proposing 'concrete international legal change' (Jones 2023: 154). To do so, this chapter avails a posthuman theoretical and methodological framework for academic as well as practice-oriented international legal work with an emphasis on the posthuman feminism. As Jones aptly puts it, there is an 'inherent tension between wanting to work within international law but then having to accept international law's constraints when doing so' (155). This emerges through 'a wider tension' between theory and the work of 'bringing theory to practice' (155). With a background in legal practice, I can add the tension in bringing practice to theory: practice comes to scholarship with its own questions and concerns. In the meeting of these different positions important changes can happen, with due respect to the constraints under which international legal scholarship and practice exist. But how does one do it?

Let me give an example: drawing on the so-called turn to history in international law I have, together with Miriam Bak McKenna, argued that history is a fundamental part of the conventional 'sources doctrine' in international law (Arvidsson and Bak McKenna 2020). The sources doctrine is one of the 'constraints' (Jones 2023: 155) that international lawyers must work with. While a 'fixed' doctrine – building on customary international law and codified in Article 38(1) of the International Court of Justice Statute – its interpretation and application remains open and indeterminate to a degree: it is a legal doctrine that must adequately describe and respond to contemporary questions and concerns, also when those shift. Posthuman feminism, I argue, avails adequate tools for both describing and addressing pressing questions and concerns in international law, to reconsider subjects, objects and aims of international law, and to do so while working with the 'constraints' of the sources doctrine. In the posthuman condition, the sources doctrine thus can be reconsidered through posthuman feminist concerns to respond adequately in the present.

Although doctrinal international law avails a 'canon' on what and whose history counts, there is a critical consensus on the need and room for change in terms of the sources and histories relied upon by international lawyers (e.g. Knop 2002; Nesiah 2018; Obrégon 2019). This includes narratives (the discursive-linguistic part that posthuman feminist methodology tends to) deselected – for ideological, racist, sexist, speciesist and other reasons. It also, as Rose Parfitt (2018) points out, includes sculptures and highways and other objects of international law (Hohmann and Joyce 2018) (the material part that posthuman feminist methodology tends to). Using the sources doctrine as an example, my point is that to accept international law's constraints is to work carefully and creatively with international law to reconfigure *what* international law is, and for *whom* and which ends it is set to work (Chinkin 2022). For this theory beyond what international law's doctrines avail is necessary – posthuman feminist is the theory I suggest responds best to the most critical concerns of our time.

I have created an image (Figure 1.1) with a highly condensed version of posthuman feminism as a theoretical and methodological approach to international law. I will return to it as I pursue the arguments of this chapter, hoping it will prove useful in allowing international legal scholars and practitioners to come back to its fundamental and 'simplified' main points in search of entries, inspiration and courage to go on to change the world into a better place.

Posthuman Feminist Methods: Some Fundamentals and Examples

I will now turn to the inter- and transdisciplinary mode of analysis in posthuman feminist theory and methodology. Empirical research methods for posthuman feminist scholarship can be drawn from any field – the humanities, social and natural sciences and beyond. Often the multiple-methods approach means 'getting down and dirty in the field of play' (Massumi 2018: 69) to not only observe but to immerse oneself within that which one analyzes as to sense it – smell, taste, hear, feel – in a situated (Haraway 1988) and

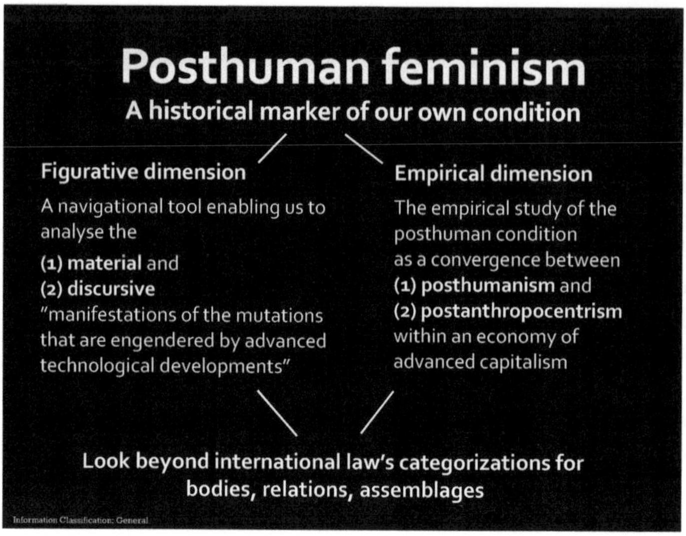

FIGURE 1.1 A simplified theoretical and methodological framework for international law scholars working with feminist posthumanism. Feminist traditions and ethics are part of the overarching framework, with methodological considerations in the figurative and empirical dimensions analyzed. Citation from Braidotti (2019: 2).

embodied (Gallop 1988) way, as often done in feminist autoethnographic and autobiographic methods (hooks 1999; Williams 1992). Research methods for the figurative dimension are more specific to posthuman feminist scholarship, which is why I will focus primarily on those here.

There is a rich interdisciplinary discussion on posthuman theory as a methodological scholarly and practice approach (e.g. Gravett and Kinchin 2020; Appleby and Pennycook 2017; Taylor and Hughes 2016). Yet in the field of law, posthuman methodology-oriented debates are limited (Davis 2017; Dekkha 2010; Grear 2023, 2017; Quiroga-Villamarín 2020). In recent years, posthuman international legal scholarship has grown in terms of the issues and fields covered as well as in the range of scholarship (e.g. Arvidsson 2018, 2020, 2023a, 2023b; Arvidsson and Sjöstedt 2023; Cirkovic 2021; Heathcote 2018; Hohmann 2021; Jones 2018, 2021, 2023; Jones and Otto 2020; Petersmann 2021a). Even so, little attention has been awarded to the methodological implications of posthuman theory for international law scholarship and practice.

As discussed in the introduction to this book (Jones and Arvidsson 2023), critical posthumanism – specifically posthuman feminism – builds on, converges and intersects with a range of issues, problems and theoretical and methodological approaches well known to international law and its scholarship: feminism (Braidotti 2021), Marxism (Braidotti 2019), post- and de-colonial theory and race (Wynter 2015), Indigenous and aboriginal knowledge (Bennett 2010; Bignall *et al* 2016), eco-feminism (Gaard 1993, 1997; Tsing 2015), gender and queer theory (Gaard 1997; Braidotti 2021), feminist science (fiction) and technology studies (Haraway 2016a, 2016b), quantum physics (Barad 2007) and related critical variants of scholarship and practices. With these a range of methodological approaches follow.

In *Posthuman Knowledge* (2019) Braidotti sets out the central methodological tenants of posthuman feminism in the following way:

> As a theoretical figuration, the posthuman is a navigational tool that enables us to survey the material and the discursive manifestations of the mutations that are engendered by advanced technological developments (am I a robot?), climate change (will I survive?), and capitalism (can I afford this?). The posthuman is a work in progress.
>
> *(2)*

In *Posthumanism Feminism* (2021) Braidotti explains this navigational tool – what we could also name as the tool for analysis of, in our case, international law in the present – as a 'chartography . . . that enables us to develop adequate understandings of our material life conditions and the complexities of the present' (212–13). This analysis is coupled with feminist figurations – 'projective anticipations about what can be done' about the material life conditions and the complexities of the present (213). 'They apply', Braidotti advises, 'and operationalize into action the epistemic insights of feminist theory, like conceptual personae, or "thinking aids" that helps us work through complex issues' (ibid). Barad, in contrast, works with a 'diffractive method':

> Diffraction is the physical phenomenon that occurs as waves emerge, when water flows across an obstacle like a rock. As opposed to reflection, which is a common metaphor for analysis that invites images of mirroring, diffraction is the process of ongoing differences. As a thinking-tool for analysis, diffraction attunes us to the differences generated by our knowledge-making practices and the effects these practices have on the world.
>
> *(Sauzet 2015: 40)*

Coming from two different methodological perspectives and traditions – Braidotti from the humanities and Barad from quantum physics – what brings the two together is a joint attention to the figurative and empirical dimensions through which the material and the discursive-linguistic come together, where relations and bodies are formed, subjects come into being and power operates in the posthuman condition. Before engaging with how the material and discursive-linguistic come together methodologically as intertwined questions of ontology and epistemology, I will expand on the two different posthuman feminist methods as examples, with some international law context.

Example 1: Posthuman Figurations

The use of figurations – described by Braidotti (2019: 2) in the preceding quote – for epistemological and ontological (normative) ends should sound familiar to the international lawyer: 'Theoretical fictions' – are often used as figurations in international law. These are idealized figures – such as the 'human in the loop' in IHL (Arvidsson 2021) or the 'victim' in international criminal law (Elander 2019) – working as metaphorical reflections rather than as matter. Through these figures international law is made to matter, concretely and normatively speaking. Posthuman figurations, in contrast – Braidotti's 'posthuman' or Haraway's 'cyborg': both of which I will turn to later – act to dismantle 'the posture of scientific objectivity, academic hierarchies and lethal binary oppositions' (Braidotti 2021: 213). Posthuman feminist international legal scholarship draws on both international legal figures and posthuman feminist traditions to provide new and altered figurations for directing law's normative effects toward less-violent, unequal and destructive ends (Arvidsson 2021; Jones 2023).

In Braidotti's work the central figuration of 'the posthuman' targets the power formations of the 'invasive nature of contemporary technologies' and 'the consequences for the production of knowledge today' (Braidotti 2021: 213). The posthuman is a 'materially embedded and embodied' signpost of 'crucial knots of knowledge and power, anticipating emergent meta-patterns of resistance and of dissonant and creative becoming' (213). The posthuman is thus not a 'thing' that can be found or constructed, but rather a mode of analysis and an operationalization 'into action' of 'the epistemic insights of feminist theory' (213). In my work on posthumanitarian international law the 'posthuman' works as a figuration questioning where and whether the distinction between human (warfighter) and semi-autonomous weapons systems can, at all, be meaningfully made (Arvidsson 2018, 2020, 2023b). If the international legal categories of 'the human' and 'the weapons systems' can no longer be distinguished from one another – given the developments in warfare and weapons technology and given the posthuman condition in which these take place, at the height of technological advancement, the intensification of advanced capitalism and the sixth extinction in the Anthropocene – then, why would IHL hold on to categorizations that neither reflect the state-of-the-world nor address the most pressing concerns of the world IHL is set to act in? In this context, 'the posthuman' is not a new kind of warfighter or way of applying IHL to make new/other distinctions and categorizations, but rather a navigational tool to map the discursive-linguistic as well as the empirical fields of IHL and contemporary technology-driven and advanced warfare. It can suggest where other ways of perceiving the world and international law – its roles and aims – are possible.

Haraway notes that posthuman feminist figurations offer 'condensed maps of contestable worlds' (1997: 11). They thus allow 'the complexity of the differential, materially embedded subject positions they represent and account for' (Braidotti 2021: 213). In Haraway's scholarship the most emblematic of these figurations – the cyborg – emerges outside of human/animal sexual reproduction, being neither fully human nor un-human (Haraway 1985, 2016b). The cyborg is 'a condensed image of both imagination and material reality, the two joined centers structuring any possibility of historical transformation' (2016b: 7). Being 'both a matter of fiction and lived experience' (ibid: 6) it functions as a 'thinking aid' to consider the 'interconnection that grounds technology into its earthly environment' (Braidotti 2021: 214). The cyborg can thus work as a thinking aid to sense 'the human in the loop' as a body of technological, biological and discursive-linguistic-legal matter (Arvidsson 2018, 2021). John Haskell (2023) invokes the cyborg to argue that the field of international law and technology is cyborgian in nature – being, as it were, both material and a matter of fiction. In understanding international law as cyborgian the scholar and practitioner of international law can approach the field with a vitality of always bringing change beyond static categorizations of old paradigms of thought and practice.

Example 2: Individuation, the 'Cut' and Diffractive Method

Taking a slightly different position, posthuman feminist methodology can also be described as highlighting what Gilbert Simondon calls the process of 'individuation' (e.g. Simondon 1980 [1958]). This is the material process through which entities are set apart, made individual, making them *one* thing and not the other. In this process a constant state of 'becoming' (a term adopted by Gilles Deleuze and Felix Guattari from Simondon) is interrupted, discursively and materially, by 'cuts' – a central idea of Barad's new materialist scholarship, by which '"the thing" "we" research, is enacted in entanglement with "the way" we research it' (Sauzet 2018). With Barad this is called 'diffractive method' (Barad 2007), a term that Barad draws from Deleuze-Guattarian philosophy. Simply put, it means that on the level of physics, things are not stable or stay within their 'categories', all the way down to atomic particles. The point about 'things' being constructs rather than objective truths and stable entities has been made several times before in history, philosophy and science – for example, by Michel Foucault and Judith Butler. Barad's scholarship brings the linguistic-psychic and historical registers *as well as* the natural science-oriented registers together to consider the continuous formation of things, persons, objects or, in short: how matter becomes through mattering. This is a mattering that Haraway expresses as '[i]t matters which stories tell stories, which concepts think concepts. Mathematically, visually, and narratively, it matters which figures figure figures, which systems systemize systems' (2016a: 160). This come to matter in international law, as Elena Cirkovic notes when arguing for an international law that 'instead of being the mirror of permanently split human subjectivity, could recognize the indeterminate nature of the world beyond it', showing how international law narrates and how carbon oxide is mathematically figuring the figure of the 'Arctic' (2021: 167).

The point is simple but crucial: there are no such things as 'things'. At least not as ready-mades. Neither in international law nor elsewhere. Instead, there are 'cuts' by which phenomena are individualized and set apart as individual entities, things or subjects. Or, in international legal terminology: subjects, objects and the many 'others' (Orford 2006). When Haraway notes that 'concepts thinks concepts' and 'figures figure figures' this is to say that (international legal) concepts and (international legal) figures can never 'mirror' anything else other than their own ontological and epistemological making of that which they seek to describe and normatively impose in the world. This is how international law operates: it 'cuts' phenomena in the world and thereby discursively and normatively sets them apart from other phenomenon, treating each differently according to its categorization and international legal definition. Illustrative international law examples include how civilians are cut apart from combatants in IHL (Articles 43(2) and 50 of the 1977 *Additional Protocol I*), and how AI is cut apart from human intelligence (the EU AI Act, Article 3(1)). Of course, nothing and no one exist in any real sense as a 'combatant' outside of international law's figurations – anyone who falls under the category of combatant only does so for the purpose of international law, and only so far as they momentarily embody the subject position of the combatant. It is a discursive-linguistic 'fiction' or, with Braidotti's words: an international legal figuration. One that has normative and material effects.

Drawing on the insights from physics – that there are no such things as things, physically speaking: there are neither subjects nor objects – the normative effects of how 'cuts' are made are substantial. How cuts – or, in international legal terminology: distinctions and categorizations – are made depends on the ontological, epistemological and ethical frameworks through which knowledge is established and legal normativity emerges. These ontological and epistemological frameworks change with time and place, history and geography: the natural law theory of the early history of international law is now abandoned for other ideals of knowledge-making in contemporary international law, scholarship and practice. How the 'cut' is made makes the difference. Making new 'cuts', and cutting in new ways, as international lawyers, enables us to understand the world in new ways, to see new problems – and old ones – and find new ways of approaching them. Posthuman feminism provides the framework through which to do this.

Another central move in Barad's method is the turn away from the 'linguistic turn' (mentioned previously):

> Language has been granted too much power. The linguistic turn, the semiotic turn, the interpretative turn, the cultural turn: it seems that at every turn lately every 'thing' – even materiality – is turned into a matter of language or some other form of cultural representation.
>
> *(Barad 2003: 801)*

Diffractive method involves taking seriously the inability of international law to 're-present' the world, as if it was simply 'reflecting' reality. Instead, as noted earlier, '[a]s opposed to reflection, which is a common metaphor for analysis that invites images of mirroring, diffraction is the process of ongoing differences' (Sauzet 2015: 40). Along these lines, Daniela Gandorfer and Zuleika Ayub emphasize the necessity for legal scholarship to move beyond the representable and to question representability as a function of international law:

> We want to think about the production of meaning in its inextricability from matter, with meaning understood not as representational (i.e. as a semiotic or symbolic quality or quantity), but rather as something constantly being carried (phora/φορά) 'with,' 'after' or 'between' (meta-/μετα-) semantic domains while also always traveling with or through an entanglement with matter – where 'matter' is understood not as fixed substance, but, following Karen Barad's claim, as 'substance in its intra-active becoming,' as such 'not situated in the world' but 'worlding in its materiality.' We are concerned with those political, aesthetic, legal, social, technological, physical, and environmental entanglements that not only shape but are onto-epistemologically constitutive of processes of knowledge and meaning production and transmission.
>
> *(Gandorfer and Ayub in Helmreich* et al *2021: 158, citing Barad 2007: 180–1, 83)*

The idea, thus, is that substance, matter, things, subjects, and so on are 'not situated *in* the world' (emphasis added) but make the world come forth and 'worlding in its materiality' (Barad 2007: 83). To capture this point, diffractive method helps as a thinking-tool for locating where international law 'cuts' subjects and objects apart, and how and where cuts can be made differently as to matter the world into a less exclusionary and violent place for the benefit of others than just some humans and their privileged pleasures.

The Material and Discursive in Posthuman Feminist Methods: How Language and Matter Come Together

In Figure 1.1 I have indicated a fundamental methodological insight that goes with all posthuman feminist scholarship: it tends to *both* material *and* discursive relations as intertwined questions of ontology and epistemology, and it does so building on feminist traditions and practices. This has also become evident in the two examples I expanded on earlier: while emphasizing matter, both Braidotti's posthuman feminism – the posthuman figurations – and Barad's new materialism – diffractive method – hinge on the work done by and through language with material effects. So, even if posthuman international legal scholarship foregrounds '*material* conditions' (Hohman 2021: 2, emphasis in original), and there has, alongside the posthuman international legal scholarship (cited in the beginning of this chapter), emerged a scholarship in international law focusing on objects (Hohmann and Joyce 2018; Kang and Kendall 2019; Parfitt 2018), attending to the material conditions is only part of the theoretical and methodological design of posthuman analysis – feminist or otherwise.

An often-appearing emphasis on 'material' – and ontology as subsuming epistemology – may be caused by it being underplayed in previous international legal scholarship – think only of the international legal scholarship on the language and grammar of international law, following Martti Koskenniemi's work (e.g. 2007, 1989). However, it is important not to lose sight of discursive-linguistic elements by overemphasizing materiality as the 'new' by which scholarship is to 'overcome' the 'old' (language). 'Overcoming' the past is a well-known trope as the glossing over of international law's colonial past and present (e.g. Hohmann and Schwöbel-Patel 2023). Moreover, when Barad (2007) states that language has been granted too much power, and when Braidotti speaks of posthumanism as refusing 'the linguistic paradigm' (Braidotti in Dolphijn and van der Tuin 2012: 21), it is understandable that some scholars have come to see posthumanism as focusing on all things material, leaving language behind (as if language somehow exists outside of the material). This, however, is to misunderstand what Barad, Braidotti and other posthuman (feminist) scholars are, and have been, doing.

In what follows I will set out the context on how language and the material come together through ontological and epistemological concerns in posthuman (feminist) theory and method. After this, I will turn the focus to the material, to then provide concrete examples of how posthuman feminist theory and methodology sits within international law, scholarship and practice.

The Discursive-Linguistic

In the so-called linguistic turns, especially its Saussurean variations and the discursive turns that followed, the problem for critical posthuman scholars, such as Barad and Braidotti and the international legal scholars and practitioners who draw on posthuman (feminist) theory, is not only the ways in which language and power become conflated – and materiality subsumed under language – but instead primarily the political hopes and agency that become invested in language (Braidotti 2021). Matter and materiality has become, in the most extreme cases in the linguistic turns, a mere product of language.

Moreover, posthuman scholars have turned away from language's mode of representationalism – for example Gandorfer and Ayoub (in Helmreich *et al* 2021: 158) as quoted earlier. Whereas language-as-representation invites a sense of language as 'mirroring' reality – and thus capable of (re)presenting reality as determined, determinable and defined through language – posthuman theory aims at 'processes of ongoing differences' (Sauzet 2015: 40). Posthuman feminist scholarship engages with language as part of the material and the relations studied rather than as its main vehicle for political hope and action. In a Koskenniemian turn, for international law the question of language, representation and the real can be translated into the question of the indeterminacy of international law. International law, Koskenniemi argues, maintains itself 'in constant movement from emphasizing concreteness to emphasizing normativity and vice-versa without being able to establish itself permanently in either position' (Koskenniemi 2007: 65). To Koskenniemi international law becomes a language and a grammar thorough which indeterminacy is operated or managed. It is done so less to 'mirror' the state of the art in the relations between states – although it does so to some degree aiming to gain a 'descriptive' force (Orford 2012) – but rather to normatively order the indeterminacy. Still, international law, scholarship and practice remain in the representational corner: ordering through a language that matters through stories telling stories, concepts thinking concepts, figures figuring figures and systems systemizing systems (paraphrasing Haraway 2016a: 160).

In sum: in approaching posthuman theory as a theoretical and methodological framework for international law the material *as well* as the discursive dimension are part of the posthuman condition. They are inseparable parts of the ontological and epistemological concerns posthuman theory takes on, *not* as dualistic or opposite ends but as non-separatable and fundamental entry points. Posthuman theory as a theoretical and methodological framework for international law requires methods that are discursively 'mapping', availing what Braidotti calls a 'cartography', while simultaneously tending to the empirical dimension through empirical methods. In terms of methodologies posthuman feminist scholarship works through the posthuman shift beyond the human as the central organizing frame, often combining a linguistic-genealogical-discursive register with empirical research methods. The first can be a method centered on the meaning and use of language, including the normative force and power attached to it. Methodologically, this is how conventional international legal doctrinal method asks the international law scholar and practitioner to approach international laws' texts: availing methods of interpretation of language and the performativity and emergence of normativity through language, of historical contextualization and anachronism, the hierarchy of sources and the ways in which general principles are made part of a discursive interpretation and argumentation.

Examples

Some examples of how critical posthuman feminist scholars have combined language oriented and feminist methods – empirical as well as discursive-linguistic – toward a critical posthuman analysis include what Jane Bennett calls 'doodling', 'decanting', 'dividuality' and 'middle-voiced verbs' (Bennett 2023). Some of these are well-known feminist and ethnographic practices, for example, 'doodling' to de-center oneself through 'automatic writing' as the researcher 'jots down' or scribbles both as a way of performing that which Jacques Derrida calls *différance* (Derrida 1981) and to write oneself forth as in Hélène Cixous' *ecriture feminine* (Cixous 1976 [1975]; Arvidsson 2022). To 'decant' is to aerate (as is with a bottle of wine): 'The "efficacy" ', Bennet notes, 'of decanting consists in an intensification of the subtle flavors, shades, tones, scents, trajectories already on the scene' (Bennet 2023: 6). All of which are part of embodied sensing in empirically oriented methods. Dividuality is the opposite of 'individuality' which harks back to the method of looking (and sensing) beyond the distinct categorizations to see figures that are neither 'individuals' nor 'everything': instead, such dividuality is comprehending 'lively elements continuously engaged in unstable and contingent relations' (8). Moving into linguistic methods of action and actionability the 'middle voice verbs' is a grammatical form of 'activities in which an actor is inside, and thus also altered by, the process . . . indicating an effectivity *amidst* a (heterogeneous, recursive) process' (9).[1] Whereas Bennett's methods are generally applicable to many scholarly fields and problems – including international law fields and topics – other posthuman feminist methods are more specific in terms of their embodied material research method, at least so on a first account: open water swimming with sharks, as Roslyn Appleby and Alastair Pennycook do in their posthuman language and education research, enables the researcher to map human–nonhuman relations in a multisensory way specific to the human–shark encounter (Appleby and Pennycook 2017). Yet, this specific relation – and the method through which it is studied – has

1 Bennet 2023 is still forthcoming when this is being written; therefore, pages refer to the pre-print version of the chapter, on file with the author.

broader implications, also for international law, its scholarship and practice. It decenters the researcher from a hierarchical anthropocentric order in which the human is – when in open water – out of her element, and instead in that of the 'object of study'. The latter is in Appleby and Pennycook sharks, but to study AI as an international lawyer the 'open water swimming' method may be translated into 'swimming' in the 'deep waters' of designing an AI-driven application (Arvidsson and Noll 2023). So, even as open water swimming is a method specific to its topic studied, the method of de-centering is central and generally applicable to all posthuman feminist work.

The Material

What, then, is the 'material' of posthuman scholarship? The question has been less materially bent in scholarly discussions, as it has come to focus on how the 'ism' stands in relation to previous scholarship dedicated to the material, materiality and materialisms. While Braidotti's posthuman feminism is straightforward as to how it deals with matter – it is a central part of that which constitutes the field of study (see Figure 1.1) as well as how it is studied – scholars and scholarships under the banner of new materialism have received a less straightforward response: a persistent suggestion in scholarship is that new materialism builds on, or seeks to supplant, *historical* materialism, and that it should stand more closely in conversation with historical materialism than it currently does (Jones and Arvidsson 2023). While new materialist scholarship may or may not gain from closer conversations with historical materialism, it is – as is critical posthumanism more broadly – not specifically a Marxist or post-Marxist field. There are, to be precise, relations between posthuman feminist scholarship and Marxism – relations widely acknowledged in posthuman feminist scholarship. Yet, the 'new' of new materialism is not a reference to a materialism that is 'new' in relation to historical materialism. Instead, new materialism(s) primarily builds on matter and materiality such as it has been considered in physics – in Barad's case quantum physics – philosophy of science, and philosophy broadly conceived. Most variants of posthumanism – including its critical, feminist and new materialist – harks back to the Spinozian philosophical tradition, especially as popularized and interpreted by Gilles Deleuze and Felix Guattari. The materialism in relation to which 'new' materialism is new is thus not historical materialism or Marxism, but the much broader and 'older' field of physics and the philosophical question of matter as it is considered in, for example, Aristotle, Spinoza, Nietzsche, Freud and not the least by Deleuze and Guattari. Moreover, new materialism, as Anna Grear explains it (2023), is a plurality of 'isms'. Some materialisms draw on and pursue conversations with historical materialism and its scholarship as their primary interlocutor. However, the main and shared methodological and theoretical point for posthuman- and new material-'isms' is the centrality of ontology and epistemology to the mattering of matter.

Matter and Discourse as Part of International Law: The Discursive-Linguistic and Material When Taken to International Law

But what does this material *and* discursive of posthuman feminist theory and method mean to international legal scholarship? In international legal scholarship the various approaches I have touched on already are all part of the emerging field of scholarship. In terms of empirically practice-oriented international legal scholarship, I have, together with Gregor Noll, combined conventional doctrinal international legal analysis with intersectional and posthuman feminist theory while taking on the task of designing an algorithm as part of the study of AI, international law and automatic legal decision-making (Arvidsson and Noll 2023). In a less hands-on, yet still materially and empirically interdisciplinary analysis, Gina Heathcote draws on feminist theory and methods to study the material design of military uniforms to enquire about the posthuman convergence of gender, technology and (dis)ability in warfare and its laws (2018). In a similarly interdisciplinary mode Elena Cirkovic has studied methane craters, Arctic greenhouse gas emissions and orbital debris in space as 'unpredictable and disruptive agents' (2021). This while employing empirical methods drawn from natural sciences as well as doctrinal international legal methods to argue for a cosmolegal understanding of 'the process of learning and lawmaking through which the law would recognize the unpredictability of human and non-human relations' (2021: 149). Another example, where interdisciplinarity in terms of both theory and method serves as the guiding framework, is Jones *et al* who draw on Haraway's 'speculative fabulation' as a method inspired by speculative fiction in which 'a mode of attention, a theory of history, and a practice of worlding' (Haraway 2016ba: 230) takes place as a 'practice, a way of disrupting ways of knowing and thinking otherwise' (2023: xx). Like Heathcote, Jones *et al* explicitly draw on feminist theory and practice. Yet another example is drawn from a proposition I have made together with Britta Sjöstedt for IHL to cover not only armed conflicts, with its specific distinctions and hierarchizations, but to instead ontologically and normatively move toward a merger with international disaster management law and policy. Toward this end we have argued for 'a more cross-species and multiaspect, embracive, and non-exclusionary IHL legal ordering [. . .] engaging with violent outbursts', of a potentially lethal character – regardless of if these are man-made or 'natural' disasters (Arvidsson and Sjöstedt 2023: 133). Drawing on doctrinal legal argumentation and method, post-anthropocentric mapping of the discursive and figurative dimensions of distinctions – invoking the Deleuze-Guattarian 'war machine' – as well as empirically grounded research (in the fields of, for example, ecology, immunology and AI swarming engineering), the theoretical and methodological design in Arvidsson and Sjöstedt is an illustrative example of how international legal doctrinal argumentation can be made to work toward posthuman feminist practice-oriented ends when combined with posthuman theory and method.

Taken all together, posthuman international legal scholarship, following on the examples already set out, is indebted to, draw on and converge with a broad field of scholarships, the basic setting of which are the concerns I began this chapter with: the posthuman convergence – the posthuman condition as a convergence between posthumanism and post-anthropocentrism within an economy of advanced capitalism – such as it becomes manifested both materially and discursively in our present times. From the scholarship I have referred to this far, it is thus clear that there is not *one* method that we call posthuman or *the* posthuman methodology to which international legal scholarship heeds or should look to. Instead, posthuman scholarships employ a range of interwoven methods, methodological approaches and emphases. Consequently, posthuman international legal scholarship has developed, and continues to do so, through methodological alliances.

In the following I will focus on the practical aspect of 'how to do it' of two posthuman feminist methodological approaches. The first is the method of invoking posthuman figurations, and the second is of individuation, cuts and diffraction.

How to Do Posthuman Feminist Methods in International Law, Scholarship and Practice

So, how to 'do' it all? The first step is always a step back, looking at the world as if we did not already know the answers that doctrinal international legal analysis provides us with, or how it allows us to *see* certain things as 'relevant' to the analysis, while others remain outside the framework of analysis. Or, for that matter, let us move beyond the limit of 'seeing' as the only sense useful to the international lawyer: there is touch, taste, smell, hearing and more.

Conventional doctrinal international law answers and categorizations are relevant to keep in mind when approaching a new question because those are the ones all international lawyers and scholars must relate to when making interventions into central international legal debates. Accepting international law's constraints, as Jones argues, means to know doctrinal international law well, without conflating oneself and ones' scholarship with its aims. To push the debates in new directions it is necessary to know against what to push. Yet, once we momentarily let go of the categorizations and distinctions through which we, as international lawyers, are taught to navigate the world to identify international legal problems and possibilities, we can 'cut' a particular field or issue of analysis differently.

Example 1: A Grid, a Field of International Law or a De-Selection?

To provide a practical example I have provided Figure 1.2. It depicts *something*, yet what do we 'see'?

Before answering the question it is helpful to ask where a 'cut' is made between the 'one' and the 'other' – in 'everyday' language as well as in international law's categorizations in the image. What are the subjects and objects we can describe, and how do they relate: where do they start and end? Do they have any pre-set 'limits' or are their beginning and ends linguistic, material or otherwise defined? What do we have in front of us, and how can we see as to *not* repeat what others have told us to look for? How do we make a methodological 'cut' to approach the material and figurative in the image? And who, *or what*, are we, in relation to this image, and what difference can we make in the world of international law, scholarship and practice – based on what we see in the image? At this stage, it is helpful to recall Bennett's methods of doodling, decanting and dividuation (2023). Stay with the image to see what transpires once it is aerated, doodle on the image and de-individuate yourself from it.

FIGURE 1.2 To make a 'cut'.

The cut I have made in the image (Figure 1.2) is made from a particular angle, using several different media (a camera, digital and printing technology). With Haraway's words it emerges as 'situated knowledge' from which we perform our knowledge-making (1988). Since no one, Haraway argues, can see from all directions simultaneously it follows that we all see what we see from a particular point of view. In Figure 1.2 the cut is made from a terrestrial situated position, forcing our gazes to see and analyze from an angle where the 'self' – the gaze as well as the analysis – is the same as the situatedness and position. Any knowledge derived from Figure 1.2 – in other words, any analysis or international legal norm – is therefore privileging *one* particular perspective above others: a terrestrial, human – we assume – perspective, de-prioritizing – while still recognizing – some other perspectives while 'de-selecting' yet others (Braidotti 2019: 164; Arvidsson in Arvidsson *et al* 2024). Drawing on the methodological insights presented earlier, what happens if we probe the limits of the perspective to see from within the position the metal of the steel-frame in the image? Does that change our point of view? Does it change what we can see, feel, smell and hear? Does it matter? Yes. In international law terms it matters if the departure point is enabling human free and equal trade in steel for profit, or if it is from the perspective of metals as ending planetary resources – its industrial refinery methods being ecologically unsustainable. What happens if we 'edit in' and make visible the humans whose labor made the construction possible? Does it make a difference? Yes. It becomes a question of international labor and human rights law. Or, furthermore, if we were to make a relational chart of all the individuals and entities connected through the technology embedded in and made possible through the construction pictured in the image? And the ones affected, as they walk or fly by, sensing the vibrations of metal and electricity? Would we then have an entirely different material set of problems for our international law and technology analysis? Yes. What if we decant the image until the nonhuman encounters transpires and are made to matter (to us, to international law)? And if we, furthermore, add the camera itself as a mediator and as a diffractive tool, does it change the international legal analysis? Yes. Of course. Which human and nonhuman creatures taste the metal and its afterlives? Which fleshy changes do the radio waves enact on different bodies? How are earth and air felt/imagined in this image? What laws might be invoked against my trespass under the structure – and who or what may pass the frameworks of international law unseen, unheard and unrecognized?

The image *can* be of a field of international law. But it can also be of international legal 'things'. It can be an international legal question, principle or topic – the subject in international law or obligations *erga omnes*. Can you see it? The image may further be one of issues, problem and phenomena that doctrinal international law does not cover, have ready-made answers to or have a language for, at least not explicitly so: the image may be analyzed in terms of inter-species communication, international data harvesting or international trade in digital identities made possible through what is 'there', within the cut we made. There is, in principle, no limit to what we can consider or sense. And: whose survival is at stake in the cuts made, and the differentiations and hierarchizations that follow? Who, in Braidotti's words, is 'de-selected' (Braidotti 2019: 164)? Posthuman feminist ethics involves not only locating those power relations played out through the cuts/differentiations/hierarchizations/de-selections made but also to address them with an aim to make a change for a better and fairer world.

While other theoretical and methodological frameworks – such as Third World Approaches to International Law (TWAIL), Marxism and feminism – offer possibilities of other ways of 'cutting', posthuman feminism allows the ontological and epistemological moves of the cut to be part of the analysis. Thus, in contrast to parts of TWAIL, Marxist and feminist international legal scholarship, posthuman feminism offers international law, its scholarship and practice an analytical tool with, on the one hand, a situated, transparent and self-reflexive theoretical and methodological framework of analysis and, on the other hand, a multidisciplinary/multi-methodological analytic approach to the posthuman condition – the conjunction of posthumanism and post-anthropocentricism defined by three related phenomena: the height of technological advancement, the intensification of advanced capitalism and the catastrophic sixth extinction in the Anthropocene.

Example 2: Posthumanitarian International Law

The next two images move us into the field of IHL, technology and AI, a field where posthuman international legal scholarship have expanded exponentially (Arvidsson 2018, 2020, 2021, 2023b; Arvidsson and Sjöstedt 2023; Heathcote 2018; Jones 2018, 2023; Wilcox 2017). It features all of that which has brought about the posthuman condition: the conjunction of posthumanism and post-anthropocentricism defined by the height of technological advancement – including international law's response to autonomous weapons (Jones 2021, 2023) and AI (Arvidsson *et al* 2024; Arvidsson and Noll 2023), the intensification of advanced capitalism – and international law's entanglement with it (Tzouvala 2019; Käll 2022) not the least as part of the military industrial complex (Arvidsson 2018, 2020), and the catastrophic sixth extinction in the Anthropocene (Jones 2023; Petersmann 2021b).

In Figure 1.3, we may think that we see a human warfighter. But do we? We see a helmet, parts of a uniform, a weapon and we see a few human fingertips – or so it seems. Taking the basic categories of human/nonhuman into consideration: where does the human start, and where does the 'other', the weapon and the uniform, begin (Arvidsson 2018, 2021; Heathcote 2018; Noll 2014; Parsley 2021)? These are question easy to answer in doctrinal international law . . . or are they? There is, in fact, no definition of 'the human' in IHL (Arvidsson

FIGURE 1.3 A 'human' warfighter.

2018. Compare: *The Geneva Conventions of 1949* and *Additional Protocols I and II of 1977*; Henckaerts and Doswald-Beck 2005), yet in IHL targeting and the use of semi-autonomous weapon systems there must be a 'human in the loop'. Who, or what, is 'human' in the human warfighter-uniform-neurostimulation-pharmaceutically enhanced-technological-media-mud-air body performing IHL targeting in contemporary technology-intensive warfare? Even with the best and sharpest of distinctions, doctrines and international legal arguments the question is not easy to answer. The suggestion from posthuman feminist jurisprudence is that the question is not the one that international law, scholarship and practice should be most concerned about. Instead, I and many other scholars with me have argued, the relevant question for international law is to how to curb lethal planetary destructive violence on all levels – regardless of it is 'artificial', 'human', 'natural', combined or otherwise (Arvidsson 2018, 2020, 2021, 2023b; Arvidsson and Sjöstedt 2023; Jones 2023; Parsley 2021).

Much of the weapons technology debates – but also those of AI – have centered on understanding the technology, *assuming* it to be different from, and distinctly not, human. But do we already know what the 'human' is or can be? A posthuman feminist answer is that 'the human' is not a stable category, but one often used to exclude and dominate both human and 'non-human' others (Arvidsson 2018, 2020).

Can the figure in Figure 1.3 be 'human'? Is it a 'human in the loop' of IHL and targeting? Or is that figure rather a posthuman entity of material agencies, relations, and technologies: that of a material human body, of a military uniform providing an exoskeleton to enhance the physical capacity of the human body (Heathcote 2018), and of a neuro-enhanced human brain using pharmaceutical drugs and electro-stimulation to elevate the human capacity to interact with the weapons-system it is part of (Noll 2014)? Is it rather a weapon that acts in concert with the neuro-enhanced brain? The list could go on: where does the human subject start and end, and where is the agency of nonhuman entities creating something entirely new: a posthuman, rather than a human, in the loop. The question is relevant to international law as humans are regulated in an entirely different way compared to weapons systems. Who, or what, is it? What would be a better way of regulating 'it'– better than to just 'assume' that the established categories are the best available?

If we look at Figure 1.4, the cut is made differently as compared to Figure 1.3. The human warfighter emerges as part of a broader field: as a field of grass, as part of the human and nonhuman environment (Arvidsson and Sjöstedt 2023). Or should we see this as a body of water (Neimanis 2017; Heathcote 2023) and hydrospheric legal relations? Whose private or public property emerge in the image? What minerals, atoms and germs are forming the dividual relations the image reflects? Who and what is de-selected through the international legal normativities in the cuts we make in analyzing the image? What about the smells, tastes, and sounds? The earthly vibrations as heavy tanks roll by, making the straws of grass tremble?

Posthuman feminism always pushes the sensing toward reconsidering the present in new ontological and epistemological registers: of human–nonhuman relations, of nature–technology relations, of the makings of advanced capitalism through the resourcification of nonhumans, of the ongoing climate changes, and of planetary destruction and the extinction of ever-more species. Posthuman feminism asks of you to consider the figurative as well as the empirical dimension, regardless of what you decide to analyze: and to go on and act. Do so as part of posthuman feminist alliances because, as Braidotti puts it, 'We-Are-All-In-This-Together-But-We-Are-Not-One-And-The-Same' (Braidotti 2009: 32).

Conclusions

One of the reasons international law lends itself so well to posthuman feminist analysis is that it builds on abstract categories of distinctions, separations and ordering. These have for the most part some, but not necessarily convincing, relations of descriptive force to that which international law seeks

FIGURE 1.4 A human–nonhuman environment.

to order. In other words, international law seeks to describe that which it orders in ways that are convincing to those who are to recognize international law's normative power (Orford 2012). This means that international law's categorizations and distinctions are only relevant if, and to the degree that, they can convincingly describe that which it seeks it order. For this reason, international law is in a constant need of theoretical and methodological frameworks that can offer opportunities for the international legal scholar and practitioner to see, sense, cut and (re)describe the new – and old – in more relevant ways (Aristodemou 2014). As the world changes – through scientific findings and technological innovations, geopolitical disruptions or 'natural' and human-created disasters – international law adapts, it stretches and bends. It is the task of international lawyers – scholars and practitioners – to 'bend' creatively, critically and ethically.

In this chapter I have shown how posthuman feminism can work as a theoretical and methodological approach to international law to stretch and bend, probe and reconfigure it – while staying within, as Jones puts it, 'international law's constraints when doing so' (2023: 155). Setting out some fundamentals about posthuman feminism, I have argued that that it can help international legal scholars and practitioners to pursue new ways of seeing and sensing our contemporary world, with its problems and possibilities: to cut the frames of analysis differently, to probe international law's categories to reconsider and reconfigure dichotomic and hierarchical notions of oppression, exclusion and predatory violence. Toward this end, I have provided some examples, primarily from the field of IHL and technology.

Drawing on posthuman feminist theory, and working within the current posthuman condition, the aim of this chapter has been to attend more carefully to methodology in posthuman feminist international law. Thus, when working as international lawyers, in this world, what I have argued that we can do is no less than to *not* repeat the mistakes of those who came before us; to make use of posthuman figurations and make new methodological 'cuts' in international law to approach the material and figurative anew and toward less destructive aims; and to take serious the questions of what difference we can make in the world of international law, scholarship, practice and beyond for a more hopeful present and futures.

Acknowledgments

The research for this chapter has been generously funded by the WASP-HS research grant *AI, The Social Contract, and Democracy*. I want to thank Emily Jones and Gina Heathcote for their generous comments on the chapter, as well as the participants of the Asser Institute Spring Academy on AI and International Law, 2023, the Hague, for their engaged comments and discussions.

References

Appleby, R. and A. Pennycook (2017) 'Swimming with Sharks, Ecological Feminism and Posthuman Language Politics', *Critical Inquiry in Language Studies*, 14(2–3): 239–61.

Aristodemou, M. (2014) 'A Constant Craving for Fresh Brains and a Taste for Decaffeinated Neighbours', *The European Journal of International Law*, 25(1): 35–58.

Arvidsson, M. (2018) 'Targeting, Gender, and International *Posthuman*itarian Law and Practice: Framing the Question of the Human in International Humanitarian Law', *Australian Feminist Law Journal*, 44(1): 9–28.

Arvidsson, M. (2020) 'The Swarm That We Already Are: Artificially Intelligent (AI) Swarming "Insect Drones", Targeting and International Humanitarian Law in a Posthuman Ecology', *Journal of Human Rights and the Environment*, 11(1): 114–37.

Arvidsson, M. (2021) 'Who or What Is the Human of International Humanitarian Law?', in C. Chalmers and S. Pahuja (eds) *Routledge Handbook on International Law and the Humanities*, Abingdon: Routledge, 422–31.

Arvidsson, M. (2022) 'Laugh All You Medusas! *Écriture Feminine* as Feminist Legal Translation, Transformation, Transgression, and Translactation in the Age of AI and the Anthropocene', *Australian Feminist Law Journal*, 47(2): 283–97.

Arvidsson, M. (2023a [Forthcoming]) 'On Gardens of the Anthropocene: Gendered Violence, Colonial Legal Enclosures, and Feminist Posthuman Kinship', in A. Grear and D. Kwek (eds) *New Materialist Tangles in and for the Anthropocene*, Bristol: Bristol University Press.

Arvidsson, M. (2023b) 'Post-Humanitarian International Law', in R. Braidotti, E. Jones and G. Klumbyte (eds) *More Posthuman Glossary*, London: Bloomsbury, 113–15.

Arvidsson, M. and M. Bak McKenna (2020) 'The Turn to History in International Law and the Sources Doctrine: Critical Approaches and Methodological Imaginaries', *Leiden Journal of International Law*, 33(1): 37–56.

Arvidsson, M., D. Gandorfer and D. McQuillan (2024 [Forthcoming]) 'New Digital Technologies, Law, and a Non-Fascist Life? On Global Governance, Digital Networks, and the Molecular Unconscious', in F. Johns, G. Sullivan and D. Van Den Meerssche (eds) *Global Governance by Data: Infrastructures of Algorithmic Rule*, Oxford: Oxford University Press.

Arvidsson, M. and G. Noll (2023) 'Decision Making in Asylum Law and Machine Learning: Autoethnographic Lessons Learned on Data Wrangling and Human Discretion', *Nordic Journal of International Law*, 92(84): 133–69.

Arvidsson, M. and B. Sjöstedt (2023) 'Ordering Human-Other Relationships: International Humanitarian Law and Ecologies of Armed Conflicts in the Anthropocene', in V. Chapeaux, F. Mégret and U. Natarajan (eds) *International Law and Anthropocentrism*, Abingdon: Routledge, 122–41.

Baars, G. (2019) *The Corporation, Law and Capitalism: A Radical Perspective on the Role of Law in the Global Political Economy*, Leiden: Brill.

Barad, K. (2003) 'Posthumanist Performativity', *Signs*, 28(3): 801–31.

Barad, K. (2007) *Meeting the Universe Halfway*, Durham: Duke University Press.

Bennett, J. (2010) *Vibrant Matter: A Political Ecology of Things*, Durham: Duke University Press.

Bennett, J. (2023 [Forthcoming]) 'Acting Amidst: Some Concepts and Practices', in A. Grear and D. Kwek (eds) *New Materialist Tangles in and for the Anthropocene*, Bristol: Bristol University Press.

Bignall, S., S. Hemming and D. Rigney (2016) 'Three Ecosophies for the Anthropocene: Environmental Governance, Continental Posthumanism and Indigenous Expressivism', *Deleuze Studies*, 10: 455–78. DOI: https://doi.org/10.3366/dls.2016.0239

Bostrom, N. and J. Savulescu (2009) 'Introduction: Human Enhancement Ethics: The State of the Debate', in J. Savulescu and N. Bostrom (eds) *Human Enhancement*, Oxford: Oxford University Press.

Braidotti, R. (2009) 'Non-Fascist Ethics', in M. Hlavajova and W. Maas (eds) *Propositions for Non-Fascist Living: Tentative and Urgent*, Utrecht: BAK.

Braidotti, R. (2013) *The Posthuman*, Cambridge: Polity Press.

Braidotti, R. (2019) *Posthuman Knowledge*, Cambridge: Polity Press.

Braidotti, R. (2020) '"We" Are In This Together, But We Are Not One and the Same', *Journal of Bioethical Inquiry*, 17: 465–9. https://doi.org/10.1007/s11673-020-10017-8

Braidotti, R. (2021) *Feminist Posthumanism*, Cambridge: Polity Press.

Chinkin, C. (2022) *Women, Peace and Security and International Law*, Cambridge: Cambridge University Press.

Cirkovic, E. (2021) 'The Next Generation of International Law: Space, Ice, and the Cosmolegal Proposal', *German Law Review*, 22: 147–67.

Cixous, H. (1976 [1975]) 'The Laugh of the Medusa [*Le Rire de la Meduse*]', Translated by Keith Cohen and Paula Cohen, *Signs*, 1(4): 875–93.

Davis, M. (2017) *Law Unlimited: Materialism, Pluralism, and Legal Theory*, Abingdon: Routledge.

Dekkha, M. (2010) 'Teaching Posthumanist Ethics in Law School: The Race, Culture, and Gender Dimensions of Student Resistance', *Animal Law*, 16: 287–315.

Derrida, J. (1981 [1972]) *Positions*, Translated by Alan Bass, Chicago: University of Chicago Press (Paris: Editions du Minuit).

Dolphijn, R. and I. van der Tuin (2012) *New Materialism: Interviews and Cartographies*, Ann Arbor: Open Humanities Press.

Elander, M. (2019) *Figuring Victims in International Criminal Justice*, Abingdon: Routledge.

Gaard, G. (ed) (1993) *Ecofeminism: Women, Animals, Nature*, Philadelphia: Temple University Press.

Gaard, G. (1997) 'Toward a Queer Ecofeminism', *Hypatia*, 12(1): 114–37.

Gallop, J. (1988) *Thinking Through the Body*, New York: Colombia University Press.

Gilbert, J., E. Mcpherson, E. Jones and J. Dehm (2023) 'The Rights of Nature as a Legal Response to the Global Environmental Crisis? A Critical Review of International Law's "Greening" Agenda', in D. Dam-de Jong and F. Amtenbrink (eds) *Netherlands Yearbook of International Law 2021*, The Hague: T.M.C. Asser Press, 47–74. DOI: https://doi.org/10.1007/978-94-6265-587-4_3

Gravett, K. and I. Kinchin (2020) 'Revisiting "a 'Teaching Excellence' for the Times We Live in": Posthuman Possibilities', *Teaching in Higher Education: Critical Perspectives*, 25(8): 1028–34.

Grear, A. (2017) 'Foregrounding Vulnerability: Materiality's Porous Affectability as a Methodological Platform', in A. Philippopoulos-Mihalopoulos and V. Brooks (eds) *Research Methods in Environmental Law*, Cheltenham: Edward Elgar, 3–28.

Grear, A. (2023) 'Flat Ontology and Differentiation: In Defence of Bennett's Vital Materialism, and Some Thoughts Towards Decolonial New Materialisms', in M. Arvidsson and E. Jones (eds) *International Law and Posthuman Theory*, Abingdon: Routledge.

Haraway, D. (1985) 'Manifesto for Cyborgs: Science, Technology, and Socialist Feminism in the 1980s', *Socialist Review*, 80: 65–108.

Haraway, D. (1988) 'Situated Knowledges: The Science Question in Feminism and the Privilege of Partial Perspective', *Feminist Studies*, 14(3): 575–99.

Haraway, D. (1997) *ModestWitness@SecondMillennium.FemaleMan©_MeetsOncoMouse™: Feminism and Technoscience*, New York: Routledge.

Haraway, D. (2011) 'SF: Science Fiction, Speculative Fabulation, String Figures, so Far', Pilgrim Award Acceptance Comments, 7 July. https://people.ucsc.edu/~haraway/Files/PilgrimAcceptanceHaraway.pdf

Haraway, D. (2016a) *Staying with the Trouble: Making Kin in the Chthulucene*, Durham: Duke University Press.
Haraway, D. (2016b) *A Cyborg Manifesto: Science, Technology, and Socialist-Feminism in the Late Twentieth Century*, Minneapolis: University of Minnesota Press.
Harris, A. (2022) 'Decolonizing the Legal Subject in Climate Chaos', *The South Atlantic Quarterly*, 359–75.
Haskell, J. (2023) 'International Law as Cyborg Science', *Nordic Journal of International Law*, 92: 9–30. DOI: https://doi.org/10.1163/15718107-bja10054
Heathcote, G. (2018) 'War's Perpetuity: Disabled Bodies of War and the Exoskeleton of Equality', *Australian Feminist Law Journal*, 44(1): 71–91.
Heathcote, G. (2023) 'Terraqueous Feminisms and the International Law of the Sea' in M. Arvidsson and E. Jones (eds) *International Law and Posthuman Theory*, Abingdon: Routledge.
Helmreich, S., D. Gandorfer and Z. Ayub (2021) 'Doing Theory: Life, Ethics, and Force', *Theory & Event*, 24(1): 158–91.
Henckaerts, J.M. and L. Doswald-Beck (2005) *Customary International Humanitarian Law. Volume 1: Rules*, Cambridge: Cambridge University Press.
Hohmann, J. (2021) 'Diffuse Subjects and Dispersed Power: New Materialist Insights and Cautionary Lessons for International Law', *Leiden Journal of International Law*, 34(3): 585–606.
Hohmann, J. and D. Joyce (eds) (2018) *International Law's Objects*, Oxford: Oxford University Press.
Hohmann, J. and C. Schwöbel-Patel (2023) 'A Monument to E.G. Wakefield: New and Historical Materialist Dialogues for a Posthuman International Law', in M. Arvidsson and E. Jones (eds) *International Law and Posthuman Theory*, Abingdon: Routledge.
hooks, b. (1999) *Yearning: Race, Gender, and Cultural Politics*, Chicago: South End Press.
Jones, E. (2018) 'A Posthuman-Xenofeminist Analysis of the Discourse on Autonomous Weapons Systems and Other Killing Machines', *Australian Feminist Law Journal*, 44(1): 93–118.
Jones, E. (2021) 'Posthuman International Law and the Rights of Nature', *Journal of Human Rights and the Environment*, 12: 76–101.
Jones, E. (2023) *Feminist Theory and International Law*, Abingdon: Routledge.
Jones, E. and M. Arvidsson (2023) 'Introduction to Posthuman Theory and International Law', in M. Arvidsson and E. Jones (eds) *International Law and Posthuman Theory*, Abingdon: Routledge.
Jones, E. and D. Otto (2020) 'Thinking Through Anthropocentrism in International Law: Queer Theory, Posthuman Feminism and the Postcolonial', *LSE Center for Women Peace and Security*. https://repository.essex.ac.uk/26574/
Käll, J. (2022) *Posthuman Property and Law Commodification and Control through Information, Smart Spaces and Artificial Intelligence*, Abingdon: Routledge.
Kang, H.Y. and S. Kendall (2019) 'Contents, Introduction & Contributors', *Law Text Culture*, 23: 1–15.
Knop, K. (2002) *Diversity and Self-Determination in International Law*, Cambridge: Cambridge University Press.
Korhonnen, O., M. Bruncevic and M. Arvidsson (2023) 'Subjecthood in Cyberspace and the Uncanny Valley of International Law', *Nordic Journal of International Law*, 94: 82–113. DOI: https://doi.org/10.1163/15718107-bja10058

Koskenniemi, M. (1989) *From Apology to Utopia*, Cambridge: Cambridge University Press.

Koskenniemi, M. (2007) 'The Fate of Public International Law: Between Technique and Politics', *Modern Law Review*, 70(1): 1–30.

Massumi, B. (2018) *99 Theses on the Revaluation of Value: A Postcapitalist Manifesto*, Minneapolis: University of Minnesota Press.

Neimanis, A. (2017) *Bodies of Water: Posthuman Feminist Phenomenology*, London: Bloomsbury.

Nesiah, V. (2018) 'Decolonial CIL: TWAIL, Feminism, and an Insurgent Jurisprudence', *AJIL Unbound*, 313–18. DOI: https://doi.org/10.1017/aju.2018.82

Noll, G. (2014) 'Weaponising Neurotechnology: International Humanitarian Law and the Loss of Language', *London Review of International Law*, 2(2): 201–31.

Obrégon, L. (2019) 'Peripheral Histories of International Law', *Annual Review of Law and Social Science*, 15: 437–51.

Orford, A. (2006) *International Law and Its Others*, Cambridge: Cambridge University Press.

Orford, A. (2012) 'In Praise of Description', *Leiden Journal of International Law*, 25: 609–25.

Parfitt, R. (2018) 'Fascism, Imperialism and International Law: An Arch Met a Motorway and the Rest Is History . . .', *Leiden Journal of International Law*, 31(3): 509–38.

Parsley, C. (2021) 'Automating Authority: The Human and Automation in Legal Discourse on the Meaningful Human Control of Lethal Autonomous Weapons Systems', in C. Chalmers and S. Pahuja (eds) *Routledge Handbook of International Law and the Humanities*, London: Routledge, 432–45.

Petersmann, M.-C. (2021a) 'Response-abilities of Care in More-Than Human Worlds', *Journal of Human Rights and the Environment*, 12: 102–24.

Petersmann, M.-C. (2021b) '"I Wish There Was A Treaty We Could Sign": An Inquiry into the Making of the Global Pact for the Environment', *Indiana Journal of Global Legal Studies*, 28(2): 7–80.

Quiroga-Villamarín, D. (2020) 'Domains of Objects, Rituals of Truth: Mapping Intersections Between International Legal History and the New Materialisms', *International Politics Reviews*, 8: 129–51.

Sauzet, S. (2015) 'Thinking Through Picturing', in P. Hinton and P. Treusch (eds) *Teaching with Feminist Materialisms*, Utrecht: At Gender, 37–51.

Sauzet, S. (2018) 'Phenomena – Agential Realism', *New Materialism: How Matter Come to Matter*. https://newmaterialism.eu/almanac/p/phenomena-agential-realism.html

Simondon, G. (1980 [1958]) *On the Mode of Existence of Technical Objects*, Translated by N. Mellamphy, Richmond: University of Western Ontario [Paris: Aubier, Editions Montaigne].

Taylor, C.A. and C. Hughes (2016) *Posthuman Research Practices in Education*, New York: Palgrave.

Tsing, A. (2015) *The Mushroom at the End of the World*, Princeton: Princeton University Press.

Tzouvala, N. (2019) *Capitalism as Civilization: A History of International Law*, Cambridge: Cambridge University Press.

Wilcox, L. (2017) 'Drones, Swarms and Becoming-Insect: Feminist Utopias and Posthuman Politics', *Feminist Review*, 117: 25–45.
Williams, P. (1992) *The Alchemy of Race and Rights*, Boston: Harvard University Press.
Wynter, S. (2015) 'The Ceremony Found: Towards the Autopoetic Turn/Overturn, Its Autonomy of Human Agency and Extraterritoriality of (Self-)Cognition', in J.R. Ambroise and S. Broeck (eds) *Black Knowledges/Black Struggles: Essays in Critical Epistemology*, Liverpool: Liverpool University Press, 184–252.

International Acts and Treaties

The Geneva Conventions of 1949: *Convention (I) for the Amelioration of the Condition of the Wounded and Sick in Armed Forces in the Field. Geneva, 12 August 1949*; *Convention (II) for the Amelioration of the Condition of Wounded, Sick and Shipwrecked Members of Armed Forces at Sea. Geneva, 12 August 1949*; *Convention (III) relative to the Treatment of Prisoners of War. Geneva, 12 August 1949*; and *Convention (IV) relative to the Protection of Civilian Persons in Time of War. Geneva, 12 August 1949.*

Additional Protocol II and II: *Protocol Additional to the Geneva Conventions of 12 August 1949, and relating to the Protection of Victims of International Armed Conflicts (Protocol I), 8 June 1977; and Protocol Additional to the Geneva Conventions of 12 August 1949, and relating to the Protection of Victims of Non-International Armed Conflicts (Protocol II), 8 June 1977.*

The EU AI Act: The European Commission Proposal for a *Regulation of the European Parliament and of the Council Laying Down Harmonised Rules on Artificial Intelligence (Artificial Intelligence Act) and Amending Certain Union Legislative Acts*, Brussels, 21.4.2021 COM(2021) 206 final, 2021/0106 (COD).

The International Court of Justice Statute: *Statute of the International Court of Justice*, 18 April 1946 (integral part of the *United Nations Charter* (Chapter XIV).

2

FLAT ONTOLOGY AND DIFFERENTIATION

In Defense of Bennett's Vital Materialism, and Some Thoughts Toward Decolonial New Materialisms for International Law

Anna Grear

New Materialisms – Critiques and Reflections

While there is no need for the purposes of a chapter in this particular book to rehearse a general introduction to new materialisms, definitional questions and the identification of 'new materialism' form a necessary component of this chapter if only because the book's editorial framing distinguishes 'new materialism' from 'posthumanism' to suggest that certain strands of 'new materialism' are insensitive to questions of structural injustice. In this connection, the editors by implication draw into the book's foundational framing the resonance of a wider critique concerning 'new materialism's' alleged lack of conceptual resources for critiques of power – including in respect of international law (Hohmann 2021). What, then, is the concern underlying such a distinction between new materialism and posthumanism? And how might the distinction be established? Relatedly, does new materialism really lack the conceptual resources for critiques of power now so necessary for decolonial international legal praxes? Is it possible that new materialism, on the contrary, could offer a unique contribution to such efforts? And if so, how?

To address these questions, this chapter reflects on the implications of a difference of ontological inflection that could ground a nuanced distinction between 'posthumanism' and 'new materialism' for the purposes of analyzing 'new materialism's' alleged lack of capacity to offer critiques of structural injustice. Jane Bennett's work is often a core target of such critiques, accused of producing a 'systemic blindness to the inequalities, asymmetries and hierarchies enacted in vital materializations' (Lemke 2018: 31). The chapter explores this critique before reframing Bennett's work as a potentially

DOI: 10.4324/9781032658032-4

promising new materialist contribution to the critical project of replacing the Euro-modernist onto-epistemology currently underwriting the patterned injustices of the international legal order.

New Materialism/Posthumanism – What's the Fuss/zz?

The first challenge facing the drawing of the distinction in question between new materialism and posthumanism is presented by the energetic heterogeneity of the 'new materialisms', which makes definitional settlement challenging. Distinctions – however – need not be closures and – if anything – the various nuances and inflections of posthumanist and new materialist work add energy to their generative possibilities. The very heterogeneity of 'new materialism' is a core feature reflecting 'the emergence of new paradigms for which no overall orthodoxy has yet been established' (Coole and Frost 2010: 4), and the 'overlapping, contradictory, and unstable insights of the renewed materialisms' (Quiroga-Villamarín 2020: 129) suggest that meanings are up for grabs, unsettled and invigoratingly open. I welcome that. I imagine that the editors do, too, and I therefore suggest that the editorial framing of this book is best conceived of not as an attempt to fix a boundary so much as an invitation to think further into emergent nuances and tensions of a highly dynamic field. And yet, a distinction is invoked. And it is a distinction not without connection to the more unqualified claim (which the editors do not make) that 'new materialism' lacks the conceptual resources to contribute to critiques of structural power.

The contemporary origins of the terms 'new materialism'/'neo-materialism' (Dolphijn and van der Tuin 2012: 13) are to be found in the 'second half of the 1990s', in their deployment by Rosi Braidotti and Manuel De Landa (ibid: 48). In an interview published in *New Materialism: Interviews and Cartography* (ibid: 19–37), Braidotti said that her interviewers were 'right in pointing out the progressive development of and identification with the label "neo-materialism" within the corpus of [her] nomadic thought' (ibid: 20). Central to neo-materialism, Braidotti explained, is its function as 'a method, a conceptual frame and a political stand, which refuses the linguistic paradigm, stressing instead the concrete yet complex materiality of bodies immersed in social relations of power' (ibid: 21). The need to reimagine/renew materialism was a response, she noted, to 'recent scientific insights, notably psychoanalysis, but also in terms of the critical inquiry into the mutations of advanced capitalism' (ibid: 20). Accordingly, in its emergence as an explicit referent, 'new' or 'neo-' materialism was a development emphatically embracing critical inquiry into the uneven power dynamics intrinsic to advanced/neoliberal capitalism.

The centrality to new materialism of (uneven) socio-material processes is also made clear by De Landa, who argued in the same set of interviews that materialism 'must take as its point of departure the existence of a material world that is independent of our minds' (ibid: 39) and that once one confronts the need to explain the 'enduring identity' of material entities and rejects the idea of 'essences', it necessarily follows that 'all objective entities are products of a historical process, that is, their identity is synthesized or produced as part of cosmological, geological, biological or social history' (ibid). While 'neo-materialism is based on the idea that matter has morphogenetic capacities of its own and does not need to be commanded into generating form' (ibid: 43), some of the historical processes that have 'synthesized or produced' 'objective entities' are emphatically 'social': new materialism thus assumes (arguably *foregrounds*) formations of the socio-material. In a sense, then, the theoretical centrality to new materialism of social relations of power in which the 'concrete yet complex materiality of bodies is immersed' (Braidotti, ibid: 21) is inevitable. *How could it be otherwise?*

Is there, then, a more precisely focused inflection point at which 'new materialism' fails to retain this emphasis on the power-soaked implications of non-essentialist materialism, fails to function as 'a method, a conceptual frame and a political stand . . . [foregrounding] the concrete yet complex materiality of bodies immersed in these social relations of power' (ibid)? To my mind, the precise point of inflection turns on an ontological nuance: all new materialisms deploy a monistic ontology, and some new materialist accounts frame this monism in terms of what De Landa calls a 'flat ontology' (De Landa 2013: 47).[1] There is, accordingly, an apparent need within the field of the new materialisms 'to reconcile the tension between "flat" and differentiated, subject-oriented accounts of agency, significance and value' (Deiner 2020: 1).

I venture to suggest that if there is any single 'new materialist' whose work is most frequently targeted by critiques of a 'flat' 'new materialist' ontology, it is Jane Bennett, author of *Vibrant Matter: Towards a Political Ecology of Things* (Bennett 2010). Similar critiques have been leveled against Object Oriented Ontology (OOO), but since OOO is often distinguished from 'new materialism', I focus here on Bennett's work. And while De Landa famously employs a flat ontology, it is Bennett who has attracted particularly sustained criticism concerning the implications of her 'vital materialism'. Bennett is obviously an influential new materialist scholar – in that sense, a natural target for reflection and critique. Interestingly, however, unlike Braidotti – who

1 De Landa defines 'flat ontology' in the following terms: 'while an ontology based on relations between general types and particular instances is *hierarchical*, each level representing a different ontological category (organism, species, genera), an approach in terms of interacting parts and emergent wholes leads to a *flat ontology*, one made exclusively of unique, singular individuals, differing in spatio-temporal scale but not in ontological status' (De Landa 2013: 47, emphasis original).

overtly aligns herself with neo-materialism – Bennett has not to my knowledge (or to hers)[2] used the term 'new materialist' of herself. Setting Bennett's work apart from other broadly posthumanist/new materialist work is not, however, always straightforward.

First, with regard to the distinction between 'new materialism' and posthumanism as it bears upon power relations, as noted earlier *all* new materialisms (as *materialisms*) presuppose historically accumulated/evolved formations of materiality and socio-materiality. And as concerns the latter in particular, these processes can meaningfully be called 'power-soaked' – ineluctably marked as they are by long-standing patterns of unevenness.

Second, critics of new materialism, including critics of Bennett, frequently take simultaneous aim at posthumanism. Some – perhaps many – seem to use the concepts interchangeably – which is another factor emphasizing the fuzzy elusiveness of the distinction between them. In this regard, Bennett's work is certainly not always a clearly distinguished target. One well-known critique of new materialism (Rekret 2016) for example, takes direct aim at what the author calls the 'growing constellation of "new materialist" theories of ethics and politics' precisely by taking 'as exemplary the work of Jane Bennett, Rosi Braidotti [a leading affirmative posthumanist theorist], and Karen Barad' (Rekret 2016: 225). Even Thomas Lemke, who offers a sustained critique of Bennett's work (Lemke 2018), and to whose criticisms this chapter will shortly turn, describes Bennett's work as being dedicated to 'elaborating the implications of the material turn and posthumanist conceptions for politics and political theory for a long time' (ibid: 32).

Without attempting to produce an analytical cartography and having positioned Bennett as a key target of critiques of 'new materialism' against the fuzziness attending questions of identification more generally, it is time to turn closer attention to the question of the difference in inflection at issue. It seems that the editorial framing of this book drives at a nuanced distinction between 'new materialism' as a monist position deploying a 'flat ontology' and 'posthumanism' (as distinct from *this* version of 'new materialism') as a monism allowing for (and focusing on to a significant degree) a 'differentiated, subject-oriented account of agency, significance and value' (Deiner 2020: 1). Closely related to addressing that distinction, therefore – and some related criticisms of Bennett's work – is the question of whether, *even if* 'new materialism' is to be distinguished by its 'flat' ontology, such an ontology renders differentially constructed forms of agentic responsibility – including differentially constructed forms of human agentic responsibility – impossible/

2 Personal conversation with Jane Bennett: Cardiff University, 2020, at the 'New Materialist Imaginaries for the Anthropocene' final event with Jane Bennett and William Connolly in the School of Law and Politics; funded by the Centre of Law and Society.

difficult to account for and respond to. Does *differentiation*, and any related theory of legal/political/ethical responsibility, moreover, necessarily rely upon a *subject-oriented* account of agency, significance and value? And does Bennett's 'flattish'[3] ontology necessarily rule out processes of differential subjectivization despite her wariness concerning the subject of the subject? And even *if* Bennett's work (as my putatively archetypical critical target) adopts a putatively 'flat ontology', does it follow that there would be no conceptual resources within her work from which to address questions of power and patterns of injustice? Is such a conclusion inevitable? Or is the matter more nuanced?

Lemke's Critique of Bennett

In 'An Alternative Model of Politics: Prospects and Problems of Jane Bennett's *Vital Materialism*', Lemke offers a sustained reflection on the implications of Bennett's ontology and ethical approach, reflecting on 'some problems and limitations' of her theoretical perspective (Lemke 2018: 31).

Lemke sets out to analyze the 'ontological underpinnings of Bennett's materialist account', focusing on two examples that Bennett uses to 'illustrate [her] notion of a "force of things"' (ibid). He argues that Bennett's

> notion of an all-encompassing vitality of matter is insufficient to explain the relationality of matter; it is also empirically limited and provides only a selective account of agency. These shortcomings and limitations affect the political perspectives of Bennett's version of vital materialism. . . . Being attentive to the vitality of things translates into a systemic blindness concerning the inequalities, asymmetries and hierarchies enacted in vital materializations.
>
> *(ibid)*

Space will not here permit an entirely satisfying discussion of Lemke's critique nor offer room for detailed, contextualized answers drawn from Bennett's work. A few indicative arguments will have to suffice. Accordingly, in this segment of the chapter, I introduce Lemke's arguments and indicate some potential responses to his critique.

Lemke contextualizes his analysis of Bennett's ontology by citing Braun and Whatmore's observation that 'the matter of politics and the politics of matter have never seemed so thoroughly entwined' (ibid: 32), noting the breadth of new materialisms and their promise 'to provide a very different

3 Bennett's preferred terminology and characterization of her ontology: email correspondence with the author, 2021.

account of agency and ontology, one that fundamentally affects political categories and concepts' (ibid). Importantly, Lemke notes that the 'reappraisal of matter is *intrinsically connected* to a rethinking of the composition of the political collective and [to] the question of how non-human entities, from algorithms to cell phones and genes, shape and govern political practices and social conduct' (ibid: emphasis added). Indeed, such a new materialist deconstruction of the centrality of human agency is, Lemke (rightly) suggests, a precondition for addressing contemporary economic and environmental crises (ibid).

Notwithstanding the inherently political implications of new materialism, for Lemke, Bennett's new materialist ontology translates into a 'systemic blindness' concerning patterns of inequality, asymmetry and hierarchy (ibid: 33). It is this conclusion – and the criticisms offered in support of it – that I seek now to address.

Lemke notes that Bennett's alternative 'onto-story', with its central emphasis on 'thing power' and distributive agency, has an overtly affirmative political ambition (ibid: 34). Bennett argues that attention to the vibrancy of matter, and a 'positive ontology' embracing the 'shared materiality of all things' (ibid, citing Bennett 2010: vii–x), will encourage 'the emergence of more ecological and more materially sustainable modes of production and consumption' (Bennett, ibid). Folded into seeking more materially sustainable modes of production and consumption, of course, is a concern to move away from the eco-destructive, consumptive priorities of the current neoliberal market order. Politics – with all that it implies about questions of injustice and responsibility – lies at the heart of Bennett's aims and the 'guiding question' of Bennett's work is: 'How would political responses to public problems change were we to take seriously the vitality of (nonhuman) bodies?' (Lemke 2018: 34, citing Bennett 2010: viii). Although Lemke certainly does not frame Bennett's aim in these terms, Bennett's focus seems shaped by an unerring concern to generate a materialist onto-politics going to the very heart of the capitalist order (the unsustainable order of 'production and consumption' endangering planetary life) (see Bennett 2021: 204). As I read her, Bennett directs attention to what has been there all along but which has been marginalized/occluded by an almost exclusive focus on human agency and on the objectification of 'nature'. Such onto-political matters are always inherently interwoven with and freighted by questions concerning the social power structures and socio-material histories through which inequalities, injustices, asymmetries, hierarchies and deeply uneven processes of subjectification, subjectivization and objectification have been constructed and are sustained (Grear 2015) – not least, in the Eurocentric life-colonizing materialities of the international juridical order (Blanco and Grear 2019).

Lemke is clearly aware that Bennett cannot fairly be said to be inadvertent to structural injustices. Indeed, he notes that Bennett assumes the exposure of social hegemonies typical of earlier materialist critiques and directly addresses 'the limits of strategies of "demystification" prominent in the materialist tradition, which often buy into the anthropocentric imaginary according to which human agency "has illicitly been projected into things"' (Lemke 2018: 34, citing Bennett 2010: xiv, 2001: 111–30; see also Khan 2009: 93–5). Bennett thus *supplements*, rather than seeks to supplant, earlier historical materialist critiques. As Lemke puts it:

> For Bennett it is not sufficient to 'expose social hegemonies' as historical materialists did; we *also* need to address 'nonhuman, thingly power'. Thus the negative critique of existing institutions must be corrected and complemented by designing 'positive, even utopian alternatives'.
>
> *(Lemke 2018: 34)*

Bennett's account thus *assumes* social hegemonies and their critiques but also has a prefigurative aim. Her project is one of correction and supplementation – a project that aims '*also*' to include the agentic force of nonhuman things. Bennett does not therefore reject or ignore the material realities of hierarchies and asymmetries. Rather, she re-positions and re-contextualizes the human (and the agentic) in service of an affirmative post-anthropocentric politics. Where, then, does the real issue lie?

Lemke's critique takes aim at Bennett's ontology. Bennett's problem, it seems, lies in a putative theoretical inconsistency: Bennett must either be inadvertent to the implications of her own ontology (if it lacks the resources to undergird differential forms of agentic responsibility; to respond to the structural injustices she is so clearly aware of; and to generate an alternative politics by collapsing politics into ethics) or Bennett is simply naïve and/or selective concerning the implications of her vital materialist imaginary by producing a 'systemic blindness' to the more pernicious potentialities of vital materializations. Questions – including these – therefore arise. Is Bennett's ontology incapable of delivering the political imagination and sensitivity to injustice that she so clearly aspires to? Is she simply out of touch with the implications of her own theorizations?

Lemke supports his claim that Bennett's ontology is systemically blind to inequalities, asymmetries and hierarchies by first analyzing two case studies provided by Bennett to illustrate her political ecology of things.

Lemke uses the first example to illustrate Bennett's account of distributive agency: Bennett resists the traditional construct of 'the agent' by deploying Latour's 'actant', identified by its ability to produce effects – an approach that renders visible 'affinities' (Lemke 2018: 35; Bennett 2010: 98) between human and nonhuman actions and acts. Bennett is clear that not all actants exhibit the 'same kind of agency' (Bennett, ibid). Differential agency thus emerges in distributive agency, and for Bennett, nonhuman actants display a kind of 'choice' irreducible to either a mechanical instinct or to a divine plan (Lemke 2018: 35) and 'things' are more than 'objects'. Indeed, Bennett explicitly *rejects* the language of the 'object' for the nonhuman thing precisely because it enables 'the political parsing that yields only active (manly, American) subjects [set against] passive objects' (Bennett 2015: 234). Indeed, Bennett's reservation about the language of the 'object' as a tool of structural oppression is an important point of departure between Bennett and OOO. Bennett prefers the terms 'things' and 'bodies', precisely for the purpose of offering resistive disruption of the gendered (racial) assumptions and asymmetries built into the traditional subject-object dichotomy. To illustrate Bennett's concept of distributive agency for the purposes of his critique, the first case study that Lemke introduces is Bennett's analysis of an infamous power blackout in North America (Lemke 2018: 36) (offered by Bennett as a central case of '*distributive* agency' – Bennett 2010: 21, emphasis original).

The blackout affected 50 million people in the United States and Canada for 24 hours, involving the shutdown of 100 power plants and 22 nuclear reactors. For Bennett, the grid is an 'agentic assemblage' (ibid), and a multitude of actants converged to produce the blackout:

> The electric power grid assemblage includes human actors that build and manage power sites, maintain the networks, supervise the operations, consume the electricity, and pass the regulatory laws, but it also contains a different species of actants: electrons, trees, wind, fire, coal, sweat, computer programs, plastic, wire, wood and electromagnetic fields.
>
> *(Bennett 2010: 24–5)*

The blackout, in short, was the 'endpoint' of a 'cascade' of human *and* nonhuman affects (ibid: 25). Lemke records that '[t]he participants not only included human decisions, motives and omissions such as profit interests and insufficient maintenance programs, but also trees and computer programs, regulatory environments such as the neoliberal organization of the energy market . . . [and more besides]' (Lemke 2018: 36).

What is immediately clear here is that Bennett's account necessarily invokes actants at multiple scales (including underlying neoliberal injustice patterns) and does not exclude questions of differentially constructed agentic responsibility – including human responsibility. What Bennett's account *does* demand is a more complexity-sensitive, less reductive and less linear account of causality and therefore of the construction of responsibility. Bennett's 'distributive agency' thus clearly situates human embodiment/agentic force as '*one* site of agency within and across a multiplicity of other material bodies and formations' (Khan 2012: 42). She certainly does not ignore power structures – the neoliberal market, after all, is positioned as a highly visible actant in the assemblage. And while Bennett rightly concludes of distributive agency that it 'makes it more difficult to engage in the "blame game" ' (Bennett 2010: 37, cited by Lemke 2018: 36), her argument, in the end, illustrates the (highly plausible) claim that there is no simple answer to questions of responsibility for the blackout. In my view, it would be misleading to read Bennett's account of distributive agency as if it undermines the possibility of differentially sensitive theories and accounts of responsibility: Bennett's 'actants' do not exercise 'the same kind[s] of agency': differentiated agency is thus explicit in her ontology – and is highly relevant for any theory of responsibility built upon it. What Bennett *does* do here is (rightly) factor in nonhuman actants in a way that (rightly) complicates linear legal notions of constructed causal agency based on selective empirical omissions (common in the legal construction of liability chains, for example) that are *themselves* re-enactments of well-worn patterns of law-constructed social and structural injustices, inequalities and asymmetries.

Having provided a description of Bennett's case study of the blackout, Lemke moves on to the second case study: Bennett's account of the 'agency of a particular kind of fatty acid that is prevalent in some fish' (Omega 3) (Lemke 2018: 36), offered in an article called 'Edible Matter' (Bennett 2007) and in a chapter in *Vibrant Matter* (Bennett 2010: 39–51). Noting that Omega 3 seems to modulate 'human behaviour, affective states and cognitive abilities', Bennett deploys the fatty acid as an illustration of the agentic force of nutrients as bodies interacting with human bodies, 'forming assemblages that [she] proposes to call "American consumption" or the "crisis of obesity" '(Lemke 2018: 36 citing Bennett 2010: 39). Bennett explicitly includes in this assemblage the social, cultural and economic factors that mediate dietary and nutritional regimes and other actants – not just the nutrients themselves:

> the problem of obesity would have to index not only the large humans and their economic-cultural prostheses (agribusiness, snack-food vending machines, insulin injections, bariatric surgery, serving sizes, systems of food marking and distribution, microwave ovens) but also the strivings and trajectories of fats as they weaken or enhance the power of human wills, habits, and ideas.
>
> *(Lemke 2018: 37, citing Bennett 2010: 42–3)*

Here again, Bennett signals toward pernicious (consumer-capitalist) social hegemonies and by de-centering the 'agency' of the human actant as eater-consumer draws into the frame the patterned (quasi-coercive and predatory) systems of marketing, distribution and corporate-industrial food production that make up the entangled dynamics of the distributive agency in play.

Without analyzing the implications of either of Bennett's examples in depth, Lemke moves on to evaluate Bennett's production of an alternative political imaginary. He suggests that she re-invents democratic theory, radicalizing Ranciere's political theory by offering a 'posthumanist reading' (Lemke 2018: 37) and converging with Latour to broaden the 'demos' to include the nonhuman. Bennett's work, as Lemke puts it, problematizes the ontological hierarchy that elevates the human above all else, 'proposing a flattened conception that regards humans "merely" as a "particularly *rich and complex* collection of materials"' (ibid, citing Bennett 2010: 11. Emphasis in original (Bennett)). Not only is this 'flattened conception' 'helpful in displacing liberal accounts of agency by favouring assemblages and associations' (Lemke 2018: 38) but, combined with Bennett's vital materialist ontology, cuts across the life/matter binary – a move that Lemke welcomes for undermining 'any normative attempt to differentiate between socially and political recognized forms of life and devalued forms of life that are considered not worth killing or risk being killed' and extending biopolitics beyond the human (ibid: 38). Bennett's work also, Lemke notes, challenges the human/environment binary while simultaneously disrupting 'conventional ideas of exteriority and externality: it forces humans to recognize alterity in their own humanness, thereby going beyond traditional concepts of embodiment' (ibid: 37–8).

Where then, are the ambiguities and shortcomings of Bennett's ontology? What explains Lemke's claim that Bennett's attention to vital materializations produces systemic blindness to inequalities, hierarchies and asymmetries?

Lemke raises a series of criticisms, citing in support (and without analysis) the work of other critics of Bennett from whom he partially draws his arguments.

The first problem, Lemke argues, is that Bennett assumes too much concerning the automatism/mechanism of matter in existing political thought and practice. In support, he cites work that demonstrates the 'profound entanglements of matter and information in contemporary societies' (ibid: 49). It is difficult to see how this counterpoint offers an insurmountable critique of Bennett's ontology though: it seems to amount to a claim that 'matter is already more entangled than you allow for, Jane Bennett'. In Bennett's defense, however, it is clear that the existing (dominant) ontology undergirding the realm of the political/juridical *still* presents matter as object/mechanism *notwithstanding* mounting empirical evidence of profound entanglements of matter and information. In terms of the dominant political imaginary, and of the dominant international juridical imaginary, Bennett is absolutely correct. Additionally, if anything, proof of the profound entanglements of matter and information (even *if* under-addressed by Bennett in her book) underlines the reach and potency of her ontology. Moreover, Bennett could surely argue with considerable warrant that the entanglement of matter and information was *always* the underlying empirical reality: that matter and information have *never* been separate in the way that the criticism assumes. Indeed, her new materialist ontology makes such a view of matter-information inevitable as an expression of 'material-semiosis'/'semiotic materiality' (Haraway 2008: 136).

The next objection that Lemke presents is potentially more serious, and amounts to the claim that Bennett

> cherishes vitality and enchantment as 'a positive resource' while neglecting or ignoring destructive tendencies. Material surprises may not always be sources of delight and pleasure, but include dangerous and possibly fatal consequences such as those exhibited in natural disasters, climate change, or materials like asbestos.
>
> *(Lemke 2018: 40)*

With all due respect to Lemke and to other critics who take this view, it is important not to overlook the implications of the two examples that Lemke himself selects. A major blackout is hardly a case of vital matter's sheer positivity. And nor is the obesity crisis (a 'dangerous' and 'possibly fatal' manifestation of vital matter's agentic force in the form of degraded food types/toxic preservatives, pernicious industrial corporate and consumer food regimes and much more besides). I struggle to see how it is possible fairly to read Bennett's enthusiasm for an affirmative theory of the politically radical, positive possibilities of vital materialism as ignoring potentially 'dangerous' vital materializations. And does Bennett's appraisal of 'generosity' and 'joy' (Lemke's next point) necessarily 'discard hostility, boredom, disappointment or rejection' as political forces (ibid: 40)? It is important to be assiduously fair to Bennett's project. Bennett does not, as she points out, set out to provide an 'apodictic account' (Bennett 2004: 357). She is telling an 'onto-story' (ibid), inviting a 'mode of perception', searching for a 'vocabulary' that might 'allow nonhumanity to appear on the ethical radar screen' (ibid). Bennett seeks an imaginative shift facilitating an affirmative posthuman politics responsive to the conative energies of vital matter in *full awareness* of the structural pathologies of the existing system and of the importance of older materialist critiques of hegemonic power and patterns of exploitation. Bennett's account is – recall – explicitly supplementary and corrective. She turns attention '*also*' to the agentic powers of nonhuman things in the search for a positive prefigurative posthuman politics, and it seems difficult fairly to conclude that her account in any way forecloses the possibility of 'dangerous and fatal' material surprises. Her work, after all, as Lemke's first example itself demonstrates, points directly to a potentially dangerous and fatal material surprise in the form of a massive electricity blackout.

Lemke next criticizes Bennett's duality-shifting concept of 'life', arguing that it might be more accurate to allow the distinction between animate and inanimate bodies to play a role. Citing Braun and Whatmore for support,

Lemke confronts Bennett's ontology with the question of whether 'more is gained from closer attention to the specificity of the matter at hand, as opposed to a generic analogy to "life" that could be described as a metaphysics' (Lemke 2018: 40, citing Braun and Whatmore 2010: xxix). Responding to this point, I merely underline, again, Bennett's attentiveness to the fact that actants possess agencies of different kinds and that multiple actants with differing intensities and patterns of (unfixed but potentially habituated) capacities and tendencies form the various mutating and shifting assemblages that make up vital matter. Breaking down the boundary between the animate and inanimate does *not* necessitate a loss of close attention to specificity or to the ways in which actants 'come to matter'. It is entirely possible both to deny a fundamental division between animate and inanimate vital matter *and* to attend to 'differential patterns of mattering' (as Barad might put the point (Barad 2007: 394)).

Lemke next argues that 'similar reservations apply to the concept of "things"', because Bennett's encounter with matter 'necessitates visual contact and bodily presence': 'The ontological spectre of things Bennett presents only seems to include natural entities and technological objects, thereby excluding a large variety of other "things" beyond these categories or below the threshold of visibility and physicality' (Lemke 2018: 41). Here, Lemke suggests that 'we are left to wonder about how to encounter vibrant matters that unsettle distinctions between near and far, presence and absence, and might take place with properties and capacities closer to a liquid or gas, water or air' (ibid) and encounters with financial systems and other flows of force. Again, I think this is overstated. It is true that Bennett speaks of a range of objects encountered in mundane life as examples of vital materiality, but it is equally true that she adverts (even according to Lemke's own examples) to thing-powers not so immediate or mundane. After all, Bennett defines 'things' as 'quasi-agents or forces with trajectories, propensities or tendencies of their own' (Bennett 2010: viii). Are we really left to wonder about other vibrant matters beyond 'natural entities and technological objects'? What about the encounters with invisible nutrients and other related things lying beyond 'the threshold of immediate visibility' and/or physicality? What about electron fields? What about all the meta-meso-micro forces and quasi-agents folded even into the multiplex layers of Bennett's two case studies? It seems puzzling to me that Lemke would use Bennett's examples of distributive agency and then appear to ignore the ontic character of the actants in the assemblages of the power cut and the obesity crisis to adopt this particular line of critique. The global and national systems, neoliberal imperatives, and the transcorporeal vectors of affect implicated by Bennett's examples underline far-reaching and complex forces and agentic flows that emphatically 'unsettle distinctions between near and far, presence and absence'. To my mind, Lemke and the critics he draws upon here miss the mark in an almost inexplicable way.

Deeper conceptual problems apparently attend an ambiguity in Bennett's concept of 'things': for Bennett, things are relational (they have no solid identity but participate in dynamic processual assemblages and they are simultaneously 'things in themselves' (Lemke 2018: 41)). This relational and more-than-relational character of 'things' seems to trouble Lemke and critics he draws upon. Interestingly, Bennett herself adverts to these complexities, suggesting that thing-power 'tends to overstate the thinginess or fixed stability of materiality' (Bennett 2010: 20). *Does it though?* If 'things' emerge out of flows and relationalities *and* find contingent identity as things-in-themselves (as differentially identifiable actants of multiple kinds – as Bennett's examples demonstrate) where is the problem? Is it really so difficult to reconcile these aspects of Bennett's ontology? I disagree with Bennett that her ontology overstates 'thinginess'. 'Thinginess', as I see it, is a contingent, not a fixed, feature of the world – no matter how 'fixed' a thing might appear to mundane human awareness. And contingency is itself a relative and mutable matter: different intensifications, intensities, stabilized patterns and destabilizing patterns and forces can coexist in any given assemblage. (Bennett's ontology on this point seems broadly consistent with Barad's intra-active monism drawn from quantum physics (Barad 2007).)

I also resist Bennett's concession concerning a 'latent individualism' in her account of actants (which in any case 'never really act alone' (ibid: 20–1)). Moreover, the 'latent individualism' here (and again, I resist the terminology and the concession) is certainly not an 'isolationist and individualist concept of agency' as Lemke asserts that it is (Lemke 2018: 41). Differentiation, after all, is an aspect of reality – and does not imply individualism, latent or otherwise. To move from the 'individuality' of differentiated actants to 'individual*ism*' is an unwarranted leap. And nor, to my mind, is there a contradiction between the vital force specific to a particular 'member or proto-member' of an assemblage and the idea that the assemblage possesses an 'effectivity proper to the grouping as such' (Lemke, ibid, citing Bennett 2010: 24). Bennett does not, therefore, *contra* Lemke, 'simply extend the category of the actor beyond humans' and her notion of the propensity of things to a willfulness and choicefulness of their own is certainly not reducible to a 'liberal' conception of the will. Nor does Bennett's notion of the agentic necessarily leave 'intact the liberal imaginary and the conceptual divide between causality and agency, external forces and inner will' (Lemke 2018: 42) (and in an apparent contradiction of Lemke's own earlier assessment that Bennett's ontology is 'helpful in displacing liberal accounts of agency by favouring assemblages and associations' (ibid: 38)). In short, it seems to me that the construct of the agentic in Bennett's work cannot fairly be reduced to the recapitulation of the liberal agent/agentic without deploying an equivocation. It might, as Lemke suggests, be better to speak in terms of 'modes of doing', but the agentic dimensions of the doingness of things in Bennett's work is most certainly not agency in any form reducible to a liberal conception. And nor does Bennett's description of things acting as 'quasi-agents or forces with trajectories, propensities or tendencies of their own' (Bennett 2010: viii) mean that 'the focus on relations is displaced by the idea of pre-established identities' (Lemke, ibid: 42). The emergent, relational quality of things is entirely compatible with the idea that things have particular propensities and tendencies of 'their own', identifiably 'theirs' (differentiated), yet relationally emergent, diffractively generated and co-generative. These are subtle and fine-grained matters, but it seems to me that what Bennett traces out is a differential intra-becoming that does not eradicate particularity.

It is these conceptual problems and ambiguities (which I suggest are not compellingly established) that for Lemke 'seriously limit the political purchase of Bennett's work' (ibid). For Lemke, Bennett 'stops halfway' because she does not account for 'how exactly forces come to be determined in one way rather than another' (ibid). Yet despite the fact that this was never Bennett's project, her ontology is not at odds with such an account. The central argument of Bennett's work, recall, is that nonhuman forces have not adequately been accounted for: she points to the forces of production, consumption and reductive humanistic liberal accounts of agency that foreclose accounts of what comes to matter. Her ontology contains rich resources for differential accounts of actants/things as 'quasi-agents' and while distributive agency has complicating implications for theories of responsibility, attentiveness to the agentic fields and assemblages that generate materializations holds out a space for highly sensitive, empirically attentive analyses of responsibility. And such analyses would be far more faithful to the complexity of causal assemblages than existing legal theories are. The fact that Bennett concludes concerning the blackout that 'no one was to blame' (which is her report of the finding of the official investigation into the event) does *not* mean that Bennett would argue that no one is ever to be held responsible for matters emerging from the distributive agentic forces at work in assemblages such as the grid. Yes, perhaps Bennett could do more, as Lemke suggests, to explore *how* vital forces are mobilized and enacted – but this was never her project. It seems to be the project that her critics wish she had engaged with, but that is a different matter entirely. The question of 'what comes to matter (and what does not)' is implicit throughout Bennett's work, and I find it intellectually impossible at this point to conclude that her 'flattened' (Lemke 2018: 37)/'flattish' (Bennett: note 3 in this chapter) ontology produces 'systemic blindness' to issues of inequality, hierarchy or asymmetry, or that her ontology makes attentiveness to such differential patterns impossible or even difficult. (Indeed, going a little further than I perhaps need to, it remains an open question whether *flat/even flatter* ontology makes such differentiation and attentiveness impossible. Even a flat ontology that celebrates the existence of 'objects' 'in their own right' such as that proposed by Levi Bryant in *The Democracy of Objects* (Bryant 2011), 'readily recognizes that humans have unique powers and capacities and that how humans relate to the world is a topic more than worthy of investigation' (ibid: 246).)

Differentiation is central to Bennett's ontology. The individual does not disappear from view as a site for the attribution of agentic responsibility, and nor do structures and patterns become immune to critical analyses of distributions of power and predation. 'Things' emerge as agentically differentiated with 'propensities of their own', and it is entirely clear that in such an onto-vision the term 'individual', as De Landa puts it, 'means simply "singular or unique", that is, not a particular member of a general category, but a unique entity that may compose larger individual entities through a relation of part-to-whole' (De Landa, in Dolphijn and van der Tuin 2012: 40). The 'individual' on this view emerges as an entangled, differential manifestation of processes of materialization – and demands precisely the 'closer attention to the specificity of the matter at hand' (Braun and Whatmore 2010: xxix) so central to the broader posthumanist task of tracing the intimacies of human–nonhuman power relations at meta-, meso- and micro-scales.

Turning now to the question of subjectivity, Braidotti has argued that subjectivity 'involves complex and continuous negotiations with dominant norms and values and hence also multiple forms of accountability' (Braidotti, in Dolphijn and van der Tuin 2012: 31). Central to Braidotti's concern is the powerful injustice-resistive question of how to co-compose the 'we' at stake (Braidotti 2020) in processes of subjectivization. Subjectivization emerges from Braidotti's work as a centrally important poietic process of formation, a dynamic process fraught with urgent political questions demanding intelligent sensitivity to patterns of past, present and future exclusions and oppressions. It is certainly true that critiques of such processes are central to posthumanist justice-seeking. It is also true that Bennett's work does not directly address such processes and that she is suspicious of the category of the 'subject'. Nevertheless, such processes are intrinsic to, and legible in, the eco-socio-material assemblages Bennett engages with and the 'thing' power central to her work is necessarily folded into processes of subjectivization. It is fair to say that Bennett's account does not explicitly account for such processes. It is not the case, however, that her ontology makes such processes difficult to account for. Certainly, one could critique Bennett for not attending to them, but it is important to recall, in this connection, Bennett's *supplemental* approach to older materialisms. Bennett's project is not to provide an apodictic response to the challenges facing the posthuman situation. Her express concern is to *better* account for the political significance of nonhuman things, things that have 'propensities of their own' – propensities that include modes of agentic becoming-with in the very formation and constitution of the 'human' itself. As Bennett herself puts it in more recent work,

> Regarding the 'equality' question or what has been called a turn toward a flattened ontology: I don't of course think that people are equal to, in the sense of being indistinguishable (with regard to capacities, styles of existence, rights, ethical importance) from technical devices or lichen or birds. My effort is rather to embed within a political-social theory a recognition of a life of things irreducible to the meanings and uses to which people put them, and also an acknowledgement of how 'non-human' forces and entities are *internal* to human powers and constitute a vibrant realm of 'it' within subjectivity. The 'flattening' is an effort to counteract the anthropocentric bait, which lures us to the (hubristic) comfort of imagining a natural hierarchy of being with people securely and definitively located at the top.
>
> *(Bennett 2021: 202)*

While it is clear that Braidotti foregrounds the vital ethico-material encounters of in/justice in the work of subject formation – which I see as a necessary and powerful contribution to the on-going work of posthumanist justice-seeking – Bennett's ontology neither undermines nor renders impossible such important work. It allows for differentiation even though the category of the 'subject' remains suspect for her and processes of subjectivization are not explicitly accounted for. Accordingly, I suggest that the distinction to be drawn here is but a *difference of inflection* between two unique and powerful posthumanist neo-materialist affirmative political imaginaries. Even short of an overt focus on processes of subjectivization, Bennett's work has much to offer critical international theory and the ongoing search for forms of posthumanist justice-seeking.

Bennett's Vital Materialism and Decolonial Possibilities?

Is it possible that far from being inadequate for thinking about power relations, Bennett's vital materialism holds particular promise for the development of decolonial alliances with Indigenous scholarships and onto-politics actively resisting the injustices of the international juridical order? Perhaps.

Indigenous peoples, scholars and activists are arguably *the* most significant critics of the expulsive extractivist logics and dynamics central to the international juridical order. As is well known in critical legal circles, Cartesian subject-object relations and their Kantian counterparts still subtend the disembedded agency of the Eurocentric 'subject at the centre' of international law (Grear 2021) (the anthropocentric 'subject', whether taking form as the state, the corporation or the individual) that dominates the onto-epistemic assumptions of the entire international legal order (Natarajan *et al* 2023). One particularly destructive result of this dominance is the imposition of hierarchies of being that operationalize a spectrum of objectifications in the service of organized plunder: wholesale land grabs; appropriation by governance conditionalities, financialization, spoliation and multiple other means; extractivism; and the relentless systemic prioritization of the Global North over the Global South. Indigenous scholars and activists, long wary of the merely facial 'inclusion' of Indigenous peoples in the international legal order by way of a 'cultural' concession made by the neoliberal 'one world world' (Escobar 2015: 348), are adopting increasingly effective forms of resistive onto-politics (ibid: 352) offering powerful creative-critical resistance to the injustices of the dominant order. Meanwhile, it has been argued that posthumanist and new materialist scholarship draws on Western philosophical resources and sciences without adequate recognition of Indigenous cosmovisions and scholarship, which have long accounted for nonhuman agentic capacities (Sundberg 2014). What then, might Bennett's ontology bring to decolonial endeavors as a potential ally?

Perhaps a good starting point for thinking about vital materialism's potential contribution to such resistive onto-political endeavors is to frame vital materialism through Braidotti's important emphasis on the intimacy of power relations. Braidotti emphasizes the importance of thinking 'of power relations simultaneously as the most "external", collective social phenomenon and also as the most intimate or "internal" one' (Braidotti 2011: 17). This is an intimacy that necessarily brings into the frame questions of the composition of 'reality', 'self' and – in particular – the kind of 'we' that must emerge if post-anthropocentric futures are to be affirmative and co-generative rather than predatory and necropolitical (Braidotti 2020).

Bennett's work is marked, for me at least, by sustained evocation of such intimacy. Her project takes form as a search precisely for new modes of perceptual openness – to attuned attentiveness. Her work also necessarily evokes the intimacies of power operative at micro-, meso- and meta-scales. For example, her study of essential fatty acids evokes not only the intimate 'internal' operation of the 'bodies' of essential fatty acids in the assemblage of the 'human body' (and thus, I would argue, processes of subject-formation – albeit *implicitly*), but also necessarily invokes multiple meta-scale dynamics (some of which Bennett mentions and some of which she does not) such as: neoliberal global food production policies; practices of organized food predation; global transits; contested understandings of 'food'; market dynamics; advertising and the materialities of information and media; corporate agricultural land grabs; trans-planetary circulations of air and water, toxins and nutrients; the politics of the glocal/local/global; the legally protected corporate plunder of Indigenous seed-lines; intellectual property rights; and much,

much more besides. In short, the material-affective flows at work in Bennett's human–nonhuman assemblages point unerringly toward the most planetary of phenomena and simultaneously to the most 'internal' and visceral of matters and to multiple scales 'between'.

And while, as noted earlier, Bennett does not attend to the formation of subjectivity, there is a deep sense in which Bennett's work allies with Braidotti's project of the 'de-familiarization' of the knowing subject – a process that Indigenous cosmovisions also potentially elicit, albeit differently. Braidotti writes that

> De-familiarization is a sobering process by which the knowing subject evolves from the normative vision of the self he or she had become accustomed to. The frame of reference becomes the 'chaosmos' – the becoming world of subjectivity itself – as . . . open-ended, interrelational, multi-sexed, and trans-species flows of becoming by interaction with multiple others. A subject thus constituted explodes the boundaries of humanism at skin level.
>
> *(Braidotti 2013: 20)*

Facing the project of defamiliarization is also the need to acknowledge and to learn from those who were never 'familiarized' as the knowing subject in the first place. There is also a related sense in which Indigenous cosmovisions do not need to *become post*-humanist because Indigenous modes of knowing never assumed the humanist subject to start with. Indigenous onto-epistemologies are richly responsive to multiplicitous open-ended interrelational flows of becoming by inter/intra-action with multiple others, in a richly entangled more-than-human 'world of worlds', multiply understood – and have been for thousands of years.

Defamiliarization must also, therefore, find an urgent and explicit decolonial register – not least for international law – and a burning question for posthumanist and new materialist international legal theory is now how to avoid replicating colonialities when pressing back against the Euro-modernist onto-epistemology of the current legal order. It is against this question, in particular, that I want to position Bennett's work as a potentially promising new materialist contribution to the building of the necessary scholarly alliances with Indigenous onto-politics.

One risk presented by posthumanist and new materialist critiques of dualistic modernist constructions of 'nature' and 'culture' is, after all, the subtle re-installation of Eurocentricity. Acknowledging the critical potency of posthumanist and new materialist thought, Juanita Sundberg has, for example, written that she is 'discomforted by the ways in which . . . engagements with posthumanism tend to reproduce colonial ways of knowing and being by enacting universalizing claims and, consequently, further subordinating other ontologies' (Sundberg 2014: 34). This is a serious charge. And it is one explicitly aimed against Bennett, among others.

Sundberg takes aim at Bennett's invocation of 'The Naive Ambition of Vital Materialism', which calls upon 'modern, secular, well-educated humans' to allow for 'moments of methodological naivete' (ibid: 42). Addressing Bennett's call 'to linger' in the service of cultivating 'the ability to discern nonhuman vitality, to become perceptually open to it', Sundberg takes issue with Bennett's expression of concern that fostering a vital materialism might invoke 'the taint of superstition, animism, vitalism, anthropomorphism, and other premodern attitudes' (noting that Bennett is here quoting WJT Mitchell) (ibid: 44).

Does Bennett's position really commit her to a Eurocentric dismissal of Indigenous ontologies? I am not so sure that it does.

Reading Bennett's words in their original context, Bennett's express aim is to 'enhance receptivity to the "impersonal life" that surrounds and infuses us [to] generate a more subtle awareness of the complicated web of dissonant connections between bodies and enable more strategic interventions into that ecology' (Bennett, in Braun and Whatmore 2010: 38). This ecological strategy is potentially in powerful alignment with decolonial aims. As Bennett puts it, in vital materialism:

> All bodies become more than mere objects, as the thing powers of resistance and protean agency are brought into sharper relief. Vital materialism would thus set up a kind of safety net for those humans who are now, in a world where Kantian morality is the standard, routinely made to suffer because they do not conform to a particular (Euro-American, bourgeois, theocentric, or other) model of personhood. The ethical aim becomes to distribute value more generously, to bodies as such. Such a newfound attentiveness to matter and its powers will not solve the problem of human exploitation or oppression, but it can inspire a greater sense of the extent to which all bodies are kin in the sense of being inextricably enmeshed in a dense network of relations.
>
> *(Bennett, ibid: 48)*

This 'safety net' against the Kantian hegemony of the person aims squarely at the imposition of suffering for non-conformity – a non-conformity typical of Indigenous cosmovisions and lifeways. Bennett's stand against quasi-hegemonic (Kantian) personhood *and* against the reduction of thing-power to a mere 'effect of culture' brings her, I think, into potential alliance with Indigenous onto-politics *and* with Braidotti's important emphasis on defamiliarization.

Bennett's embrace of 'methodological naïvete' – in its original context – is, moreover, specifically to enable 'the postponement of a genealogical critique of objects' (ibid: 53). *This* 'delay' (*this* effort to 'linger') is her attempt to open out perceptual encounters with vital matter. It is, importantly, in *this* context – set against the genealogical critique of objects and against the assumption and imposition of Kantian personhood (and the suffering that it visits on the non-conforming) – that Bennett suggests that 'one tactic' in developing the necessary capacity for naïvete (in the precise sense in which Bennett evokes it) is to 'revisit and become temporarily infected by discredited philosophies of nature, risking the "taint of superstition, animism, vitalism, anthropomorphism and other premodern attitudes"' (not her own words, recall but Mitchell 2005: 149). It is significant that where Bennett goes next is to offer a 'foray' into ancient atomism – thus directly linking her statements, not to any implied or imputed Indigenous primitivism, but to early Roman philosophy in the foundations of the Western canon (Bennett in Braun and Whatmore 2010: 53). Bennett's view, if we take context and intention into account – and especially her explicit rejection of the oppressive implications of Eurocentric personhood for those who 'do not conform to it' – makes it highly unlikely that she would disparage Indigenous or non-European onto-epistemologies. Her focus throughout is on a thoroughly Western 'fetishization of the subject, the image, the word' (ibid: 54).

Indeed, I think it is possible to read Bennett's vital materiality as a potential contribution to decolonial work. In this, I concur with Micheal Angelo Rumore's assessment that Bennett's work provides a stepping off point for decolonial work on the subaltern. Writing about the 'Postcolonial Ecologies' panel at the *Radical Materialisms* conference held at CUNY Graduate Center, in 2015, Rumore notes that at the conference Peter Mörtenböck identified two interconnected questions: (1) How do we align politically, theoretically, and aesthetically with subalterns defending their lifeworlds and ecologies against the forces of neoliberal globalization? (2) How can we better conceptualize the reciprocities between human and nonhuman agents? While these two questions live in an unresolved tension, they potentially converge in a generative nexus between Indigenous onto-politics and scholarship and new materialist attentiveness to the radical political implications of the liveliness of matter. This attentiveness to vital materializations and its political implications is a point, moreover, at which Indigenous scholarship critically engages with the broader posthumanist privileging of certain kinds of human–nonhuman assemblages over others (such as techno-scientific assemblages) and 'productively contribute[s] to discussions of the ethical and political implications of posthumanism' itself (Watson and Huntington 2008: 258). Rumore concludes of Bennett's work – rightly I think – that Bennett's aspiration for a 'political ecology of things' offers an important intervention 'in response to the persistence of dehumanization in the exercise of ecological imperialism . . . [precisely] by demanding that we take seriously the ability of nonhuman matter to resist the demiurgic ambitions of the imperial human gaze' (Rumore 2015).

In short, given the international juridical persistence of the primacy of the 'subject at the centre'; of its appropriative will; of its 'mastery' over 'objects'; of its objectification of its multiple 'others' – it seems urgently necessary to advert to the extent to which, and the ways in which, the dominance of this subject is radically interwoven with the historical and contemporary objectification and dehumanization of Indigenous peoples and to learn from (Braidotti 2020) (without essentializing or appropriating) their sophisticated onto-political scholarships of resistance. Bennett's work as Rumore puts it, holds out the hope of recognizing 'reciprocal sovereignties within an ontologically-diverse "world of matter"'. Such recognition – given juridical form – could address – head on – the onto-political erasure at the heart of Eurocentric neocoloniality (Rumore 2015).

Bennett's world of matter, a world in which 'edibles, commodities, storms and metals [and more] act as quasi-agents, with their own trajectories, potentialities and tendencies' (Watson 2013: 147) in an 'ontological field without any unequivocal demarcations between human, animal, vegetable or mineral' (Bennett 2010: 117) has an important degree of convergence with the rich relational worlds of Indigenous peoples, notwithstanding the invigorating differences and tensions between Indigenous scholarship and posthumanist and new materialist work.

Conclusion

Far from generating 'a systemic blindness concerning the inequalities, asymmetries and hierarchies enacted in vital materializations', Bennett's work offers the basis for a particularly intimate account of such materializations and their potentialities both critical and pre-figurative. Her work is thus a rich contribution to the wider liberatory project of affirmative posthumanist scholarship, such as emerges in the work of Braidotti. Bennett's work also has, potentially, a promising potential degree of reticulation with Indigenous decolonial struggles and scholarship.

If it is the case – and I would assert that it is – that posthumanist and new materialist scholars need to avoid performing a scholarly erasure of Indigenous onto-epistemologies, then Bennett's theory of lively materialization – potentially – offers a useful bridge toward that necessary shift. And, turning to international legal theory, if, as Claire Charters rightly argues, 'Indigenous Peoples have challenged the colonial association of international legality with positivism and state-centrism, [and] especially [with] Eurocentrism' (Charters 2021: 115), then Bennett's post-anthropocentric political ecology is indeed a potentially generative site for New Materialist decolonial alliances in defense of the human–nonhuman subaltern. Combined with posthumanist work such as Braidotti's on processes of subjectivization, Bennett's 'flattish' ontology is a potent source of valuation for the more-than-human worlds so violently erased by juridically mediated colonial/neocolonial plunder and erasure.

References

Barad, K. (2007) *Meeting the Universe Halfway: Quantum Physics and the Entanglement of Matter and Meaning*, Durham, NC: Duke University Press.

Bennett, J. (2001) *The Enchantment of Modern Life: Attachments, Crossings and Ethics*, Princeton: Princeton University Press.

Bennett, J. (2004) 'The Force of Things: Steps Toward an Ecology of Matter', *Political Theory*, *32*(3): 347–72. DOI: https://doi.org/10.1177/0090591703260853

Bennett, J. (2007) 'Edible Matter', *New Left Review*, 45: 133–45.

Bennett, J. (2010) *Vibrant Matter: A Political Ecology of Things*, Durham: Duke University Press.

Bennett, J. (2015) 'Systems and Things: On Vital Materialism and Object-Oriented Philosophy', in R. Grusin (ed) *The Nonhuman Turn*, Minneapolis: University of Minnesota Press.

Bennett, J. (2021) '(Why) Lucretius Matters: A Dialogue with Jane Bennett', *K Revue Trans-Européene de Philosophie et Arts*, 6(1): 193–204.

Blanco, E. and A. Grear (2019) 'Personhood, Jurisdiction and Injustice: Law, Colonialities and the Global Order', *Journal of Human Rights and the Environment*, 10(1): 86–117.

Braidotti, R. (2011) *Nomadic Subjects: Embodiment and Sexual Difference in Contemporary Feminist Theory*, 2nd ed., New York: Columbia University Press.

Braidotti, R. (2020) ' "We" Are In This Together, But We Are Not One and the Same', *Journal of Bioethical Inquiry*, 17(4): 465–9.

Braidotti, R. (2013) 'Becoming-world', in R. Braidotti, P. Hanafin and B. Blaagaard (eds) *After Cosmopolitanism*, Abingdon: Routledge.

Braun, B. and S.J. Whatmore (eds) (2010) *Political Matter: Technoscience, Democracy, and Public Life*, Minneapolis: University of Minnesota Press.

Bryant, L. (2011) *The Democracy of Objects*, Ann Arbor: University of Michigan Library.

Charters, C. (2021) 'The Sweet Spot Between Formalism and Fairness: Indigenous Peoples' Contribution to International Law', *AJIL Unbound*, 115: 123–8.

Coole, D. and S. Frost (2010) *New Materialisms: Agency, Ontology, Politics*, Durham: Duke University Press.

Deiner, S. (2020) 'New Materialisms', *The Year's Work in Critical and Cultural Theory*, 28(1): 44–65.

De Landa, M. (2013) *Intensive Science and Virtual Philosophy*, London: Bloomsbury.

Dolphijn, R. and I. van Der Tuin (2012) *New Materialism: Interviews and Cartographies*, Ann Arbor: Open Humanities Press.

Escobar, A. (2015) 'Commons in the Pluriverse', in D. Bollier and S. Helfrich (eds) *Patterns of Commoning*, Amherst, MA: The Commons Strategies Group, 348–60.

Grear, A. (2015) 'Deconstructing *Anthropos*: A Critical Legal Reflection on "Anthropocentric" Law and Anthropocene "Humanity" ', *Law and Critique*, 26(3): 225–49.

Grear, A. (2021) 'International Law, Legal Anthropocentrism and Facing the Planetary', in U. Natarajan, V. Chapaux and F. Mégret (eds) *The Handbook of Anthropocentrism and International Law*, Abingdon: Routledge.

Haraway, D. (2008) *When Species Meet*, Minneapolis: University of Minnesota Press.

Hohmann, J. (2021) 'Diffuse Subjects and Dispersed Power: New Materialist Insights and Cautionary Lessons for International Law', *Leiden Journal of International Law*, 34: 585–606.

Khan, G. (2009) 'Agency, Nature and Emergent Properties: An Interview with Jane Bennett', *Contemporary Political Theory*, 8: 90–105.

Khan, G. (2012) 'Vital Materiality and Non-Human Agency: An Interview with Jane Bennett', in G. Browning *et al* (eds) *Dialogues with Contemporary Political Theorists*, London: Palgrave Macmillan, 42–57.

Lemke, T. (2018) 'An Alternative Model of Politics? Prospects and Problems of Jane Bennett's *Vital Materialism*', *Theory, Culture and Society*, 35(6): 31–54.

Mitchell, W. J. T. (2005), *What do Pictures Want? The Lives and Loves of Images*, Chicago: University of Chicago Press.

Natarajan, U., V. Chapaux and F. Mégret (eds) (2023) *The Routledge Handbook of International Law and Anthropocentrism*, Abingdon: Routledge.

Quiroga-Villamarín, D.R. (2020) 'Domains of Objects, Rituals of Truth: Mapping Intersections Between International Legal History and the New Materialisms', *International Politics Reviews*, 8: 129–51.

Rekret, P. (2016) 'A Critique of New Materialism: Ethics and Ontology', *Subjectivity*, 9: 225–45.

Rumore, M.A. (2015) 'Provincializing Humanism: Reflections on the World of Matter'. https://socialtextjournal.org/periscope_article/provincialising-humanism-reflections-on-world-of-matter/ (Accessed: 1 September 2021).

Sundberg, J. (2014) 'Decolonizing Posthumanist Geographies', *Cultural Geographies*, 21(1): 33–47.

Watson, A. and O.H. Huntington (2008) 'They're Here – I Can Feel Them: The Epistemic Spaces of Indigenous and Western Knowledges', *Social & Cultural Geography*, 9: 257–81. DOI: https://doi.org/10.1080/14649360801990488

Watson, J. (2013) 'Eco-Sensibilities: Interview with Jane Bennett', *Minnesota Review*, 8(1): 147–58.

3

AESTHETICS, NEW MATERIALISM AND LEGAL MATTER

The 'Art' of Anglo-American Colonialism

Delaney Mitchell

Introduction: *Matter v. Material*

This chapter principally questions the ways in which aesthetic methodologies are making claims on international law through a detailed discussion of Cameron Rowland's *Depreciation* (2018), a conceptual artwork that seeks to dis/locate colonial concepts of property and broader living legacies of Anglo-American colonialism. I argue that attention to the differentiation between *matter*, as that which is-not-yet but has the potential to take legal form, and *material*, as matter that possesses 'active' legal form vis-à-vis its attainment of meaning through legal interpretation, is needed to expand knowledge of the ways that law is actively being shaped by artists. Deploying Karen Barad's conception of *intra*-action, which understands agency not as an inherent property of an individual or human to be exercised but as a dynamism of forces (2007), I explore the forces that allow artistic objects/gestures to 'appear' as legally significant, thus revealing the legal potential inherent in *matter*.

The intervention is divided into three substantive sections: '*Depreciation*', '*Intra*-action' and 'Transactionality'. In the first section, *Depreciation*, I outline Rowland's piece and introduce *aesthetic legal methodologies*, a term I develop to describe how the process of turning *matter* into *material* is deployed by artists to determine the legal meaning of an object/gesture. The second section, *Intra*-action, delves into the theoretical underpinnings of aesthetic legal methodologies. Drawing on queer philosophy and queer principles found in posthumanist theory that challenge exclusionary humanisms and anthropocentrism, this section critically considers the conditions that allow something to appear as meaningful to law, as well as how attention

DOI: 10.4324/9781032658032-5

to *intra*-active processes can expand the purview of significance. Tracing the legal contours of Rowland's *Depreciation*, I present 'transactionality' (Fauq 2020) in the third and final section as an aesthetic legal methodology born of an *intra*-action between aesthetics and contract and property law. This section examines how 'transactionality' relies on abstraction to isolate an object/gesture from its original context and reformulate its use or meaning. Specifically, I question whether Rowland's approach of isolating a land title (his object/gesture) results in a reiteration of the form of (colonial, masculine) abstraction present in contract and property law that he seeks to critique vis-à-vis transactionality. Indeed, it is this move that facilitates a claim by Rowland to United States land on behalf of non-Indigenous, Black subjects. I unpack the legal ethics of Rowland's land claim by exploring the relationship between conceptualism and abstraction in aesthetics and how this relationship is imbricated in ('new' and historic) material in/justices.

In this chapter, aesthetics refers both to the more conventional art historical and/or critical analytic devices that delineate style or composition as well as how such moves in an artistic practice are imbricated in historic materialist concerns of labor and political economy and new materialist concerns of the sensorium and human and non/human relationality (Agard-Jones 2016). I follow Daniel Matthews in taking a:

> generalised study of aesthetics to embrace a concern with a sensate subject's immersion in social space, the study of how the visive, affective and sensuous dimensions are animated through a given configuration of power relations that orders, distributes and enframes our perception of the world.
> *(2019: 4)*

Thinking aesthetics across historic and new materialist scales, I broadly examine Rowland's land claim in light of critical differentiations between the United States (as occupied land) and the United Kingdom (as the heart of Empire).

Developing interventions found in posthuman theory, this chapter contributes to an emerging international legal debate on the colonial jurispolitics[1] of race, gender and land. I engage with more established international legal debates on reparation and other forms of reparative justice to demonstrate that paying attention to *intra*-actions – and the distinction between law's *matter* and *material* that they reveal – presents opportunities to address 'new' and historic injustices of Anglo-American colonialism. Insisting upon the potentiality of this approach, I join the call for international legal theorists to 'queer' legal ethics through meaningful engagement with principles

1 The term 'jurispolitics' refers to the convergence of politics and law in particular movements among the Liberal Left; see Brown and Halley (2002) on a range of jurispolitical issues, and Halley (2008) on feminist jurispolitics.

found in posthuman theory, to rethink how we conceive of 'responsibility' as an ethical and political stance in the context of settler societies and to always orient toward *matter* in our pursuits of justice.

Depreciation

Depreciation (2018) is a piece of conceptual art that is comprised of a set of documents recording Rowland's purchase of one acre of land at 8060 Maxie Road, Edisto Island, South Carolina (United States), formerly part of the Maxcy Plantation. The documents are displayed across two large, white mats with each mat enclosed by a simple black frame; the frames hang side by side on an otherwise blank, white wall. The piece responds to a significant but brief episode in the history of slavery reparation in the United States in which property-based reparations were promised to freed slaves. For Rowland, the land draws its significance from General William Sherman's promise of '40 acres and a mule' to freed slaves in 1865 (Sunwoo 2019: 7). The piece responds to the reversal, following the assassination of Abraham Lincoln, of the proposition by Vice President Andrew Johnson who 'instructed the return of lands to dispossessed Confederate owners, leaving most former slaves no choice but to enter the sharecropping system or else risk arrest – now dually dispossessed of both land and freedom' (ibid). Rowland returns to this historic injustice in a heterodox manner. A pamphlet that accompanies the exhibition describes the piece in his own words:

> This land was purchased at market value on August 6, 2018, by 8060 Maxie Road, Inc., a nonprofit company formed for the sole purpose of buying this land and recording a restrictive covenant on its use. This covenant has as its explicit purpose the restriction of all development and use of the property by the owner.
>
> The property is now appraised at \$0. By rendering it legally unusable, this restrictive covenant eliminates the market value of the land. These restrictions run with the land, regardless of the owner. As such, they will last indefinitely.
>
> As reparation, this covenant asks how land might exist outside of the legal-economic regime of property that was instituted by slavery and colonization. Rather than redistributing the property, the restriction imposed on 8060 Maxie Road's status as valuable and transactable real estate asserts antagonism to the regime of property as a means of reparation.
>
> *(Rowland 2018: np)*[2]

2 Text is author's own and is provided on a pamphlet to viewers of the piece '*Depreciation*, 2018 – Restrictive covenant; 1 acre on Edisto Island, South Carolina'. This piece was part of the 'D37' exhibition at The Museum of Contemporary Art, Los Angeles, United States.

In his astute reflection on the legal and economic regime of property in the United States as conditioned on slavery, Rowland seeks to dis/locate colonial concepts of property. *Depreciation* enacts a move toward a new kind of reparation outside of the existing legal-economic regime – one which may be described, in José Esteban Muñoz words, as a 'pre-appearance in the world of another mode of being that is not yet here' (2009: 147), though 'knowable, to some extent, as a utopian feeling' (2009: 3). Rowland's utopia is reflected in his imagining of the futurity of the land, and his enactment of a restricted covenant to indefinitely determine the futurity of this imagining.

The pre-appearance of Rowland's utopia outside of the colonial legal-economic regime of property is, in part, communicated through his minimalist aesthetic and distinct occupation of space. The piece is exhibited on an otherwise blank, white wall, a move embedded with commentary on the racial history of the museum itself.[3] Rowland's pieces work in and against what Joan Copjec has termed 'outside art' (2002: 103), that is, art that cannot be contextualized by any museum or wall text – a notion Tavia Nyong'o has expanded upon to query Black artistry from the proposition that 'history is not its container, but that which it contains' (2018: 143). Rowland's work – especially *Encumbrance*,[4] which I will return to later – might be referred to as 'post-outside art', that is, something which continues to grapple with the limits of the museum or gallery's ability to provide context or container whilst playing with the notion that there is nothing 'outside': the artwork is endemic to the material history of the institutions themselves.

Indeed, *Depreciation* far exceeds the white walls of its container. The piece ambitiously brings the legal determinations that shape the relationship between people and land in the world outside, into the gallery. The minimalist exhibition style initially appears quite sterile, evoking little emotive response. Upon interrogating the content, this feeling of sterile-ness gives rise to the unique effect of viewing objects in a legal exhibit: a disorientating sensation that comes from viewing otherwise mundane items – a piece of paper, a household object – that have been given a perverse amount of significance through their legal meaning. As, for example, Hyo Yoon Kang has observed, 'the courtroom is "only" a room without the legal significance imbued to it' (2018: 464). I will return in detail to the process of interpretation through which a particular amalgamation of *matter* (a room, a sheet of paper) has the potential to become *material* to law (a courtroom, a document), as a series

3 This concept is drawn from Robyn Wiegman's 'Don't Look Away: Race, Sex and Kara Walker's Pornopticon' lecture delivered on 27 April 2015 at New Art Exchange in Nottingham, UK. Notes on file with author.

4 '*Encumbrance* 2020 – Mortgage; mahogany double doors: 12 Carlton House Terrace, ground floor, front entrance' by Cameron Rowland was exhibited in 3 & 4 Will. IV c. 73 at the Institute of Contemporary Arts, London, UK.

of difficult legal questions are enmeshed in this process of re/formulation. The following questions posed by Kang demand careful consideration in this regard:

> How do we identify law's constitutive ingredients? Rather than asking what acts, sounds, sights and feelings we perceive as being permeated by law, the question then becomes how these come to be regarded and felt as relevant to law and how they come to be spelled out in legal language. *Which of these elements come to matter legally and which don't?* What are the devices, instruments and procedures that make legal inscriptions material in the sense of meaningfulness? How are these materialities or meanings then performed? [emphasis added]
>
> *(2018: 462)*

With *Depreciation*, I laterally demonstrate how these materialities are being performed by and through particular *intra*-actions and, furthermore, how these *intra*-actions come to constitute what I term *aesthetic legal methodologies* that concretely impact upon international law.

Intra-*action*

Interrogating how visual practices take on legal form is pressing in the contemporary moment in which artists are layering law into their politics. The boundaries of what is taken to be 'material' to law are being pushed by contemporary art, and thus the established understanding that the 'material dimension creates and gives form to the discursive, and vice versa' (Dolphijn and van der Tuin 2012: 91) demands an explicit extension to address the question of how law's *matters* and *materials* are entangled in the reciprocal material-discursive dimension of the colonial jurispolitics of race, gender and land.

What can be known about law's entanglement in the material-discursive dimension is limited by what can 'appear' to law as significant. Sara Ahmed's queer phenomenology, which takes the significance of the objects that appear – and those that do not – as signs of orientation (2006: 1–24), offers a conceptual framework from which to contend that law's lack of orientation toward matter is limiting its knowledge of aesthetic objects that emerge in and through aesthetic legal methodologies as to become significant to law. Understanding the material-discursive dimension of law necessitates two important theoretical distinctions: (1) a conceptual distinction between *matter*, as that which is-not-yet but has the potential to take legal form, and *material*, as matter that possesses 'active' legal form vis-à-vis its attainment of meaning through legal interpretation, and (2) an understanding of the genealogy of how matter becomes material. In this configuration, *matter* is not *a priori* transformed into material by virtue of law's attention.[5] Rather, *matter* possesses the potential to be transformed into *material* if attended to through a process of legal interpretation that is backed by a normative claim through which the meaningfulness of that particular amalgamation of matter to law is substantiated. This process of interpretation is dynamic and unstable: able to be appropriated by both legal and 'non-legal' actors in ways that meaningfully impact upon law. I propose that one of the ways in which matter becomes material is through the deployment of an aesthetic legal methodology that anoints matter with meaning (legal significance). Because law is largely not attendant to matter at present, a new materialist orientation will allow objects that obtain legal form through aesthetic legal methodologies to 'appear' on the law's plane of consciousness.

As the relationship between aesthetics and law is dynamic (contingent on the particularities of its encounters), it is best theorized through its '*intra*-action(s)' (Barad 2007: 141). Of *intra*-action(s) Barad explains, 'structures are to be understood as material-discursive phenomena that are iteratively (re)produced through ongoing material-discursive *intra*-actions' (2012a: 48). Focusing on *intra*-action disrupts disciplinary knowledge by displacing bodies of scholarship as pre-established entities, and thus revealing the otherwise unknowable actions between them which require our attention. An *intra*-active approach allows a legal theorist to 'pick up' an object and examine it from all sides: analyzing how it appears and what is made available through its different encounters. Barad calls this approach, which I advocate as a tool for legal analysis, a diffraction experiment: 'a process of reading insights through one another diffractively is about experimenting with different patterns of relationality, opening things up, turning them over and over again, to see how the patterns shift' (Barad 2012b: np). Through diffractive experimentation – picking legal objects up and turning them over – *intra*-actions become visible. Limited focus on *intra*-action(s) between law and aesthetics may explain why, as of yet, aesthetic legal methodologies have not been robustly theorized.[6]

5 Here, 'attention' is akin to a meta-method, which deconstructs the set of theoretical and methodological assumptions that accompany a given process. In other words, a legal theorist can pay critical attention to the processes by which a room becomes a courtroom, a piece of paper becomes a document, and so on, without interpretively acting upon an object/gesture. Attention is not itself the process by which *matter* becomes *material*; interpretive attendance back by a normative claim is.

6 The interactions between law and aesthetics have been outlined in classical texts such as Adam Geary's (2001) work on literary aesthetics and Peggy Phelan's (1997) work on psychoanalysis, as well as in more contemporary texts such as Lucy Finchett-Maddock and Eleftheria Lekakis' (2020) edited collection on visual art and power and Cassandra Sharp and Marett Leiboff's (2015) edited collection on law's popular cultures. I maintain, however, that contemporary

A focus on *intra*-action(s) aids legal analysis in seeing beyond the law's own logic of signification, which paradoxically prefigures what is taken to be 'material' to law and conversely limits what is knowable as a legal issue. The law's logic of signification offers the subsequent (and inadequate) formulation: what is material to law is always already prefigured by its ability to be interpreted legally (i.e. law is law because it is law). One of the important ways in which new materialism exceeds law's logic of signification, and thus reveals marginalized perspectives not otherwise legally visible, is its denouncement of the dualisms that form 'the backbone of modernist thought' (Dolphijn and van der Tuin 2012: 86). Dolphijn and van der Tuin track the new materialist ways in which:

> modernity's dualisms (structured by a negative relation between terms) are traversed, and how a new conceptualization of difference (structured by an affirmative relation) comes to be constituted along the way . . . [leaving] behind all prioritizations (implicitly) involved in modern dualist thinking, since a difference structured by affirmation does not work with predetermined relations (e.g., between mind and body) nor does it involve a counter-hierarchy between terms.
>
> *(ibid)*

Here we see a particular assonance with strands of feminist philosophy, made evident by Rosi Braidotti through her genealogy of 'neo-materialism' (especially 1991, 1994). For Braidotti, feminist philosophy 'goes even further than mainstream continental philosophy in rejecting dualistic partitions of minds from bodies or nature from culture' (2012: 21). She continues:

> the embodied and embedded brand of feminist material philosophy of the subject introduces a break from both universalism and dualism. As for the former, universalist claims to a subject position that allegedly transcends spatio-temporal and geo-political specificities are criticised for being disembodied and dis-embedded, i.e., abstract. Universalism, best exemplified in the notion of 'abstract masculinity' (Hartsock 1987) and triumphant whiteness (Ware 1992), is objectionable not only on epistemological, but also ethical grounds.
>
> *(ibid: 22)*

Universalism and dualism place the white, heterosexual, able-bodied man as the central focus of Western legal thought, foreclosing a philosophy of

---

legal theory stands to benefit from a theoretical differentiation between 'interactions' and '*intra*-actions' in its thinking through of aesthetics.

difference both at the level of the subject and the (posthuman) realm beyond.[7] This is true in international legal thought, which Third World Approaches to International Law (TWAIL) scholars have rightfully argued reflects the colonial dominance of Western legal powers.[8] Questioning the colonial foundations of international law, TWAIL-influenced feminist artist and research practitioner, Helene Kazan advances that 'by examining the historical processes responsible for inequalities produced through law's enforcement, we can come to challenge its defining principles' (2020: 203). This intervention advances that examining the processes responsible for inequalities and in/justice requires attention to both historical materialism and new materialism. Of critical importance to this chapter is the way in which dualism functions to predetermine legal meaning through the prioritization of *material* over *matter*. Refusing the confines of law's orthodox logic of signification and deploying the theoretical apparatus of *intra*-action, reveals the concrete ways in which aesthetic legal methodologies turn *matter* into legal *material*, and thus have the potential to either reproduce inequalities engendered in legal enforcement or break with them entirely.

Transactionality

Depreciation is a conceptual artwork that exemplifies the use of aesthetic legal methodologies to turn *matter* into legal *material*. As it pertains to contemporary art, such as Rowland's, conceptualism refers to practices or artistic production techniques in which the concept constitutes the artwork, often taking precedent over conventional aesthetic, technical and material concerns (Wood 2002). In its denouncement of conventional practice, conceptualism often contends with the question of what art is, exploring its limits. Rowland brings these constitutive contentions to the field of law. While he does not denounce conventional practice, and indeed relies heavily on orthodox legal tools, he contends with the question of what law is, and, more importantly, he challenges law's constitutive ingredients by advancing contemporary conceptual art as a legal domain. Rowland's artistic and legal 'design' in *Depreciation* of a restrictive covenant to render the market value of the land at 8060 Maxie Road null contributes to a renewed conceptual

7 One need not look further than the cornerstone of international law, the Universal Declaration of Human Rights, or to international law's postcolonial, queer and feminist scholars such as Ratna Kapur (2017, 2018), Dianne Otto (2017), Eddie Bruce-Jones (2015) and Vanja Hamzić (2012) to corroborate that universal and particularized (i.e. against the dis-embodied and dis-embedded legal subject) international legal efforts have likewise failed in producing a meaningful philosophy of difference, at the level of the subject and the (posthuman) realm beyond.

8 I am thinking especially of Sundhya Pahuja (2011) on the politics of universality.

practice categorized by curator and art and cultural critic, Cédric Fauq as 'transactionality' (2020: np).

Fauq develops the term transactionality in relation to Rowland's work as well as in relation to the work of Carolyn Lazard, Ima-Abasi Okon and Abbas Zahedi.[9] Fauq claims that these artists have sketched the contours of an updated conceptualism: 'one that is intimately linked to social justice but doesn't try to "do justice"; one that embraces blackness without labelling it' (ibid). With regard to Rowland, Fauq develops transactionality specifically in relation to a piece titled *Encumbrance* (discussed later) but also as a characteristic of his broader portfolio. Fauq sees a notion of 'desertion' at work in Rowland's pieces, specifically, a tendency 'to desert race to get closer to blackness' or what he also calls a nonrepresentational Blackness (ibid). He explains,

> the desertion motion goes hand in hand with the minimalist aesthetic embraced by [Rowland] as well as a process of 'reformulation,' which can only happen when an object, a gesture, is being 'isolated' from its original context.
>
> *(ibid)*

Rowland has ingeniously isolated objects – a mahogany door in *Encumbrance*; leaf blowers, bicycles, prams and other items in *D37*[10] – to dis/locate objects/gestures from their original (historically colonial and/or contemporaneously racist) context.

One of the ways in which Rowland has done this is by 'renting out' objects obtained through property seizure auctions as artworks to exhibition spaces. Noting that the Police, Immigration and Customs Enforcement and Customs and Border Protection may retain 80 percent to 100 percent of the revenue generated from the auction of seized property from primarily poor and/or racial minority populations, he rents these object-turned-artworks to exhibition spaces for five years in order that the total auction price be realized (Rowland 2018). Rowland does this to (re)formulate and (re)present the object/gesture in a manner that grounds the viewer to the material history of

9 Cédric Fauq's term 'transationality' comes from 'Transactional Objects Full of Contexts in Voided Sites' (2020), a development to a previously published article titled 'Curating for the Age of Blackness' (2019). The term is derived through Fauq's personal encounters with works by Carolyn Lazard, Ima-Abasi Okon, Cameron Rowland and Abbas Zahedi; all works referenced in these essays were apart of separate exhibitions.

10 These pieces by Rowland include: '*Stihl Gas Backpack Blower – Item: 0628-002765,* 2018 Stihl Gas Backpack Blower' (Artwork); '*Group of 8 Used Bikes – Item: 1284-018213,* 2018' (Artwork); '*Summer 3d One Stroller – Item: 6781-005030,* 2018' (Artwork), in 'D37' (exhibition) at The Museum of Contemporary Art, Los Angeles, United States.

the institutions where the artwork is exhibited, the original function of the dis/located object/gesture and the intersecting financial and material imbrications which have created the conditions in which the object/gesture appears to the viewer in the particular space/place.[11] These financial and material imbrications can also be referred to as transactions. Of Rowland, Fauq theorizes transactionality as a means of speaking to the material conditions of a transaction and the power dynamics at play between different agents involved, an allegedly nonrepresentational approach to critiquing living legacies of trans-Atlantic slavery, anti-Blackness and racism more broadly.

Of the four artists from which Fauq develops transactionality, Rowland is the only one who takes the practice up in a manner that comes to constitute an aesthetic legal methodology. This claim can be evidenced by new materialism, which facilitates an analytic process of legally determining what constitutes *matter* and *material*. Here, new materialism's ability to negotiate material-discursive dynamics is critical as, for Fauq, there is no differentiation between an 'object' (material) and a 'gesture' (discursive) in transactionality, thus necessitating an orientation that is capable of theorizing their co-constitutive conditions. Central to my argument is the idea that *Depreciation* viewed *through* new materialism reveals Rowland's particular use of transactionality *as constituting* an aesthetic legal methodology. New materialism provides fertile ground for the phenomenological inquiry into how aesthetic visual practices may come to take legal form (i.e. become aesthetic legal methodologies).

Transactionality has given name to a practice (method) in aesthetics that has the power to impact upon law. However, the power to impact upon law is not *a priori* to transactionality. Rowland's transactionality constitutes an aesthetic legal methodology because he has *legally interpreted* his gesture/object: a process of interpreting *matter* through legality so that it comes to possess 'active' legal form. That is, it becomes *material*. Through this process of legal interpretation in which matter becomes material, Rowland has produced a way of doing law in which artists are able to determine the legal meaning of an object/gesture through the existing legal regime of property. This ethical disconnect between object/gesture and artist/subject is exemplified in Fauq's claim that transactional works are intimately linked to justice but do not try to do justice (2020: np).

The claim that the artist's objects are linked to justice but that neither the object nor the artist try to do justice can be troubled by a focus on

11 See, Cameron Rowland, '2015 Moca Real Estate Acquisition, 2018' in 'D37' at The Museum of Contemporary Art, Los Angeles, United States. In this piece, Rowland traces the origins of the property on which MOCA is established back to the 'low-income' and predominantly 'Mexican and Oriental' residents who were disposed of their neighborhood block in 1839.

matter in relation. Food and cultural studies scholar Annemarie Mol, for example, uses new materialism to seriously consider the interaction of eater and food-object, arguing that new materialism facilitates a focus that thwarts any straightforward distinction of agency and that 'otherly' conjures relations of subjectivity (2008). If you supplement 'eater' with 'artist' it becomes apparent that while neither the artist nor the object may be 'trying to do justice', justice is indeed being done to, by and through their *intra*-action(s). The formulation of an aesthetic legal methodology, or the process in which an artist is able to determine the legal meaning of an object/gesture, requires further interrogation. Interrogating aesthetic legal methodologies requires a phenomenological orientation, such as the one provided by new materialism, which is not locked in its own logic of signification but rather 'traverses and thereby rewrites thinking *as a whole*' (Dolphijn and van der Tuin 2012: 14). Consequently, new materialism raises (at minimum) two important questions pertaining to the role of isolation in transactionality that trouble the use of aesthetic legal methodologies: (1) what (if any) the relationship is between conceptualism and abstraction in aesthetics and (2) how this (potential) relationship is imbricated in 'new' and historic material in/justice.

Conceptualism differs from abstraction; however, there is slippage between them in Rowland's renewed conceptualism, which makes use of transactionality, an aesthetic intervention that utilizes explicit legal methodologies to impose restrictions at 8060 Maxie Road. Abstraction holds many different and contested meanings in the field of contemporary art, which this chapter cannot intervene in. I do, however, propose that Rowland's use of legal method, specifically his 'design' of a restricted covenant in his aesthetic practice, opens him up to critique on abstraction's substantive, material and historical grounds in law.

Transactionality specifically seeks to provide commentary on the idea of abstraction with the goal of distancing itself from the mere act of 'transaction' and referring to something more than the 'exchange' as an act. Transactionality 'seeks to comprehend the conditions of transaction, as well as the power dynamics at play between the different agents involved', implicitly critiquing which subjects are able to enter into the terms of an exchange (make contracts) and what their respective bargaining power is (Fauq 2020: np). Influenced by Brenna Bhandar (2015, 2018) in her transnational work on the colonial lives of property and K-Sue Park (2015, 2019) in her work on the legal history of racialized dispossession and self-deportation in the United States, Rowland is unequivocally invested in dis/locating the (colonial) legal history of contracts by critiquing who has historically been able to make, control the terms of and benefit from them. He is, in turn, attempting to dis/locate the abstract, (white) colonial male subject through reformulation. There is, however, trouble with his use of transactionality to achieve this aim, specifically in the way in which isolation is deployed to accomplish 'reformulation' (Fauq 2020: np).

In *Depreciation*, abstraction and conceptualism are revealed in Rowland's minimalist aesthetic, which seeks to yield a 'reformulation' of his gesture/object (the land title to 8060 Maxie Road) through isolation (ibid). Importantly, the reformulation only results when the object/gesture is isolated from its original context. The isolation works on two levels. The first pertains to Rowland's isolation of 8060 Maxie Road from the real estate market, rendering its value null. The second relates to how isolation operates through his minimal aesthetic, exemplified by the physical presentation of the object/gesture (the legal documents that constitute *Depreciation*) isolated in 'empty' gallery space. While also applicable to object-based work (see Renard-Painter 2017), new materialism seriously troubles transactionality's premise on isolation/desertion in relation to land. Specifically, the 'desertion motion' that is consequentially linked with the minimalist aesthetic and the process of 'reformulation' (which can only happen through abstraction/isolation) perpetuates a poor analysis of the genealogy of land from a perspective of matter in relation. Matter in relation is a precondition of theorizing land and, following Rick Dolphijn and Iris van der Tuin (2012), this theoretical orientation is incompatible with dualism.

The removal of an object/gesture from its original context implicitly works in a modern, dualist mode of thinking as it creates conditions of what 'desertion' or 'isolation' mean from the perspective of one party (be it a person, animal, thing) bilaterally in relation to another party as the need/desire for desertion of the object/gesture is born out of a perceived need to reconfigure an interaction between the two. As discussed earlier in relation to Braidotti, dualism is structured by a negative relation between terms. Isolation definitionally and conceptually follows this dualist function: isolation of X from Y. When isolation is conceptually coupled with reformulation, a series of ethical problems arise. If we think of X and Y as matter, the isolation and reformulation of X in relation to Y not only reconfigures their *intra*-action(s) but all other *intra*-action(s) which X has with other variables, by nature of its reformulation in relation to Y. Dualism functions in Rowland's work through the artists subjective orientation of what it means to remove (or abstract) the object/gesture (X) from its original context (Y). Focusing on *intra*-action(s), rather, 'queers the familiar sense of causality' and 'more generally unsettles the metaphysics of individualism' which produce dualist modes of thinking (Barad 2012b: np).

For example, in *Encumbrance*, Rowland seeks to provide what Eve Kosofsky Sedgwick (2002) has called tex/xture – the substantive, historic and material texture – to the exhibition space (Institute of Contemporary Arts), broadly, and its mahogany doors, specifically. The Institute of Contemporary Arts (ICA) has been based at 12 Carlton House Terrace since 1968 in a building owned by the Crown since 1760, which is adorned with architectural spoils of the trans-Atlantic slave trade. Of the significance of mahogany, Rowland notes:

> Mahogany became a valuable British import in the 18th century. It was used for a wide variety of architectural applications and furniture . . . the timbers were felled and milled by slaves in Jamaica, Barbados, and Honduras among other British colonies. It is one of the few commodities of the triangular trade that continues to generate value for those who currently own it.
>
> *(Rowland 2020: np)*

In response to this continued generation of value through the possession of mahogany, Rowland directly implicates the ICA in trans-Atlantic slavery. He continues by describing his aesthetic legal method:

> An encumbrance is a right or interest in real property that does not prohibit its exchange but diminishes its value. The encumbrance will remain on 12 Carlton House Terrace as long as the mahogany elements are part of the building. As reparation, this encumbrance seeks to limit the property's continued accumulation of value for the Crown Estate.
>
> *(Rowland 2020: np)*

With *Encumbrance*'s mahogany doors, Rowland directly implicates the United Kingdom in trans-Atlantic slavery – which Britain, specifically, has been reluctant to accept accountability for.[12] Thus, dualism functions successfully in this deployment of an aesthetic legal methodology (a bilateral implication of the United Kingdom in Anglo-American colonialism). However, there are critical differences that are all too often erased in the transnational anglophone flows of knowledge production such as the potentially fraught implications of aesthetic methodologies as legal claims when they involve land in light of the critical spatial differentiation between the United Kingdom (as the heart of Empire) and the United States (as occupied land).

With *Depreciation*, the reliance on dualism is fraught because it takes land as the object/gesture. For Rowland, 8060 Maxie Road is the site of a former plantation that relied on slave labor. This is unequivocally an important *matter* in the land's material-discursive dynamic that should be amplified

12 Britain's lack of accountability for colonialism is far too expansive to be addressed here, however, of particular importance to this chapter are the ways in which disputes have manifested concerning cultural institutions and legal objects. The British Museum's legal battles over the Benin Bronzes are one such example (see Kiwara-Wilson 2013; see also Lundén 2016; Adewumi 2015).

and addressed. His restrictive covenant ensures that the land will never be used for this or related purposes of racial domination and human debasement again. However, Rowland's move paradoxically only ensures this outcome as long as the current settler-colonial property regime stays in place as the restrictive covenant is safeguarded by and through the existing regime. It also transferred power to Rowland to determine the futurity of the land, functioning as a land claim. Even from a simplified, anthropocentric point of view, this is troubling if we assume that there are *at least* Black, white and Native (Indigenous) *intra*-action(s) embedded in the genealogy of the land at 8060 Maxie Road, specifically, but also all land in the United States and settler societies more broadly. Formative schools of thought such as TWAIL, postcolonial legal studies and critical Indigenous studies have sustained legal and political critique against the colonial foundations of international law and its role in continuing conditions of coloniality: international law paradoxically recognizes and legitimizes settler colonial regimes, such as the United States; it also serves as a mechanism for advancing recognition and reparation for the very Indigenous people dispossessed by the regimes it legitimates.[13]

The way in which Native dispossession was enacted in the continental United States is of critical importance here.[14] K-Sue Park explains the joint governmental and privatized approach:

> While colonial governments were making regular overtures to tribes to attempt to maintain diplomatic relations, they simultaneously engaged private citizens in the project of Indian Removal by linking settlers' private incentives to their own ends. This strategy gave private individuals an inordinately large role to play in land acquisition and Indian Removal, which constituted a single project.
>
> *(2019: 1893)*

While Rowland does not occupy the position of white-settler, it is critical to note the role of private citizens' land acquisition in Native dispossession as, with *Depreciation*, Rowland is attempting to invert the Master's Tools,[15]

13 The paradoxes of sovereignty for indigenous peoples are mired in specific histories of dispossession. For a comprehensive, compelling account of how this continues to play out in the Hawaiian context, see J. Kēhaulani Kauanui (2018); on the continental U.S./Canadian context see Audra Simpson (2014).

14 The non-continental contexts of the United States – Alaxsxa (Alaska) and Hawai'i (Hawaii) – have specific legal histories of dispossession which differ from the continental context. On Hawai'i see Noenoe Silva (2004) and Kauanui (2018), on Alaxsxa, see R.M. Huhndorf and S.M. Huhndorf (2011).

15 Referencing Audre Lorde's 1984 essay *The Master's Tools Will Never Dismantle the Master's House* (Lorde 2007).

that is, the legal-economic regime of property through the creation of 8060 Maxie Road, Inc. and legal coverture to instate a restrictive covenant on its use. Indeed, though Rowland is keenly aware of the law's violence and his highly generative artistic practice often implicitly or explicitly acknowledges the limitations of the use of legal method, the effects of this form of legal engagement – even if it is strategic – cannot be diminished precisely because the stakes are high. Rowland's approach successfully isolates the land title (his object/gesture) from what he takes to be as its original context but inadvertently relies on dualism to execute this. As a result of his strategic reliance on dualism to achieve other ends, Rowland inadvertently performs a reiteration of the form of (colonial, masculine) abstraction that he seeks to critique, with *Depreciation* functioning as a claim to land in the settler colonial context of the United States on behalf of non-Indigenous, Black subjects.

While Roland seeks to dis/locate colonial concepts of property and generate new modalities to conceive of land outside of the real-estate market, he neglects the law's inability to take into account aesthetic specificities of 'non-living matters', such as land, art works and software codes (Kang 2018: 454). Rowland's lack of a matter-based approach is a missed opportunity when so much of his work seeks to address so-called non-living matter – of land and art – as well as living matter – of Black lives (Weheliye 2014). New materialism reveals the cost of transactionality as his choice of aesthetic legal method is a dualist mode of thinking through Anglo-American colonialism that does not lend any active support to Indigenous sovereignty and stewardship of unceded land. While Rowland admirably attempts to transcend representational politics by conceiving of a 'new' anti-racist way of doing art, doing politics, doing law, it is precisely this perception of 'newness' that negates the extent to which the relationship between conceptualism and abstraction is always already imbricated in the relationship between materiality, spatiality and rights in the unceded lands of the United States. Perhaps, as matter is relational rather than representational, a matter-oriented approach could have aided in his pursuit of something otherwise.

It is precisely this differentiation between relation and representation that distinguishes legal *matters* from legal *materialities*. For Hyo Yoon Kang, there is a lack of distinction between matter and materiality of law that 'leads to facile analogies and assumptions of equivalence without affording a better understanding of legal entanglements with worlds in concrete detail' (2018: 461). Working from Hans-Jörg Rheinberger, she notes, 'matter becomes material only through representation, and representation itself is an act of interpretation, or coming into a meaning' (ibid: 462). For Kang, this means that 'law's materials are the constitutive matters that can have varying degrees of semiotic significance' (ibid). A stone, she notes, becomes a legal object if it acts as a boundary marker, implicating it in prescriptive regulation. Absent of its prescriptive regulation, it remains 'only' a stone.

Absent of the encumbrance placed by Rowland, the mahogany doors at the ICA were not legally imbricated in the spoils of Anglo-American colonialism. This is precisely because 'if there is no adequate legal form to acknowledge a matter, the matter does not exist in and for law' (ibid: 464). Rowland has thus ambitiously taken it upon himself to relate matter and legal form. He has made use of aesthetic legal methodologies that generate matter into new legal material. However, the land at 8060 Maxie Road already possessed legal significance through colonial dispossession of Native land and lifeways absent of the restrictive covenant placed by Rowland. This generates a problematic approach of abstracting and 'reformulating' the legal meaning of colonial objects/gestures inattentive of any theorization – legal or otherwise – of the land's human and more-than-human *intra*-action(s) that give rise to a more complex genealogy.[16] Following the framework set out by Kang to differentiate *matter* from *material*: not all visual art practices that engage with law or matters of concern to law constitute an aesthetic legal methodology precisely because not all legal matters are 'material' to law – but some like the restrictive covenant placed on 8060 Maxie Road are, and we need *matter* to determine this.

International legal theorists concerned with the ('new' and historic) materiality of injustice specifically need the posthuman, post-anthropocentric notion of 'matter in relation' in order to ground conceptualism so that it remains modest, finite and earth-bound (Haraway 1991), a move that has the potential to transcend the masculine, colonial tendency toward abstraction and support mutual liberation. Matter in relation begins with the acknowledgment that rights are not abstract but made material through *intra*-action(s) that implicitly and explicitly contend with the finitude of land and other earth-bound natural 'resources' (life sustenance). Beginning at the level of *matter*, material, conceptual, narrative and relational practices ought to be used concurrently by legal theorists to consider – for instance – the genealogy of mass population removal in a manner that ethically weighs the merits and demerits of competing claims to such finite 'resources' as land by differently colonized groups.

While important critical accounts of the colonial lives of property have de/constructed understandings of how modern property law contributes to the formation of racial subjects in settler colonies (Bhandar 2018), this

16 Indigenous feminists have been especially influential in providing astute, complex genealogies of how people interact and are enmeshed in land and the proliferation of lifeforms – animate and inanimate – that land gives rise to. See Simpson 2014, 2016; Silva 2004; Todd 2016; Kauanui 2018.

chapter demonstrates that there are yet moments when (new) materiality, spatiality and law converge in a manner that necessitates a posthuman legal ethic(s). *Matter* facilitates this orientation toward the more-than-human. However, the ethical dilemmas with which law contends cannot be resolved by new materialism's 'turn to matter' alone, nor its broader home in feminist science and technology studies, which often propagates an ethics characterized by the call to let the material things speak (Haraway 1991); a call often marked by the 'thorny racial privileges and biases that animate this field' (McKittrick 2020: 1). Kang has observed that simply letting material things speak sits in tension with law which is always already backed by a normative claim. I have thus been careful to advocate for new materialism as a necessary *supplement* to legal discourse, one that is attuned to the highly productive space of their *intra*-action(s): between normative ethics and lively matter.

Examining the *intra*-action(s) of law and new materialism requires an analytic approach. Kang recommends a three-tiered level of analysis to determine whether matter exists in and for law: (1) determining the 'concrete particularities of the "raw" matter as interpreted by law in relation to its abstract form'; (2) examining the legal representation of the first relationship 'through particular constellation and mis-en-scène through law's techniques and media'; and (3) interpreting the effects of legal materiality from various other interpretive viewpoints (2018: 465–6). I suggest a modification to the first level of analysis, which assumes 'raw' matter to exist in abstract form, a necessary move to transcend the pitfalls of Rowland's approach in *Depreciation*. If we assume that there is no abstract form but rather that the 'raw' matter is always already in relation, then we can trace its *intra*-action(s) to interpret the matter dynamically in relation to legal form(s).

Conclusion: Matters of Ethics

Through Cameron Rowland's *Depreciation* (2018), this chapter has argued that posthuman theory and new materialism reveal the ways in which particular visual art practices are making claims on the law and thus coming to constitute aesthetic legal methodologies. I explored 'transactionality' as an aesthetic legal methodology, which bestows upon Rowland the ability to change the legal form of his gesture/object: the land at 8060 Maxie Road. This detailed (re)reading of *Depreciation* demonstrated the ways in which legal methods are *produced through* aesthetics to become aesthetic legal methodologies, that is, how aesthetic methods of doing law *come into being*. I cautioned that Rowland has produced a way of doing law in which artists are able to determine the legal meaning of an object/gesture that is not subject to broader ethical regulation. This discussion emphasized the particularly fraught implications of aesthetic legal methodologies when it comes to land claims. I troubled the legal and land-based ethics of Rowland's reliance on abstraction and dualism to conceive of land outside of the present legal-economic regime of property – the results of which formulated a claim to land on behalf of non-Indigenous, Black subjects. Following Kang's observation that matter becomes material only through representation, and representation itself is an act of interpretation, I argued that Rowland misrepresented the vitality of the matter that constitutes 8060 Maxie Road and its extensive human (and more-than-human) genealogies.

I wish to conclude by offering a few thoughts on the ethical implications of Rowland's representational approach. The politics of living in a settler society such as the United States is a politics of responsibility that is differentially distributed across Settlers and Arrivants. Following Jodi Byrd, a politics of responsibility asks:

> How might we place the arrivals of peoples through choice and by force into historical relationship with Indigenous peoples and theorize those arrivals in ways that are legible but still attended to the conditions of settler colonialism?
>
> *(2011: xv)*

Whilst both are necessarily imbricated in Anglo-American colonialism, settler-colonialism creates political and ethical dynamics that critically differentiates the United States from the United Kingdom. *Intra*-actions are a highly productive way of thinking through this politics of responsibility. From this purview, responsibility is 'not about [the] right response, but rather a matter of inviting, welcoming, and enabling the response of the Other . . . that is, what is at issue is response-ability – the ability to respond' (Barad 2012b: np). For Barad, the conditions of possibility of response-ability include accountability for the specific histories of particular practices of engagement:

> Responsibility is not a calculation to be performed. It is a relation always already integral to the world's ongoing intra-active be-coming and not-becoming. That is, responsibility is an iterative (re)opening up to, an enabling of responsiveness.
>
> *(ibid)*

Barad's notion of response-ability, like their conception of *intra*-action, is queer: it disrupts the usual framings of ethics and opens up something radically relational and responsive. The restrictive covenant placed by Rowland at 8060 Maxie Road utilized orthodox legal tools to indefinitely determine the futurity of the land, foreclosing response-ability: the ability for others to respond, to situate and substantiate their historic and contemporary *intra*-actions with the land, their claims to place and space. This is troubling for a (post)colonial international legal agenda that seeks to address the multifarious modalities of 'new' and historic material injustices through reparation and other forms of reparative justice. Legal theorists are attuned to identifying ethical dilemmas in conventional forms, in law's *material*, but as aesthetic legal methodologies are serving to expand the international legal landscape, we need to turn our attention to *matter*, to get comfortable picking up legal objects, to 'get our hands dirty' performing diffractive experiments because the most pressing ethical dilemmas lie here in *intra*-action(s) – of which we are largely blind at present.

Reparation and reparative justice can and should take conventional legal-economic forms – land and natural resource stewardship redistribution, monetary compensation – but without an accompanying commitment to radically change our perception of international law's constitutive forms and (posthuman) elements, we risk reiterating the very universalist and dualist tendencies of the colonial legal order that we seek to critique. A shift in orientation, a queering of our sense of response-ability and ethics will render visible new stakes in our never-ending pursuit: justice-to-come.

References

Adewumi, A. (2015) 'Possessing Possession: Who Owns Benin Artefacts?', *Art Antiquity & Law*, 229–42.

Agard-Jones, V. (2016). 'Interview with Vanessa Agard-Jones', (podcast) on *Cultures of Energy: The Energy of the Humanities Podcast*, Huston, TX: Center for Energy & Environmental Research at Rice University.

Ahmed, S. (2006) *Queer Phenomenology: Orientations, Objects, Others*, Durham: Duke University Press.

Barad, K. (2007) *Meeting the Universe Halfway: Quantum Physics and the Entanglement of Matter and Meaning*, Durham: Duke University Press.

Barad, K. (2012a) 'Interview with Karen Barad', in Rick Dolphijn and Iris van der Tuin (eds) *New Materialism: Interviews and Cartographies*, London: Open Humanities Press, 48–70.

Barad, K. (2012b) 'Intra-Actions: An Interview with *Karen Barad*', *Mousse*, 34.

Bhandar, B. (2015) 'Title by Registration: Instituting Modern Property Law and Creating Racial Value in the Settler Colony', *Journal of Law and Society*, 42(2): 253–82.

Bhandar, B. (2018) *Colonial Lives of Property: Law, Land, and Racial Regimes of Ownership*, Durham: Duke University Press.

Braidotti, R. (1991) *Patterns of Dissonance: A Study of Women in Contemporary Philosophy*, Cambridge: Polity Press.

Braidotti, R. (1994) *Nomadic Subjects: Embodiment and Sexual Difference in Contemporary Feminist Theory*, New York: Columbia University Press.

Braidotti, R. (2012) 'Interview with Rosi Braidotti', in Rick Dolphijn and Iris van der Tuin (eds) *New Materialism: Interviews and Cartographies*, London: Open Humanities Press, 19–37.

Brown, W. and J. Halley (eds) (2002) *Left Legalism/Left Critique*, Durham: Duke University Press.

Bruce-Jones, E. (2015) 'German Policing at the Intersection: Race, Gender, Migrant Status and Mental Health', *Race & Class*, 56(3): 36–49.

Byrd, J. (2011) *The Transit of Empire*, Minneapolis: Minnesota University Press.

Constable, M. (2014) *Our Word Is Our Bond: How Legal Speech Acts*, Redwood City: Stanford University Press.

Copjec, J. (2002) *Imagine There's No Woman: Ethics and Sublimation*, Boston: MIT Press.

Dolphijn, R. and I. van der Tuin (2012) *New Materialism: Interviews and Cartographies*, London: Open Humanities Press.

Fauq, C. (2019) 'Curating for the Age of Blackness', *Mousse*, 66.

Fauq, C. (2020) 'Transactional Objects Full of Contexts in Voided Sites', *Mousse*, 71.

Finchett-Maddock, L. and E. Lekakis (2020) *Art, Law, Power: Perspectives on Legality and Resistance in Contemporary Aesthetics*, London: Counterpress.

Geary, A. (2001) *Law and Aesthetics*, London: Bloomsbury.

Halley, J. (2008) *Split Decisions: How and Why to Take a Break from Feminism*, Princeton: Princeton University Press.

Hamzić, V. (2012) 'Unlearning Human Rights and False Grand Dichotomies: Indonesian Archipelagic Selves Beyond Sexual/Gender Universality', *Jindal Global Law Review*, 4(1): 71–85.

Haraway, D. (1991) *Simians, Cyborgs and Women*, London: Free Association Books.

Huhndorf, R.M. and S.M. Huhndorf (2011) 'Alaska Native Politics Since the Alaska Native Claims Settlement Act', *South Atlantic Quarterly*, 110(2): 385–401.

Kang, H.Y. (2018) 'Law's Materiality: Between Concrete Matters and Abstract Forms, or How Matter Becomes Material', in A. Philippopoulos-Mihalopoulos (ed) *Routledge Handbook of Law and Theory*, Abingdon: Routledge.

Kapur, R. (2017) 'The (Im) Possibility of Queering International Human Rights Law', in D. Otto (ed) *Queering International Law: Possibilities, Alliances, Complicities, Risks*, Abingdon: Routledge, 131–47.

Kapur, R. (2018) *Gender, Alterity and Human Rights: Freedom in a Fishbowl*, London: Edward Elgar Publishing.

Kauanui, J. (2018) *Paradoxes of Hawaiian Sovereignty*, Durham: Duke University Press.

Kazan, H. (2020) 'Decolonizing Archives and Law's Frame of Accountability', *World Records Journal*, 4: 203–13.

Kiwara-Wilson, S. (2013) 'Restituting Colonial Plunder: The Case for the Benin Bronzes and Ivories', *DePaul Journal of Art, Technology & Intellectual Property Law*, 23(2): 375–425.

Lorde, A. (2007 [1984]) 'The Master's Tools Will Never Dismantle The Master's House', in A. Lorde (ed) *Sister Outsider: Essays and Speeches*, New York: Crossing Press, 110–4.

Lundén, S. (2016) 'Introduction: The Making of Benin Objects, the Edo, and the British' and 'The 1897 Edo-British War', in *Displaying Loot: The Benin Objects and the British Museum*, Göteborg: Göteborgs Universitet, 7–31.

Matthew, D. (2019) 'Law and Aesthetics in the Anthropocene: From the Rights of Nature to the Aesthesis of Obligations', *Law, Culture and the Humanities*, 1–29, online publishing. DOI: https://doi.org/10.1177/1743872119871830

McKittrick, K. (2020) *Dear Science and Other Stories*, Durham: Duke University Press.

Mol, A. (2008) *The Logic of Care: Health and the Problem of Patient Choice*, London: Routledge.

Muñoz, J.E. (2009) *Cruising Utopia: The Then and There of Queer Futurity*, New York: New York University Press.

Nyong'o, T. (2018) *Afro-Fabulations: The Queer Drama of Black Life*, New York: New York University Press.

Otto, D. (ed) (2017) *Queering International Law: Possibilities, Alliances, Complicities, Risks*, Abingdon: Routledge.

Pahuja, S. (2011) *Decolonising International Law: Development, Economic Growth and the Politics of Universality*, Cambridge: Cambridge University Press.

Renard-Painter, G. (2017) 'When Is a Haida Sphinx: Thinking About Law with Things', *Northern Ireland Law Quarterly*, 68(3): 391–402. DOI: https://doi.org/10.53386/nilq.v68i3.49

Park, K.-S. (2015) 'If Your World Was Built on Dispossession: Strategies of Conquest by Settlement in America', Doctoral Dissertation for the Department of Rhetoric at the University of California, Berkeley, Available on Department's Website.

Park, K.-S. (2019) 'Self-Deportation Nation', *Harvard Law Review*, 132(7): 1878–939.

Phelan, P. (1997) *Mourning Sex: Performing Public Memories*, London: Routledge.

Rowland, C. (2018a) '2015 Moca Real Estate Acquisition' in 'D37' (exhibition) at The Museum of Contemporary Art, Los Angeles.

Rowland, C. (2018b) '*Depreciation*, – Restrictive Covenant; 1 Acre on Edisto Island, South Carolina' in 'D37' (exhibition) at The Museum of Contemporary Art, Los Angeles.

Rowland, C. (2018c) '*Stihl Gas Backpack Blower – Item: 0628-002765*, 2018 Stihl Gas Backpack Blower' (Artwork); '*Group of 8 Used Bikes – Item: 1284-018213*, 2018' (Artwork); '*Summer 3d One Stroller – Item: 6781-005030*, 2018' (Artwork), D37, exhibition at The Museum of Contemporary Art, Los Angeles.

Rowland, C. (2020) '*Encumbrance*, 2020 – Mortgage; Mahogany Double Doors: 12 Carlton House Terrace, Ground Floor, Front Entrance', 3 & 4 Will. IV c. 73, exhibition at the Institute of Contemporary Arts, London, UK.

Sedgwick, E.K. (2002) *Touching Feeling: Affect, Pedagogy, Performativity*, Durham: Duke University Press.

Sharp, C. and M. Leiboff (eds) (2015) *Cultural Legal Studies: Law's Popular Cultures and the Metamorphosis of Law*, 1st ed., Abingdon: Routledge.

Silva, N. (2004) *Aloha Betrayed: Native Hawaiian Resistance to American Colonialism*, Durham: Duke University Press.

Simpson, A. (2016) 'The State Is a Man: Theresa Spence, Loretta Saunders and the Gender of Settler Sovereignty', *Theory & Event*, 19(4).

Simpson, L.B. (2014) 'Land as Pedagogy: Nishnaabeg Intelligence and Rebellious Transformation', *Decolonization: Indigeneity, Education & Society*, 3(3): 1–25.

Sunwoo, I. (2019) 'Burden of Proof: Cameron Rowland's D37', *The Avery Review*, 36: 1–9.

Todd, Z. (2016) 'An Indigenous Feminist's Take on the Ontological Turn: "Ontology" Is Just Another Word for Colonialism', *Journal of Historical Sociology*, 29(1): 4–22.

Weheliye, A. (2014) *Habeas Viscus: Racializing Assemblages, Biopolitics and Black Feminist Theories of the Human*, Durham: Duke University Press.
Wiegman, R. (2015) *Don't Look Away: Race, Sex and Kara Walker's Pornopticon*, Public Lecture, Nottingham, UK: New Art Exchange, 27 April.
Wood, P. (2002) *Conceptual Art (Movements in Modern Art)*, New York: Delano Greenidge Editions.

4

THE COMMON HERITAGE OF KIN-KIND

Emily Jones, Cristian van Eijk and Gina Heathcote

Introduction

The common heritage of [hu]mankind (CHM) is a principle of international law that is primarily used to regulate areas beyond national jurisdiction. Applied, therefore, to regions beyond the territorial jurisdiction of any one state, legal application includes the deep-seabed and subsoil of the high seas, the law of outer space and, to a lesser degree, Antarctica. The principle, in its plain wording, invokes hope in the face of a dominant global order structured through the state and state obligations. The notion that certain areas are to be held by all as part of humankind's common heritage offers a disruption to traditional international legal models of property and sovereignty, while fostering an environmental imaginary around a shared sense of responsibility. However, in reality, the principle of CHM was primarily created and has been used to promote the fair distribution of economic resources between states, supposedly ensuring that Global South states benefit equally with Global North states from extraction in these zones. While such use is potentially disruptive, creating a hopeful notion of fair distribution and economic access between Global North and South states, in practice, the principle ultimately stops short of challenging problematic models of sovereignty and property, let alone environmental extractivism (Natarajan 2023). Rather, the principle, in its current framing, is anthropocentric and deeply implicated in capitalist extractivism, albeit sometimes working to distribute the plenty in a more equitable way. 'Heritage' in this sense is narrowly defined as resource that detracts from the hope imagined in a plain word reading of CHM.

In this chapter, we begin by outlining the way the CHM has been defined and used in international law to argue that the legal definition and use of the

DOI: 10.4324/9781032658032-6

principle is anthropocentric. We draw on Donna Haraway's speculative fabulation as a critical posthuman method, alongside concepts of reworlding from queer theory, to reimagine the CHM through an ecological and posthuman lens (Haraway 2016; Tallbear and Willey 2019). In undertaking this process, noting Haraway's focus on how the past, present and future are all equally part of speculative fabulation, we draw on a combination of historical and contemporary re-imaginings of the CHM, alongside critical posthuman theoretical insights, to understand how such a method may be deployed in international law.

While there is much literature on the CHM, we argue that this literature focuses on the where and what, and less on the who. In this chapter, we question whose heritage we are or should be talking about. Taking heed of posthuman theory's call for the necessity of dismantling hierarchies, not only between humans, such as between people in Global North and Global South states, but also between humans and nonhumans, alongside the focus in posthuman theory on challenging dominant models of subjectivity (Braidotti 2015), we reimagine the CHM through the lens of the common heritage of kin-kind (CHKK). We define the shift to kin-kind as a reworlding process that rethinks articulations of mankind, subsequently humankind, to consider legal relations beyond the human. This reworlding helps us define the *who* of the CHM principle to include the interests of nonhuman subjects, allowing for the principle to simultaneously be reimagined beyond its current framing through the subject/object dichotomy (Jones 2023).

The chapter concludes with some reflections on the use of speculative fabulation as a method to reworld international law. While we find hope in the use of this method we acknowledge limitations rooted in the constant focus on a Eurocentric past and precedents in international law. The tensions between hope and hopelessness that emerge thus encourage, in the words of Haraway, the necessity to 'stay with the trouble' (Haraway 2016).

The Common Heritage of Humankind in International Law

The common heritage of humankind, which somewhat tellingly began as the common heritage of *mankind* (hence the still widely used acronym CHM – which we adopt here for ease of understanding) is used in international law to define and regulate multiple international territories, including the deep seabed,[1] outer space,[2] and arguably Antarctica (Keyuan 1991; Frakes 2003),

1 See: United Nations General Assembly, Convention on the Law of the Sea, 10 December 1982, Article 136; Declaration of Principles Governing the Seabed and the Ocean Floor, and the Subsoil Thereof, beyond the Limits of National Jurisdiction, 17 December 1970, UNGA 118, A/RES/2749 (XXV); Agreement Relating to the Implementation of Part XI of the United Nations Convention on the Law of the Sea of 10 December 1982, adopted July 28, 1994, 1836 UNTS 3.

2 The idea, or perhaps legal principle, that outer space is part of the global commons to be held by all mankind is suggested in The Treaty on Principles Governing the Activities of States

human genomes and plant genetic resources (FAO Res 8/83, 1983, Article 1; cf. Mgbeoji 2003: 837; Aoki and Luvai 2007) and, potentially, the atmosphere (Mayer 2019). On a plain reading, the CHM invokes a sense of hope or solidarity in the notion of a shared responsibility for the nonhuman. This is especially the case when it is applied to areas beyond national jurisdiction – areas not owned by one state alone but held by all in common. The idea that 'humanity' might bear responsibility for an area conflicts with orthodox doctrines of statehood and property, suggesting a system more akin to the Roman concept of the commons as a shared model of ownership. The term connotes a notion of common responsibility, suggesting that humanity is, as a whole, the custodian of these areas (Harden-Davies *et al* 2020). By designating these areas as part of humankind's *heritage*, the implication is that they are part of *our* heritage, and thus in need of preservation. However, the sense of hope evoked by the language of the CHM is not reflected by the principle's contemporary application at international law. In practice, the CHM has failed to meaningfully transform notions of common responsibility and protection in shared environments.

The international legal principle of the CHM developed in stages, and at very specific historical moments. Many of its iterations have been used to promote a privileged access to 'shared' land and resources. International lawyers often trace the commons back to Grotius' *Mare Liberum*, which was published in 1618 on commission from the Dutch East India Company as a tool of the Dutch imperialist project (Wilson 2006; Vervliet 2010: ix; Natarajan 2023). Almost 150 years later, Vattel wrote *The Law of Nations* to justify the colonial dispossession – a novel synonym for 'theft' – of lands and resources from Indigenous peoples (Vattel 1834 [1758]). For Vattel, the exploitation of areas and resources within *and* beyond national jurisdiction for 'common' benefit was both a legal *and* a moral obligation (Anghie 2014: 84–91). These are keystone citations for early genealogies of the commons, but they also demonstrate the recurring emphasis upon resource and territory, rather than solidarity or protection.

Vattel's moral-legal obligation to exploit for common benefit came into new use in the early twentieth century, as the 'Second Wave' of Antarctic Imperialism began in earnest (Howkins 2015: 221–31; Scott 2019: 2–3). As certain states turned their gaze southward, international legal scholars began framing Antarctica as a 'common possession [. . .] of all of the family

in the Exploration and Use of Outer Space, including the Moon and Other Celestial Bodies (signed 27 January 1967, entered into force 10 October 1967) 610 UNTS 205, preambular para 1 and Article 1; and was further developed in Agreement Governing the Activities of States on the Moon and Other Celestial Bodies (The Moon Agreement) (signed 5 December 1979, entered into force 11 January 1984) 1363 UNTS 3, Article 11. The United States has recently contested the notion of space as a global commons, and the applicability of the Moon Agreement: see Exec Order No. 13914, 85 FR 20381 (2020), ss 1–2.

of nations' (Balch 1910: 265); as a 'plural condominium', to be shared by 'brothers of the family of nations' (Fauchille 1925: 658–9). Likewise, the first complete English translation of *Mare Liberum* was published in 1916, where it found new relevance to projects seeking to profit from the oceans. Two League of Nations reports, in 1926 and 1930, on the *Exploitation of Products of the High Sea* framed ocean resources as the 'common patrimony of the whole human race'.[3] Then, two decades later, space exploration became conceivable, and the commons was repurposed once again. British lawyer Ralph Andrew Smith wrote in 1949 that 'the Moon is not their [US] property . . . it is the common heritage of man' (Andrew Smith 1949); French jurist Lionel Laming wondered the next year if 'all the solar system . . . deserves to be considered as the heritage of mankind' (Laming 1950: 94); and in 1953 Joseph Kroell called space the 'common patrimony of humanity' (Kroell 1953: 233). The use of 'patrimony', like the later 'mankind', reveals a continuity of the sense of masculine entitlement to resources and inherited wealth. Moreover, from its very beginning, the language of common heritage has advanced in tandem with projects to extract resources beyond national jurisdiction.

Before we move to a critical reimagination of the CHM, it is necessary to outline its specific foundations in international law. The chronological beginning of this story is Antarctica. The Antarctic Treaty (AT) was concluded in 1959 by a handful of states claiming putative interests in the continent. However, the Antarctic Treaty sits uncomfortably in the history of the commons: its 12 original parties began negotiations in secret, after India attempted to add Antarctica to the 1956 UNGA agenda (Howkins 2008: 5; Storr 2021). It was negotiated outside the UN framework by states explicitly hoping to preserve their own rights and restrict those of third parties (AT 1959: Article IV). Nevertheless, the Antarctic Treaty was a key moment in commons lawmaking. The Treaty stipulates that Antarctica should be used for peaceful purposes (AT 1959: Article I), providing for a general freedom of scientific investigation (Article II), and limiting new territorial claims (Article IV(2)). The treaty's preamble refers to the 'interest of all mankind', that Antarctica be used peacefully, and does not become the subject of international discord. In contrast to the OST, the Antarctic Treaty has a dispute settlement clause (XI) and a review process via Consultative Meetings (Article IX). The latter clause allowed the addition of several protocols to provide for, among others, environmental impact assessment (Madrid Protocol 1991: Article 3, 8), liability for environmental harm (Madrid Protocol 1991: Article 16,

3 League of Nations Committee of Experts for the Progressive Codification of International Law, 'Questionnaire No. 7 adopted by the Committee at its Second Session, held in January 1926: Exploitation of the Products of the Sea' (1926), *AJIL Special Supplement*, Annex 233, 236; League of Nations Doc. C.228.M.115.1930.v, Part III (2 May 1930), 17.

Annex IV) and a moratorium on mineral resource extraction (Madrid Protocol 1991: Article 7, 25(5)). The Madrid Protocol therefore fills some of the gaps between the original treaty and the CHM as it had developed by 1991 (Keyuan 1991: 196–8). The operation of the Madrid Protocol, including its environmental provisions, may become open to review in 2048 (Madrid Protocol 1991: Article 25(2)). However, the mineral extraction moratorium cannot be removed without a binding legal regime to replace it (Madrid Protocol 1997: Article 25(5)), and the Antarctic Treaty provisions limiting territorial claims are not part of this review process. Still, the widespread discourse framing Antarctica as an impending and inevitable land-grab is concerning. Such framings also enact a certain kind of reworlding, potentially facilitating the making of the very world warned against (Abdel-Motaal 2020).

While the question of whether the CHM applies to outer space remains contested within space law, the term and constituent elements of the CHM arose often during space lawmaking (Tronchetti and Liu 2021; van Eijk 2022). The Outer Space Treaty (OST 1967) recognizes the 'common interest of all mankind' in its Preamble, and it provides that outer space 'shall be the province of all mankind' in Article 1,[4] which also obliges states to explore and use outer space 'for the benefit and in the interests of all countries' (OST 1967: Article I). The 1979 Moon Agreement was more explicit in referring to 'the Moon and its natural resources' as being part of the CHM (Moon Agreement: Article 11), and in obliging states to equitably distribute its benefits (ibid: Article 11(7)(d)). However, in the 12 years between the Outer Space Treaty and Moon Agreement, the CHM became a battleground in a wider discourse on global distributive justice (Vadrot *et al* 2022: 230–1). As a result, the Moon Agreement only has 18 states party and four signatories (Craven 2019).[5]

Perhaps the most prominent legal application of the CHM is in the primary treaty governing the ocean, the 1982 United Nations Convention on the Law of the Sea (UNCLOS 1982). UNCLOS does not, however, designate the entirety of the ocean as the CHM; rather, 'The Area and its resources are the common heritage of mankind' (ibid: Article 136),[6] with 'The Area' referring to the 'seabed, ocean floor, and subsoil thereof, beyond the limits of national jurisdiction' (ibid: Article 1(1)). 'The Area' does not include, therefore, the water above the 'seabed, the ocean floor, and subsoil' (ibid).

4 There is some debate among space lawyers as to whether Article I designates *space* as the 'province of mankind', or its exploration and use. The *travaux preparatoires* indicate the former, for example, United Arab Republic, 'Working Paper No. 8' (22 July 1966) UN Doc A/AC.105/35, 6.

5 This will become 17 ratifications with the withdrawal of Saudi Arabia, effective 5 January 2024.

6 Article 136 UNCLOS Part XI, S.2; the application of the CHM principle to The Area was reaffirmed in the 1994 Implementation Agreement to UNCLOS.

In other words, the High Seas are still subject to Grotius' freedom of the High Seas (ibid: Article 87). For context, a state's territory extends up to 12 nautical miles from the baseline of a country's coast (ibid: Article 3). Beyond the territorial zone lies the exclusive economic zone (EEZ) which a state may claim up to 200 nautical miles (ibid: Articles 55, 57), with a few exceptions (ibid: Article 76). The EEZ allows coastal states to claim certain rights and duties beyond their territorial sea over matters including exploration, exploitation, and conservation and management (ibid: Articles 56(1)(a), 61–2). Waters that lie beyond this area are the High Seas – international territory held by all in common (ibid: Article 86) and are subject to the freedom of the High Seas.

The legal governance of the ocean enacts the CHM across several provisions. First, the areas that constitute the CHM can only be used for 'peaceful purposes' (ibid: Article 88). Second, Article 137(1) states that 'No State shall claim or exercise sovereignty or sovereign rights over any part of the Area or its resources' (ibid: Article 137(1)). The exception is where such action is authorized by the International Seabed Authority (ISA), which was established by the UNCLOS Implementation Agreement under Part XI to regulate activities in the Area on behalf of mankind as a whole (ibid: Article 153(1); Implementation Agreement 1994). UNCLOS Article 140(2) states that the ISA must provide for the equitable sharing of financial and other economic benefits derived from the Area and appropriate mechanisms must be taken, following Article 160(2)(f)(i) on a nondiscriminatory basis. Thus, it is clear that 'the concept of the benefit of mankind as a whole and the equitable sharing of benefits are intimately intwined' (Tanaka 2019: 219).

The connection between the CHM, its economic goals and distributive justice was no accident. As Surabhi Ranganathan astutely examines, the CHM was developed in the context of a wider 'ocean floor grab' (Ranganathan 2019). Central to this grab, particularly during the UNCLOS negotiations in the 1960s and 70s, were calls from Global South states for a New International Economic Order and for the concrete recognition of their right to self-determination. These were calls to rethink international relations, which sought more just models – economic and otherwise – between all states (UNGA 1974). Various proposals during the UNCLOS negotiations included provisions to ensure a fairer distribution of the gains from extraction; some, including subsidies for developing states, were successful and included in the treaty. However, many such provisions were challenged by Global North states, particularly the United States, and subsequently rolled back in the 1994 Agreement on Part XI of UNCLOS (Ranganathan 2014: 154–61). In 2023, as this chapter was finalized, states are once more asserting the common heritage of humankind as a principle in the (Draft) Agreement on the conservation and sustainable use of marine biological diversity of areas beyond national jurisdiction (UN General Assembly, 2023: Article

5 (b)) – also known as the BBNJ Agreement, with negotiations focusing on fair and equitable access to resources (including marine genetic resources) as central to the inclusion of CHM (Vadrot *et al* 2022).

It becomes clear from this brief overview of the CHM as applied in the law of the sea that the principle has been defined in a way that focuses on the exploitation of resources and economic interests (see also Ranganathan 2019; Ranganathan *et al* 2019; Storr 2022; Feichtner and Ranganathan 2019). While some balancing act is present in terms of ensuring a fairer distribution of resources between Global North and South states, the CHM principle, despite alternative readings based on its plain meaning, is certainly not envisaged in an environmental sense, in a way that sees the environment and nonhuman animals as part of humanity's (or the planet's) common heritage in and of themselves. Rather, the CHM has come to be used to focus on economic value. This financial understanding of the CHM is deeply anthropocentric.

However, the financializaton of the CHM is only one of the two anthropocentric elements that underpin the CHM. The second becomes evident from what the principle regulates, and what it does not. While the CHM requires States to take measures to protect the marine environment (UNCLOS: Article 145), the principle itself is limited to a certain array of listed matter and species. For instance, while UNCLOS defines the Area as including the 'seabed, ocean floor, and subsoil thereof' (ibid: Article 1(1)), the reality is more complicated. In short, there are some parts of this environment that are deemed to be covered under the CHM, and others that fall under the wider legal regime of the High Seas. For example, we can examine the manganese nodules on the deep-seabed: balls of metals and minerals that form over millions of years. These nodules are one of the core targets of (as of yet not authorized) deep-sea mining. Manganese nodules are deemed to fall under the CHM, as do all 'solid, liquid of gaseous mineral resources' (UNCLOS 1982: Article 133(a)). However, *all* 'living resources' (to use the anthropocentric language of UNCLOS) are excluded from the CHM, meaning that they therefore fall under the regime of the High Seas. This strange separation between the Area and the water above, however, makes little sense in terms of the species who inhabit these spaces. For example, incirrate octopods (without fins, most often found on the ocean seabed) have been observed using the dead sponges attached to manganese nodules resting on the deep-seabed to lay and brood their eggs (Purser *et al* 2016). While the nodules are part of the CHM, the sponges, the eggs and the octopods are all regulated under the High Seas regime, despite their attachment to, and dependence upon, the specially regulated nodules. This strange separation has led Ranganathan to argue that the law thereby disregards the 'complex and symbiotic ecosystems within which such resources, both living and non-living, develop' (Ranganathan 2019: 590).

Likewise, the recent BBNJ Agreement applies the CHM principle for all living materials and species in the High Seas (Articles 5, 9(5)), while establishing a regime for the fair and equitable sharing of benefits (Article 11). However, like UNCLOS, the BBNJ is focused on the economic dimension of marine resources. The four component regime, which focuses on marine genetic resources, area based management tools, environmental impact assessments and capacity-building and technology transfer, does not significantly address the interconnected and intertwined relations between matter and living organisms, or their relation to humans (Vadrot *et al* 2022). This anthropocentric disregard for the intertwined relations between matter and living organisms ensures that the 'resources' that matter most to states in terms of financial value are deemed to be the common heritage of all of humanity, while the nonhuman animals that live and rely on them are not. This inclusion and exclusion that underpins the way the CHM is defined in the law of the sea directly exposes the epistemological underpinnings of the CHM principle, those underpinnings being about financial interests and the exploitation of resources.

The anthropocentric underpinnings of the CHM are not only a theoretical problem. This can be seen in ongoing negotiations at the ISA on the possible authorization and regulation of deep-sea mining, where the protection of the marine environment is interpreted as a means of governing seabed mining in an 'environmentally friendly' way. A similar model also flows through the new BBNJ Agreement on the use of marine genetic resources. The ISA approach sits in contrast with scientific literature concluding that deep-sea mining risks severe negative environmental harm (Dover *et al* 2017; Kim 2017; Niner *et al* 2018), and joining the chorus of civil society organizations in questioning whether mining should happen at all (e.g. the Deep-Sea Conservation Coalition). However, as Ranganathan points out, the question of whether mining should be allowed, given environmental risks, 'is not a question that the ISA was set up to ask' (Ranganathan 2019: 597). Overall, these dynamics have led Feichtner and Ranganathan to argue that the governance of the Area under UNCLOS should be seen as constructed through a political economy in which governments compete for growth, rather than to pursue social justice or environmental agendas (Feichtner and Ranganathan 2019: 632).

Ultimately, despite its emergence across several specialized regimes, it becomes exceedingly clear that commitments to CHM are primarily concerned with protecting and promoting economic gain. On plain reading, the CHM seems to offer a global commitment to sharing responsibility for environmental protection. But CHM in its legal meaning is less about substantial environmental protection, and more about regulating priority in who can extract natural resources first. In describing speculative fabulation as method and developing a critical posthuman feminist reworlding of the principle into the 'common heritage of kin-kind', we will use this chapter to navigate together from the hopelessness engendered by existing practice, toward a world that recognizes the shared commonalities of human and nonhuman alike as the common heritage of kin-kind.

Speculative Fabulation as Method in International Law

While the CHM has a particular meaning at law, in this chapter we are interested in how a posthuman analysis changes the principle. While there are many stands of posthuman theory, as outlined in the introduction to this volume, we apply critical posthuman theory. Critical posthuman theory, inspired by intersectional feminism (Braidotti 2021), is defined as a body of thought that seeks to dismantle exclusionary humanist hierarchies upheld between humans, including gender, sexuality, race, ableism and class, while also rethinking the anthropocentric assumption that humans sit in hierarchy over nonhuman subjects (Braidotti 2021; Jones 2023). In this section, we entwine the critical posthuman techniques of speculative fabulation, reworlding and making kin as a method to reconsider the CHM (Haraway 2015, 2016; Tallbear and Willey 2019).

Central to our analysis is the work of Donna Haraway on speculative fabulation and her theorizing on making kin. Haraway's concept of speculative fabulation begins with the premise that:

> It matters what matters we use to think other matters with; it matters what stories we tell to tell other stories with; it matters what knots knot knots, what thoughts think thoughts, what ties tie ties. It matters what stories make worlds, what worlds make stories.
>
> *(Haraway 2011)*

Inspired by speculative fiction and the way this body of work helps analyze the world in new and imaginative ways, Haraway's speculative fabulation is defined by her as 'a mode of attention, a theory of history, and a practice of worlding' (Haraway 2016: 230). Speculative fabulation is a practice, a way of disrupting ways of knowing and thinking otherwise. However, speculative fabulation is not a mere 'clearing away of the present and the past in order to make futures' (ibid: 1). Rather, for Haraway, speculative fabulation is very much about 'staying with the trouble'. Haraway therefore seeks to understand the world as being full of 'beginnings' and 'comings, nurturing what might still be' however, these beginnings do not suggest a 'wiping out of what has come before' but, rather, these are full of 'inheritances' and 'of remembering' (ibid: 2). Later we actively remember – and insert – alternative histories of the commons, before thinking with kin to articulate a CHKK.

To give an example the practice of speculative fabulation, Haraway highlights the increased 'comic faith' in the turn to techno-fixes to address the climate emergency. While remaining skeptical of the idea that 'technology will somehow come to the rescue', Haraway also argues for the need to 'remember that it remains important to embrace situated technical projects'. Haraway writes: 'They are not the enemy . . . they can do many important things from staying with the trouble and for making generative oddkin' (ibid: 3). Therefore, for Haraway, speculative fabulation is about telling stories and imagining new worlds into being. Noting that each story risks making 'terrible political and ecological mistakes', Haraway stays with the trouble while writing these stories, seeking to 'propose near futures, possible futures, and implausible but real nows' (ibid: 236). These stories represent an attempt to imagine worlds otherwise, noting the contradictions and pitfalls inherent in any proposal, but trying anyway in the hope of creating a better world.

Haraway theorizes perceptions of kinship to address inter-species relations, writing '[n]o species, not even our own arrogant one pretending to be good individuals in so-called modern Western scripts, acts alone; assemblages of organic species and of abiotic actors make history, the evolutionary kind and the other kinds too' (Haraway 2015: 159). Haraway connects the process of making kin beyond biological families and making kin beyond humankind, what we term kin-kind, to address 'care, relatives without ties by birth, lateral relatives, lots of other echoes' while embarking on 'imagination, theory, and action to unravel the ties of both genealogy and kin, and kin and species' (ibid: 161). Elsewhere, Usha Natarajan's analysis of the commons speaks for a need to embrace 'the richness, plurality and hybridity of cultures and draw from them diverse knowledge about sustainability and equity instead of disciplining them into attempting futile emulation of Western culture' (Natarajan 2023: 15). It is clear that speculative fabulation or reworlding is not merely something that remains in the realm of the imagination: it is also a material as well as linguistic-discursive practice (Haraway 2016). This is a point queer theorist José Esteban Muñoz makes, highlighting the power of reworlding through his concept of the brown commons. This 'commons of brown people, places, feelings, sounds, animals, minerals, flora, and other objects' (Muñoz 2018: 395) is defined by Muñoz as fostering 'a process of thinking, imagining otherwiseness' (Jose Esteban Muñoz 2012, quoted in Luciano and Chen 2015). Making kin as reworlding is a practice that enables the construction of futures otherwise through both linguistic and ontological change (see also Arvidsson 2023: this volume) and which we imagine through the formation of the common heritage of kin-kind where nonhuman species, matter and organisms have a shared (common) interest (heritage) for all kin-(kind).

Speculative fabulation has much potential when applied to international law, which is a discipline supposedly governed by rules, or ways of determining what the law is and what it is not. These rules include the doctrine of precedent, rules on how to interpret treaties, rules on how to attribute responsibility,[7] and so on. Each of these sets of rules contribute to fostering an idea that international law is a science, a technical and objective discipline. Of course, disagreements on interpretation can occur, as evidenced by dissenting opinions in judicial decisions. Overall, how far such dissent can go is ultimately governed by set constraints on what international law is and can be. International law is a knowledge project produced by an interpretive community of international lawyers, often trained at a limited group of academies in specific legal traditions (Waibel 2015). This is true even as the academy begins to 'diversify' (de Carvalho and Uriburu 2022; Kulamadayil 2023). In fact, as Sara Kendall notes, projects to diversify international law can come with their own risks, including the 'shoring up [of] dominant legal forms through extending the frame of international law to what was previously excluded or marginalized' (Kendall 2016: 623–4). In short, representation alone is not enough and, without the corresponding epistemic shift, can help reinforce and legitimate the dominant epistemologies that underlie international law (see Táíwò 2021), despite challenges from feminist, Third World and other critical scholars for enacting exclusion and other harms (Anghie 2007; Charlesworth and Chinkin 2000; Heathcote 2019a; Tzouvala 2020).

Speculative fabulation is about reworlding, about thinking otherwise – not toward extending the 'frame of international law to what was previously excluded or marginalized' (Kendall 2016: 623–4), but instead reworlding its ontological and epistemological foundations. Speculative fabulation provides a means to challenge the epistemic basis of international law, by populating international law not only with 'more' and 'others', but also re-ordering the relations between international legal subjects, new and old. A CHKK, by definition, requires a rethinking of the relational encounter of humans and the nonhuman. Like all science fiction, speculative fabulation does not seek to imagine new worlds for the sake of it, but to use them to better understand the foundational workings of our own, for kin-kind thinking with the nonhuman to address the climate emergency. International law routinely works to prioritize humans over nonhuman subjects. This has been shown by multiple authors (e.g. Cirkovic 2021) but is perhaps best exemplified through the work of critical international environmental law scholars who examine how the law operates, not to protect the environment but to transform nature into a resource to be exploited for human profit and pleasure (Grear 2020c; Jones 2021, 2023; Natarajan and Dehm 2022). International law's underlying anthropocentrism can also be exemplified by looking at the dominant

7 ILC (2001) 'Draft Articles on the Responsibility of States for Internationally Wrongful Acts', *YILC*, 2: 95.

use and definition of the CHM, which, as we outlined earlier, has come to be defined and used in a way that reinforces extractive capitalism.

In contrast, Haraway draws on posthuman theory's focus on subjectivity (see: Braidotti 2013) through her use of speculative fabulation to challenge anthropocentric and autopoietic modes of thought, specifically through her use of the term 'kin'. For Haraway, the word 'kin' encompasses many ideas, asking 'to whom one is actually responsible' (Haraway 2016: 2). The concept of kin challenges familial ties associated to biology and genetics, troubling the concept of family by both noting the connections between all humans but also between humans and nonhumans as part of what Haraway terms 'multispecies flourishing' (ibid). For Haraway then, kin is about fostering connections and response-abilities between symbiotic human and nonhuman subjects, noting the need to dismantle hierarchies and better consider, for example, the environmental challenges of our times in a way that best allows all subjects to flourish, human and nonhuman (ibid: 99–103).

Next, we outline in more detail how the posthuman notion of kin can help reframe international law. Prior to this we consider past and present accounts of the commons that fall outside of dominant legal imaginaries, acknowledging Haraway's method as engaging what exists past and present. Noting the anthropocentricity of international law, as embedded in the CHM, we consider the CHM otherwise. First, we begin with some existing alternative imaginaries of the CHM for international law, including historical imaginations and contemporary attempts. We then draw upon speculative fabulation as a posthuman method, and Haraway's concept of kin, to rethink the CHM in international law as the CHKK.

Alternative Visions of the Common Heritage of Humankind in International Law

As we have already shown, the CHM has been used to evoke a sense of hope in international law and scholarship – but actually further reinforces the anthropocentric notions of property and extractive capitalism. Many international legal scholars have sought to rethink this principle, though such projects are by no means new. The commons and common heritage have storied histories of re-association, through which they have taken on new meanings and have been used to address contemporary needs through international law (Getachew 2019: 40–2). These re-associative processes are ongoing: for some, realizing the promise of the CHM involves reinterpreting the CHM through international law. Such projects are inspiring, but also necessarily constrained by the international legal discourse in which they operate – and, as we argue, the limits of humankind as the inheritor of the commons.

This section will begin by outlining and assessing some of these projects, commencing with some alternative historical understandings of the commons and moving onto contemporary rethinkings of the CHM in international law. It is key to distinguish here, however, between the CHM and ideas of 'the commons' or *res communis*. These ideas are often conflated in academic literature, and the meanings of both are variant and often ambiguous, but they are nevertheless distinct concepts that have arisen in response to different contexts and needs (Storr 2022). While broader ideas of the commons, or alternative models of shared ownership and property, do indeed hold much promise for posthuman legal theorists (Grear 2020b), these ideas have been developed separately from the CHM. In this section, we draw on these wider understandings of the commons to lead toward speculative fabulation as method and to reimagine the CHM through the lens of kin-kind.

According to the Justinian Code, 'these things are common to mankind – the air, running water, the sea, and consequently the shores of the sea'.[8] But the Byzantines understood this conception of the commons as a shared *jurisdictional* 'ownership' (*imperium*), and not a *proprietary* ownership (*dominium*) that conveyed exclusive rights or claims (Fenn 1925). It was also not original to the Byzantines: Aristotle had cynically critiqued collective property ownership 800 years earlier.[9] It is also contained in the Qu'ran,[10] which says that God subjected (or made serviceable to) 'us' – all of humanity – the heavens and the earth (Khalilieh 2019: 32–6). Writing in 1418, Islamic legal scholar Ibn Qayyim al-Jawziyya explicitly qualified large rivers as 'a common heritage of mankind' beyond private ownership (Khalilieh 2019: 28, fn 4). Buddhist jurisprudence likewise considers that 'the birds of the air and the beasts have as equal a right to live and move about in any part of the land as thou. The land belongs to the people and all living beings; thou art only the guardian of it'.[11] This emphasis on shared custodial responsibilities is also present in knowledge systems of many Indigenous peoples, including Aboriginal and Torres Strait Islander peoples (Sharp 2002: 10–11; recognized in the Croker Island Sea Cases). These imaginings of the commons jar with modernist Western understandings of individual proprietary rights as

8 *Institutes of Justinian* (529 AD) 91–2, Book 2, Title 1.1.

9 'For that which is common to the greatest number has the least care bestowed upon it. Every one thinks chiefly of his own, hardly at all of the common interest; and only when he is himself concerned as an individual'. Aristotle, *Politics*, Vol. 2 (orig ca 350 BCE, Translated by Benjamin, Clarendon Press 1885), Book 2, Ch 3.

10 Qu'ran (translator Mustafa Khattab 2015), 31:20 ('Have you not seen that Allah has subjected for you whatever is in the heavens and whatever is on the earth, and has lavished His favours upon you, both seen and unseen?'); 45:13: ('He [also] subjected for you whatever is in the heavens and whatever is on the earth – all by His grace. Surely in this are signs for people who reflect'.)

11 Arahat Mahinda to King Devanampiya Tissa (223 BCE), recorded in *Mahavamsa* (223 BCE), ch 14, cited in *Gabčíkovo-Nagymaros Project (Hungary/Slovakia)* (Sep Op Weeramantry) [1997] ICJ Rep 78, 99.

the ideal form of ownership – understandings that also underpin international law. They also begin to trouble the notion that the CHM is, in fact, 'common' – as Edwin Egede argues, jurists from the many African jurisdictions based upon collective ownership might have very different, culturally informed interpretations of 'common heritage' (Egede 2014). This tension between collective and individualized concepts of responsibility continues to impact the meaning of the commons today.

The commons have a similarly long history as places governed by collective duties or efforts to preserve. Samira Idllalène describes the Islamic legal concept of the *ḥima* as an early form of environmental common – an area regulated and protected for collective use, usually for animal husbandry (Idllalène 2021: 52). A 1983 IUCN review of Islamic jurisprudence described the 'common and shared right' to use and benefit from 'all environmental elements' as balanced with a careful and holistic assessment of 'needs and wants' (Ba Kader *et al* 1983, sec. 4, para 4). Elsewhere, a shared duty to preserve has long brought about reimaginings of the commons into explicit tension with private industry, including within Western states. For example, in 1913, American conservationist George Dorr argued that more beautiful tracts of nature should be 'inalienably public, forever free to all', but that

> with increasing private ownership and rapidly increasing population, the [national parks] movement . . . will need to go far eventually. The earth is our common heritage. It is both right and needful that it should be kept widely free in the portions that the homes of men, industry and agriculture do not claim.
>
> *(Dorr 1913: 8)*

Half a century later, Lord Wilberforce reminded the UK House of Lords that, while 'conservation is not of course a new problem', the '*res communis*' resources of the high seas, air, space, and the poles were 'not inexhaustible, and if not protected they [will be] exposed to . . . the predatory instincts of man'.[12]

This deep and complex history of the commons is not the traditional origin story of the CHM as an international legal principle. Instead, international lawyers generally historicize the beginning of the CHM in international law to a 1967 a speech by Arvid Pardo, Malta's UN Ambassador, to the UN General Assembly. Pardo, joined by Elisabeth Borgese Mann (Mickelson 2019: 640–1; Meyer 2022; Seck 2023), called for the deep seabed beyond national jurisdiction and its resources to be deemed to be part of the CHM. This was necessary, they argued, because the 'needs of poor countries, representing

12 HL Deb 1 May 1967 vol. 282 cols 738–66.

that part of mankind that is most in need of assistance, should receive preferential consideration in the event of financial benefits being derived from the exploitation of the sea-bed and ocean floor for commercial purposes'.[13] At first, Pardo proposed that all ocean spaces would be the CHM – a broad reimagination of the Grotian freedom of the seas (Grotius 1916: 25). But he quickly came to realize that such a radical proposal would not be popular with powerful Global North states seeking to expand their territorial sovereignty. Instead, Pardo limited his proposal to the seabed alone (Taylor 2012). Pardo's speech was motivated by reports of the vast resources on the seafloor, rather than environmental concern (Ranganathan 2016: 706–13). Pardo saw the CHM as a means to redistribute the profits from commercial exploitation of the seabed, including to the Global South. Pardo knew his audience – he spoke as decolonial projects coalesced into a transnational movement, with enough solidarity and moral force to counter both Cold War powers (Ranganathan 2021). Pardo's reimagination of the commons critically transformed the relationships and contestations of the Global North and South, but the CHM has not resolved or mitigated the lasting harms and inequities of colonialism (Anghie 2007, 2023; Tzouvala 2020). In fact, Pardo's CHM has enabled the persistence of colonial forms of law, through reinforcing notions of property and extractive capitalism (Storr 2022).

While the CHM was, in the end, defined in financial and extractive terms, what is clear from the alternative histories of the preceding principle is that the principle itself, and understandings of the commons generally, have long been contested, diverse and plural in origin and expression. Against this backdrop, the modern CHM principle can be seen as one of the most recent incarnations of an idea that has transformed many times to fit the needs and the imagined futures of specific contexts.

Contestations over the meaning of the CHM are by no means solely historical: there have also been many contemporary attempts to re-assess the principle. These includes doctrinal approaches that analyze how the principle, as framed in international law as it is, may be used to bolster the regulation of certain issues, such as marine management (Wang and Chang 2020), as well as more critical literature. For example, Cris van Eijk tells a counter-history of the space commons as a means to contest the erasure of radical Global South attempts to contribute to the legal governance of the space commons (van Eijk 2022). Other scholars have sought to push the principle in an environmental direction. For example, one argument that has been put forward is that the principle of the common heritage of humankind should be applied to that which is essential to the shared interest of all humans, with

13 Arvid Pardo (Malta), UNGA (1st), 'Verbatim Record of the 1516th Meeting' (1 November 1967), para 13.

arguments being made around the need to preserve for future generations (Sands and Peel 2018: 552). However, the idea that the principle should be applied within the territorial jurisdiction of sovereign states has proven controversial (Noyes 2012: 450; Wolfrum 2009). While the principle has been used in international environmental law, the term more commonly used here is the 'common concern of mankind',[14] which 'seems to call predominantly for co-operation and equitable burden sharing, and does not cover the full spectrum of the common heritage principle' (Wolfrum 2009; Cottier 2021). In short, formal arguments that have called for a reframing of the principle have largely avoided any significant transformation or development of mainstream understandings of CHM at a structural level or in terms of focus on the 'who'.

There are those who have already begun to reframe areas beyond national jurisdiction through a more ecological lens, drawing on the emerging rights of nature movement to do so. While they have had little success in terms of legal application, these approaches are of great interest from the perspective of speculative fabulation as method and our focus on kin-kind. The rights of nature is an emerging global movement, in international law and beyond, seeking to tackle climate change and environmental degradation. Around the world, states including Aotearoa/New Zealand, Bangladesh, the United States and Ecuador have begun to recognize the rights of nature through various paradigms (Jones 2021), by recognizing either the rights themselves or the legal personality of a specific ecosystem. While the rights of nature have been recognized in multiple countries in their domestic law, they have not yet been applied in international law, despite recent attempts (Kauffman and Martin 2016; Gilbert *et al* 2023). This means that calls for the recognition of the rights of nature in international law remain, for now, speculative. It is interesting to note, however, that the majority of calls for the rights of nature to be recognized come from those seeking to recognize these rights in relation to areas beyond national jurisdiction, that is, zones where the principle of the CHM applies, at least in part. This is not surprising. State sovereignty is a core obstacle when it comes to recognizing the rights of nature in international law, with sovereign states having to consent to such a framework for it to come into place, with states being unlikely to do so. Recognizing the rights of nature in areas beyond national jurisdiction could therefore be a strategic proposal, being a means by which to sidestep the problem of sovereignty (Gilbert *et al* 2023). Rights of nature advocates have sought to call for the recognition of the rights of nature in multiple areas beyond national jurisdiction. For example, Harriet Harden-Davies *et al* call for the application of a rights

14 See Protection of Global Climate for Present and Future Generations of Mankind, UNGA Res 43/53, 6 December 1988, GAOR 43rd Session Supp. 49 vol. 1, 133.

of nature approach to the field of global ocean governance (Harden-Davies *et al* 2020) and, since 2018, there have been ongoing discussions regarding the creation a Regional Convention for the Rights of the Pacific Ocean that would recognize the Pacific Ocean as having rights (ibid). Interestingly, the 'Statement of Principle' which outlines the ongoing work on this Convention, draws on the language of kinship, acknowledging 'our kinship with the Ocean, and our responsibilities to the Ocean' (Tilot *et al* 2021).

Likewise, a proposal was put forward by a group of advocates and academics in 2021 to recognize the rights of Antarctica (Cullinan *et al* 2021). Similar approaches have also been called for in relation to the moon, with the proposed Declaration for the Rights of the Moon being released in early 2021 (Australian Earth Laws Alliance 2021; Altabef 2021). While we cannot examine these proposals here in detail (though see: Gilbert *et al* 2023), they share many similarities: they focus on how such approaches may help tackle environmental exploitation (Rogers and Maloney 2022: 4), while also arguing that a rights of nature approach may help foster a better understanding of the connection between humans and these environments (Harden-Davies *et al* 2020). It is also clear that many thinkers involved in these projects are, like us, concerned with the way the environment is currently treated by international law as a resource to be extracted, with Slatter, for example, arguing in relation to the possibility of deep-sea mining in the Pacific, that '[a]chieving legal personhood status for the Pacific Ocean may be the only way to protect it and its life systems from being ravaged for short term gains by rapacious corporate interests and complicit, short-sighted leaders' (Slatter 2020: 20).

Many of these approaches share much with the critiques we have already outlined of the CHM and with the concept of kin that we seek to deploy in this chapter. However, there are a few key differences. First, these approaches, while each focusing on areas beyond national jurisdiction, do not necessarily focus on or solely on areas deemed to be the CHM. For example, as discussed earlier, only certain parts of the ocean are currently designated as the CHM, with the rest falling under the High Seas regime and potentially the BBNJ Agreement. Furthermore, as already noted, it is debatable whether outer space or the moon fall under the CHM or, at least, how the principle impacts legal regulation of these spaces.

Second, rights of nature initiatives have different objectives than we do here. The aforementioned initiatives each seek to propose something new – a new declaration, agreement or approach that recognizes the legal personality of a new entity. This chapter focuses on an existing principle within international law, rather than on a specific area or environment where it applies. We seek to understand how it could be reworlded otherwise, through the posthuman method of speculative fabulation, to better account for the interests of nonhuman subjects. This aim is precisely why the method of speculative fabulation is so important; speculative fabulation, according to Haraway, focuses on and works with the past and the present, while seeking to foster new futures.

Furthermore, existing literature on the CHM primarily focuses on the what and where, but not the who. Not only does this further enable the CHM's emphasis on territory and resource extraction, but it limits discourse on the boundaries of subjectivity, including whether and how nonhumans should become stakeholders in this common heritage. In parallel, the many ongoing efforts to recognize the rights of nonhumans in shared spaces are not advocating for changes to the CHM principle itself, but rather are proposing new forms of regulation for these areas. We see an opportunity for the literature on the CHM to learn from critical work, scholarly and otherwise, on the commons and the rights of nature – work that has examined the 'who', that has asked the nonhuman question, and work that re-places human and nonhuman kin alike as stakeholders in our planet (Grear 2020b; Petersmann 2023). So far, ecological attempts to rework the commons and CHM have struggled to be recognized by mainstream international legal literature. While the CHM is now referred to as the common heritage of *human*kind, finally broadening the term to include other genders beyond men, international law is a long way from accepting the *conceptual* expansion of the principle to include nonhuman subjects.

Toward the Common Heritage of Kin-Kind: Practicing Speculative Fabulation in International Law

In this section, we analyze the CHM in international law through the lens of posthuman theory, applying speculative fabulation as a method to evaluate whether and how the principle might be used to challenge anthropocentric visions of extractive capitalism in international law. Noting that the literature seeking to re-assess the CHM in international law, until now, primarily focuses on the what or the where, and if it does ask the who question, it does so by focusing on human inequalities, we argue for the need to focus on a further expansion of the who in nonhuman terms. Speculative fabulation and the application of posthuman theories of kin, we argue, can be used to reworld and recreate the CHM beyond the constraints of existing international law, allowing for a more imaginative, promising and emancipatory vision of the principle to come to the fore. However, as we will discuss in our conclusion, such reworlding comes with its own limitations.

In order to evaluate how speculative fabulation could apply to the principle of the CHM, there is a need to identify the problems of the past, or the paths that were drawn but not taken. As outlined earlier, the method of speculative fabulation is not merely about rethinking the present but is, rather, a mode of thought that recognizes and engages with the past and present while seeking more hopeful futures. With this in mind, while the CHM has come to be legally defined in a way that focuses on extractivism, this was never the sole proposal put forward to understand the legal principle. Indeed, the CHM has always been a contested notion in international law, and while an extractivist and anthropocentric definition has come to dominate how CHM in international law is understood and applied, the use of the CHM in this way has long been contested, including by those who have sought to define the principle in an ecological way.

Haraway's work on kin calls into question 'to whom one is actually responsible' (Haraway 2016: 2). Kin, for Haraway, is a way of reconceiving relationships between humans and between humans and nonhumans, as part of her multispecies becoming (Haraway 2016). The idea of kin is therefore central to Haraway's concept of speculative fabulation and her ideas of reworlding, challenging anthropocentric notions of human domination and calling for alternative onto-epistemological futures. Haraway is by no means the only person to challenge anthropocentric thought through a focus on the relationships between human and nonhuman subjects, with other theorists associated with the posthuman turn discussing similar themes in their work on, for example, 'onto-epistemology' (Barad 2007), 'agential-realism' (ibid), 'vibrant matter' (Bennett 2010) or 'vitalist materialism' (Braidotti 2013). We are also by no means the first authors to bring these ideas to international law, with several scholars having discussed the required epistemic shift toward better understanding human–nonhuman relations in environmental law (Adelman 2021; Boulot and Sterlin 2022; Jones 2021, 2023; Petersmann 2021), with others offering similar analysis of the law of the sea (Heathcote 2019b; Ollino 2019), in discussions of technology and international law (Arvidsson 2018, 2020; Grear 2017, 2020a; Wilcox 2017a, 2017b), or in relation to outer space law (Cirkovic 2021, 2022; Cocca 1964; Haley 1957). We have chosen to focus on Haraway's use of the term 'kin' when seeking to disrupt and rethink the anthropocentric epistemological underpinnings of the CHM precisely because this term calls into question, not only how the CHM is and should be defined but also who the subject of the principle is and should be, seeking to move the principle away from a focus on humankind by looking, instead, toward understandings of human and nonhuman relations, as embodied in the idea of kin-kind. Furthermore, the focus on kin-kind recognizes queer reworlding projects that straddle non-biological and nonhuman kin as central to queer ecologies (McGarry *et al* 2021).

While the current principle of the CHM invokes a particular, anthropocentric and extractivist imagery, our proposed principle of the CHKK disrupts and contests that definition, arguing that human and nonhuman subjects alike are, and need to be, legally recognized as stakeholders in the common heritage that is our planet. While mindful that the CHM is still contested in terms of which *human* subjects are included, or at least which states have a voice when it comes to regulating these areas (van Eijk 2022), nevertheless posthuman theory seeks to dismantle hierarchies between humans as well as of the human over the nonhuman. The CHKK as a legal principle would address all humans and nonhumans in future proposals for legal regulation. This may require some shift in legal forms to ensure that the interests of present and future generations of humans and nonhumans are centered in any discussion over how to regulate areas that fall under the CHM, or an unlearning of Western and Eurocentric legal traditions to think with the diverse legal conceptions of the commons we have drawn on throughout this chapter.

Thinking with kin-kind might require us to return to nodules and incirrate octopods or perhaps armor footed snails, which thrive in gases released from the thermal vents on the deep seabed. Both exist in the commons but, at present, offer no economic value to humans. Research suggests deep sea mining would have significant consequences for both species, amongst others (Dover *et al* 2017; van Reusel *et al* 2016). A legal principle based on the CHKK would hold the relationship between humans and ocean kin as central to legal decision-making, as well as the dependencies of ocean kin, animal, fauna and mineral organisms, on the matter to be mined as a form of heritage – proprietary in a way. Human encounters with these critters might seem unlikely, and yet humans are already shaping the future for ocean kin as we sit at the ISA and think on how to regulate deep sea mining or as signatures to the BBNJ Agreement are sought. A legal account of kin-kind in common would ask different questions of interspecies relationships, including of our own expectation that the habitat of kin are available for the economic gain of humans. Recognizing that incirrate octopods cannot speak, at least not to humans, leads to subsequent questions on how their subjectivity would be exercised, but a principle of CHKK asks what humans will do about the relationship we have already forged with ocean-kin. CHKK returns the commons to a mode of shared ownership and shared livelihoods: acknowledging that the matter on the deep-sea bed matters to ocean-kin and matters to humans. In the forms of legal regulation, that is the CHKK, the mining of manganese nodules must see and respond to the matter–non-matter dependencies, making nodules, as seemingly inert matter, alive for the worlds they engender.

How might a CHKK avoid the of risk being deployed in the services of extractivist capital? Perhaps a more important question is: can a code for mining regulation, as is in the process of being drawn, or exploration, as currently exists, acknowledge the interspecies dependencies of humans and the nonhuman? The CHKK provides requirements for expanding understandings of human–nonhuman dependencies in a precautionary manner and in line with the environmental law precautionary principle, recognizing, similarly, Sustainable Development Goal 14 and the existing commitment of the international community to 'conserve and sustainably use the oceans'

(SDG 14). As the ISA debates and drafts the mining code, a world can be imagined – reworlded – where the incirrate octopod's existence is valued as intrinsically of worth, regardless of any absence of monetary value to men, or states. Legal tools already exist to engender these reworldings, including Article 192 of the UNCLOS which commits states to protect and preserve the marine environment (UNCLOS), while non-European legal traditions offer plural encounters with the commons that see the nonhuman as legal entities and as invoking alternative forms of property, ownership and responsibility. Furthermore, while debates over who has standing to respond to a breach under a kin-kind regime might raise further questions, the CHKK, especially in relation to the deep seabed or marine genetic resources, can impose obligations, overseen by the International Tribunal for the Law of the Sea and the ISA, a frame of values that dictate action rather than waiting for violations. In swimming with kin-kind and thinking with nonhuman species to make them matter before the law, CHKK permits the harms inflicted on the nonhuman to be the concern – to matter – under international law. As queer as this may seem to dominant legal imaginaries, we have used alternative speculations and conceptions of the commons to render this possible and to engender hope for kin-kind, now and for the future.

The Limits of Speculative Fabulation as Method

Speculative fabulation calls for reworlding while being mindful of the past and present. Throughout this chapter we have drawn inspiration from various sources, including alternative visions of the commons from the past alongside contemporary international law to reimagine the CHM. This has included proposals for the rights of nature to be recognized in international law in relation to areas beyond national jurisdiction. While each of these projects has sought to better account for the nonhuman subject when it comes to human–environmental relations, and while we were inspired by these projects, as noted earlier, our focus, as inspired by the method of speculative fabulation, differs to these projects. It does so in that it focuses, not on providing new ways of thinking or completely new legal models (as the various rights of nature proposals for areas beyond national jurisdiction do) but, rather, instead analyzes an existing principle in international law, the CHM, seeking to imagine it otherwise while still staying within the limits of international law. In this sense, we remain more tethered to international law than these other projects, seeking to stay in conversation with mainstream international lawyers and international legal doctrine as part of our speculative fabulation method. This is important given the skepticism many international lawyers have when it comes to discussions of the rights of nature. Nevertheless, there are also limitations to our approach and arguably to speculative fabulation methods for international lawyers that we review in this section.

The first limitation is international law itself. International law, as explored through our preceding analysis of the CHM, is based upon a set of assumptions or 'structural biases', limiting the range of possible outcomes (Modirzadeh 2023: 41). This can be exemplified when considering the sources of international law. Despite attempts to broaden the range of sources of international law beyond those listed in Article 38(1) of the Statute of the International Court of Justice, Article 38(1) remains the authoritative list of sources articulated as international conventions, customary international law and general principles (Charlesworth 2012; see also Saunders 2020). What is interesting is that each of these sources create a framework that is deeply rooted in the past, resulting in a system that is reactive and conservative in character. International law's perpetual turn toward its own past slows down its capacity to act on contemporary challenges and imagine futures yet to come, rendering it hostile to any attempts to address these challenges and imagine otherwise (Arvidsson and Bak-McKenna 2020; Parfitt 2014). The CHKK must surmount these difficulties to be realized as an international legal tool. Nevertheless, the urgency of climate change and its relationship to extractivist histories of the commons propels a reworlding for precisely these reasons, and furthermore, underscores our commitment to reworlding and speculative fabulation as engaged via existing alternative imaginaries.

The second limitation to our reworlding of the CHM relates more to the distinction between language and action. Among the most visible developments to the CHM in the last few decades, at least until 2023, has been the shift to the 'common heritage of *hu*mankind'. While it is encouraging that 'mankind' is no longer acceptable shorthand for the breadth of human interests (Steer 2021), adjusting our terminology does not of itself result in the 'inclusion' of women and other gendered subjects, especially without correlative progress on a conceptual level. Likewise, it is difficult to propose the 'inclusion' of nonhuman subjects through a linguistic shift. The concern here is that by calling upon existing legal constructs that we claim are anthropocentric, and by trying to work within international law – even when seeking to include new nonhuman subjects – we risk extending the existing paradigm without challenging it sufficiently (Jones 2023; Kendall 2016).

This is yet another example of the limits of speculative fabulation as applied to international law or, in other words, the limitations one faces when seeking to rethink from within international law. As Ratna Kapur has argued, many of international law's key principles and ideas, including those found in international human rights law, are deeply liberal. By adding a new subject to liberal international law, the risk becomes that that subject is added and stirred into existing legal structures, thus extending liberalism without challenging it (Kapur 2019). While this critique strongly resonates with international human rights law, arguably, it applies less to the CHM.

This is because of the way the principle has been defined until now in a way that justifies and normalizes the economic exploitation of the environment. The foundations of the CHM, unlike international human rights law, thereby seem less liberal, especially given the principles *lack* of focus on the subject beyond some, in practice, limited attempts to better distribute the wealth of these areas between Global North and South states. In this sense, the CHM is based more on extractivist values than liberal, even if these extractivist underpinnings are, at least, framed in a slightly more just way in terms of global human interests. 'Adding' the nonhuman subject as an interest-holder to the principle, therefore, has the potential to challenge the core of the principle. Forcing international lawyers and states to think about the interests of the nonhuman requires a direct disruption to extractivst values. In this sense, therefore, the critique of 'just add and stir' seems less relevant here as we imagine a 'revolutionary reconfigure[ing] from within' (Kendall 2016; Jones 2023). The speculative fabulation of a kin-kind rather than a humankind of CHM in international law works, in our reading, as a means to reworld international law, and to do so from within.

Conclusion

In this chapter, we push against the anthropocentric nature of the CHM, using Haraway's speculative fabulation as a method to reworld the CHM to better account for the interests of nonhumans. Reworlding through speculative fabulation starts by looking backwards – as Haraway put it, to stay with the past and the present when reworlding the future. Accordingly, we began by historicizing the history of the CHM beyond the orthodox narrative in existing literature. Specifically, we argued that the CHM has historically been a reworlding project; it has been made and remade many times over to fit the needs of various particular moments. In the space created by this history of reimagination, we have proposed a novel, more radical attempt at world-making. Drawing upon Haraway's use of 'kin', we call for the CHM to be transformed into the common heritage of kin-kind (CHKK).

In applying speculative fabulation as method, we encountered two limitations. The first was international law itself. International law may be indeterminate, but it nevertheless limits the array of possible futures (Koskenniemi 2006). This means that critical approaches that seek to engage international law, to imagine alternative futures from within international law, may find success limited to concepts where they reaffirm the existing parameters of legal thought. Centering nonhuman interests in the CHM is necessary, but we also argue that it may be aspirational, given the very limited options it allows through which to reinterpret the CHM. The discomfort of outlining hope despite a sense of hopeless imbues our study of the CMH. The second limitation is the danger of superficial adjustment without real change.

Our worldviews, priorities, and actions must rise to meet the promise of our words – otherwise, they will remain just that.

So far, 'common heritage of humankind' has been, to quote Duncan French, '[m]uch more an adjective than a noun' (Stoll *et al* 2021: 434–5). To think of the commons as a noun, to expand its legal subjectivity, requires a CHKK that disrupts both genealogical and anthropocentric conceptions of kinship and kin-making. To reconsider the CHM as a story of reimagination, tracing how its meaning has adapted to fit the needs, values, and imagined futures of various particular 'nows', opens the possibility (hope) of new imaginings. By conjuring the CHM from adjective to noun, by imagining otherwise, we are reworlding with kin, both queer and nonhuman.

Though the CHM is often read as a failed attempt at radical worldmaking, the 'radical' world it produced is all around us – one that privileges exploitation and expansion at the cost of kin. Our predecessors have left us a common heritage that is, as they themselves predicted, a 'betrayal of the objectives it had been meant to further'.[15] But beneath those layers of comic hope and despair is a promise. The past's dead worlds need not bind us, so long as we, as earthly kin, can 'stay with the trouble' – and, through reimagining, make better ones (Haraway 2016).

References

Abdel-Motaal, D. (2020) 'High North and the Antarctic', in J. Weber (ed) *Handbook on Geopolitics and Security in the Arctic: The High North Between Cooperation and Confrontation*, Cham: Springer International Publishing, 363–78.

Adelman, S. (2021) 'A Legal Paradigm Shift Towards Climate Justice in the Anthropocene', *Oñati Socio-Legal Series*, 11(1): 44–68. DOI: https://doi.org/10.35295/osls.iisl/0000-0000-0000-1177

Altabef, W. (2021) 'The Legal Man in the Moon: Exploring Environmental Personhood for Celestial Bodies', *Chicago Journal of International Law*, 21(2). https://chicagounbound.uchicago.edu/cjil/vol21/iss2/7

Andrew Smith, R. (1949) 'Man and His Mark', *Journal of the British Interplanetary Society*, 8(3): 131–2.

Anghie, A. (2007) *Imperialism, Sovereignty and the Making of International Law*, Cambridge: Cambridge University Press.

Anghie, A. (2014) 'Vattel, Internal Colonialism, and the Rights of Indigenous Peoples', in *Freedom and Democracy in an Imperial Context*, Abingdon: Routledge.

Anghie, A. (2023) 'Rethinking International Law: A TWAIL Retrospective', *European Journal of International Law*: chad005. DOI: https://doi.org/10.1093/ejil/chad005

Aoki, K. and K. Luvai (2007) 'Reclaiming "Common Heritage" Treatment in the International Plant Genetic Resource Regime Complex', *Michigan State Law Review*, 35: 36–70.

15 Stefano D'Andrea (Italy), Legal Subcommittee, UN Committee on the Peaceful Uses of Outer Space (7 May 1976) UN Doc A/AC.105/C.2/SR.250, 3.

Arvidsson, M. (2018) 'Targeting, Gender, and International Posthuman itarian Law and Practice: Framing the Question of the Human in International Humanitarian Law', *Australian Feminist Law Journal*, 44(1): 9–28. DOI: https://doi.org/10.1080/13200968.2018.1465331

Arvidsson, M. (2020) 'The Swarm That We Already Are: Artificially Intelligent (AI) Swarming "Insect Drones", Targeting and International Humanitarian Law in a Posthuman Ecology', *Journal of Human Rights and the Environment*, 11(1): 114–37. DOI: https://doi.org/10.4337/jhre.2020.01.05

Arvidsson, M. (2023) 'Posthuman Feminism as a Theoretical and Methodological Approach to International Law', in M. Arvidsson and E. Jones (eds) *International Law and Posthuman Theory*, Abingdon: Routledge.

Arvidsson, M. and M. Bak McKenna (2020) 'The Turn to History in International Law and the Sources Doctrine: Critical Approaches and Methodological Imaginaries', *Leiden Journal of International Law*, 33(1): 37–56. DOI: https://doi.org/10.1017/S0922156519000542

Australian Earth Laws Alliance (2021) Version of 11 February 2021, online at: https://www.earthlaws.org.au/moon-declaration/

Ba Kader, A.B.A. *et al* (1983) *Basic Paper on the Islamic Principles for the Conservation of the Natural Environment*. IUCN. https://portals.iucn.org/library/node/6307 (Accessed: 8 April 2023).

Balch, T.W. (1910) 'The Arctic and Antarctic Regions and the Law of Nations', *American Journal of International Law*, 4(2): 265–75. DOI: https://doi.org/10.2307/2186613

Barad, K. (2007) *Meeting the Universe Halfway: Quantum Physics and the Entanglement of Matter and Meaning*, Durham: Duke University Press.

Bennett, J. (2010) *Vibrant Matter: A Political Ecology of Things*, Durham: Duke University Press (a John Hope Franklin Center Book).

Boulot, E. and J. Sterlin (2022) 'Steps Towards a Legal Ontological Turn: Proposals for Law's Place beyond the Human', *Transnational Environmental Law*, 11(1): 13–38. DOI: https://doi.org/10.1017/S2047102521000145

Braidotti, R. (2013) *The Posthuman*, Cambridge: Polity.

Braidotti, R. (2015) 'Posthuman Feminist Theory', in L. Disch and M. Hawkesworth (eds) *The Oxford Handbook of Feminist Theory*, Oxford: Oxford University Press, 673–98. DOI: https://doi.org/10.1093/oxfordhb/9780199328581.013.35

Braidotti, R. (2021) *Posthuman Feminism*, 1st ed., Cambridge: Polity.

de Carvalho, J.S. and J. Uriburu (2022) 'Problematising Diversity: The Change That International Lawyers (Do Not) Want for International Courts', *London Review of International Law*, 10(3): 391–425. DOI: https://doi.org/10.1093/lril/lrac020

Charlesworth, H. (2012) 'Law-Making and Sources', in J. Crawford and M. Koskenniemi (eds) *The Cambridge Companion to International Law*, Cambridge: Cambridge University Press (Cambridge Companions to Law), 187–202. DOI: https://doi.org/10.1017/CCO9781139035651.013

Charlesworth, H. and C. Chinkin (2000) *The Boundaries of International Law: A Feminist Analysis*, Manchester: Manchester University Press.

Cirkovic, E. (2021) 'The Next Generation of International Law: Space, Ice, and the Cosmolegal Proposal', *German Law Journal*, 22(2): 147–67. DOI: https://doi.org/10.1017/glj.2021.4

Cirkovic, E. (2022) 'The Cosmolegal of Outer Space Governance', in C. Cockell and F. von der Dunk (eds) *Institutions of Extraterrestrial Liberty*, Oxford: Oxford University Press.

Cocca, A.A. (1964) 'General Principles for the Utilization of Outer Space: Determination of the Meaning of the Expression Res Communes Humanitatis in Space Law', Proceedings on the Law of Outer Space, Paris, 1–6.

Commonwealth v. Yarmirr; Yarmirr v. Northern Territory [2001] HCA 56, 11 October.

Cottier, T. (2021) 'The Principle of Common Concern of Humankind', in T. Cottier and Z. Ahmad (eds) *The Prospects of Common Concern of Humankind in International Law*, Cambridge: Cambridge University Press, 3–92. DOI: https://doi.org/10.1017/9781108878739.003

Craven, M. (2019) '"Other Spaces": Constructing the Legal Architecture of a Cold War Commons and the Scientific-Technical Imaginary of Outer Space', *European Journal of International Law*, 30(2): 547–72. DOI: https://doi.org/10.1093/ejil/chz024

Cullinan, C. *et al* (2021) 'Declaration for the Rights of Antarctica'. www.antarcticarights.org/ (Accessed: 13 June 2023).

Dorr, G.B. (1913) *Man and Nature*, Bar Harbor, Maine: Wild Gardens of Acadia, Sieur de Monts Publications, 7.

Dover, C. *et al* (2017) 'Biodiversity Loss from Deep-Sea Mining', *Nature Geoscience*, 10: 464–5. DOI: https://doi.org/10.1038/ngeo2983

Egede, E. (2014) 'The Common Heritage of Mankind and the Sub-Saharan African Native Land Tenure System: A "Clash of Cultures" in the Interpretation of Concepts in International Law?', *Journal of African Law*, 58(1): 71–88. DOI: https://doi.org/10.1017/S0021855313000144

Fauchille, P. (1925) *Traité de Droit International Public*, 8th ed., Paris: Rousseau.

Feichtner, I. and S. Ranganathan (2019) 'International Law and Economic Exploitation in the Global Commons: Introduction', *European Journal of International Law*, 30(2): 541–6.

Fenn, T. (1925) 'Justinian and the Freedom of the Sea', *The American Journal of International Law*, 19(4): 716–27. DOI: https://doi.org/10.2307/2188310

Frakes, J. (2003) 'The Common Heritage of Mankind Principle and the Deep Seabed, Outer Space, and Antarctica: Will Developed and Developing Nations Reach a Compromise?', *Wisconsin International Law Journal*, 21(2): 409–34.

Getachew, A. (2019) *Worldmaking After Empire: The Rise and Fall of Self-Determination*, Princeton: Princeton University Press.

Gilbert, J. *et al* (2023) 'The Rights of Nature as a Legal Response to the Global Environmental Crisis? A Critical Review of International Law's "Greening" Agenda', in D. Dam-de Jong and F. Amtenbrink (eds) *Netherlands Yearbook of International Law 2021, vol 52*. The Hague: T.M.C. Asser Press: 47–74.

Grear, A. (2017) '"Anthropocene, Capitalocene, Chthulucene": Re-encountering Environmental Law and Its "Subject" with Haraway and New Materialism', in L.J. Kotzé (ed) *Environmental Law and Governance for the Anthropocene*, London: Hart Publishing: 77–95.

Grear, A. (2020a) 'Legal Imaginaries and the Anthropocene: "Of" and "For"', *Law and Critique*, 31(3): 351–66. DOI: https://doi.org/10.1007/s10978-020-09275-7

Grear, A. (2020b) 'Resisting Anthropocene Neoliberalism: Towards New Materialist Commoning?', in A. Grear and D. Bollier (eds) *The Great Awakening: New Modes of Life Amidst Capitalist Ruins*, Brooklyn: Punctum Press, 317–56. https://orca.cardiff.ac.uk/id/eprint/122785/ (Accessed: 28 June 2023).

Grear, A. (2020c) *The Great Awakening: New Modes of Life Amidst Capitalist Ruins*, Brooklyn: Punctum Books.

Grotius, H. (1916) *The Freedom of the Seas, or the Right Which Belongs to the Dutch to Take Part in the East Indian Trade*, Oxford: Oxford University Press.
Haley, A.G. (1957) 'Space Law and Metalaw – Jurisdiction Defined', *Journal of Air Law and Commerce*, 24(3): 286–303.
Haraway, D. (2011) 'Speech Accepting the Pilgrim Award', 7 July. https://people.ucsc.edu/~haraway/Files/PilgrimAcceptanceHaraway.pdf
Haraway, D. (2015) 'Anthropocene, Capitalocene, Plantationocene, Chthulucene: Making Kin', *Environmental Humanities*, 6(1): 159–65. DOI: https://doi.org/10.1215/22011919-3615934
Haraway, D. (2016) *Staying with the Trouble: Making Kin in the Chthulucene*, Durham: Duke University Press.
Harden-Davies, H. *et al* (2020) 'Rights of Nature: Perspectives for Global Ocean Stewardship', *Marine Policy*, 122: 104059. DOI: https://doi.org/10.1016/j.marpol.2020.104059
Heathcote, G. (2019a) 'Feminist Dialogues', in *Feminist Dialogues on International Law*, Oxford: Oxford University Press. DOI: https://doi.org/10.1093/oso/9780199685103.003.0001
Heathcote, G. (2019b) 'Feminism and the Law of the Sea: A Preliminary Inquiry', in I. Papanicolopulu (ed) *Gender and the Law of the Sea*, The Hague: Brill Nijhoff, 83–105. DOI: https://doi.org/10.1163/9789004375178_004
Howkins, A. (2008) 'Defending Polar Empire: Opposition to India's Proposal to Raise the "Antarctic Question" at the United Nations in 1956', *Polar Record*, 44(1): 35–44. DOI: https://doi.org/10.1017/S0032247407006766
Howkins, A. (2015) *The Polar Regions: An Environmental History*, Hoboken, NJ: John Wiley & Sons.
Idllalène, S. (2021) *Rediscovery and Revival in Islamic Environmental Law: Back to the Future of Nature's Trust*, Cambridge: Cambridge University Press. DOI: https://doi.org/10.1017/9781108772082
Jones, E. (2021) 'Posthuman International Law and the Rights of Nature', *Journal of Human Rights and the Environment*, 12(2): 76–101. DOI: https://doi.org/10.4337/jhre.2021.00.04
Jones, E. (2023) *Feminist Theory and International Law: Posthuman Perspectives*, Abingdon: Routledge. DOI: https://doi.org/10.4324/9781003363798
Kapur, R. (2019) 'On Gender, Alterity and Human Rights: Freedom in a Fishbowl', *Feminist Review*, 122(1): 167–71. DOI: https://doi.org/10.1177/0141778919847398
Kauffman, C.M. and L. Martin (2016) *Testing Ecuador's Rights of Nature: Why Some Lawsuits Succeed and Others Fail*, Atlanta: International Studies Association Annual Convention, 18 March. http://files.harmonywithnatureun.org/uploads/upload471.pdf
Kendall, S. (2016) 'On Academic Production and the Politics of Inclusion', *Leiden Journal of International Law*, 29(3): 617–24. DOI: https://doi.org/10.1017/S0922156516000224
Keyuan, Z. (1991) 'The Common Heritage of Mankind and the Antarctic Treaty System', *Netherlands International Law Review*, 38(2): 173–98. DOI: https://doi.org/10.1017/S0165070X00003740
Khalilieh, H.S. (2019) *Islamic Law of the Sea: Freedom of Navigation and Passage Rights in Islamic Thought*, Cambridge: Cambridge University Press.

Kim, R.E. (2017) 'Should Deep Seabed Mining Be Allowed?', *Marine Policy*, 82: 134–7. DOI: https://doi.org/10.1016/j.marpol.2017.05.010

Koskenniemi, M. (2006) *From Apology to Utopia: The Structure of International Legal Argument*, Cambridge: Cambridge University Press.

Kroell, J. (1953) 'Eléments Créateurs d'un Droit Astronautique', *Revue Générale de l'Air*, 16: 233.

Kulamadayil, L. (2023) 'Ableism in the College of International Lawyers: On Disabling Differences in the Professional Field', *Leiden Journal of International Law*, 1–15. DOI: https://doi.org/10.1017/S0922156523000171

Laming, L. (1950) *L'Astronautique*, Paris: Presses Universitaires de France.

Luciano, D. and M. Chen (2015) 'Has the Queer Ever Been Human?', *GLQ: A Journal of Lesbian and Gay Studies*, 21: 183–207. DOI: https://doi.org/10.1215/10642684-2843215

Mayer, B. (2019) 'A Review of the International Law Commission's Guidelines on the Protection of the Atmosphere', *Melbourne Journal of International Law*, 20: 453.

McGarry, D. *et al* (2021) 'The Pluriversity for Stuck Humxns: A Queer EcoPedagogy & Decolonial School', in J. Russell (ed) *Queer Ecopedagogies: Explorations in Nature, Sexuality, and Education*, Cham: Springer International Publishing, 183–218. DOI: https://doi.org/10.1007/978-3-030-65368-2_10

Meyer, T. (2022) *Elisabeth Mann Borgese and the Law of the Sea*, The Hague: Brill Nijhoff. https://brill.com/view/title/61104 (Accessed: 4 August 2022).

Mgbeoji, I. (2003) 'Beyond Rhetoric: State Sovereignty, Common Concern, and the Inapplicability of the Common Heritage Concept to Plant Genetic Resources', *Leiden Journal of International Law*, 16: 821–37.

Mickelson, K. (2019) 'Common Heritage of Mankind as a Limit to Exploitation of the Global Commons', *European Journal of International Law*, 30(2): 635–63. DOI: https://doi.org/10.1093/ejil/chz023

Modirzadeh, N.K. (2023) '"[L]et Us All Agree to Die a Little": TWAIL's Unfulfilled Promise', *Harvard International Law Journal*, 65. DOI: https://dx.doi.org/10.2139/ssrn.4406477

Muñoz, J.E. (2012) *The Brown Commons: The Sense of Wildness*, San Juan, Puerto Rico: American Studies Association Convention, 16 November.

Muñoz, J.E. (2018) 'Preface: Fragment from the Sense of Brown Manuscript', *GLQ: A Journal of Lesbian and Gay Studies*, 24(4): 395–7. DOI: https://doi.org/10.1215/10642684-6957730

Natarajan, U. (2023) 'The Global Commons: Deep Sea, Outer Space and Beyond', *Ocean Yearbook Online*, 37(1): 1–16. DOI: https://doi.org/10.1163/22116001-03701002

Natarajan, U. and J. Dehm (eds) (2022) *Locating Nature: Making and Unmaking International Law*, Cambridge: Cambridge University Press. DOI: https://doi.org/10.1017/9781108667289

Niner, H.J. *et al* (2018) 'Deep-Sea Mining with No Net Loss of Biodiversity: An Impossible Aim', *Frontiers in Marine Science*, 5(1).

Noyes, J.E. (2012) 'The Common Heritage of Mankind: Past, Present, and Future', *Denver Journal of International Law and Policy*, 40(1): 447.

Ollino, A. (2019) 'Feminism, Nature and the Post-Human: Toward a Critical Analysis of the International Law of the Sea Governing Marine Living Resources Management', in G.V. Heathcote (ed) *Gender and the Law of the Sea*, The Hague: Brill Nijhoff, 204–28. DOI: https://doi.org/10.1163/9789004375178_004

Parfitt, R. (2014) 'The Spectre of Sources', *European Journal of International Law*, 25(1): 297–306. DOI: https://doi.org/10.1093/ejil/chu011

Petersmann, E.-U. (2023) 'How to Constitute a Global Community Through International Law and Jurisprudence?', in G. Ziccardi Capaldo (ed) *The Global Community Yearbook of International Law and Jurisprudence 2021*, Oxford: Oxford University Press. DOI: https://doi.org/10.1093/oso/9780197659083.003.0035

Petersmann, M.-C. (2021) 'Response-abilities of Care in More-Than-Human Worlds', *Journal of Human Rights and the Environment*, 12: 102–24. DOI: https://doi.org/10.4337/jhre.2021.00.05

Purser, A. *et al* (2016) 'Association of Deep-Sea Incirrate Octopods with Manganese Crusts and Nodule Fields in the Pacific Ocean', *Current Biology*, 26(24): R1268–9. DOI: https://doi.org/10.1016/j.cub.2016.10.052

Ranganathan, S. (2014) *Strategically Created Treaty Conflicts and the Politics of International Law*, Cambridge: Cambridge University Press. DOI: https://doi.org/10.1017/CBO9781107338005

Ranganathan, S. (2016) 'Global Commons', *European Journal of International Law*, 27(3): 693–717. DOI: https://doi.org/10.1093/ejil/chw037

Ranganathan, S. (2019) 'Ocean Floor Grab: International Law and the Making of an Extractive Imaginary', *European Journal of International Law*, 30(2): 573–600.

Ranganathan, S. (2021) 'What if Arvid Pardo Had Not Made His Famous Speech? (False) Contingency in the Making of the Law of the Sea', in I. Venzke *et al* (eds) *Contingency in International Law: On the Possibility of Different Legal Histories*, Oxford: Oxford University Press.

Ranganathan, S., J. von Bernstorff and P. Dann (2019) 'The Common Heritage of Mankind: Annotations on a Battle', in *The Battle for International Law*, Oxford: Oxford University Press. DOI: https://doi.org/10.1093/oso/9780198849636.003.0002

Rogers, N. and M. Maloney (2022) 'The Anthropocene Judgments Project: A Thought Experiment in Futureproofing the Common Law', *Alternative Law Journal*, 47(3): 173–8. DOI: https://doi.org/10.1177/1037969X211062306

Sands, P. and J. Peel (2018) *Principles of International Environmental Law*, 4th ed., Cambridge: Cambridge University Press. DOI: https://doi.org/10.1017/9781108355728

Saunders, I. (2020) *General Principles as a Source of International Law: Art 38(1)(c) of the Statute of the International Court of Justice*, 1st ed., Oxford: Hart Publishing. DOI: https://doi.org/10.5040/9781509936090

Scott, S.V. (2019) 'Imperialism in Antarctica', in I. Ness and Z. Cope (eds) *The Palgrave Encyclopedia of Imperialism and Anti-Imperialism*, Cham: Springer International Publishing, 1–8. DOI: https://doi.org/10.1007/978-3-319-91206-6_142-1

Seck, S. (2023) 'Elisabeth Mann Borgese: Ecology, Relationality, and Law of the Sea', in I. Tallgren (ed) *Portraits of Women in International Law: New Names and Forgotten Faces?*, Oxford: Oxford University Press. DOI: https://doi.org/10.1093/oso/9780198868453.003.0031

Sharp, N. (2002) *Saltwater People: The Waves of Memory*, Crows Nest: Allen & Unwin.

Slatter, C. (2020) 'Securing the Pacific in a Globalised World: New and Emerging Developments in International Law', *Canterbury Law Review*, 27(1): 5.

Steer, C. (2021) '"The Province of all Humankind" – A Feminist Analysis of Space Law', in M. de Zwart and S. Henderson (eds) *Commercial and Military Uses of Outer Space*, Singapore: Springer, 169–88. DOI: https://doi.org/10.1007/978-981-15-8924-9_12

Stoll, T., D. French and O. Suttle (2021) 'Comments: The Doctrinal Approach of Common Concern', in T. Cottier and Z. Ahmad (eds) *The Prospects of Common Concern of Humankind in International Law*, Cambridge: Cambridge University Press, 431–46. DOI: https://doi.org/10.1017/9781108878739.013

Storr, C. (2021) 'Critical Minerals: Australia's Role in Negotiations Over Resource Extraction in Domains Beyond National Jurisdiction, 1958–1991', in *Australia in the International Legal System: From Empire to the Contemporary World*, London: Hart Publishing.

Storr, C. (2022) *From Sacred Trust to Common Heritage: An Uncommons History*, University of Essex Public International Law Lecture Series, 8 February. https://youtu.be/0HhC80qrtSA

Táíwò, O.O. (2021) 'Being-in-the-Room Privilege: Elite Capture and Epistemic Deference', *The Philosopher*. www.thephilosopher1923.org/post/being-in-the-room-privilege-elite-capture-and-epistemic-deference (Accessed: 20 June 2023).

Tallbear, K. and A. Willey (2019) 'Critical Relationality: Queer, Indigenous, and Multispecies Belonging Beyond Settler Sex & Nature', *Imaginations: Journal of Cross-Cultural Image Studies*, 10(1): 5–15. DOI: https://doi.org/10.17742/IMAGE.CR.10.1.1

Tanaka, Y. (2019) *The International Law of the Sea*, Cambridge: Cambridge University Press.

Taylor, P. (2012) 'The Common Heritage of Mankind: A Bold Doctrine Kept Within Strict Boundaries', in D. Bollier and S. Helfrich (eds) *The Wealth of the Commons: A World Beyond Market and State*, Amherst, MA: Levellers Press, 353–60. https://wealthofthecommons.org/essay/common-heritage-mankind-bold-doctrine-kept-within-strict-boundaries (Accessed: 28 June 2023).

Tilot, V.C. *et al* (2021) 'The Concept of Oceanian Sovereignty in the Context of Deep Sea Mining in the Pacific Region', *Frontiers in Marine Science*, 8. DOI: https://doi.org/10.3389/fmars.2021.756072

The Treaty on Principles Governing the Activities of States in the Exploration and Use of Outer Space, including the Moon and Other Celestial Bodies (signed 27 January 1967, entered into force 10 October 1967) 610 UNTS 205 (OST).

Tronchetti, F. and H. Liu (2021) 'The White House Executive Order on the Recovery and Use of Space Resources: Pushing the Boundaries of International Space Law?', *Space Policy*, 57: 101448. DOI: https://doi.org/10/gmx4rs

Tzouvala, N. (2020) *Capitalism as Civilisation: A History of International Law*, Cambridge: Cambridge University Press.

UN General Assembly, 'Declaration on the Establishment of a New International Economic Order' (UN 1974) UN Doc A/RES/3201(S-VI).

United Nations General Assembly, Convention on the Law of the Sea (UNCLOS) (1982, 10 December).

Vadrot, A.B.M., A. Langlet and I. Tessnow-von Wysocki (2022) 'Who Owns Marine Biodiversity? Contesting the World Order Through the "Common Heritage of Humankind" Principle', *Environmental Politics*, 31(2): 226–50. DOI: https://doi.org/10.1080/09644016.2021.1911442

van Eijk, C. (2022) 'Unstealing the Sky: Third World Equity in the Orbital Commons', *Air and Space Law*, 47(1): 25–44.

van Reusel, A. *et al* (2016) 'Threatened by Mining, Polymetallic Nodules Are Required to Preserve Abyssal Epifauna', *Scientific Reports*, 6(1): 1–6.
Vattel, E.D. (1834) *The Law of Nations: Or, Principles of the Law of Nature, Applied to the Conduct and Affairs of Nations and Sovereigns*. Edited by J. Chitty, Cambridge: Cambridge University Press. DOI: https://doi.org/10.1017/CBO9781139095396
Vervliet, J. (2010) 'General Introduction', in *Hugo Grotius Mare Liberum 1609–2009*, The Hague: Brill Nijhoff, ix–xxx. https://brill.com/display/book/9789047430452/Bej.9789004177017.i-178_002.xml (Accessed: 31 May 2023).
Waibel, M. (2015) 'Interpretive Communities in International Law', in *Interpretation in International Law*, Oxford: Oxford University Press.
Wang, C. and Y.-C. Chang (2020) 'A New Interpretation of the Common Heritage of Mankind in the Context of the International Law of the Sea', *Ocean & Coastal Management*, 191: 105191. DOI: https://doi.org/10.1016/j.ocecoaman.2020.105191
Wilcox, L. (2017a) 'Drones, Swarms and Becoming-Insect: Feminist Utopias and Posthuman Politics', *Feminist Review*, 116(1): 25–45. DOI: https://doi.org/10.1057/s41305-017-0071-x
Wilcox, L. (2017b) 'Practising Gender, Queering Theory', *Review of International Studies*, 43(5): 789–808. DOI: https://doi.org/10.1017/S0260210517000183
Wilson, E. (2006) 'Erasing the Corporate Sovereign Inter-Textuality and an Alternative Explanation for the Publication of Hugo Grotius' Mare Liberum (1609)', *Itinerario*, 30(2): 78–103. DOI: https://doi.org/10.1017/S0165115300013978
Wolfrum, R. (2009) 'Common Heritage of Mankind', in *Max Planck Encyclopedia of Public International Law*, Oxford: Oxford University Press.

PART 2

Political Economy, History and Colonialism

5

A MONUMENT TO E.G. WAKEFIELD

New and Historical Materialist Dialogues for a Posthuman International Law

Jessie Hohmann and Christine Schwöbel-Patel

Introduction

Edward Gibbon Wakefield's story has all the trappings of a dramatic film script: it includes abduction, imprisonment, deceit, prestige and memorialization. Despite this, Wakefield's story, if remembered at all, is mostly remembered in a much-truncated way, making only the latter two features prominent. If searching for a commemoration of the man, one might visit Adelaide, Australia, where one would find a small, bronze plaque with a bas-relief bust of its subject on the foundation stones of South Australia's Parliament building. The monument faces North Terrace 'the major symbolic edifice of Adelaide' (Hay *et al* 2004: 201–3) site of venerable colonial institutions, including the museum and art gallery, state library, war memorial and University of Adelaide. The monument was unveiled in April 1952 by the then Governor of South Australia. At the ceremony, Wakefield was referred to as 'the father of self-government in South Australia' and described as 'a warm-hearted man of great public spirit' (Adelaide Advertiser 1952: 1). Wakefield's legacy is his theory of systematic colonization, with its rejection of convict labor, and its ingenious proposal for a productive settler colony that would rid the mother country of her unwanted pauper population. These views, the governor noted at the unveiling, Wakefield had expounded in *A Letter from Sydney* published while in prison there in 1829. Yet Wakefield never set foot in Sydney – not even to serve a prison sentence. Nor did he ever visit South Australia. In fact, Wakefield's letter, no matter how evocative of the colony of New South Wales, was in one way an elaborate work of fiction – at least as regards his own role as a settler. In another way, the *Letter from Sydney* was

DOI: 10.4324/9781032658032-8

a factual account of the political economy of the expanding British Empire (Chalmers 2022: 8–9).

For our engagement with new materialism and historical materialism and its relationship to posthumanism and international law, Wakefield's plaque offers an excellent point of departure. It is not a plaque that has aroused protests or discussions of the kind concerning Cecil Rhodes, Winston Churchill, Edward Colston and other famous colonialists and apologists of empire, as recently problematized through the Rhodes Must Fall and Black Lives Matter movements; however, we argue that it deserves attention alongside similar colonial history and memory practices in public spaces. Monuments deserve attention both in their material form and for what they represent. E.G. Wakefield attracted our (materialist) interest for several reasons: Due to his role in the colonization of Australia and his theory of 'systematic colonisation', his reputation as a 'humanitarian' prompted by his rejection of convict and slave labor, because Karl Marx discusses Wakefield's insights about colonization in *Capital volume 1* (1867: 932) and because of the simple fact that his never having set foot in Australia makes his memorialization as its 'founding father' curious and interesting. Our aim is to identify the relevance of international law in the context of monuments and their material life. In international law monuments are variously objects of remembrance and reconciliation in post-conflict spaces; protected as objects of art, culture and human achievement; or seen to reflect broader cultural and historical significance. When monuments symbolize and record significant moments in a nation's history, often moments of peace and war, they both reinscribe the importance of the event and of international law itself. When those events are structured by international legal rules and agreements, they are 'archival sites of law' (Peevers 2017: 167). The protection of (historical) monuments is encoded in multiple international legal regimes from the laws of war, to human rights, to international criminal law, to international cultural heritage law (see e.g. Spijkers 2021; Vrdoljak 2011; Lixinski 2018; Office of the United Nations High Commissioner for Human Rights 2014, 1907 Hague Convention respecting the Laws and Customs of War and Land; 1954 Hague Convention on Cultural Property; 1977 Additional Protocol I to the 1949 Geneva Conventions; Article 8 (b) (ix); Rome Statute of the International Criminal Court). Their position in international law – protected as objects with universal value – mirrors international law itself, with its universalist ambitions and underpinnings. The assumption made, both as regards monuments and international law, is that they are reparative of past wrongs.

We suggest a different reading of monuments in connection with international law to this dominant frame, namely one brought to life by a dialogue between new and historical materialism.[1] For us, an invitation to consider

1 Notable exceptions to the mainstream approach to monuments and international law are Parfitt (2018), Drumbl (2020) and Grady (2019).

posthumanism and international law is an invitation for a critical engagement with the material world. In this chapter, we turn our dual materialist lenses to the legacies of colonial domination and extraction, and the continuing role of international law in the capitalist exploitation of the world. Bringing the explanatory power of new and historical materialist approaches to the Wakefield monument can deepen our understanding of these processes.

This includes a problematization of international law's progress narrative, its complicity in (settler) colonialism, and its entanglement with the global capitalist order. What we seek of posthumanism is a critical engagement with law, and international law, in ways that destabilize powerful forces: forces such as imperialism, capitalism and racialization and the exploitative practices they rest on, perpetuate and excuse. Posthumanism's challenge, as Braidotti and Hlavajova note, is

> how to represent . . . the profound interconnections between humans and non-human factors and agents. And how to fulfil this task, moreover, while keeping in mind the structural inequalities that control access to the dominant category of the 'human' to begin with.
>
> *(Braidotti and Hlavajova 2018: 8, see also 11–12)*

Bignall, Hemming and Rigney, describe a posthuman ethics as:

> far less concerned with defining the principles and rules of human right and obligation that derive from innate qualities that mark the human as an exceptional kind of being, than it is with attending to ecological principles underscoring the complex patterns of connectivity that produce worldly outcomes of justice and injustice, and potentially can be directed positively and artistically towards the enhancement of creativity to benefit life.
>
> *(2016: 466–7)*

Whether posthumanism can satisfy these ambitious questions is tested by bringing new materialism into conversation with historical materialism – a theory of history that centers materialist conditions and social relations and has, since the work of political economists, theorists and revolutionaries such as Karl Marx and Rosa Luxemburg, offered a critique of capitalism and imperialism. We aim not to collapse or synthesize them into 'one materialism', or argue that historical materialism can be read as, in fact, new materialism (for which see e.g. Nail 2020). We also do not argue that the 'new' has replaced the 'old', or that they stand in opposition, but build on the acknowledgment of the link between historical and 'new' materialism by posthuman and new materialist scholars (see e.g. Bennett 2010: xiii–xix; see also Coole and Frost 2010: 4), while acknowledging and further exploring their ambivalences (Cole 2018: 170). We aim to lay them against each other as overlapping lenses and to bring out their synergies and tensions or points of incommensurability. Our position is that new materialism's insights are most powerful when they are coupled with and engage the legacies of historical materialism, on which they build.[2]

In the following, we begin with the curious story of Edward Gibbon Wakefield's role in the foundation of South Australia as a British settler colony. We then provide an overview of new materialism and a new materialist reading of the Wakefield monument, followed by an overview of historical materialism and a historical materialist reading of the Wakefield monument. This allows us to provide a richly textured reading of the monument, which aids in letting different facets of the relationship between the monument and international law emerge. We use this material(ist) dialogue to provide some initial insights into the utility of posthuman theory for international law.

Edward Gibbon Wakefield, 'Father' of the Colony of South Australia

Wakefield was born in London in 1796. He was admitted to Gray's Inn in 1813 but became secretary to the British Envoy in Turin in 1814, serving in a diplomatic capacity for a number of years. His early career does not reveal much of his interest in the British colonies, but 'Wakefield's imprisonment in Newgate was to transform his whole career' (Pretty 1967). It was in Newgate Prison that he wrote his *A Letter from Sydney*, originally published as a series in the *Morning Chronicle* and later as a book. Wakefield was serving a three-year sentence for abducting a 15-year-old heiress, Ellen Turner (ibid). Turner, who had been lured from her school, was married to Wakefield at Gretna Green in Scotland and taken to Calais before Wakefield was brought back to London to stand trial (ibid). Interestingly, a second monument to Wakefield stands in Gretna Green, Scotland, presumably commemorating his status as a 'celebrated' abductor (Beautiful Britain).[3] It should nevertheless be noted that Wakefield's crime meant that during his lifetime, his public reputation was tarnished (Pretty 1967), meaning he penned many of writings anonymously, including *A Letter from Sydney*.

In prison, Wakefield met inmates, many of whom had been sentenced to transportation to Britain's penal colonies in Australia. Wakefield became intensely interested in the plight and prospects of the inmates. In Newgate, Wakefield appears to have seen, through the prism of the wretched convicts, a simultaneous solution to the cost of colonization, Britain's excess pauper population, and the problem of making a colony profitable for the capitalist.

2 See also Hohmann 2021.

3 A further monument, 'a beautiful Italian sculpture' in the church in Winwick Lancaster, was set up by Turner's later husband, to commemorate Turner and her infant daughter. She died in childbirth during this marriage in 1831. See Beaumont (1873).

In *A Letter from Sydney*, he wove an elaborate narrative, from the perspective of a colonial land holder disappointed in his inability to profit from his land. In full character, he fictionalized his trip to New South Wales, describing the 'coal and iron of which my estate is supposed to abound' (Wakefield 1829: 4). He wrote of the 'magnificent timber' (ibid). He recounted his impressions of the land as fertile, with 'trees scattered over the whole property, as in an English Park' (ibid).[4] And yet of his inability to profit from and exploit it:

> I was told that an estate of 10,000 acres might be obtained for a mere trifle. This was true. I have got 20,000 acres, and they did not cost me more than 2*s*. per acre. But I imagined that a domain of that extent would be very valuable. In this I was wholly mistaken. As my estate cost me next to nothing, so it is worth next to nothing.
>
> *(Wakefield 1829: 4)*

A Letter from Sydney and Wakefield's subsequent writings contained his proposal to overcome this problem, and to make land in the colony valuable (ibid; see also Wakefield 1833). He diagnosed the root of the problem to lie in the fact that land was inexpensive. With land being inexpensive, anyone could purchase it, but no one would want to work the land. Essentially, the wage laborers who would otherwise be taking on this role themselves bought land. This need for laborers in the colonies, Wakefield saw in contrast to the pauperization of laborers in Britain. Here, workers had been forced off the land due to enclosure, moving to cities in search for work, with nothing to sell but their labor power. Hand in hand with the poor working conditions, unemployment and poverty came a 'heightened worker militancy' (Ince 2018: 114). Profits were driven down with less purchasing power of the population. Wakefield devised a 'solution' to the excess of English capital and labor through systematizing colonization. The proposal was to control the sale of land, raise the price of it so that the common laborer could no longer afford it, and to introduce adequate wages for laborers – because after all, it had to be attractive for British laborers to move to Australia. Wakefield was celebrated as a humanitarian and progressive because he was writing in the aftermath of the abolition of the slave trade and was opposed to 'shoveling out paupers' to Britain's settler dominions. As Birchall writes, while the plan and its execution involved private enterprise, it was underpinned by state sovereignty over property, making the state central to the scheme (Birchall 2021: 144; see also Wakefield 1831; Chalmers 2022).

Though major figures, including South Australia's first Governor, and Torrens, proponent of the famous land titling system, apparently credited

4 For a critical account of the 'English Park' impression of Australia see Pascoe (2014).

Wakefield with a major role in the establishment of South Australia as a colony, 'Wakefield's name appears rarely in contemporary manuscripts, though his personal influence must have been very great' (Pretty 1967). Nevertheless, Wakefield has been mythologized as a founding father of South Australia. Even in 1952 when his plaque was unveiled, Wakefield's skillful blend of fact and fiction had convinced the state governor.

Such mythologizing is reminiscent of international law's Whiggish progress narrative and protection of property rights. What has been termed the 'Great Man' narratives of international law portray the discipline as influenced through the ideas of remarkable men, who were visionaries of a peaceful and united world. Such focus on ideas has come at the expense of understanding the material conditions that structure inequality. It also mostly omits the story of the Global South, which was exploited for the enrichment and progress of the Global North, as notably problematized by the growing body of Third World Approaches to International Law scholarship (Eslava *et al* 2017; Chimni 2021; Gathii 2022). Global North enrichment through colonialism was justified by employing universalized and juridified terms such as 'sovereignty' (Anghie 2005), and also 'territory' – aptly explained by Cait Storr as 'a fundamentally Eurocentric construction of the rightful relationship between community, authority and place' (Storr 2023). Erasure of physical earth through abstraction hides very real material inequalities. As the immaterial ideas of progress take center stage, the relationships created through international legal norms and institutions that contribute to sustaining the structures of imperialism, capitalism, racialization and patriarchy become less visible. Both historical materialism and new materialism offer potential tools to critique the mythologizing of disciplines and people and to bring structural questions to the fore.

New Materialism

What Is New Materialism?

Although the contours of new materialism remain contested, new materialism offers a theory, an ontology and a research methodology. It seeks to recognize and understand the world in a way that rejects and overcomes the dualistic pairings (such as mind/matter, nature/culture) on which Enlightenment thought is structured. New materialism stresses the need to understand that 'matter, the world and humans themselves are not dualistic entities structured according to dialectical principles of internal or external opposition, but rather materially embedded subjects-in-process circulating within webs of relation with forces, entities and encounters' (Braidotti and Hlavajova 2018: 8). It is posthuman in the sense that it is post-anthropocentric, and posthumanist, but as Braidotti and Hlavajova write in introducing their

Posthuman Glossary, posthumanism is more than the sum of these two 'post-s' and aims to a 'qualitative leap' in new critical directions (Braidotti and Hlavajova 2018: 8; see also Braidotti 2013). New materialism is closely aligned with posthumanism in its aims, its methods and its politics, but it is not coterminous with it. In fact, as Braidotti argues, neo-materialisms function as methodology and a creative cartography *for* a critical posthumanism (Braidotti 2019: 31–5).

Next, we expand on the main contours of new materialism as we understand it (see further Hohmann 2021: 591–4). That is, we see new materialism as making three key contributions. First, new materialism seeks to give serious attention to matter in its physicality (Coole and Frost 2010: 1). Thus, new materialism turns attention to things and objects, nature and the (human) body, which Western idealist philosophy have so often ignored, or treated primarily as the binary foils for human action and subjectivity (Hohmann 2018: 40–5). It is committed to 'raising the profile of the physical world as an integral part of the social' (Davies 2017: 57). As Barad puts it simply: in investigating 'how matter comes to matter. How matter makes itself felt' (Dolphijn and van der Tuin 2012: 59). This entails seeking to understand the work objects or things, matter and materials, do in the world without, so far as possible, an overlay of preconceptions built up through the received categories established from the Enlightenment onwards in Western thought and the traditional disciplines. But there is no rigid distinction between the human subject regarding the world, and the things regarded. Instead, new materialism's second point is that we are tangled together, or co-constituted, as entities in the world.

In new materialist thought, the meaning of the subject is intelligible only in relation to the object, not in the sense of a binary either/or, but through engagement or entanglement. A central undertaking for new materialisms is to question that there are discrete, fixed and preexisting units that can be understood to relate to each other. Instead, as Barad writes, in *intra-active* engagement, entities emerge from their relating (Barad 2007: 137–41, original emphasis). Barad writes that the 'primary ontological units are not "things" but phenomena – dynamic topological reconfigurings/entanglements/relationalities/(re)articulations of the world' (ibid: 141). Thus '[a]gency is not an attribute but the ongoing reconfigurings of the world' (ibid). New materialism brings everything into relation (Davies 2017: 58).

This leads to the third important aspect of new materialism, which identifies matter as actant, even agentic. Bennett writes that matter is *vibrant* and full of 'energetic vitality' (Bennett 2010: 5). She suggests that considering material things to act is to notice and insist that they are also 'quasi agents or forces with trajectories, propensities, or tendencies of their own' (ibid: viii). Things always have the capacity to exceed our understanding of them, to break free of their human-designated status, and in doing so, they 'manifest traces of independence or aliveness' (Bennett 2010: xvi). Other new materialist thinkers are more resistant to categorizing matter as having agency or an 'actant' status. For example, although Barad's work is often described as 'agential realism' they avoid using the terms agent or even actant, because these terms work against their relational ontology (Dolphijn and van der Tuin 2012: 54; see also Philippopoulos-Mihalopoulos 2016: 194). Rather than agency as something held as a property of things or persons, they see it as 'an enactment, a matter of possibilities for reconfiguring entanglements' (Dolphijn and van der Tuin 2012).

The Wakefield Statue Through a New Materialist Lens

The monument to Wakefield, dark copper set against the smooth grey stone, *looks* quintessentially like matter, in the sense of passive object. The plaque, with its bas-relief bust staring toward the west, appears inert and stable, a representation of a person long dead.

However, from a new materialist position, the idea that this monument is outside us, inert, separate, monolithic, is destabilized. A new materialist approach focuses attention on the plaque not as a representation or symbol, but as a vibrant or agentive force. The Wakefield monument can be read as a node along a web of shifting and intra-acting forces, of relational, contested, process stretching through time and space. Materialism disrupts the idea that monuments freeze time in a moment that divides the past from the future along a trajectory. For example, as Parfitt has written in relation to international law, monuments can collapse the distinction between the past and the present, and help us read international law as '*embedded in* and *rebounding from*, the physicality of a particular location, contributing to the constitution of particular kinds of subjectivity' (Parfitt 2018: 514, emphasis in original). A monument can, through the coming together of its materials, its location and its symbolism enact a 'fold' in time that simultaneously emphasizes and hides (Parfitt 2018: 517; see also Grady 2019: 368).

The trajectory of history as proceeding along a progressive line, with distinct marks that divide past from present, is one that international law is heavily invested in, with its progress narratives and Whiggish view of history. The recent sustained attention – anger, rage, sentimentality, loyalty – directed to monuments, among them those of Rhodes, Colston and Churchill, is, in a new materialist reading, testament to the agentic node monuments are. Monuments are not just what appears on the plinth. They spread roots into the landscape. They crystallize power and resistance. In this sense, we can also understand them as manifestations of international law's effects and legacies in our daily lives, often in the background to our daily commute, a walk through the park, or a visit to a new city (see e.g. Eslava 2015; Hohmann and Joyce 2018; Vos 2019). Monuments can be read in a new materialist vein to mark the ways that power and agency coalesces and shifts. We begin with the Wakefield monument, and offer two angles on a new materialist reading of it. In both, we treat the Wakefield monument as a node where, in the first reading, certain things are made present. And in second, things are pushed under or hidden.

Wakefield, who never did visit South Australia, is surprisingly *present*. The Wakefield Monument on the South Australian Parliament building is modest, far from the picture 'monumental' connotes. However, despite its modest presentation, it is connected with other references which are powerfully inscribed on the land. Just a few blocks south, beginning at the colonial city's heart, Victoria Square (Tarntanya or Tarndanyangga, heart of the unceded land of the Kaurna Peoples), runs Wakefield Street, constructed as one of the city's widest boulevards in honor of its namesake. Moving along the road, past the 20-story brutalist 'Wakefield House' (a government building) and the Wakefield Hotel, Wakefield Street becomes Wakefield Road where it joins the city's ring of Parklands. Turn the other way however, and you will still find Wakefield, by joining Main South Road, and traveling 100 km northwest to Port Wakefield – the first government-established town outside the capital. There, in the late 1840s, copper ore mined at Burra, as well as wheat and other agricultural products, were shipped to buyers around the world, before the Port was bypassed in 1857 by a railway. Naming practices map onto the land, and stamp references and associations. These roads were colonial infrastructure. They were arteries that physically channel goods, settlers, diseases and ideas across a landscape that the colonizers deemed as previously unmarked and uninhabited. At the same time, these roads, ports, towns and buildings demarcate land. They are arteries but also boundaries. They were part of the processes of turning territory into property, a vital part of making the colony profitable, as Wakefield insisted (see also Bhandar 2018; Keenan 2015 on the intersection between property and territory in the settler colonial context). Thirdly, they are also, themselves, monuments, as Wakefield Street's stately breadth and central position in the planned cityscape of Adelaide attests. Port Wakefield too named not only a port and town, but the very processes by which the land was made to yield up wealth: those minerals and grains which Wakefield wrote of in his *A Letter from Sydney*.

Port Wakefield's website interestingly identifies the town as a node that marks the confluence of transport artery, resource extraction and exploitation, and colonial marking of the land: 'Port Wakefield . . . is seen as a major transportation corridor for both commercial and domestic travelers and provides numerous services to support such an industry. The town itself is a hidden treasure . . . steeped in colonial history' (Port Wakefield Community Management Committee 2022). The town was

> created to cater for the needs of the early settlers. With the development of the agricultural, mining and later the fishing industries of South Australia, Port Wakefield became the pivot point for such products. A port was developed to cater for the increased production of such commodities as ore from the mines at Burra, hay and wheat.
>
> *(ibid)*

We read Port Wakefield as the point in space where things become commodities available to the global capitalist order, where, in Bennett's terms, they become 'animated' and play into a profoundly problematic 'enchantment' with commodity culture (Bennett 2001). Copper, wheat and hay are no longer parts of the earth or tenuous roots, stalks and grains, but the beginnings of supply chains, objects of capital valuation and exploitation for commercial profit.

Not only a spatial, but a temporal connection exists here. The town's website echoes Wakefield's proposal for colonization. The tourism board notes that the town's

> major developments in recent years have included the Pork Industry with intensive farming and meat processing, poultry farms, Hay processing and exporting plants, An Intermodal Transport Hub, Quarry mines, and numerous housing developments. . . . With these economic indicators the town is on the verge of economic and population boom – watch this space.
>
> *(Port Wakefield Community Management Committee 2021)*

Port Wakefield's future streams along the same channels as its past: intensive resource extraction to reap profit from the land, a 'population boom' and housing development. Wakefield himself was centrally concerned with population concentration: dispersal was bad for capital. He pictured territory divided up for dense settled, population, where the land was made to bear profit but also house people in a mirror of England (Birchall 2021: 144; see also Chalmers 2022).

The monument to Wakefield on the South Australian Parliament can be read as a knot where the material world converges with colonial myths of foundation and progress, and the global capitalist order. The posthumous celebration of Wakefield and his contribution to South Australia made tangible in the monument reinscribe Wakefield's role as the 'father' of systematic colonization, but it also connects to other memorializations of Wakefield – in streets, towns and buildings stretching out from the symbolic center of Adelaide. These nodes connect Wakefield's to the current iterations of extractive capitalism that his theory rested on, from mining to intensive agriculture in introduced species.

The monument hides as well as marks things out. We turn now to a second reading of the Wakefield monument, in which we focus on what is obscured, unseen or denied, but can be brought to light in a new materialist reading.

The first act of obscuring, the deepest and most fundamental, takes place through the doctrine of discovery and the legal categorization of Australia as *terra nullius* in international law. A foundational precondition for the land now claimed as South Australia was its emptiness. British assertions of sovereignty, and characterization of the land as 'wasteland', grounded Wakefield's proposal of systematic colonization (Wakefield 1829: xvi; *South Australia Act* 1834). This was despite significant and undeniable Indigenous presence. The landscape was a managed one, with open tracts, such as the Adelaide plains themselves, created and maintained by careful land management (Clarke 1991: 58–60). In addition, the colonizers encountered substantial tracks in frequent use, covering significant distances, which the colonizers took over first as cart tracks, and 'many of them [are] almost certainly preserved today as bitumen roads' (ibid: 60). Early missionaries, among the most avid documenters of Aboriginal culture, recorded that Aboriginal names were tied to particular lands, and served as a prominent link with a particular territory (ibid: 61).

The Indigenous presence ruptures the foundational documents and the 'smooth' presentation of a Wakefieldian history in the city. Indeed, subsequent colonial documents were forced to acknowledge the 'natives', and their rights, and declare their protection (The Proclamation of South Australia 1836; Letters Patent 1836). Nevertheless, successive colonial laws enabled a physical emptying of South Australia, effecting a retrospective 'fit' with the legal assertion of sovereignty and the colony as 'waste' (Owen and Cowie 2015; Watson 2015: 56; Foster 2000). But, as prominent Indigenous international law scholar Irene Watson argues, attempts to make Indigenous peoples vanish fail: Indigenous identity is 'reflected back to us from the land' and 'the land has enabled us to survive' (Watson 2015: 57). A deep and living interconnection among all beings animates and sustains First Nations' law in what is now Australia (see Kwaymullina and Kwaymullina 2010; Bignall *et al* 2016; Gay'wu Group of Women 2019), one that the imposition of 'subjects' and 'objects', and static memorials to founding fathers cannot erase. At the same time, the monument to Wakefield, embedded into the seat of colonial lawmaking, serves as a point around which resistance and erasure coalesce. Posthumanism and Indigenous law and knowledge can meet here: at an insistence that the land is not open to legal categorization as a 'passive resource for endless exploitation' (Bignall, Hemming and Rigney 2016: 459; see also Graham and Pittavino 2021: 345–50). Rather, in the philosophy of South Australia's Ngarrindjeri Nation, explained by Bignall, Hemming and

Rigney as a posthuman philosophy with a powerful ancient existence (2016: 467), where the Ngarrindjeri speak 'as Country': 'land and waters is a living body. We the Ngarrindjeri people are part of its existence' (ibid: 468). International law as a living posthuman practice and experience emerges strongly here: as Bignall, Hemming and Rigney explain:

> Ngarrindjeri are not content to wait for the Westphalian system of the law of states to decide the terms under which their Nation's governmental authority is recognised by a principle of right, and instead are immediately mobilising their own (traditional) Aboriginal understanding of sovereignty as a power to negotiate relational conduct, in this case engaged by bringing the settler state to abide by clearly defined protocols of interaction. Here, right is not well conceived as a universal precedent for legitimate practice; instead agreed principles of rightful entitlement and action emerge *in situ*, from justly negotiated practices of political coexistence.
>
> *(ibid: 469)*

From a new materialist perspective, monuments to colonial founding fathers – from statues to boulevards – cannot effect an erasure of Indigenous presence, law and continued existence, because Indigenous presence cannot be separated from the land and lawful relationships embedded in and emerging out of it. Neither can the extraction of commodities and the marking of the land render it 'mere' property open for exploitation and capitalist accumulation under international and domestic laws. As Irene Watson writes, the relationship between land, law and people, in Indigenous ontology is more complex: '[w]e live as part of the natural world; we are in the natural world. The natural world is us' (Watson 2015: 15). The statue of Wakefield emerges as a space where resistant agency coalesces and emerges from other ancient knowledges of intra-active being and becoming.

Historical Materialism

What Is Historical Materialism (and How Does It Relate to International Law)?

Historical materialism is a theory employed (by Marx and by extension Marxists) to critique the capitalist mode of production, in particular by focusing on class struggle. The capitalist mode of production – how things are made – refers to the accumulation of surplus value through exploitation of labor. Central to understanding capitalism is the role of the wage laborer and her alienation from what she produces in relation to the so-called capitalist. In international (legal) terms, this can be demonstrated through the status of the wage laborer in global value chains. The accumulation of value along the chain – from raw material to finished product – requires many steps with the final product remaining far removed from the laborer. Meanwhile, the capitalist accumulates the profits from the relationship. The pattern that has been reproduced through global capitalism is that raw materials and wage labor are typically exploited in the Global South, or in historical materialist terms, the 'periphery' to the capitalist 'metropole'. The global economic order is organized through capitalist relations, but it is not only an economic order; it is a political and legal order too. Central to the creation, structure, geography, distributive effects and governance of global value chains are legal regimes (The IGLP Law and Global Production Working Group 2016). In global value chains, this is demonstrated through international economic law and investment law and their institutions that uphold the unequal order.

The spilling over of the capitalist order into other (historically not strictly economic) social forms of organization, such as education, health and public services, is often referred to as the neoliberal order. Terms such as neoliberal legality have been adopted to explain the role of law in creating and upholding capitalism (Brabazon 2017). Although Marxists differ in their focus on economic determinism (how much relations are defined through strictly economic relations), ultimately, historical materialism is a theory for understanding social relations. Scholars influenced by Marx and interested in international law and political economy often refer to the upholding of the global capitalist order through international legal institutions such as the World Trade Organization, the International Monetary Fund, the World Bank and even the International Criminal Court (Slobodian 2018; Martin 2022; Tzouvala 2020; Baars 2019; Schwöbel-Patel 2021). These institutions do not merely protect capital, they also create continuations of racialized forms of capitalism, most acutely and devastatingly evidenced in the inequalities between the Global North and the Global South. Marxists, Socialists and other radical thinkers such as Socialist Feminists and Anarchists in the field of international law have sought not only to highlight the inequalities of this global order but have also sought to identify ways and means of redistribution.

A Historical Materialist Reading of the Wakefield Monument

There are several possible readings of the monument to Wakefield from a historical materialist perspective; we propose two possible emphases. First, the Wakefield monument is a reminder that settler colonialism can best be understood through the lens of the political economy of imperialism. Second, the monument as representative of 'humanitarianism' is based on a truncated understanding of history that eliminates the understanding of exploitative social relations. Let us explore these in turn.

First, political economy: political economy is often associated in critical circles with the critique of capitalism. E.G. Wakefield, however, employed classical political economy as a tool *for* not against capital accumulation. Indeed, 'Wakefield explicitly intended his colonial reform agenda to save capitalism in the metropole and to secure it in the colonies' (Ince 2018: 114). Karl Marx wrote admiringly about Wakefield that he had understood capitalist relations in the colonies, because he had discovered 'the truth about capitalist relations in the mother country' (Marx 1867: 932). What Wakefield had correctly identified, according to Marx, was that the means of production (money, machines, land) do not yet make a capitalist; a capitalist is dependent on the wage-laborer, 'the other man, who is compelled to sell himself of his own free will' (ibid). Capital, Marx summarizes, is not a *thing*, and it is not to *have things*; it is 'a social relation between persons which is mediated through things' (ibid). The means of production and subsistence described by Wakefield in *A Letter from Sydney* – such as a large acreage of an estate – only become capital 'under circumstances in which they serve at the same time as a means of exploitation of, and domination over, the worker' (Marx 1867: 933). Wakefield's idea for systematic colonization was to export capitalist relations to the colonies. This is an important lesson for studies of international law, even critical studies, which at times focus on the violence of colonization, statehood and sovereignty, without considering the social relations that were being established – and that continue today in the global capitalist order. Social (class) relations are entrenched in human relations. Wakefield was not only promoting colonization through settlers; the aspect that was 'systematic' was the export of conditions that would lead to a distinct capitalist class that could profit from the land. A *post*humanism that insists on looking beyond social relations as being too fixated on the human (too anthropocentric) may miss this crucial insight.

But this is not to say that Marx got it all right. Marx also had a blind spot in regards to Indigenous peoples. He assumed that in the colonies, the soil was 'public property' (Marx 1867: 934) – which he contrasted with the private property of Western European relations to land. As well as assuming the propertization of land, this chimes with the idea of Australia as 'waste land', rather than a land that was lived on and with by Indigenous peoples, who may have had different ways of relating to the land. Marx therefore recognized the social relations between the capitalist and the worker, but omitted the forceful displacement of the Indigenous peoples. Moreover, although Marx insisted that existing societies were 'not the owners of the globe. They are only its possessors, its usufructuaries' (Marx 1867: chapter 46), he has been accused of promoting a crude developmentalism, particularly in what would become the colonized world. To understand the racial relations of capitalism, Fanon coined the term 'stretched Marxism':

> Marxist analysis should always be slightly stretched every time we have to do with the colonial problem. Everything up to and including the very

> nature of pre-capitalist society, so well explained by Marx, must here be thought out again.
>
> *(Fanon 1963: 40)*

What he meant by this was a material understanding of social relations that included the *constitutive* role of racialization in capitalist relations. Arguably, Fanon's views on (racial) capitalism can be further stretched to include an understanding of the relationship to the land that is more complex in Indigenous thought – a posthuman stretching of stretched Marxism, if you will. Indigenous scholars such as Glen Sean Coulthard have powerfully argued that Marx's blind spot was that only people could be exploited. Coulthard argues that aside from workers, *land* must also be seen as exploitable and exploited, particularly when considering colonial relations (Coulthard 2014).

Second, humanitarianism: figures of the nineteenth century continue to be memorialized for their *humanitarianism*, particularly if, like Wakefield, they were circulating their ideas after the abolition of the slave trade. Wakefield came from a family of Quakers. This background is often cited as an explanation for his desire for social reform (Woollacott 2015). However, his exporting of domination through capitalist relations stands in stark contrast with any progressive social reform agenda. As Jane Lydon has observed, E.G. Wakefield was part of a generation of ruling classes for whom the anti-slavery movement performed an important purpose by 'simultaneously accruing moral authority and sanctioning oppressive new forms of disciplined labour' (Lydon 2021: 112). The theory of systematic colonization, which was intended to create the role of the wage-laborer in the colonies, was a type of disciplined labor drawn from plantations. The idea for new disciplined labor in combination with new techniques of land commoditization was able to satisfy both the abolitionist reform agenda as well as pro-slavery interests of racial superiority (Lydon 2021: 112). Systematic colonization was, in other words, a response to the economic losses of slavery, but with the added moral capital afforded 'humanitarians'. Humanitarianism is a form of social problem-solving that often falls short of taking structural inequality into account. Contemporary forms of humanitarianism that work on the basis of moral capital but are sustaining of structural inequality are celebrity humanitarianism or philanthro-capitalism (Schwöbel-Patel 2021). Here, those in the public eye, from celebrities to large corporations, will take advantage of the stage that the attention economy grants them in order to center their social reform agendas. A specific form of this is 'green-washing', where corporations attest to their climate credentials whilst continuing to be involved in extractive and polluting industries – and ultimately climate catastrophe (Schwöbel-Patel 2023). In the case of Wakefield, his idea drew interest because of his insistence on the difference between slave and 'free' labor; yet, as Lydon notes, this overlooked 'the harsh conditions under which laborers lived and worked in Britain' (Lydon 2021). He promoted his 'systemic colonization' as a humanitarian fix: a solution to the overpopulation of the metropole, the bubbling labor unrest of exploited workers and their pauperization. With his suggestion for sending wage-laborers to the colonies, or in other words his 'humanitarian expansion of empire' (Lydon 2021), Wakefield not only embedded the given structural inequalities; he also helped constitute new inequalities. This reading of the monument disrupts the linear progress narrative often displayed in international law as it insists on a critical view of exploitation. The struggle of wage-laborers in the nineteenth century can be connected to the struggle of the exploited today – whether that is Indigenous peoples struggling for land or workers exploited in greenwashing corporations. International law's role has not exclusively improved the lives of the oppressed; rather, it has facilitated oppression by supporting capitalist conditions. A historical materialist lens is, then, a means to take seriously the structural analysis – to see beyond the quick fixes of problem-solving.

Marx's relationship to *humanism*, however, is hotly contested.[5] Suffice to say for our purposes that historical materialism is a theory to understand social relations. For posthumanists, this might be limiting as they (also) direct attention to nonhuman entities. That is not to say that Marx didn't also consider the effects and power of nonhuman entities – 'thing-power' as it has been described by contemporary theorists (Bennet 2010). Arguably, Marx was describing 'thing-power' both in relation to capital and commodities. As a nonhuman entity, capital can go 'in search of' more capital for accumulation and commodities have the power to enchant and alienate.[6] Capital itself may, according to Moishe Postone, therefore 'be constitutive of forms of social practice and subjectivity' (Postone 2003: 86). Ultimately, though, despite the nonhuman serving the critique of social relations, for Marxists, the common key to overcoming exploitation or oppression is through political *struggle*, which requires an identification of the social classes involved and their access to material resources. From this vantage point, a focus on matter at the expense of the social does not readily reveal inequalities and is therefore a less useful tool for undoing the biases of the global order that are structured through race, class and gender. Such a critique, as voiced for example by the sociologist Thomas Lemke, is concerned that the posthuman attribution of 'thing-power' as a political theory provides no 'substantive analysis of the specificities of power relations' (Lemke 2018: 53).

In its focus on humans and their social relations – with class struggle being the most notable – historical materialism is therefore in a sense distinctly humanist. Although there is some scope to critique the labor relations that led to the monument being erected (how the bronze was cast, and by whom

5 The publication of György Lukás's *History and Class Consciousness* and Karl Korsch's *Marxism and Philosophy* started the thought and praxis around Marxist humanism.
6 Capital, vol. I, see 'commodity fetishism'.

the raw materials were extracted), in a historical materialist reading, the monument to Wakefield remains most powerful in its *representation* rather than in its matter. The preoccupation of historical materialism is with the capitalist and imperial history (of the representation of Wakefield) and how these exploitative social relations continue to the present. The 'matter' of the monument, whilst interesting, would likely not be a preoccupation for answering the question of international law and its relationship to progress narratives, its complicity in (settler) colonialism, and its entanglement with the global capitalist order.

Conclusion

We sum up by re-emphasizing that our engagement with new and historical materialism brings us to the conclusion that the two are not counterposed in that the 'new' has replaced the 'old'. In bringing our new and historical materialist readings of the monument to Edward Gibbon Wakefield into dialogue, we show that both theories offer forms of critique with different emphases. Both materialisms are analytical tools that help us understand monuments not only as representing the past but also the present economic, social and political order, and the role of international law and legal regimes in constructing and perpetuating that order.

Monuments look quintessentially like matter, in the sense that they are passive objects, rather than active subjects, by their very nature static, inert. But, both new and historical materialism would insist, monuments are not just about what you see on the plinth. In international law, monuments are variously objects of remembrance and reconciliation in post-conflict spaces; protected as objects of art, culture and human achievement; or reflect broader cultural and historical significance. Like international law, monuments are often considered as reparative of political and societal ills.

From a new materialist perspective, monuments might serve as nodes where confluences of attention and inattention, power and resistance coalesce and, potentially, shift or are displaced. They are markers on the land that are rooted into and made out of networks of human and nonhuman relations, which remain present in their materials, even when such relations are denied or obscured. In this sense, they manifest the excess or agentive forces that new materialists find in objects. The Wakefield monument read from a new materialist perspective provides interpretations of arteries and boundaries and makes visible that which would be deemed empty, invisible or unseen. A new materialist reading – as part of a posthumanist ontology – also meets Indigenous worldviews in this process, where law, land and people are formed in an entangled and co-constitutive process that makes visible processes of dispossession and denial that monuments to founding fathers seek to smooth over. From a historical materialist perspective, we chose to highlight the political economy and humanitarianism critiques so as to show that Wakefield's monument is a symbol of the humanitarian expansion of empire. The expansion of capitalist relations to the colonies is the prioritization of capital over labor, underpinned by (international) legal regimes. Such a reading dislodges the calcified view of a linear progress narrative with international law at its helm. A historical materialist perspective ultimately emphasizes that symbolism of monuments – even if they are reconciliatory with the past – is insufficient. Reckoning with monuments and colonial pasts from a decolonial Marxist perspective must include discussions on material reparations (Schwöbel-Patel 2022). Monuments do not have redistributive features per se and often lead to truncated historical accounts.

Bringing a new and historical materialist reading of monuments and international law into dialogue helps us make the point that international law itself has always been, in a sense, in-human or anti-human. Critical tools have been employed to draw attention to this inhumanity at different junctures. Posthumanism aims to respond to the current advanced capitalist and advanced technological moment, not by centering the human, but by questioning anthropocentricism, and by insisting on the importance of those aspects of the world that have been rendered *non*-human and *in*human (Braidotti and Hlavajova 2018: 2–3, original emphasis). This helps to bring to the fore some key assumptions informing the field of international law, in particular assumptions around the propertization of nature, the denial of other ways of being in the world, and the consequences of these assumptions, such as the climate catastrophe. From a historical materialist lens, such an insight must be complemented by a robust understanding of the underlying capitalist relations driving the international legal order. From a new materialist lens, it must be complemented by a recovery of those aspects of the world that have been denied agency, subjectivity and vitality, but which are central to existence. We return then to our initial point that new and historical materialism are not in competition, rather they converge on certain important points and can even be considered as complementary in destabilizing international law's imperialist, capitalist, racialized and patriarchal structures.

References

1907 Hague Convention.

1954 Hague Convention on Cultural Property.

Additional Protocol I to the 1949 Geneva Conventions.

Adelaide Advertiser (1952) *Memorial Plaque to Wakefield Unveiled*, Adelaide, South Australia, 19 April.

Anghie, A. (2005) *Imperialism, Sovereignty, and the Making of International Law*, Cambridge University Press.

Baars, G. (2019) *The Corporation, Law and Capitalism*, Leiden: Brill.

Barad, K. (2007) *Meeting the Universe Halfway: Quantum Physics and the Entanglement of Matter and Meaning*, Durham: Duke University Press.

Beaumont, W. (1873) 'The Fee of Materfield: Part II', in *Transactions of the Historic Society of Lancashire and Cheshire, New Series Vol. XIII Session 1872–73*, Liverpool.

Beautiful Britain, 'On This Day – 20th March'. www.beautifulbritain.uk/htm/onthisday/March/a420.htm (Accessed: 7 September 2022).

Bennett, J. (2001) 'Commodity Fetishism and Commodity Enchantment', *Theory and Event*, 5(1): np. DOI: https://doi.org/10.1353/tae.2001.0006

Bennett, J. (2010) *Vibrant Matter: A Political Ecology of Things*, Durham: Duke University Press.

Bhandar, B. (2018) *Colonial Lives of Property*, Durham: Duke University Press.

Bignall, S., S. Hemming and D. Rigney (2016) 'Three Ecosophies for the Anthropocene: Environmental Governance, Continental Posthumanism and Indigenous Expressivism', *Deleuze Studies*, 10(4): 455–76.

Birchall, M. (2021) 'History, Sovereignty, Capital: Company Colonization in South Australia and New Zealand', *Journal of Global History*, 16(1): 141–57.

Brabazon, H. (ed) (2017) *Neoliberal Legality: Understanding the Role of Law in the Neoliberal Project*, New York: Routledge.

Braidotti, R. (2013) *The Posthuman*, Cambridge: Polity Press.

Braidotti, R. (2019) 'A Theoretical Framework for the Critical Posthumanities', *Theory, Culture and Society*, 36(6): 31–61.

Braidotti, R. and M. Hlavajova (2018) 'Introduction', in R. Braidotti and M. Hlavajova (eds) *Posthuman Glossary*, London: Bloomsbury.

Chalmers, S. (2022) 'The Utopian Law and Literature of Systematic Colonisation', *Law & Literature*, 35(2): 179–99. DOI: https://doi.org/10.1080/1535685X.2021.2011046

Chimni, B.S. (2021) 'The International Law of Jurisdiction: A TWAIL Perspective', *Leiden Journal of International Law*, 35(1): 29–54.

Clarke, Philip (1991) 'Adelaide as an Aboriginal Landscape', *Aboriginal History*, 15: 54–72.

Cole, A. (2017) 'The Subject of Objects: Marx, New Materialism, and Queer Forms of Life', *Journal for Cultural Research*, 22(2): 167–79. DOI: https://doi.org/10.1080/14797585.2018.1461348

Coole, D. and S. Frost (eds) (2010) *New Materialisms: Ontology, Agency, and Politics*, Durham: Duke University Press.

Coulthard, G.S. (2014) *Red Skin, White Masks*, Iowa: University of Minnesota Press.

Davies, M. (2017) *Law Unlimited: Materialism, Pluralism and Legal Theory*, Abingdon: Routledge.

Dolphijn, R. and I. van der Tuin (eds) (2012) *New Materialism: Interviews & Cartographies*, Ann Arbor: Open Humanities Press.

Drumbl, M. (2020) 'Memorializing Dissent: Justice Pal in Tokyo', *American Journal of International Law Unbound*, 114: 111–16.

Eslava, L. (2015) *Local Space, Global Life: The Everyday Operation of International Law and Development*, Cambridge: Cambridge University Press.

Eslava, L., M. Fakhri and V. Nesiah (eds) (2017) *Bandung, Global History, and International Law: Critical Pasts and Pending Futures*, Cambridge: Cambridge University Press.

Fanon, F. (1963) *Wretched of the Earth*, New York: Grove Press.

Foster, R. (2000) 'Endless Trouble and Agitation: Aboriginal Activism in the Protectionist Era', *Journal of the Historical Society of South Australia*, 28: 15–27.

Gandorfer, D. and Z. Ayub (eds) (2021) 'Matterphorical', *Theory & Event*, 24(1): 1–410.

Gathii, J.T. (2022) 'The Agenda of Third World Approaches to International Law (TWAIL)', in J.L. Dunoff and M.A. Pollack (eds) *International Legal Theory*, Cambridge: Cambridge University Press, 153–73.

Gay'wu Group of Women (2019) *Song Spirals: Sharing Women's Wisdom of Country Through Songlines*, Sydney: Allen and Unwin.

Grady, K. (2019) 'For Whom the Bell Tolls: London's Iraq and Afghanistan Memorial 1990–2015', *London Review of International Law*, 7(3): 353–76.

Graham, N. and D.A. Pittavino (2021) 'Bauxite and Boundaries: 50 Years Since *Milirrpum v. Nabalco Pty Ltd (1971) 17 FLR 141*', *Australian Property Law Journal*, 29(3): 335–51.

Hay, I., A. Hughes and M. Tutton (2004) 'Monuments, Memory and Marginalisation in Adelaide's Prince Henry Gardens', *Geografiska Annaler: Series B, Human Geography*, 86(3): 201–16.

Hohmann, J. (2018) 'The Lives of Objects', in J. Hohmann and D. Joyce (eds) *International Law's Objects*, Oxford: Oxford University Press.

Hohmann, J. (2021) 'Diffuse Subjects and Dispersed Power: New Materialist Insights and Cautionary Lessons for International Law', *Leiden Journal of International Law*, 34(3): 585–606.

Hohmann, J. and D. Joyce (2018) 'Introduction', in J. Hohmann and D. Joyce (eds) *International Law's Objects*, Oxford: Oxford University Press.

The IGLP Law and Global Production Working Group (2016) 'The Role of Law in Global Value Chains: A Research Manifesto', *London Review of International Law*, 4(1): 57–79.

Ince, O.U. (2018) *Colonial Capitalism and the Dilemmas of Liberalism*, Oxford: Oxford University Press.

Keenan, S. (2015) *Subversive Property: Law and the Production of Spaces of Belonging*, London: Routledge.

Kwaymullina, A. and B. Kwaymullina (2010) 'Learning to Read the Signs: Law in an Indigenous Reality', *Journal of Australian Studies*, 34(2): 195–208. DOI: https://doi.org/10.1080/14443051003721189

Lemke, T. (2018) 'An Alternative Model of Politics? Prospects and Problems of Jane Bennett's Vital Materialism', *Theory, Culture and Society*, 35(6): 31–54. DOI: https://doi.org/10.1177/0263276418757316

Lixinski, L. (2018) 'Confederate Monuments and International Law', *Wisconsin Journal of International Law*, 35(3): 549–607.

Lydon, J. (2021) ' "Mr Wakefield's Speaking Trumpets": Abolishing Slavery and Colonising Systematically', *The Journal of Imperial and Commonwealth History*, 50: 81–112.

Martin, J. (2022) *The Meddlers*, Cambridge: Harvard University Press.

Marx, K. (1867) *Capital*, Vol. III, London: Penguin Classics.

Nail, T. (2020) *Marx in Motion: A New Materialist Marxism*, Oxford: Oxford University Press.

Owen, T. and K. Cowie (2015) *Stories from Kaurna*, Surrey Hills: GLM Heritage.

Parfitt, R. (2018) 'Fascism, Imperialism and International Law: An Arch Met a Motorway and the Rest Is History . . .', *Leiden Journal of International Law*, 31(3): 509–38.

Parliament of the United Kingdom (1834) 'An Act to Empower His Majesty to Erect South Australia into a British Province or Provinces, and to Provide for the Colonization and Government Thereof' (assented 15 August 1834) 4&5 Wm. IV, c 95.

Pascoe, B. (2014) *Dark Emu*, Broome: Magabala Books.

Peevers, C. (2017) 'A Deathless Story: The ANZAC Memorial, Memory and International Law', *London Review of International Law*, 5(1): 153–84.

Philippopoulos-Mihalopoulos, A. (2016) 'Lively Agency: Life and Law in the Anthropocene', in I. Braverman (ed) *Animals, Biopolitics, Law: Lively Legalities*, London: Routledge.

Port Wakefield Community Management Committee. www.portwakefield.sa.au/ (Accessed: 7 September 2022).

Postone, M. (2003) 'Lukács and the Dialectical Critique of Capitalism', in R. Albritton and J. Simoulidis (eds) *New Dialectics and Political Economy*, London: Palgave Macmillan.

Pretty, G.L. (1967) 'Wakefield, Edward Gibbon (1796–1862)', in *Australian Dictionary of Biography*, Vol. 2. https://adb.anu.edu.au/biography/wakefield-edward-gibbon-2763 (Accessed: 7 September 2022).

Privy Council of the United Kingdom (1836) *Letters Patent Under the Seal of the United Kingdom Erecting and Establishing the Province of South Australia and Fixing the Boundaries Thereof*, 19 February.

Proclamation by His Excellency John Hindmarsh (1836) *Knight of the Royal Hanoverian and Guelphic Order, Governor and Commander-in-Chief of His Majesty's Province of South Australia, Glenelg*, 28 December.

Rome Statute of the International Criminal Court.

Schwöbel-Patel, C. (2021) *Marketing Global Justice*, Cambridge: Cambridge University Press.

Schwöbel-Patel, C. (2022) 'The Precarious Agency of Racialised Recaptives', *London Review of International Law*, 10(1): 151–8.

Schwöbel-Patel, C. (2023) 'Real (E)State – Valuing a Nation Under Imperial Rentier Capitalism', in I. Feichtner and G. Gordon (eds) *Law and the Global Constitution of Value: Ecology, Governance and Political Economy*, Abingdon: Routledge.

Slobodian, S. (2018) *Globalists*, Cambridge: Harvard University Press.

Spijkers, O. (2021) 'Legal Monuments for Srebrenica in the Hague', *Utrecht Journal of International and European Law*, 36(2): 118–26.

Storr, C. (2023) 'Denaturalising the Concept of Territory in International Law', in J. Dehm and U. Natarajan (eds) *Locating Nature: Making and Unmaking International Law*, Cambridge: Cambridge University Press.

Tzouvala, N. (2020) *Capitalism as Civilization*, Cambridge: Cambridge University Press.

United Nations Office of the United Nations High Commissioner for Human Rights (2014) 'Report of the UN Special Rapporteur on Cultural Rights', *Report on Memorialization Processes in Post-Conflict and Divided Societies*, UN Doc A/HRC/25/49, 23 January.

Vos, R. (2019) 'A Walk Along the Rue de la Loi: EU Facades as Front- and Backstage of Transnational Legal Practice', in L.J.M. Boer and S. Stolk (eds) *Backstage Practices of Transnational Law*, Abingdon: Routledge.

Vrdoljak, A.F. (2011) 'Cultural Heritage in Human Rights and Humanitarian Law', *International Humanitarian Law and International Human Rights Law*, 250–302.

Wakefield, E.G. (1829a) *Sketch of a Proposal for Colonizing Australasia, &c., &c., &c*, J.F. Dove.
Wakefield, E.G. (1829b) *A Letter from Sydney: The Principal Town of Australasia*, London: J Cross.
Wakefield, E.G. (1831) *Plan of a Company to Be Established for the Purpose of Founding a Colony in Southern Australia, Purchasing Land Therein, and Preparing the Land so Purchased for the Reception of Immigrants*, London: Ridgway and Sons.
Wakefield, E.G. (1833) *England and America: A Comparison of the Social and Political State of Both Nations*, London: Richard Bentley.
Watson, I. (2015) *Aboriginal Peoples, Colonialism and International Law: Raw Law*, London: Routledge.
Woollacott, A. (2015) *Settler Society in the Australian Colonies: Self-Government and Imperial Culture*, Oxford: Oxford University Press.

6

NEITHER NATIONAL NOR INTERNATIONAL

A Posthumanist Retelling of Tax Sovereignty

Hedvig Lärka

In her book *Woman, Native, Other*, Trinh T. Minh-Ha tells of an old witch turning loose a horrid story upon the world (1989: 134). Her audience, their excitement turned into fright, pleads the witch to call her story back – but she cannot. Minh-Ha speaks for the witch: 'A story is not just a story. Once the forces have been aroused and set into motion, they can't simply be stopped at someone's request' (ibid). In this chapter, I recall the dominant coming-of-age stories of international tax law, and counter them with a story of my own. With the posthumanist tradition of mainly Minh-Ha, Haraway and Barad, I hold that while my story cannot call the old ones back, it might advance agency differently (Barad 2007: 353). At the moment of writing, in 2023, corporate income tax law is undergoing the transformation of a century. A first of its kind, global, top-up minimum tax is descending upon the world, guided by the steady hands of the Organization of Economic Cooperation and Development (OECD). In this moment I find it vital to pause and to ask: by what forces have this great change been aroused?

This chapter is about corporate income tax (CIT) regimes. According to common narrative, these regimes are structured by tax competition between sovereigns, defined by their autonomous nature and self-interest. The particular forms of sovereign autonomy and the autonomy of legal subjects alike are, of course, performed by global legal regimes upheld by sovereigns themselves. This is not explicit in scholarly discourse, where the blame for aggressive tax evasion is often put on different actors, be they either tax havens – alleged abusers of tax sovereignty, large multinational enterprises or the well-meaning sovereigns competing for capitalist value (Dagan 2017).

Using posthumanist theory and its concept of agency (Barad 2007; Braidotti 2013, 2019; Kirby 1997, 2011; Dolphijn and van der Tuin 2012),

DOI: 10.4324/9781032658032-9

drawing on posthumanist and posthuman jurisprudential work on the legal subject (Arvidsson 2020; Davies 2012; Grear 2015, 2017, 2020; Hohmann 2021), I will critically examine the naturalization of autonomy that defines tax sovereignty and legal subjectivity throughout these accounts.[1] In the first section, I will outline how change and agency within CIT regimes are storied by the OECD and within tax law scholarship. Following this section, I will describe and apply the posthumanism that I use, in telling a different story of tax sovereignty and of change. In a final section, I analyze the global top-up minimum tax in the light of this new story.

Each year, around 37 percent of global profits go untaxed and the effective tax rates that *are* levied on multinational corporate income are plummeting (Tørsløv *et al* 2023). Placing the blame for tax base erosion squarely on sovereign autonomy, actors such as the OECD argue that only international tax cooperation – that is, international tax law in general, and the top-up minimum tax in particular – can save tax sovereignty from itself. Using posthumanist theory I will destabilize this common argument, by questioning both the naturalization of sovereign autonomy and the premises of what constitutes international law. I will do this by shifting the center of agency (and blame) from sovereign nations competing over capitalist value to the formation of sovereign autonomy. At the same time affirming and sublating contemporary tax law scholarship, posthumanism questions why tax competition, tax evasion and tax havens are all performed by the current, global legal regimes in the first place. These regimes are, after all, created and upheld by the community of states themselves.

Once Upon a Time . . .

In the winter of 2021, the Organization for Economic Co-operation and Development (OECD) released the model rules for a global, top-up minimum tax. In line with the common narrative recounted in the previous section, these rules were claimed to salvage tax sovereignty from itself (OECD 2021). The release of these model rules marked the culmination of years of work led by the OECD and the G20 and was aimed at reforming corporate income tax regimes worldwide. This work has been and is still flanked by stories.

The OECD's work on reforming global CIT regimes hit a critical note in 2013, with the launch of the Base Erosion and Profit Shifting (BEPS) project (OECD 2015). The initial work of BEPS culminated in a report, released

1 In line with Karen Barad, I use the term 'posthumanist' rather than 'posthuman' (Barad 2007: 428, 414, 136). Pursuing a critical engagement precisely with the limits of humanism and humanist notions of subjectivity and autonomy, Barad's terminology indicates a sublation rather than a rejection of understandings of humanist (and legal) notions of subjectivity and autonomy.

in 2015, that listed 15 actions on how, in the OECD's wording, the base-eroding and profit-shifting activities of multinational corporate groups could be combatted in an increasingly digitalized and globalized economy (ibid). In 2016, in order to monitor implementation of their 15 actions, the OECD initiated the BEPS Inclusive Framework (OECD 2015: 3, 2017: 4). Shortly thereafter, in early 2018, the OECD invited work within the BEPS IF toward a 'consensus solution' on how to realign taxing rights with value creation within the highly digitalized economy (OECD 2018: 166).

Early work on this issue incited much hope for a principled solution, and several different ideas on what principles would best bring CIT law regimes into the twenty-first century were put on the table. Notably, the G24 contributed with a proposal focusing on the concept of Significant Economic Presence. Broadening the concept of Permanent Establishment, this new concept would enhance the taxing powers of predominantly capital importing states. This proposal thus represented an advancement of non-OECD member states interests (G24 2019a, 2019b; OECD 2019: 16) and these states repeatedly stated their opinions on the global minimum tax (G24 2021). However, when the OECD presented the first blueprints of for their 'international consensus' solution in late 2019, there was no trace to be found of the G24 proposal (G24 2021; ICRICT 2020). Instead, and as I will explain later, the global minimum tax has been designed in a way that was directly harmful to non-OECD member states' taxing powers (ICRICT 2020).

The proposal that was delivered in 2021 – the OECD and G20 top-up minimum tax – entails that the few large multinational enterprises that carry 90 percent of profits of the globalized and digitalized economy would be taxed at headquarter level up to a minimum rate of 15 percent (OECD 2020: 41, 2021). Today, every multinational enterprise is taxed not as a unitary group but as aggregates of autonomous entities. This is in line with what is called the separate entity principle. An abandonment of the separate entity principle to the benefit of unitary taxation is one that economically impoverished countries have long called for (Picciotto 2012). However, rather than being apportioned according to some agreed upon formula, tax levied at headquarter or residence level will not be distributed to other countries. Furthermore, this tax being a top-up tax, it will not replace the loophole ridden global CIT regimes currently in place, but simply layer a residual minimum tax on top of them (ICTRICT 2020).

Today, the separate entity principle enables multinational enterprises to minimize their tax burden by shifting profits to tax haven jurisdictions. This is because entities of the same multinational groups, deemed separate for tax purposes, can plan their transfer pricing in such ways that profit is shifted toward low tax jurisdictions. In order to counteract profit shifting, transactions between separate entities of the same multinational enterprises can be adjusted by tax authorities through transfer pricing rules and the arm's length standard. However, such adjustments require comparable transactions under comparable circumstances between unrelated enterprises (World Bank 2020: 92). These transactions are often-most missing in a globalized economy characterized by a high level of planning and non-market relations.

At the moment of writing, Global Value Chains dominate somewhere around 50 to 80 percent of global trade (Ergen *et al* 2023; UN 2013; World Bank 2020: 14). Characterized by hyper-specialization, intrafirm- or highly coordinated inter-firm transactions, these chains and the few enterprises that control them are far flung from the metaphor of the market square. Still, the separate entity principle and the arm's length standard assume a global 'market' of transactions between unrelated enterprises. Conservatively, intrafirm trade is estimated to make up one third of world trade flows (World Bank 2020: 33). According to a recent study, over half of cross-border trade in India is estimated to be conducted within-firm, a large part of transactions being directly linked to tax haven jurisdictions (Verma 2022). To conclude, the separate entity principle and the arm's length standard both large scale enable profit shifting by pretending toward a form of global trade that does not exist. Consequently, the regimes affect how sovereignty takes form. In the following section, I will return to this point.

Acting as a self-proclaimed, informal world tax organization, the OECD celebrated the release of the model rules for the top-up minimum tax, as a win for international cooperation at large. It seems the minimum tax will be broadly in place by 2024. Within the EU implementation of the model rules are ongoing (Council of the EU 2022). The tax, however, is designed to profit OECD countries at the expense of non-OECD countries. It is expected to drive down effective tax rates in non-OECD nation-states, to match the floor of the minimum tax, while also circumventing the present powers of those states not to tax and to tax alike (Sacchi 2021; Titus 2022). Notably, the GloBE rules have been named 'a direct transfer of revenue from developing countries, which are generally only hosts to foreign (multinational enterprise), to the rich home countries' (ICRICT 2020). Even though 'developing' countries are heaviest hit by large scale profit shifting, the minimum tax will be levied by countries where multinational headquarters are resident, that is, generally speaking, OECD countries.

In response to the disappointments delivered by the OECD's BEPS Inclusive Framework project, non-OECD countries have started pushing for the United Nations to form a world tax organization (FFD Group 2022). In addition, Nigeria, Sri Lanka, Pakistan and Kenya have said no to global consensus within the BEPS IF (OECD 2021). Most of these countries, and around 20 other non-OECD states, have enacted their own legislation to push the boundaries of their sovereign taxing rights (KPMG 2022; Magwape 2022: 15; Stanley-Smith 2019: 1). The legislative projects shared by non-OECD countries have been branded 'unilateral measures' by the OECD in a discursive move that seeks to grant exclusive legitimacy to the self-appointed 'international consensus' that the OECD and G20 countries are working toward (Cui 2020). This move renders invisible legislative projects ongoing outside of OECD and G20-led negotiations, curtailing change within global corporate income tax law regimes other than that emanating from OECD and G20.

As Minh-Ha notes, stories flowing from the OECD are hegemonic, linear and based on civilizing tropes, with well-defined actors and seemingly clear causes and effects (Minh-Ha 1989: 123 ff). They are 'stor(ies) for primitive man, deigned to "teach children the tales their fathers knew," to mold ideals, and to "illuminate facts"' (ibid). The stories delivered by the OECD and other actors, through which 'international cooperation' reestablishes tax sovereignty in the face of global tax competition, are nuanced through tax scholarship.

Today, bilateral tax treaties are up to 80 percent identical in content, to the most part corresponding to the OECD model bilateral tax treaty (Ash and Marian 2019). This uniformity is often traced as a result of the intellectual labor of five economists who met a century ago to draw up the basic principles of what would evolve into global corporate income tax law regimes. However, according to Allison Christians, contemporary CIT law regimes have emerged over time as a matter of power rather than principle (Christians 2017) Christians and others argue that bilateral tax treaty networks are not needed to counter the risk of double taxation through achieving harmonization of CIT law regimes, since tax competition and the mobility of capital that it presupposes will drive states to act in a coordinated manner (Avi-Yonah 2005; Dagan 2017: 82 ff; Hearson 2021; Hertzfeld 2016; IMF 2014). According to these views, bilateral tax treaty networks and the principles they enshrine are mainly the results of OECD countries leveraging their collective strength and unrivalled organization to perpetually broaden their collective taxing powers.

Notably, Tsilly Dagan's work casts states as actors in a market of bilateral tax treaties in which the OECD leverages cartelist behavior to tilt the market in their favor (Dagan 2017: 60, 145). According to her account, the bilateral tax treaty networks, dominated to a great extent in their content and interpretation by the OECD, create network effects. It is the benefit brought by these effects, rather than the treaties themselves, that drive states to enter into bilateral tax treaty networks. Miranda Stewart and Sol Picciotto, in turn, emphasize the emergence of a 'global bureaucracy' of bilateral exchange of information on tax matters, fully available only to OECD countries, as bolstering this cartelist behavior (Picciotto 2013; Stewart 2013).

To conclude, this tax scholarship excels in describing how OECD states leverage their powerful position to collectively enforce stronger taxing powers for predominantly capital exporting states, at the cost of the taxing powers of capital importing states. In so doing, this scholarship builds on the stories of, for example, the OECD, changing the role of agency in these stories by questioning and denaturalizing their assumptions, for example, that corporate income tax regimes are built on legal principles based either on ideals of just distribution of taxing powers, or on negotiations held on equal footing. In the next section of this chapter, I will use posthumanist thought to, in turn, build on tax scholarship by way of the cuts or assumptions on which their stories rest. In short, and in line with my posthumanist approach, I will denaturalize the concept of the tax sovereign. In so doing, I propose that international law is as much about the formation of the sovereign state and their agency, as it is about the treaties that states enter into as consequence of this agency.

There is truth in the telling of stories served by tax scholarship and by institutions such as the OECD. With the witch that introduced this chapter, I agree that these stories cannot be 'called back' (Minh-Ha 1989: 133). As material-semiotic constructs (Haraway 1988: 595) they, just like any story, flow from casual structures (Barad 2007: 140) beyond the reach of humanist intentionality. In other words, what the OECD lack in nuance they gain in *de facto* power over the transformation of CIT law regimes, however the institution chooses to present this power. According to international tax scholarship, this power stems from the privileged position that OECD states enjoy in the sort of gamified negotiations that structure CIT law regimes. In this context, posthumanist thinking will shift focus from the players toward the rules of the game. This sublation performs a denaturalization of both sovereign autonomy and international law.

A Story Is Not Just a Story

Every story begins at the middle and is, as such, begun before ever spoken. For me, the very middle of posthumanist thought is the position of absolute immanence which this body of work presupposes and toward which it always returns. Throughout this section, the posthumanist concepts of immanence, ethics and agency will be outlined. The concept of agency – already put to work earlier – will be explained, this concept being central to how posthuman theory comes to be operationalized. Instead of casting tax sovereigns as actors who tax their subjects in line with certain defined interests I will, in this this section, describe global CIT law regimes – legislation at national and regional level, as well as bilateral treaty networks – as *expressions of a larger agency* of which tax sovereignty is part and by which tax sovereignty is iteratively given form. I will do this with the help of the posthumanist concept of agency, as well as posthumanist scholarship on the legal subject.

On Posthumanist Immanence, Ethics and Agency

At its core, posthumanism provides a certain metaphysical or methodological position from which the whole of the world comes differently to matter, and concepts such as objectivity, causality and agency all take on a new meaning (Barad 2007: 33; Braidotti 2013: 163 ff). The basic ontological, objective referent for a posthumanist understanding is not things or objects but phenomena or, in the terminology of Barad, 'relationalities without relata' (Barad 2007: 333, 244, 2003; Braidotti 2019: 59). Relata, writes Barad, 'do not preexist relations; rather, relata-within-phenomena emerge through specific intra-actions' (2007: 140). This point is crucial, as it marks and operationalizes the iterative movement from idealism toward immanence or from transcendence toward materialism that a posthumanist method of knowing pursues (Barad 2007: 183 ff). Rather than being posited, relata – and here we can think for example of the concept of sovereignty – emerges and dissolves from relationalities or phenomena. In short, it is through relationality that a world sprouts, and implicit in any one phenomenon is the unfolding of agency.

From the posthumanist position of radical immanence, practices of knowing can be imagined as expressions rather than a representation of their fields of research (Barad 2007: 342; Braidotti 2013: 136; Haraway 1988; Kirby 1997: 161). In every story, in every datum that flows from the field, there is truth in the telling. To subject oneself to a posthumanist method of knowing is to make the affirmative and ethical call on how these stories and data are to be ordered, in ways through which they are made to matter. This is not ordering under representation – aiming to achieve 'objectivity' through correspondence of 'facts'. Rather, concepts and abstractions are invented in order to reactivate and recast difference, so that phenomena go beautifully together, expanding the relational present, and making difference matter (Barad 2010; Braidotti 2019: 132–3; Kirby 1997: 161).

Within the inventive process of relational epistemology, and with every claim to knowledge, the researcher embodies but the middle of an iterative articulation of the world in open-ended becoming, and there is not much the researcher can do but to sense, and to act (Braidotti 2019: 68 ff; Barad 2007: 269 ff). There is a levity, if properly practiced, to this trust in the iterative and truthful becoming of the research through the researcher, but there is also much at stake. Every move and every doing are normative, in that they establish how the world will come to be (Barad 2007: 391 ff). There is no escaping posthumanist ethics; there is no representation, no 'fact' or 'thing' or 'givenness', behind which to hide (Barad 2007: 353). Moreover, every *cut* the researcher makes in their material – the questions they pose, the peoples they listen to, the books they read, etcetera – will perform a normative knowledge that will in turn have normative impacts, and the researcher must take full responsibility and be mindful through the whole process (Barad 2007: 391 ff; Braidotti 2019: 136 ff, 68 ff).

Through trust in immanence and the choices made, *agency* emerges and takes form (Barad 2007: 215). Every phenomenon emerges as the expression of some common agency, that rises as if from underneath the field of research. From the standpoint of ontological relationality, it is this agency that enacts change rather than the individual actors – be it the nation-state, the corporation or the people. *These actors are only appearances of the agency at hand.* In this way agency, as mediator, strives incessantly to overcome itself, thus avoiding the naturalization of identity precisely through attention to relationality/phenomena. Every object or actor surfacing from agency will do so only in order to return dissolved, and difference is minded through the careful creation on a plane of immanence, of a moving whole without parts (Braidotti 2013: 136 ff; Dolphijn and van der Tuin 2012: 19). Finally, it is the agency of a presentation of agency itself, as phenomena, that determines objectivity, by the way the field of research comes more fully to matter.

Posthumanism and Legal Subjectivity

Posthumanism marks a move away from humanist ideals and specifically humanist imaginaries of subjectivity (Barad 2007: 428, 414, 136; Braidotti 2013: 101 ff, 54). The geological epoch of the Anthropocene is by humanist accounts one of 'autonomous man', a humanist subject moved by reason and as ontological supremacy and independence. Considering the ontological relationality regarded in the previous section, that story is no longer thinkable: it is '(s)eriously unthinkable: not available to think with' (Haraway 2016: 30). Yet, the autonomous man of humanist imaginaries is alive and kicking. This is especially so in law where the legal subject – such as it surfaces through legal practice – finds its apotheosis in the corporation (Davies 2012; Grear 2015, 2020; Hohmann 2021). Posthumanist scholarship does not negate this subject but sublates it by denaturalizing its autonomous form, seeing this form as an appearance of agency. In other words, posthumanism affirms the validity of, for example, tax scholarship and game theory modeling, while questioning the *cuts* that have been made to agency in these accounts.

In their affirmative critique of the humanist subject, posthumanist scholars have found the rational and autonomous 'man' to flow from capitalist relations of production, through the corporation as subject. The corporation being the contemporary form that 'can be thought of as the ultimate instantiation of disembodied Anthropos' or as the very personification of capital (Grear 2015: 293, 2010). The legal subject, at its most sublime, is simply the embodiment of capitalist value. This means that it only exists to the extent it embodies value. Showing how the 'autonomous man' is really the corporation in the era of the Anthropocene, Donna Haraway poses that 'if we could only have one word for these [Science Fiction] times, surely it must be the Capitalocene' (2016: 47). Posthumanist thought considers the capitalist subject poised at the center of the geological epoch of the Anthropocene, swarming the earth to the detriment of all life (Arvidsson 2020: 133).

The swarm of legal subjectivity, then, moves in accordance with the laws of capitalist value. These laws are ever changing. In the context of the corporation and of tax law, this is nothing out of the ordinary. Multinational enterprises are assumed by tax scholarship to move through the world reactively, guided by the sole motive of profit (Dagan 2017). As mentioned, Dagan applies the metaphor of the market when discussing how states come together to barter the best tax deals. At this market, the bilateral tax treaty is the commodity, and the deal is pretty much set well before negotiations start. The deal is set because of the particular positions that the sovereigns enjoy within a context of mobile capital that the sovereigns are insulated from affecting. From Dagan's work, it is clear that sovereign powers are driven solely by 'economical' motives. My posthumanist approach affirms this notion, while questioning the cuts made – the assumptions and premises posed – in agency. Why are tax sovereigns assumed powerless when confronted with mobile capital, with the rules of the game? By what forces do these particular sovereign autonomies, and their tax subjects, take form?

Affirming the drive toward capital accumulation as the locust of agency for multinational enterprises and sovereign states alike, such as it appears in Dagan's work, I would like to shortly rest on the point of capitalist value. Value is a relation often-most ignored or taken for granted in scholarly literature. Posthumanism however builds on the Marxian scholarly tradition, which has the purpose of explicating value as a social form (*inter alia* Bhandar 2018; Hohmann 2021; Knox 2021; Marx 1976; Murray 2021; Pashukanis 2002; Holloway and Picciotto 1977). This scholarship falls outside the scope of this short chapter. Suffice to say, however, that the value form is a social relation, grounded in the all-pervading struggle over socially necessary labor time. Simply put, value can only produce a surplus in relation to itself, i.e. by devaluing itself. This is because value is a social relation that exists only in the competition amongst capitalist forces (Murray 2021; Holloway and Picciotto 1977).

In the context of a hyperspecialized and highly integrated global economy characterized to a large extent by nonmarket relations, the abstraction of *value* mobilizes a massive totality of relations: global value chains, data, legal regimes, colonial heritage and imperial domination, cartel formation, racialization, consumption, profit shifting, etc. The state is of course central in the emergence of these relations. Whilst multinational enterprises are wholly defined by the value they embody, however, sovereigns embody value only indirectly, through these subjects. Thus, while multinational enterprises are driven toward the accumulation of the social relation of capitalist value, sovereigns are driven to control the formation of the relations of value production and, consequently, of the multinational corporation and of their global activities. The drive toward controlling the laws of motion of surplus value creation is the sine qua non imperative for states, as they exist only to the extent they indirectly embody the value form by way of – at the moment on writing – multinational enterprises.

In the metaphor of Dagan's seminal work, that which I describe can still be called a game. But it is too massive a game to fully fathom or stylize. Every 'player' will affect the agency of every other. They will do so to the extent and real-time complexity that the players dissolve in the relational performance by which they emerged, all growing into one another, all centered around the production of the social relation of capitalist value. It is a game on a global scale of emptying forms, it is a swarm of pure reaction.

. . . *Returning to the Story*

Within CIT law's globally harmonized regimes, two core tax subjects are constructed and recognized as central in international tax law scholarship: permanent establishment (of corporations) and residence (of corporations) (Avi-Yonah 2005). With some exceptions, non-OECD countries are generally only hosts to foreign multinational enterprise through permanent establishments, while OECD countries generally host such enterprise through the legal fiction of residence (Mosquera Valderrama 2015; Burgers and Mosquera 2017; Sacchi 2021: 6). At the core of these subjects lies a geopolitical conflict over their formulation. This is a conflict that has also been expressed as that between *residence countries* and *host-* or *source countries*, or between *capital importing* and *capital exporting countries* or sometimes between '*developed*' and '*developing countries*'.

Over the last century, the power non-OECD states have been able to exercise in terms of taxing have steadily dwindled, enhancing OECD state taxing powers (Avi-Yonah 2005). The high rate of mobility of capital for tax purposes, which have pushed non-OECD states to give up taxing powers over the last century, is facilitated by the design of globally harmonized corporate income tax law regimes. As mentioned, the separate entity principle and arm's length standard invite multinational enterprise to shift their profits to tax havens. The majority of the prevalent tax haven jurisdictions are OECD member states (TJN 2021). Most other tax havens have been put in place by OECD states during colonial times (Ogle 2017). However, tax havens owe their existence as much to the OECD and to colonialization as they do to global legal regimes. In this section, I explore how these regimes have been put in place by OECD countries (Cobham *et al* 2018; Picciotto 2013; Calderón Carrero 2007).

The around 37 percent of profit that goes untaxed yearly is often spoken of as 'missing' or 'hidden' (Tørsløv *et al* 2023). However, this is misleading. Using the concept of posthumanist agency, I argue that tax law must be embedded in larger narratives of international law, illuminating a contemporary history of imperialist extractivism and neocolonial exploitation. Over the last century, former slave traders and colonial powers have seen to it that rule of law is constitutionally enforced worldwide, enabling exploitation through the corporate form (Baars 2019; Chimni 2022; Nanopoulos 2023). Since independence, non-OECD countries that were robbed of sovereign control over their natural resources and shackled by debt have experienced a critical loss of policy space. This critical loss is a direct effect of policies enforced by the hands of organizations such as the IMF, WTO, World Bank, the OECD and for example bilateral investment regimes (Chimni 2022).

At the UN, primarily non-OECD states have made strong attempts at forcing the fulfillment of the ideological promise of de facto sovereignty but have had little to no success (Cobham *et al* 2018). In the shadow of these struggles and with slow, glacial force, both low tax jurisdictions and the particular form of the multinational enterprise have grown to set into the nooks and crannies of global, Western, state-led regimes. The multinational enterprises, alongside the countries in which they are headquartered, and characterized by intrafirm or highly specialized inter-firm trade, have divided the world into categories based not on industry but on position within global production processes. These positions range from exporters of raw materials to what the world bank calls 'innovative activities', carried on mainly by North America and the EU. The cementation of these positions are vital for the production of surplus value within multinational enterprises (World Bank 2020).

At the time of writing, the sheer immensity of the multinational groups that lift over 90 percent of global corporate revenues has capital mobility varying vertically across corporate chains (Clausing 2018; Clifford 2018; OECD 2020: 41). 'Resident' and with GloBE top-up minimum taxation, 'headquarter' or 'ultimate parent entity', capital is not as mobile as the capital personified through permanent establishments. This form that the multinational enterprise has taken enables the OECD to implement the top-up minimum tax. Over the last 20 years or so, OECD countries have furthermore seen to it that information on the global activities of multinational enterprises is collected, processed and shared effectively only amongst the OECD states themselves (Stewart 2013). This information is pivotal for the power to properly tax globally mobile profits.

In conclusion, OECD states have systematically diminished the sovereign taxing abilities of non-OECD states over the last century. They have done so by not taxing resident and headquarter multinationals (ICRICT 2020); by not sharing with non-OECD states information, for tax purposes, on the activities of resident multinational enterprises (Cobham *et al* 2018); by historically insisting on a corporate income tax system that treats every corporation as an individual tax subject, rather than as part of a unitary multinational group, thus enabling profit shifting on a massive scale (IFA 1976); and by refusing to better the arm's-length principle that guides the legal treatment of multinational transfer pricing.

Tax levied on corporate income accounts for about 6 percent of total tax revenue of OECD countries whilst tax levied on labor and consumption bring their total revenue to an average of 30 to 40 percent of GDP (Hearson 2021: 7 ff). However, outside the OECD the ratio of tax revenue to GDP averages about 15 percent, with corporate income tax being at least twice as important (ibid). By focusing tax revenue on labor and consumption rather than capital, OECD states are not only able to suppress production costs domestically. Extended on an international level, this base enables OECD states to protect their own revenue whilst eroding the tax bases of low-income countries that rely on corporate income tax. By diminishing taxing powers of non-OECD states, OECD states have enabled vast capital accumulation by exported capital. With the top-up minimum tax, OECD states are getting ready to collect the tax revenue that they have – over the last century – hidden away.

In the following and final section of the chapter, I return to the global, top-up minimum tax. With this tax, G20/OECD states further affect the formation of the tax subjectivity that they as tax sovereigns personify. The OECD/G20 top-up minimum tax pushes the boundaries of OECD member state tax sovereignty to further expand them – and to diminish the tax sovereignty of non-OECD states. As we leave this section of the chapter behind, and as the top-up minimum tax brings the so-called missing profits under OECD rule, it must be remembered why and through what agency the profits were made 'missing' in the first place.

. . . Once Turned Loose, It Cannot Be Called Back

Under the recent OECD/G20 initiative to bring corporate tax governance into international law through global minimum taxation, the loophole-ridden CIT regimes and the relative mobility of capital is being leveraged by OECD nation-states to further affect the formation of the subjects of tax law. Global top-up minimum taxation will not replace the current global tax regime, but only add a new layer of complexity, to tilt – under the threat of double taxation – the flow of capital value yet steeper in the direction of OECD nation-states.

The historically groundbreaking, common consolidated global tax base of the minimum tax accepts only certain taxes as 'covered taxes'. For example, both the OECD model rules and the EU Commission proposal for a directive on their implementation state that a permanent establishment of a multinational corporation – a core tax subject of non-OECD states – must be fashioned in accordance with the OECD model tax treaty in order to be acknowledged by the common consolidated tax base (OECD 2021: 63). This is only true, however, if there is a bilateral tax treaty in force between the host of the permanent establishment and the home country of the resident corporation (ibid). Thus, one could argue, that in order to avoid double taxation, countries that wish to broaden their concept of permanent establishment could simply terminate their bilateral tax treaty networks. However – and as I explain in the next paragraph – due to the design of the top-up minimum tax, countries that forego bilateral tax treaty networks will miss out on important revenue from gross-based withholding taxes.

Since the top-up minimum tax base accepts only taxes levied on a net basis, withholding taxes, and most new taxes levied on digital activity on a gross basis, won't be covered. To make up for the revenue lost by 'source' or non-OECD countries, the OECD have included a new, standalone rule called Subject to Tax Rule in the top-up minimum tax package. Unlike the top-up minimum tax, that can be applied unilaterally, the Subject to Tax Rule must be negotiated between the parties and entered into tax treaties. Effectively, the only way for non-OECD countries to be able to levy tax on gross basis, in a way that is considered covered by the global tax base, is to incorporate the new Subject to Tax Rule through tax treaties. Today, tax treaties cover 81 percent of Foreign Direct Investment stocks (Hearson 2021: 4). As mentioned, tax treaty networks are already biased in favor of OECD countries. Due to the design of the global tax base, tax treaties are unlikely to become less prevalent, in the way argued for by, for example, Hearson.

By exerting control over what is an unprecedented, global consolidated tax base, non-OECD states that have and will have expanded the reach of permanent establishments and other tax subjects, will see these subjects taxed doubly on the income subject to tax. This, in effect, means that the capital subject to tax will be diminished and that inbound investment flows will wane. If OECD nation-states hadn't made this move, non-OECD states could have leveraged the top-up minimum tax to enhance their tax powers through Permanent Establishments, other burgeoning forms of tax subjectivity, like for example Significant Economic Presence, or types of withholding tax, and forced investor states through collective bargaining to credit this tax. They can still do this, and are still doing it, but it requires an unprecedented level of coordination amongst non-OECD taxing powers. If the OECD/G20 plans for a multilateral tax convention with effective dispute resolution mechanisms are realized, however, the agency of non-OECD taxing powers will be diminished to an even greater extent.

Finally, there is an interesting point to be made about the low tax rate of the minimum tax. Being set at only 15 percent, this minimum tax might very well become a maximum tax – but only for some countries. In the interest of curbing profit shifting, non-OECD states might lower their effective tax rates to match or underbid the minimum rate. There could even be incentive for high tax countries to bifurcate their tax regimes and effectively become tax havens for mobile capital (Wardell-Burrus 2022: 27). This development could affect a critical loss of revenue for these countries, especially considering the plunge that effective tax rates have already taken in, for example, India (Verma 2022). In comparison, OECD states will not run as high a risk. Other than being able to tax resident headquarters on the top-up minimum tax, OECD-states can leverage Controlled Foreign Corporation regimes to tax not only their own but also foreign capital according to their own, higher rates.

As the wealthy states of the world leverage a complexity ridden patchwork of harmonized regimes to enforce top-up minimum taxation and, with it, an enhanced control over the reformulation of such legal regimes, what is at stake is nothing less than the redrawing of sovereign boundaries (Chimni 2022). While tax sovereignty is only part of what sovereign boundaries are and does in terms of international law, the way in which the redrawing – or, rather, the constant diminishing – of non-OECD nation-state's tax sovereignty and thus sovereign boundaries makes this a core concern of international law. Especially so in its critical scholarly iterations, and with a posthumanist view of international law as encompassing all that which grants form to sovereign autonomies and legal subjectivities.

In light of this bleak vision, the 'historical step' promoted by the OECD from tax governance to international tax law engendered in the installation of top-up minimum taxation seem not quite as transformative as the OECD will have it sound. Instead, it marks simply the continued streamlining of agency and a continued colonial appropriation of jurisdiction (Chimni 2022). With top-up minimum taxation, tax 'sovereignty' is not 're-established' by 'international cooperation' in the way that the OECD would argue. Rather, tax sovereignty is reordered – to the detriment of non-OECD nation-states – by the agency from which capitalist value, tax subjects, and their tax sovereigns spring – as expressed through CIT regimes worldwide. Finally, then, the OECD/G20 imposition of global top-up minimum taxation hegemonically pictured as a 'new age of interventionism (bringing) the big state is back in business (to) bend companies to their will' (Shanbhogue 2022: 1) simply makes for 'a shift in the form of capitalist domination (and in no sense a shift away from capitalist domination)' (Holloway and Picciotto 1977: 95).

Concluding Remarks

Once in the world, the acts of the OECD cannot be called back. However, the stories that surround these acts can be unmasked, bringing alight new agency. The good beginnings and the heroes of a story can be made to implode by the force of their own creation. In the words of Trinh T. Minh-Ha: 'Words (. . .) are no more than dry dung' (1989: 53).

Posthuman theory has allowed me to make three major claims in this chapter about how change is enacted within CIT law regimes. *First*, tax havens and the tax evading practices of large multinational groups emerge as the expression of states, primarily OECD states, exerting control over the way that the relation of surplus value is recreated. Large-scale profit shifting is made possible by OECD states, in the interests of these states. *Second*, the ontological agency of international tax law is simply the struggle over the creation of the relation of surplus value. This relation grants form to, and is granted form by, autonomous sovereigns and legal subjects alike. *Third*, the global minimum tax is another expression of this agency, and in advancing OECD taxing powers, at the expense of non-OECD taxing powers, it will reform what it means for different countries to possess tax sovereignty. Shifting the focus from autonomy to the formation of the different autonomous forms, posthumanism brings to light the role of OECD states and the OECD/G20 in the ongoing, colonial and extractivist reconfiguring of sovereign boundaries.

Through the application of posthuman theory, which allows for a demystification of tax competition, international tax scholars can acquire the tools to regard, not only OECD and OECD member state acts as formative for international law but also those counterhegemonic legislative projects that emerge from non-OECD nation-states. Concepts like Significant Economic Presence, Digital Service Tax and Equalization Levy are rapidly spreading amongst non-OECD taxing powers (KPMG 2022). In the context of heightened coordination outside the OECD, the recently approved article 12B in the UN tax convention offers great promise (Ovonji-Odida *et al* 2022: 32). Discursively constructed as 'unilateral measures' by the OECD, these legislative projects represent a counterforce to developments otherwise led by the OECD and reiterated in much of international tax law scholarship.

References

Arvidsson, M. (2020) 'The Swarm That We Already Are: Artificially Intelligent (AI) Swarming "Insect Drones", Targeting and International Humanitarian Law in a Posthuman Ecology', *Journal of Human Rights and the Environment*, 11(1): 114–37.

Ash, E. and O.Y. Marian (2019) *The Making of International Tax Law: Empirical Evidence from Natural Language Processing*, UC Irvine School of Law Research Paper No. 2019-02. https://ssrn.com/abstract=3314310

Avi-Yonah, R.S. (2005) 'All of a Piece Throughout: The Four Ages of U.S. International Taxation', *Vancouver Tax Review*, 25(2): 313–38.

Baars, G. (2019) *The Corporation, Law and Capitalism*, The Hague: Brill.

Barad, K. (2003) 'Posthumanist Performativity: Toward an Understanding of How Matter Comes to Matter', *Signs*, 28(3): 801–31.

Barad, K. (2007) *Meeting the Universe Halfway: Quantum Physics and the Entanglement of Matter and Meaning*, Durham: Duke University Press.

Barad, K. (2010) 'Quantum Entanglements and Hauntological Relations of Inheritance: Dis/continuities, SpaceTime Enfoldings, and Justice-to-Come', *Derrida Today*, 3(2): 240–68.

Bhandar, B. (2018) *Colonial Lives of Property: Law, Land, and Racial Regimes of Ownership*, Durham: Duke University Press.

Braidotti, R. (2013) *The Posthuman*, New York: Polity Press.

Braidotti, R. (2019) *Posthuman Knowledge*, New York: Polity Press.

Burgers, I. and I. Mosquera (2017) 'Corporate Taxation and BEPS: A Fair Slice for Developing Countries?', *Erasmus Law Review*, 10(1), 29–47. DOI: https://doi.org/10.5553/ELR.000077

Calderón Carrero, J.M. (2007) 'The OECD Transfer Pricing Guidelines as a Source of Tax Law: Is Globalization Reaching the Tax Law?', *Intertax*, 35(1): 4–29.

Chimni, B.S. (2022) 'The International Law of Jurisdiction: A TWAIL Perspective', *Leiden Journal of International Law*, 35(1): 29–54.

Christians, A. (2017) 'BEPS and the Power to Tax', in S.A. Rocha and A. Christians (eds) *Tax Sovereignty in the BEPS Era*, The Hague: Kluwer Law International.

Clausing, K. (2018) 'Does Tax Drive the Headquarter Decisions of the World's Biggest Companies?', *Transnational Corporations*, 25(2): 37–65.

Clifford, S. (2018) 'Taxing Multinationals Beyond Borders: Financial and Locational Responses to CFC Rules', *Journal of Public Economics*, 173: 44–71.

Cobham, A., P. Janský and M. Meinzer (2018) 'A Half-Century of Resistance to Corporate Disclosure', *Transnational Corporations*, 25(3): 1–26.

Council of the EU (2022) Council Directive (EU) 2022/2523 of 15 December 2022 on ensuring a global minimum level of taxation for multinational enterprise groups and large-scale domestic groups in the Union, available at http://data.europa.eu/eli/dir/2022/2523/2022-12-22.

Cui, W. (2020) 'What Is Unilateralism in International Taxation?', *AJIL Unbound*, 114: 260–4.

Dagan, T. (2017) *International Tax Policy: Between Competition and Cooperation*, Cambridge: Cambridge University Press.

Davies, M. (2012) 'Persons, Property, and Community', *Feminists@Law*, 2(2): 1–21. DOI: https://doi.org/10.22024/UniKent/03/fal.37

Dolphijn, R. and I. van der Tuin (eds) (2012) *New Materialism: Interviews & Cartographies*, Ann Arbor: Open Humanities Press.

Ergen, T., S. Kohl and B. Braun (2023) 'Firm Foundations: The Statistical Footprint of Multinational Corporations as a Problem for Political Economy', *Competition & Change*, 27(1): 44–73.

G-24 Working Group on Tax Policy and International Tax Cooperation (2019a) 'Proposal for Addressing Tax Challenges Arising from Digitalisation', G-24, 17 January. https://www.g24.org/wp-content/uploads/2019/03/G-24_proposal_for_Taxation_of_Digital_Economy_Jan17_Special_Session_2.pdf

G-24 Working Group on Tax Policy and International Tax Cooperation (2019b) 'Comments of the G-24 on the OECD Secretariat Proposal for a Unified Approach to the Nexus and Profit Allocation Challenges Arising from the Digitalisation (Pillar 1)', G-24. https://www.g24.org/press/comments-of-the-g-24-on-the-oecd-secretariat-proposal-for-a-unified-approach-to-the-nexus-and-profit-allocation-challenges-arising-from-the-digitalisation-pillar-1-2/

G-24 Working Group on Tax Policy and International Tax Cooperation (2021) 'Comments of the G-24 on the Statement on a Two-Pillar Solution to Address the Tax Challenges Arising from the Digitalisation of the Economy Agreed by 134 Jurisdictions of the Inclusive Framework on the 1st of July 2021', G-24. https://www.g24.org/wp-content/uploads/2022/03/Comments-of-the-G24-on-the-IF-July-Statement.pdf

Grear, A. (2010) *Redirecting Human Rights: Facing the Challenge of Corporate Legal Humanity*, London: Palgrave Macmillan. DOI: https://doi.org/10.1057/9780230274631

Grear, A. (2015) 'Deconstructing Anthropos: A Critical Legal Reflection on "Anthropocentric" Law and Anthropocene "Humanity"', *Law & Critique*, 26: 225–49.

Grear, A. (2017) '"Anthropocene, Capitalocene, Chthulucene": Re-Encountering Environmental Law and Its "Subject" with Haraway and New Materialism', in L.J. Kotze (ed) *Re-Imagining Environmental Law and Governance for the Anthropocene*, London: Bloomsbury, 77–99. DOI: https://doi.org/10.5040/9781509906574.ch-004

Grear, A. (2020) 'Legal Imaginaries and the Anthropocene: "Of" and "For"', *Law Critique*, 31: 351–66.

Haraway, D. (1988) 'Situated Knowledges: The Science Question in Feminism and the Privilege of Partial Perspective', *Feminist Studies*, 14(3): 575–99.

Haraway, D. (2016) *Anthropocene, Capitolocene, Chthulucene: Staying with the Trouble*, Durham: Duke University Press.

Hearson, M. (2021) *Imposing Standards: The North-South Dimension to Global Tax Politics*, Ithaca: Cornell University Press.

Hertzfeld, M. (2016) 'The Backlash Against Tax Treaties and Free Trade', *TaxNotes International*, 84: 438.

Hohmann, J. (2021) 'Diffuse Subjects and Dispersed Power: New Materialist Insights and Cautionary Lessons for International Law', *Leiden Journal of International Law*, 34: 1–22.

Holloway, J. and S. Picciotto (1977) 'Capital, Crisis and the State', *Capital & Class*, 1(2): 76–101.

ICRICT (2020) 'ICRICT Response to the OECD consultation on the Pillar One and Pillar Two Blueprints', ICRICT Documents. https://www.icrict.com/press-release/2020/12/16/oecd-response-to-the-oecd-consultation-on-the-review-of-country-by-country-reporting-beps-action-13

IMF (2014) *Spillovers in International Corporate Taxation*, IMF Policy Paper 28–29, IMF. https://www.imf.org/external/np/pp/eng/2014/050914.pdf

International Fiscal Association IFA (1976) 'Statement Made by E. Gnazzo', Work in Intergovernmental Organizations on Transnational Companies, Proceedings of a Seminar Held in Jerusalem During the 30th Conference of IFA.

Kirby, V. (1997) *Telling Flesh: The Substance of the Corporeal*, London: Routledge.

Kirby, V. (2011) *Quantum Anthropologies: Life at Large*, Durham: Duke University Press.

Knox, R. (2021) 'Law', in B. Skeggs, S.R. Farris, A. Toscano and S. Bromberg (eds) *Sage Handbook on Marxism*, London: Sage Publications.

KPMG (2022) 'KPMG's Summary of Taxation of the Digital Economy Developments', https://home.kpmg/xx/en/home/insights/2019/06/tnfdigital-economy0.html (Accessed 4 March 2022).

Magwape, Mbakiso. (2022) 'Debate: Unilateral Digital Services Tax in Africa; Legislative Challenges and Opportunities', *Intertax*, 50: 444–58.

Marx, K. (1976) *Capital. Volume One: A Critique of Political Economy*, Penguin in Association with New Left Review London.

Minh-Ha, T.T. (1989) *Woman, Native, Other: Writing Postcoloniality and Feminism*, Bloomington: Indiana University Press.

Mosquera Valderrama, I.J. (2015) 'Legitimacy and the Making of International Tax Law: The Challenges of Multilateralism', *World Tax Journal*, 7(3): 344–66.

Murray, P. (2021) 'Methods', in B. Skeggs, S.R. Farris, A. Toscano and S. Bromberg (eds) *Sage Handbook on Marxism*, London: Sage Publications.

Nanopoulos, E. (2023) 'The Material Constitution and Imperialism', in M. Goldoni and M. Wilkinson (eds) *Cambridge Handbook on the Material Constitution*, Cambridge: Cambridge University Publishing, 171–87.

The Netherlands Civil Society Financing for Development (FFD) Group (2022) 'Database: Governments Supporting an Intergovernmental UN Tax Body and/or UN Tax Convention'. https://csoforffd.org/2021/10/27/database-governments-supporting-an-intergovernmental-untax-body-and-or-un-tax-convention/

OECD (2015) *Addressing the Tax Challenges of the Digital Economy, Action 1–2015 Final Report*, OECD/G20 Base Erosion and Profit Shifting Project, Paris: OECD Publishing.

OECD (2017) *Inclusive Framework on BEPS: Progress Report July 2016–June 2017*, OECD/G20 Base Erosion and Profit Shifting Project, Paris: OECD Publishing.

OECD (2018) *Tax Challenges Arising from Digitalisation – Interim Report 2018: Inclusive Framework on BEPS*, OECD/G20 Base Erosion and Profit Shifting Project, Paris: OECD Publishing.

OECD (2019) *Public Consultation Document Addressing the Tax Challenges of the Digitalisation of the Economy 13 February–6 March 2019*, OECD/G20 Inclusive Framework on BEPS, Paris: OECD Publishing.

OECD (2020) *Tax Challenges Arising from Digitalisation – Report on Pillar Two Blueprint: Inclusive Framework on BEPS*, OECD/G20 Base Erosion and Profit Shifting Project, Paris: OECD Publishing.

OECD (2021) *Tax Challenges Arising from the Digitalisation of the Economy – Global Anti-Base Erosion Model Rules (Pillar Two): Inclusive Framework on BEPS*, Paris: OECD Publishing.

Ogle, V. (2017) 'Archipelago Capitalism: Tax Havens, Offshore Money, and the State, 1950s–1970s', *The American Historical Review*, 122(5): 1431–58. DOI: https://doi.org/10.1093/ahr/122.5.1431

Ovonji-Odida, I., V. Grondona and A. Muheet Chowdhary (2022) *Two Pillar Solution for Taxing the Digitalized Economy: Policy Implications and Guidance for the Global South*, Research Paper 161, Geneva: South Centre.

Pashukanis, E. (2002) *General Theory of Law and Marxism*, London: Routledge.

Picciotto, S. (2012) 'Towards Unitary Taxation of Transnational Corporations', *Tax Justice Network*, 1–25.

Picciotto, S. (2013) *International Business Taxation: A Study in the Internationalization of Business Regulation*, Cambridge: Cambridge University Press.

Sacchi, A.R. (2021) *Implementing a (Global?) Minimum Corporate Income Tax: An Assessment from the Perspective of Developing Countries*, Copenhagen Business School, CBS LAW Research Paper No. 20-15. https://papers.ssrn.com/sol3/papers.cfm?abstract_id=3668096

Shanbhogue, R. (2022) 'The New Age of Interventionism – the Big State Is Back in Business', *The Economist*, Podcast, 12 January. www.economist.com/podcasts/2022/01/12/the-new-age-of-interventionism-the-big-state-is-back-in-business

Stanley-Smith, J. (2019) *India Happy to Be Leader in Tax but Still Craves Consensus*, London: International Tax Review, 21 March.

Stewart, M. (2013) 'Global Tax Information Networks: Legitimacy in a Global Administrative State', in Y. Brauner and M. Stewart (eds) *Tax Law and Development*, Cheltenham: Edward Elgar, 316–44. DOI: https://doi.org/10.4337/9780857930019.00025

Tax Justice Network (2021) 'Corporate Tax Haven Index – 2021 Results'. https://cthi.taxjustice.net/en/ (Accessed: 2 May 2022).

Titus, A. (2022) 'Global Minimum Corporate Tax: A Death Knell For African Country Tax Policies? [Pre-Publication]', *Intertax*, 50(5): 1–10.

Tørsløv, T., L. Wier and G. Zucman (2023) 'The Missing Profits of Nations', *The Review of Economic Studies*, 90(3): 1499–534.

United Nations (2013) *World Investment Report 2013: Global Value Chains: Investment and Trade for Development*, Geneva: United Nations Publications.

Verma, S. (2022) *Related Party Trade and Transfer to Tax Havens: A Study of Select Manufacturing Foreign Subsidiaries in India*, ISID Working Paper 242, New Delhi. https://isid.org.in/pdf/WP242.pdf

Wardell-Burrus, H. (2022) *State Strategic Responses to the GloBE Rules*, Working Paper, Oxford: Oxford University Centre for Business Taxation, 1 December.

World Bank (2020) *World Development Report 2020*, Books 32437, The World Bank Group, Washington, DC: World Bank Publications.

7

AFTER *HOMO NARRANS*

Botany, International Law and Senegambia in Early Racial Capitalist Worldmaking

Vanja Hamzić

The making of the human as 'we' know it – as a distinct species that appeared between five million and seven million years ago on a continent that came to be known as Africa – invokes nowadays an ordinary Enlightenment imagery, replete with such (r)evolutionary actions as the flaking of crude stone tools, or the discovery of fire, or the invention of the wheel. Migration, language and a whole host of anatomical 'particularities' come to mind, too, until one reaches, almost seamlessly, the epochs of such 'sophisticated' markers of humanness as 'civilization' or 'culture'. The warm and fuzzy platitudes of our common ancestry notwithstanding, this story has been born out of the violence of an explicitly hierarchal view of life – with *some* humans seen as more worthy or 'advanced' than others, and with all other forms of life subservient to the preservation of those *selected* forms of human existence.

Critical studies of the human and its environment have long quarreled with this originatory narrative, debunking at various stages its foundational presumptions: that there is or should be a vertical scientific view of 'human types', or 'civilizational progress', or of human and nonhuman life. Less frequently, however, such studies questioned our distinct speciation – our self-designation as a species – or looked into the way this watershed moment in a would-be scientific understanding of the human coincided with numerous other forms of onto-epistemic violence and subjugation of diverse forms of life, human or otherwise. While critiques of the making of the Enlightenment (hu)man abound, they rarely center on the two axes of the Enlightenment project: that of international law and the racialized gender binary.

This chapter engages an emergent science of categorization and speciation and its reverberations and affordances in European international law in the long eighteenth century. I focus on a distinct material locale – that

DOI: 10.4324/9781032658032-10

of 'proto-colonial' Senegambia – so as to reveal a circum-Atlantic capitalist economy of enslavement and human fungibility in the making, and its attendant, forcible sexing, gendering and racializing regimes. The reductive, hierarchical 'human' such regimes sought to advance stood in stark contrast to eighteenth-century West African conceptualizations of human, nonhuman and more-than-human being-in-the-world – and I dwell on the example of Mande griots (*jeliw*, sing. *jeli*) and their increasingly precarious lifeworlds to underline the importance of *storytelling* as a mode of survival and resistance to gendered and racial capitalist violence.

According to Sylvia Wynter (2015), such oppressive, racial capitalist *worldings* – the figurations of the human as onto-epistemically divisible and governable along the imposed racialized, gendered, sexed, classed, abled and other fault lines – were either explicitly legal or *lawlike*. This chapter, in turn, reveals that eighteenth-century international law's technologies of subjectivation relied precisely on such worldings and touted them as both universal and natural. Against the abiding violence of racial capitalist Man – the Christian *homo politicus* gradually morphing into the colonial-Enlightenment *homo oeconomicus* (Wynter 2006: 123) – Wynter proposed a turn to 'the human as a figure on the horizon, rooted in anticolonial struggle and thought' (Alagraa 2018: 164): the storytelling insurrectionary *homo narrans*. Following Aimé Césaire's (1945) clarion call to decenter the colonial and postcolonial natural sciences in our understanding of humanity – returning, instead, to the 'science of the Word' – Wynter's *homo narrans* served to remind us of the foundational power of storytelling. Because the stories we tell ourselves co-create the world's past, present and future we learn to inhabit, they can trouble 'an order of knowledge that is indispensable to the continued reproduction of our present neoliberal/neo-imperial, secularly biocentric, global order of words and of things' (Wynter and McKittrick 2015: 30).

I take up Wynter's challenge to show both how the present racial capitalist order of knowledge was being forged in eighteenth-century natural and legal sciences, and the French and English entrepôts in Senegal and the Gambia, as well as how it was resisted there and then, including by gender-nonconforming *jeliw* through their worlding of the storytelling Senegambian human, nonhuman and more-than-human. Learning from the Black radical tradition and decolonial trans/feminist critique, this chapter calls for new, materialist figurations of posthuman *homo narrans*, away from legal or lawlike biocentricity. It argues, with Donna Haraway, for 'thick copresence' (2016: 4) of earthlings in time(s) – situated, entangled and worldly – but, instead of her 'multispecies storytelling' (13), it attends to the problem of (Enlightenment, colonial) species-making in the first place. My intent, too, is to demonstrate that a substantive, decolonial 'turn to history' and other abiding temporalities can be productive for posthuman theory and other critical studies for a range of reasons, not least because it calls into question the ordering implicit in the 'human-as-species' that centers in perpetuum only certain forms of life (so much so that scholars of queer inhumanisms, for instance, could aptly ask whether the queer has ever been human; Luciano and Chen 2015: 186). Critiques of such violent making of the human – and other species – seem incomplete without due attention paid to its forceful ossification – naturalization, historicization – in linear time, thus rendering innumerable arrays of human, nonhuman and more-than-human lifeworlds unnatural, unlivable and unworthy of remembrance – of the very existence in time.

Botanical Binaries, Human Variations

Racial capitalism has been proposed (Robinson 1983) as a useful descriptor for a range of systemic, world-destroying and worldmaking efforts of Euro-American imperial powers to colonize not only earth's populations and resources but also the ideas about the world(s) and life, their ordering, worth and temporalities. The racialized colonial dispossession of labor, land and livelihoods included, right from the start, concerted attempts at building a 'system of expropriating violence on collective life itself' (Melamed 2015: 76), which, in order to be controlled and exploited, needed to be classified and 'made sense of' in accordance with the rising Enlightenment ideas about such life. As Alexander Weheliye (2014: 8) has averred, this crucially occasioned the making of the 'modern' human:

> first, there exists no portion of the modern human that is not subject to racialization, which determines the hierarchical ordering of Homo Sapiens species into humans, not-quite-humans, and nonhumans; second, as a result, humanity has held a very different status for the traditions of the radically oppressed.

Such coterminous birth of Man and his many Others formed the basis for the Enlightenment subject of ethical consideration (Yusoff 2018: 55), delineating and stereotyping the forms of hierarchical life, not only among the *homo sapiens* (with some 'naturally selected' to live, lead and prosper, and others dispossessed of their humanity and reduced to 'flesh', as Hortense Spillers (1987) has it) but also the environment and all forms of nonhuman life. Thus, not only were humans racialized, disciplined into the ubiquitous procreative ('productive') sexual unit that would later be named the (cisheternormative) 'nuclear family', and ordered into the gender binary – so, too, were plants, animals and other biologically determined 'species'.

Thus, the famed Swedish botanist Carl Linnaeus, whose *Systema naturae* (1735, 1758, 1766–68) left an indelible mark on botanical nomenclature and prompted the rise of zoological nomenclature, advanced taxonomies of natural life in which 'the most basic division is between male and female – exactly the same distinction as in the highly chauvinistic society of late 18th-century Europe' – always giving priority to would-be 'male' characteristics (Fara 2003: 21). Thus, his first level of plant ordering depended on the number of 'male' stamens, while only the subgroups were determined by the number of 'female' pistils. Such hierarchical sexing was given an explicit marital connotation: he named stamens and pistils as *andria* and *gynia*, respectively, which he derived from Greek for 'husband' and 'wife'. He imagined that plants had penises and vaginas and reproduced on 'marriage beds' (Schiebinger 2013 [1993]: 1, 22–3). The focus on the 'marriages of plants' (*nuptiae plantarum*) served, in part, to distract the reader from more troublesome – if ubiquitous – characteristics of 'sexuality' in plants, such as their reproductive 'dimorphism' and 'hermaphrodism'. Because the reproductive parts of the plant – as well as those of the human – were increasingly seen as its 'essence' (Balani 2018: 233), they needed to follow the binary logic of such sexing as seamlessly as possible. Therefore, in the first edition of *Systema naturae*, Linnaeus felt compelled to explain that '[t]he calyx is the bedchamber', while 'the filaments the spermatic vessels, the anthers the testes, the pollen the sperm, the stigma the vulva, the style the vagina' (Fara 2003: 38–9; Linnaeus 1737: 146). Marriage, seemingly divinely ordained as between one man and one woman, had to make sense in the plant world, too. Linnaeus thus named his first class of plants *monandria* (from the Greek for 'one man'), reserved for plants with equal numbers of stamens and pistils, and nicknamed his own wife a monandrian lily (Fara 2003: 24). Plants with unequal numbers of stamens and pistils needed to be ordered differently, for their 'marriage' was to be seen as irregular. For instance, ferns, mosses, algae and fungi were classified as *cryptogamia* (meaning, 'plants that marry secretly').

Somewhat controversially, *Systema naturae* placed humans within the animal kingdom, but it distinguished them for their ability to 'know thyself' (*nosce te ipsum*). This sole faculty seemed to guide Linnaeus when he began to experiment with a binominal nomenclature in the 1850s editions of the treatise, which lead to his genus *homo* acquiring the epithet *sapiens*. He then designated the taxon below the species as 'varieties of (hu)man' (*homo variat*) and initially used the perceived difference in skin color and geographic location to distinguish between *Europaeus albus* ('white'), *Americanus rubescens* ('reddish'), *Asiaticus fuscus* ('tawny') and *Africanus niger* ('black'). The hierarchical order between the first three human 'varieties' changed from one edition of *Systema naturae* to another, but *Africanus* always remained at the bottom of the list. Sometime in the 1750s – concomitant with his invention of *homo sapiens* – Linnaeus proceeded to assign further descriptors to his *homo variat*, centering on an imagined array of physical and moral differences as well as those that purported to indicate a particular variety's quintessential form of governance and legality. In the tenth edition of *Systema naturae*, published in 1758, the difference between the *Europaeus* and the *Africanus* 'variety', which Linnaeus now called *Afer*, were described in a language that would later form the basis for scientific racism:

Europaeus b. white, sanguine, muscular.
Hair flowing, long. *Eyes* blue.
Gentle, acute, inventive.
Covered with close vestments.
Governed by laws. [. . .]

Afer d. black, phlegmatic, relaxed.
Hair black, frizzled. *Skin* silky. *Nose* flat. *Lips* tumid.
Women without shame. *Mammae* lactate profusely.
Crafty, indolent, negligent.
Anoints himself with grease.
Governed by caprice.

(Lafleur 2018: 3, 46; Linnaeus 1758: 20–2)

There can be little doubt that Linnaeus' phenotypic descriptions relied on diverse European Enlightenment literature, including botany, human anatomy and philosophy, along with proto-anthropological observations commonly found in vastly popular travelogues that also supplied information on commerce and natural resources in distant lands. Once he even managed to persuade his sovereign to task the Swedish East India Company to 'search the world over for a specimen of the *Homo troglodytes*' (Schiebinger 2013 [1993]: 81), whom he imagined having descended from the Atlas community of cave dwellers, based on an ancient Roman description. What is significant, however, is that in Linnaeus' *magnum opus*, as of 1758, racial and gender stereotypes attain the status of scientific facts. Of all his *homo variat*, Linnaeus chooses to discuss and typify only the *Afer* women's sexual-*cum*-moral disposition. The ambiguous Latin phrasing is particularly telling: '*feminis sinus pudoris*' can be translated both as 'women without shame' and 'in women: stretched labia' (Lafleur 2018: 48). In a similar manner, the diverse *homo variat*'s would-be 'natural' proclivity toward different forms of governance and legality points out to the wider Enlightenment bias against non-European politics and law. Whereas the *Europaeus* is governed by laws, the *Afer* is helplessly governed by caprice.

Although Linnaeus' status as the Enlightenment era's 'taxonomer-in-chief' is perhaps singular, his was by no means a lone voice in 'the project of taxonomizing human variety', which became 'so central to early modern colonial enterprise and so instrumental in the development of universalizing languages of Enlightenment personhood' (ibid: 4). For instance, Linnaeus' celebrated

French contemporary, Georges-Louis Leclerc, Comte de Buffon, rejected the concept of species as advanced by Linnaeus and his many followers, but he also elaborated an environmental view of human 'variation', owing to 'divers changes, from the influence of climate, from the difference of food, and of the mode of living, from epidemical distempers' (Banton 1998: 21). The Scottish encyclopedist and naturalist William Smellie, who translated Buffon's voluminous *Histoire naturelle* (1749–89; 1788–1804), wrote that, 'independently of all political institutions, Nature herself has formed the human species into castes and ranks' (Smellie 1790, I: 521–2). 'To some', he continued suggestively, 'she gives superior genius and mental abilities'. These views were also sustained and given a distinct, legal-philosophical veneer by key eighteenth-century European thinkers of international law.

International Law, *Philosophes* and the Making of the Colonial Difference

International law and European legal philosophy had their own distinct genealogy of racism and colonial sentiments stretching back into Renaissance humanist thought. Notable examples include the *Junta de Valladolid* (1550–51), the first moral debate in European history to discuss the rights and treatment of colonized Indigenous populations in the Americas. In it, the humanist scholar Juan Ginés de Sepúlveda argued that Indigenous 'were naturally predisposed to slavery' (Bunge 2017: 50) due to their 'inferior' cultural practices and what he specifically termed as 'crimes against nature' (Sepúlveda 1941 [1547]: 155). Alberico Gentili, the Regius professor of civil law at the University of Oxford, who criticized the Spanish for aiming in their American conquests 'not at commerce, but at dominion', nonetheless wrote, in 1598, that it is just to wage war against those who, 'wearing the human form, live the life of the most brutal of beasts', adding that 'some men differ very little from the brutes' (Gentili 1933 [1598], I: 89, 41; Fitzmaurice 2012: 843). The famed Dutch humanist Hugo Grotius himself, often credited as one of the 'greats' of international law, sustained, as Mikki Stelder (2021: 4) recently put it, 'the ontological colonial difference at the heart of his thinking about the sovereign subject'. His international legal framework aimed at deliberately preempting Indigenous resistance and revolts of enslaved people, demonstrating that, for him, the Indigenous 'is always already constituted as external to universal Man' (ibid: 15). Even when he invoked the rights of Indigenous populations not to be treated 'too harshly' – most famously, in his belatedly discovered *De rebus Indicis* (1603–09) – Grotius had in mind, first and foremost, the interests of the Dutch East India Company, which commissioned him to write this treatise in the first place.

In the Enlightenment era, natural law theories still shaped mainstream understandings of international law, with an ever more pronounced instrumentalist undercurrent. Bemoaning the decline of a Christian *corpus mysticum politicum*, 'the universal juridical community of the Middle Ages' (Klenner 1996: 200) (or, as Wynter has it, the Christian *homo politicus*), the German jurist Samuel Freiherr von Pufendorf saw not only 'men' as moral entities, but also vested sovereign states with compound moral personhood (Fiorillo 2017: 200). Since 'Man alone understands the Nature and Constitution of *Peace*', this is what distinguishes 'him' from beasts and gives 'him' absolute control over them (Pufendorf 1698 [1672]: 432). States' rights were similar and related to those of (Enlightened) 'men'. Another German jurist and philosopher, Christian Wolff, who – in high Enlightenment fashion – took it upon himself to excel as an encyclopedic 'systematizer of all areas of knowledge' (Haakonssen 2012: 1106), dubbed also as an apologist for the mercantilist welfare and the police state (Bloch 1986: 50–1; Kleinlein 2017: 220). His *Jus gentium methodo scientifica pertractum* stipulated that nations, just like people, 'ought to be cultured and civilized, not barbarous. For nations ought to perfect themselves and consequently their intelligence' (Wolff 2017 [1749]: 50). Further, both individuals and nations could be prone to vices, and treated accordingly: A nation is said to be vicious, if a very great number pollute themselves by every kind of vice; it is said to be intemperate, if it is a common custom to delight in excessive drinking; it is said to be licentious, if its common vice has been lust (ibid: 41).

And one such nation, featuring prominently in all treatises on international law and relations, was the Ottoman Empire. There, most commentators agreed, same-sex attraction 'being rampant, the population was on a steady decline. Women subverted the "just" rule of men, while darker races subverted the more "natural" rule of whites' (Kaiser 2000: 8). Therefore, Wolff's epistolary correspondent, the philosopher Gottfried Wilhelm von Leibniz, saw 'Muslims as enemies of reason and civilization' and spoke 'of the Turkish pestilence, the nest of Saracens, [and] the plague of Islam' (Almond 2006: 468, 480). As far as Wolff was concerned, he may have been ousted from his first university chair at Halle for his 'ungodly' admiration of Confucianism, and his views of certain non-European nations *as* nations may have set off alarm bells in some quarters of European academia, but he never questioned an inherent moral and rational hierarchy among nations. 'Hence it is plain', Wolff concluded, 'that what has been approved by the more civilized nations is the law of nations' (Wolff 2017 [1749]: 24).

Another famous eighteenth-century international lawyer, Emer de Vattel, also saw the Prophet Muḥammad 'and his successors', including the Ottomans, as having 'desolated and subdued Asia' (Vattel 1916 [1758], II: 115).

He appeared to reject European imperialism, but he advocated that 'non-productive' nations be stripped of their land and sovereignty:

> Every nation is [. . .] obliged by the law of nature to cultivate the land that has fallen to its share; and it has no right to enlarge its boundaries, or to have recourse to the assistance of other nations, but in proportion as the land in its possession is incapable of furnishing it with necessaries. Those nations (such as [. . .] some modern Tartars) who inhabit fertile countries but disdain to cultivate their lands [. . .] deserve to be extirpated as savages and pernicious beasts.
>
> *(ibid, I: 37)*

Furthermore, 'although the conquest of the civilized empires of Peru and Mexico was a notorious usurpation, the establishment of many colonies on the continent of North America might, on their confining themselves within just bounds, be extremely lawful'; in part, because, according to Vattel, the Indigenous 'people of those extensive tracts ranged through rather than inhabited them' (ibid, I: 38). His obligation to cultivate the land extended, effectively, to dispossession or 'appropriation of a public nature' and conquest in all but name (Craven 2012: 878). As Anthony Anghie has argued (2011: 251), Vattel's approach to imperialism was dual: he condemned the kind of imperialism that Grotius justified (giving states license to use force to remedy a 'wrong' against natural law), but he approved of settler colonialism. In Vattel's own words, European settlers 'have not [. . .] deviated from the views of Nature in confining the Indians within narrow limits' (Vattel 1916 [1758], I: 160–1).

Such views were, of course, largely congruent with those of the *philosophes* of Enlightenment. Montesquieu, too, rejected Spanish colonial behavior, calling it 'one of the most dangerous wounds that the human species ever received' (Montesquieu 1989 [1748]: 37), and – somewhat ambiguously – he rejected enslavement: 'As all men are born equal, one must say that slavery [*l'esclavage*] is against nature, although in certain countries it is founded on a natural reason' (ibid: 252). But he tended to avoid the subject of the French trade in enslaved Africans and use his acerbic irony to mask state responsibility for such a trade (Miller 2008: 65). Voltaire – who, tellingly, funded the French East India Company in the 1740s – admired such a 'humorous' treatment of enslavement, noting that Montesquieu 'painted Black slavery with the brush of Molière' (Voltaire 1876–83: XVIII, 604). For his own part, Voltaire drolly wrote:

> It is a serious question among [Africans] whether they are descended from monkeys or whether the monkeys come from them. Our wise men have said that man was created in the image of God. Now here is a lovely

image of the Divine Maker: a flat and black nose with little or hardly any intelligence.

(Voltaire 1876–83: XXI, 462)

Meanwhile, Rousseau contended that Linnaeus' nomenclature was as great an invention as algebra had been for mathematicians (Schiebinger 2013 [1993]: 12). He, too, rejected 'the right to enslave', while contradictorily remaining almost completely aloof to the trans-Atlantic trade in enslaved human beings. Besides, his writings reveal an explicit disdain for anyone who has been enslaved, using the epithets such as 'vile', 'groveling' and 'obedient' to describe such persons (Miller 2008: 69). Thus, the *philosophes* reserved such Enlightenment commodities as freedom and knowledge for some, while making grand pronouncements that they belonged to everyone. And the humanity of those whom European colonizers exploited the most was always construed as suspect, fleeting or contingent.

Early Racial Capitalism in Senegambia and Its Many Others

European Enlightenment literature and the attendant hierarchical ordering of human and nonhuman lifeforms in natural and legal sciences had a cumulative and lasting effect on the inextricable ways racial capitalism and the gender binary were being forged in eighteenth-century Senegambia. While extractive (un)gendering and racialization-*cum*-dehumanization were increasingly used in the French and English enslavement-centered entrepôts in Senegal and the Gambia 'to position economics as the site of rationality and knowability' (Morgan 2021: 8), Enlightenment sciences tasked with other forms of knowledge in/of the world, such as botany and legal philosophy, all helped sustain this course. Speciation, for example, assisted the processes of vertical categorization of both humans and their environs, with 'native' lifeworlds deemed 'naturally' ripe for dispossession. And natural law theories, with their distinct and deadly power to project 'a single and coherent reality' (Koskenniemi 2007: 30), made such dispossession lawful and morally justifiable.

Officers, traders, enslavers and occasional clergymen who found themselves in the service of European chartered companies or managing their states' broader imperial interests in West Africa largely considered themselves 'cultivated' people, with the literature of their time, such as the complete works of Rousseau and Voltaire, often found on their shelves (Miller 2008: 62). Voltaire's *Alzire, ou les Américains: Tragédie en cinq actes et en vers* was performed in the summer of 1766, exactly 30 years after its premiere in Paris, onboard the enslavers' ship *Le Comte d'Hérouville*, stationed on Île de Gorée, a strategically important French entrepôt that operated its own network of trading villages along the Senegalese Petite Côte. The amateur performers – all men, according to a contemporary account, engaged in the trans-Atlantic trade in enslaved Senegambians – saw nothing particularly ironic or troubling, given their daily work, in acting both 'male' and 'female' roles in a play that extolled 'the "civilized" quality of the Incas' and their efforts against Spanish enslavers (ibid: 73). Nor would, presumably, Voltaire, who 'completely elide[d] African slavery in *Alzire*' and welcomed, with 'delight', the naming of another enslavers' ship after him – *Le Voltaire* (ibid: 74, 77). Similar standards applied to the sphere of proto-colonial law and politics. For instance, that same summer of 1766, Colonel Charles O'Hara, the royal governor of the newly created but ultimately ill-fated British Province of Senegambia, advocated in a dispatch to London the necessity of direct rule and 'making the Native dependent on [British] Government', including by means of unenforceable and fraudulent treaties (something the French had already practiced in the region), or 'by putting ammunition into the Hands of any one [Senegambian] Nation, by this means keep[ing] the rest in Order' (O'Hara 1766: 103–18; Dziennik 2015; Newton 2013).

While deceit, warmongering and double standards were routinely employed to further French and British commercial and military interests, it was the new science of gender-binary racial capitalist categorization – employed to aid the trans-Atlantic trade in enslaved Africans – that intervened most fundamentally into Senegambian lifeworlds. One category, in particular, emerged to describe those deemed legally/socially/naturally enslaveable. Senegambians from diverse social strata and polities could become 'captives' (*captifs*) – a term the French ordinarily used when they referred to the enslaved bound for the trans-oceanic commerce. Michel Jajolet de la Courbe, a French aristocrat who lived and worked in Senegambia in the last decades of the seventeenth and first decades of the eighteenth centuries, provided a handy definition for this term-of-art that emphasized the alleged criminality and inferior social markers of the enslaved: 'The *captifs* are either people taken in war, or others who have committed some crime, or who are accused of sorcery, or who are of captive race' (Courbe 1913: 194).

Once so categorized, the *captifs* were ordered into 'men', 'women' and, occasionally, children, or 'boys' and 'girls' – sometimes even before they would reach a European trading post. But it was primarily a French or British entrepôt in Senegambia and then, an enslavers' ship, that would serve as the spaces of heightened and forceful (un)gendering and racialization of the *captifs*. As for racialized descriptions, the designation *nègre*, along with its age-stratified and gender-binary variants, was ubiquitous. And with regards to the process that Jessica Marie Johnson has described as 'the violent ungendering of the slave trade' (2020: 81), the enslaved would be ordinarily denied the bodily markers of their cosmological, social or gender difference and assigned a place on the ship, with 'men' given the most and 'girls' the least space, before they were sent onto the perilous voyage through the Middle Passage. So rationalized, the enslaved's gender was reduced to a mere spatial and commercial category, based on the enslaver's crude observations of their rudimentary physique. A unit of value known as *pièce d'Indie* was then used to establish quotas and tariffs, which undergirded an early capitalist type of domination that ushered in the mode of production based on a highly reductive and forceful concept of personhood of the enslaved (Hamzić 2023 [Forthcoming]).

Such would-be personhood of the enslaved stood in stark contrast to eighteenth-century Senegambian conceptualizations of human, nonhuman and more-than-human being-in-the-world. Mande oral traditions, for example, attested to the existence of a gender-variant water spirit, called Faro, who was central to Bamana selfhood and spirituality (Dieterlen 1951: 40–56). Bamana societies also harbored a positionality that a rare anthropological source describes as '[t]he hermaphrodite, [who,] being both male and female, is themself, materially, their own twin' (ibid: 87). Several Senegambian communities also included a gender-nonconforming role denoted in Fulfulde as *samarooka* and in Wolof as *gôr djiguène* (Regis 2003: 53; M'Baye 2019: 166). Among Fulɓe, a pre-Muslim genesis story suggested that the Supreme Being, called Geno, created the world from a single drop of milk, populating it at first with an array of gender-nonspecific lesser deities (*laareeji*) and then with Kiikala, the first man, Naagara, the first woman, and Ndurbeele, the first bovine, a 'hermaphrodite' who gave birth to the first 22 zebu cattle (Bah 2011: 96–100; Sow 1966). Thus, the ordering and distinction between deities, humans and animals, or with respect to an assumed sex or gender, eluded and exceeded drastically the European gender binary and speciation.

Another clear manifestation of Senegambian gender, sexual and cosmological diversity occurred among members of the endogamous artisanal status group – a 'caste' with its roots in Mande, Wolof and Soninke societies and hieropraxis, which by the eighteenth century was also common among the Fulɓe, Arabo-Berbers and other populations in the region. As *ɲamakalaw* – their collective name in Mande languages – suggests, members of the artisanal status group were believed to possess extraordinary access to the foundational life force, *ɲama*, and be the beings with their own special temporality, contact with history, and bodily and gender-variant properties. The *ɲamakalaw* occupied a deeply ambiguous position in society and were contradictorily described as feared, loathed, desired, necessary and respected – all at the same time. Their internal sub-divisions, based on specialized services they provided to society, were many, of which *jeliw*, or griots, were perhaps the most idiosyncratic subgroup. *Jeliw*'s artistry (*jeliya*) extended wide and deep – from music, dance, companionship to warriors and advice to nobles and local leaders to the art of storytelling and oral history proper, with its many mystical properties.

There were multiple forms of speech a *jeli* could resort to; from an ordinary, 'clear speech' (*kuma jɛ*) to the dark (*dibi*) and mysterious language of the diviner (*dibikan*, lit. 'dark language'), spoken in a series of conjoined nouns and noun phrases (such as *jugu-ni-dimi*, 'evil-and-pain') that ordinary people could not understand without an interpreter (Hoffman 2000: 82–3). An accomplished griot storyteller (*ŋara*) was expected to perform a wide variety of ritualized speech (*kilisi*), which could either benefit or harm the target. The power of *kilisiw* could also be enhanced using various substances known to possess *ɲama*, including those that may cause physical harm (*korote*). The essence of speech (*kuma kise*) as such – and especially the variants of speech that belonged to griots' vocabulary proper – was that it contained *ɲama*. And, because of this maxim (*ɲama bɛ kuma la*, 'there is *ɲama* in speech'), the Mande believed, as their saying goes, that *kuma tɛ mɔgɔ bolo, mɔgɔ de bɛ kuma bolo* ('speech is not in people's hands, people are in the hands of speech') (ibid: 18). Imbued with knowledge of the *ɲa* ('the means to harness *ɲama*'), the griot was not just a social historian, but also a direct – if mystical – link with the past. Temporality was, in fact, griots' chief domain, since past events were often believed to be in a causal relationship with present and future happenings. Owing to griots' *ɲama*-laden storytelling, oral histories were socially constructed and understood as both the history of today and the history of tomorrow – with the *body* of the oral historian mediating any potential temporal and mystical borders between them. *Jeliw*'s unique wordsmithry also meant that their *ɲama*-laden bodies were considered volatile. They could be a blessing, or they could wreak havoc. It is for this reason that *jeliw* were endogamous, often lived their separate lives and were sometimes disposed of in baobab trees upon their death (Conrad 1981).

Griots' bodily and lingual difference was also reflected in the way they expressed their gender(s). In marked contrast to nobles (*hɔrɔnw*) in a Mande community, whose propriety and decorum were subject to strict social control, *jeliw* could behave 'outrageously' and dress 'showily', with no particular regard to what may have been socially construed as 'male' or 'female' attire, manners and hairstyles. Because of their half-outcast, half-otherworldly status, griots were also allowed to 'mock with impunity' anyone they considered unworthy of their praise (ibid: 15).

Unsurprisingly, griots' social segregation and behavioral difference caused disbelief, anguish and – sometimes – ire in European travelogues and commercial literature of the time. John (Jean) Barbot, an employee of the Compagnie du Sénégal, called them 'a sort of sycophants', who, being considered 'infamous', were 'much despis'd by all the other Blacks' (1732: 55). Dominique Harcourt Lamiral, a commercial agent in the French outpost of Saint-Louis, described with indignation a griot always accompanying the local ruler, for whom 'the King cares very much' (1789: 100). René-Claude Geoffroy de

Villeneuve, who spent a total of four years in the region in the 1780s as aide de camp to a French governor and penned a four-tome bestseller on Senegal, similarly depicted the griots in constant presence of the *damel* of Kayor as 'a species of histrions', and remarked of another aristocrat's 'incapacity' as being related to his 'passing his days surrounded with *guiriots* and *guiriottes*' (1814, III: 36, 166). Indeed, many observers wondered exactly what went on between aristocrats and their *griot* advisors and entertainers. Thus, Armand Corre alarmingly wrote that, '[i]n Boké, I saw a griot in the company of a Fulɓe prince, whose lascivious dances reflected the more intimate role he had to fulfil in the house of His Highness' (1894: 80, n1).

This curiosity, however, did not translate into any form of special status ascribed to the *ɲamakalaw* who entered as *captifs* the gender-binary ledgers and logs of European enslavers. If anything, they were feared as potential instigators and leaders of enslaved's revolts and punished harshly for any insubordination. Thus, onboard *Le Courrier de Bourbon*, sailing in 1723 from Senegambia to Louisiana, a 45-year-old enslaved was identified as 'the sorcerer (*sorcier*) who raised [the other *captifs*'] vain hopes' of liberation, for which, according to the ship's pilot, this likely *griot* was hoisted 'to the top of the main mast and fire[d] on with rifles, until death ensued' (Directeurs de la Compagnie [des Indes] à St Robert: 1723).

Epilogue: Unlivable Pasts, Unbelievable Subjectivities

Histories of race and gender tend to overlook such Senegambian complexities of being-in-the-world, not least because these narratives do not fit neatly either 'recuperational' or strictly identitarian approaches to the eighteenth-century Black Atlantic or Senegambia proper. To begin with, there is an irreconcilable difference in method. What can be 'recovered' are but scattered remnants of the past that was either purposely disappeared in the (proto-)colonial archive – a history that was, in C. Riley Snorton's words, rendered 'unlivable' (2017: 7) – or subjected to an abiding Enlightenment-inspired empiricism in which the storytelling Senegambian human, nonhuman and more-than-human – as the forms of life and knowledge incongruent with the categories invented to prop up the racialized, gender-binary colonial difference – were seen as outright *unbelievable*. After all, it was not so long ago that a 'leading Africanist' bemoaned the would-be 'historical inaccuracy' of West African oral histories – and griots, presumably, as their oft principal purveyors – despite them once arousing 'high expectations [. . .] among historians' (Curtin 1975: 201). Furthermore, there is an insurmountable distance in language. To invest *jelikan*, the Mande griots' language proper, or their senses of the self-in-the-world, with the meaning and identitary terms-of-art of an elsewhere that is 'here and now' would not be that dissimilar to a telltale linguistic and semantic exercise in (binary) gendering at the end of the eighteenth century. Traditionally, the word *jeli* had no gender, either formal or semantic. But, as that century was drawing to a close, the gendered forms of the Mande word for griot (*jelimuso* for 'female griot' and *jelike* for 'male griot') slowly came to use, as a reflection of the new dominant gender politics at play and so as to help in translation from other languages, most commonly from French and Arabic. To the best of my knowledge, the male-gendered word *jelike* made its first appearance in the Scottish explorer Mungo Park's popular narrative, published in 1799, where it was transcribed as *Jilli kea* in reference to a 'singing man' (1799: 239).

Instead, what eighteenth-century Senegambian storytelling and lifeworlds seem to suggest is the need, in Lisa Lowe's words, for a 'history hesitant' method; for '[h]esitation, rather than rushing to recover what has been lost'; for '[h]esitation [that] may provide a space, a different temporality, so that we may [. . .] reckon with the connections that could have been but were lost and are thus not yet' (2018: 98). *Blackness* and *transness* – two of today's critical terms-of-art that seem relatable to the experiences of eighteenth-century Senegambians resisting the gender-binary racialized colonial difference – invite precisely this form of generative hesitation. Instead of them being hastily applied, or dismissed, perhaps it would be more fitting to ask, along with Snorton (2017: 7), 'What pasts have been submerged and discarded to solidify – or, more precisely, indemnify – a set of procedures that would render blackness and transness as distinct categories of social valuation?' Such differentiation, although related to the Enlightenment grammar of race and gender, also provided for a wide variety of counter-politics of (un)belonging – the strategies of survival and resistance that accounted for 'an originary irruption' (Bey 2020: 67), an *uninscribed* (Fleischmann 2019: 64) elsewhere of Blackness and transness in the aftermath of colonial and racial capitalist dispossession and distemporalization.

To account for such interruptive senses of the self and/in the past, in Senegambia or elsewhere, it might be instructive to recall Wynter's insurrectionary *homo narrans*, with its rootedness in language that was worldmaking (Wynter and McKittrick 2015: 31). Her focus on the *genres* in being human, rather than the more prevalent (and colonially inflected) categories of social difference such as race and gender, culminates in an understanding that 'with being human *everything is praxis*' (ibid: 34). To that end, her 'invocations of a humanity rooted in narration' (Alagraa 2018: 165) that disrupt the centrality, or 'overrepresentation', of racial capitalist Man chime well with posthumanist tendencies to displace Leonardo da Vinci's 'Virtuvian ideal of Man as the standard of both perfection and perfectibility' (Braidotti 2013: 23) by focusing on matter and the material free from dialectical oppositions, including those resultant in categorical binaries, and on rethinking difference as *differing*, that is, 'as a complex process [. . .] based on the centrality of the relation to multiple others' (ibid: 56). Turning to praxis and process reveals, in both cases, the fallacy of hitherto dominant orders of truth about one's selfhood, body and environs (Wynter and McKittrick 2015: 32) and throws into crisis the presumed boundaries between them. Suddenly, for example, in a true Groszian sense, bodies become volatile and leaky (Grosz 1994), and their knowability is not predicated on (the knowability of) gender (Braidotti 2013: 99; Wynter and McKittrick 2015: 33; Hamzić 2019: 143–4). Their existence becomes processual, escaping any narrow categorization, akin to 'a system, or series of open-ended systems, functioning within other huge systems [that bodies] cannot control through which [bodies] can access and acquire [their] abilities and capacities' (Grosz 2004: 3). Differing – lingual or otherwise – is something 'we' do, or it is done to 'us', to make sense of such complex symbiotic relationships.

But, as recent works in decolonial Black/trans/feminist critique affirm, even if so open-ended, bodies can imprison and cause harm. Marquis Bey, for example, has argued for an engagement that is not determined wholly by or confined to the surface of corporeality. And if aspects of the body have come to be that which are formed by violent forces, it is necessary to find liberation in the aspects that are not confined to the body, that is to say, 'it is necessary to find liberation in the aspects of subjectivity that exceed and ooze out of the body' (2022: 3–4). A Groszian turn, to be sure, and materialist at that, albeit one that cautions 'that matter and materiality are not to be equated with mere being, a transparent and unmediated facticity of "the body"' (ibid: 8), whatever this might entail. Instead, having displaced the material body as an 'unmitigated bearer and disseminator of truth, as if matter cannot be and has not been touched, as it were', Bey proposes to study and experiment with how materialization has and can occur differently (ibid). To that end, Bey sees neither transness nor Blackness as 'tied to a specific kind of body or identity'; rather, they are 'inflections of mutinous subjectivities that have been captured and consolidated into bodily legibilities' (ibid: 9). Returning to the eighteenth century, one can see how such capturing and consolidation had been wrought out through legal or lawlike biocentricity bent on the colonial difference. And, in the present or the immediate future, as Rosi Braidotti warns, the logic of advanced capitalism might no longer rely on the production of difference 'as we know it' but on new, rhizomatic commodification of life (2013: 60).

While modes of capitalist commodification change in time, there's little hope that international law will 'evolve away' from being one if its chief helpers; the way Enlightenment international lawyers legitimized and naturalized the colonial difference – inclusive of the racialized gender binary – did not substantially differ that much from international law's role in upholding and reproducing cisheteropatriarchy today (Baars 2019a). If working toward law's withering away – or law's abolition – remains a constant of radical politics (Pashukanis 2001 [1924]; Knox 2016; Hamzić 2017; Baars 2019b), so, too, should an understanding of law's continuously violent role in sustaining deeply hierarchical and contingent forms of would-be 'natural' life. To that end, as this chapter has shown, the challenge for posthumanist critique concerned with law might be twofold: first, how to include material, localized, multiple senses of the past in any ongoing reworldings and re-imaginations of the present and the future, so as to rethink temporalities and recount anew (porosely, fragmentally) – rather than 'recover' – insurrectionary times; and second, how to retell critically law's manyfold complicity in systemic world-destroying and worldmaking projects – such as that of racial capitalism – without succumbing to the false promise of law's salvatory powers.

In each case, certain hesitancy might be in order, so as to stave off 'the compulsion to make visible' – or to inscribe, capture and consolidate – within any past or current onto-epistemic orthodoxy (Lowe 2018: 98). Insofar as this work still entails telling (foundational) stories, à la *jeliw* and countless others, it might be instructive to keep an eye on diverse materializations – and temporalities – of the 'figure on the horizon' (Alagraa 2018: 164), some of which, as we have seen, invite more sustained thinking toward new figurations of posthuman *homo narrans*.

References

Alagraa, B. (2018) '*Homo Narrans* and the Science of the Word: Toward a Caribbean Radical Imagination', *Critical Ethnic Studies*, 4(2): 164–81.

Almond, I. (2006) 'Leibniz, Historicism, and the "Plague of Islam"', *Eighteenth-Century Studies*, 39(4): 463–83.

Anghie, A. (2011) 'Vattel and Colonialism: Some Preliminary Observations', in V. Chetail and P. Haggenmacher (eds) *Vattel's International Law from a XXIst Century Perspective/Le Droit International de Vattel vu du XXIe Siècle*, The Hague: Brill | Nijhoff, 237–53.

Baars, G. (2019a) 'Queer Cases Unmake Gendered Law, or, Fucking Law's Gendering Function', *Australian Feminist Law Journal*, 45(1): 15–62. DOI: https://doi.org/10.1080/13200968.2019.1667777

Baars, G. (2019b) *The Corporation, Law and Capitalism: A Radical Perspective on the Role of Law in the Global Political Economy*, Leiden: Brill.

Bah, T.S. (2011) 'Fulɓe', in J.A. Shoup (ed) *Ethnic Groups of Africa and the Middle East: An Encyclopedia*, Santa Barbara: ABC-CLIO, 96–100.

Balani, S. (2018) 'From Botany to Community: A Legacy of Classification', in S. Sheikh and U. Orlow (eds) *Uriel Orlow: Theatrum Botanicum*, Tilburg: Sternberg Press.

Banton, M. (1998) *Racial Theories*, Cambridge: Cambridge University Press.

Barbot, J. (1732) *A Description of the Coasts of North and South-Guinea, and of Ethiopia Inferior, Vulgarly Angola, Being a New and Accurate Account of the Western Maritime Countries of Africa*, London: Churchill.

Bey, M. (2020) *The Problem of the Negro as a Problem for Gender*, Minneapolis: University of Minnesota Press.

Bey, M. (2022) *Black Trans Feminism*, Durham: Duke University Press.

Bloch, E. (1986) *Natural Law and Human Dignity*, Translated by D.J. Schmidt, Cambridge: MIT Press.

Braidotti, R. (2013) *The Posthuman*, Cambridge: Polity Press.

Bunge, K. (2017) 'Francisco de Vitoria: A Redesign of Global Order on the Threshold of the Middle Ages to Modern Times', in S. Kadelbach, T. Kleinlein and D. Roth-Isigkeit (eds) *System, Order, and International Law: Legal Thought from Machiavelli to Hegel*, Oxford: Oxford University Press, 38–55.

Césaire, A. (1945) 'Poésie et Connaissance', *Tropiques*, 12: 158–70.

Conrad, D.C. (1981) 'The Role of Oral Artists in the History of Mali', PhD Thesis, SOAS University of London, London.

Corre, A. (1894) *L'Ethnographie Criminelle D'après Les Observations et Les Statistiques Judiciaires Recueillies Dans Les Colonies Françaises*, Paris: C. Reinwald & Cie.

Courbe, M.J.D.L. (1913) *Premier voyage du sieur de La Courbe fait à la coste d'Afrique en 1685*, Paris: E. Champion.

Craven, M. (2012) 'Colonialism and Domination', in B. Fassbender and A. Peters (eds) *The Oxford Handbook of the History of International Law*, Oxford: Oxford University Press, 862–89.

Curtin, P.D. (1975) 'The Uses of Oral Tradition in Senegambia: Maalik Sii and the Foundation of Bundu', *Cahiers d'Études Africaines*, 58(15): 189–202.

Dieterlen, G. (1951) *Essai sur la religion Bambara*, Paris: Presses universitaires de France.

Directeurs de la Compagnie [des Indes] à St Robert (1723) 'Directeurs de la Compagnie [des Indes] à St. Robert, Directeur [de la concession du] Sénégal', the *Archives nationales d'outre-mer*, Aix-en-Provence, COL C6 7, February.

Dziennik, M.P. (2015) ' "Till These Experiments Be Made": Senegambia and British Imperial Policy in the Eighteenth Century', *English Historical Review*, 130(546): 1132–61.

Fara, P. (2003) *The Story of Carl Linnaeus and Joseph Banks: Sex, Botany & Empire*, Cambridge: Icon Books.

Fiorillo, V. (2017) 'States, as Ethico-Political Subjects of International Law: The Relationship between Theory and Practice in the International Politics of Samuel Pufendorf', in S. Kadelbach, T. Kleinlein and D. Roth-Isigkeit (eds) *System, Order, and International Law: Legal Thought from Machiavelli to Hegel*, Oxford: Oxford University Press, 199–215.

Fitzmaurice, A. (2012) 'Discovery, Conquest, and Occupation of Territory', in B. Fassbender and A. Peters (eds) *The Oxford Handbook of the History of International Law*, Oxford: Oxford University Press, 840–61.

Fleischmann, T. (2019) *Time Is the Thing a Body Moves Through*, Minneapolis: Coffee House Press.

Gentili, A. (1933 [1598]) 'De jure belli, libri tres', in J.B. Scott (ed) *The Classics of International Law*, Vol. I, Oxford: Oxford University Press.

Grosz, E. (1994) *Volatile Bodies: Towards a Corporeal Feminism*, Bloomington: Indiana University Press.

Grosz, E. (2004) *The Nick of Time*, Durham: Duke University Press.

Haakonssen, K. (2012) 'Christian Wolff (1679–1754)', in B. Fassbender and A. Peters (eds) *The Oxford Handbook of the History of International Law*, Oxford: Oxford University Press, 1106–9.

Hamzić, V. (2017) 'Alegality: Outside and Beyond the Legal Logic of Late Capitalism', in H. Brabazon (ed) *Neoliberal Legality: Understanding the Role of Law in the Neoliberal Project*, Abingdon: Routledge, 190–209.

Hamzić, V. (2019) 'What's Left of the Real?', in D. Fassin and B.E. Harcourt (eds) *A Time for Critique*, New York: Columbia University Press, 132–49.

Hamzić, V. (2023 [Forthcoming]) 'Labors in Time and Subjectivity: Gender Nonconformity and Racial Capitalism in the Making of Eighteenth-Century New Orleans', in K. Engle and N. Hoad (eds) *Beyond Inequality: New Paradigms for Addressing the Future of Work*, New York: Columbia University Press.

Haraway, D.J. (2016) *Staying with the Trouble: Making Kin in the Chthulucene*, Durham: Duke University Press.

Hoffman, B.G. (2000) *Griots at War: Conflict, Conciliation, and Caste in Mande*, Bloomington: Indiana University Press.

Johnson, J.M. (2020) *Wicked Flesh: Black Women, Intimacy, and Freedom in the Atlantic World*, Philadelphia: University of Pennsylvania Press.

Kaiser, T. (2000) 'The Evil Empire? The Debate on Turkish Despotism in Eighteenth-Century French Political Culture', *Journal of Modern History*, 72(1): 6–34.

Kleinlein, T. (2017) 'Christian Wolff: System as an Episode?', in S. Kadelbach, T. Kleinlein and D. Roth-Isigkeit (eds) *System, Order, and International Law: Legal Thought from Machiavelli to Hegel*, Oxford: Oxford University Press, 216–39.

Klenner, H. (1996) 'Bileams Pferd auf die Kanzeln! Zur Naturrechts- und Völkerrechtslehre des Samuel Pufendorf', in B. Geyer and H. Goerlich (eds) *Samuel Pufendorf und seine Wirkungen bis auf die heutige Zeit*, Baden-Baden: Nomos, 195–208.

Knox, R. (2016) 'Valuing Race? Stretched Marxism and the Logic of Imperialism', *London Review of International Law*, 4(1): 81–126.

Koskenniemi, M. (2007) *"Not Excepting the Iroquois Themselves . . .": Machiavelli, Pufendorf and the Prehistory of International Law*, Max Weber Lecture Series, Florence: European University Institute.

Lafleur, G. (2018) *The Natural History of Sexuality in Early America*, Baltimore: Johns Hopkins University Press.

Linnaeus, C. (1735) *Systema Naturae Per Regna Tria Naturae Systematice Proposita Per Classes, Ordines, Genera, & Species*, Leiden: Lugduni Batavorum.

Linnaeus, C. (1737) *Genera Plantarum*, Leiden: Conrad Wishoff.

Linnaeus, C. (1758) *Systema Naturae Per Regna Tria Naturae, Secundum Classes, Ordines, Genera, Species, Cum Characteribus, Differentiis, Synonymis, Locis*, Stockholm: Holmiae.

Linnaeus, C. (1766–68) *Systema naturae per regna tria naturae, secundum classes, ordines, genera, species, cum characteribus, differentiis, synonymis, locis*, Stockholm: Holmiae.

Lowe, L. (2018) 'History Hesitant', *Social Text*, 33(4): 85–107.

Luciano, D. and M.Y. Chen (2015) 'Has the Queer Ever Been Human?', *Gay and Lesbian Quarterly*, 21(2–3): 182–207.

M'Baye, B. (2019) 'Afropolitan Sexual and Gender Identities in Colonial Senegal', *Humanities*, 8(4): 1–16. DOI: https://doi.org/10.3390/h8040166

Melamed, J. (2015) 'Racial Capitalism', *Critical Ethnic Studies*, 1(1): 76–85.

Miller, C.L. (2008) *The French Atlantic Triangle: Literature and Culture of the Slave Trade*, Durham: Duke University Press.
Montesquieu, C.D. (1989 [1748]) *The Spirit of the Laws*, Translated and edited by A.M. Cohler, B.C. Miller and H.S. Stone, Cambridge: Cambridge University Press.
Morgan, J.L. (2021) *Reckoning with Slavery: Gender, Kinship, and Capitalism in the Early Black Atlantic*, Durham: Duke University Press.
Newton, J.D. (2013) 'Naval Power and the Province of Senegambia, 1758–1779', *Journal of Maritime Research*, 15(2): 129–47.
O'Hara, C. (1766) 'O'Hara to Secretary Conway', *Shelburne Papers*, William L. Clemens Library, Ann Arbor, MI, vol. 81, fos 103–18, 28 May.
Park, M. (1799) *Travels in the Interior Districts of Africa: Performed Under the Direction and Patronage of the African Association, in the Years 1795, 1796, and 1797*, London: W. Bulmer & Co.
Pashukanis, E. (2001 [1924]) *The General Theory of Law and Marxism*, Somerset: Transaction Publishers.
Pufendorf, S.F.V. (1698 [1672]) *De jure naturae et gentium, libri octo*, Amsterdam: Johann Paul.
Regis, H.A. (2003) *Fulbe Voices: Marriage, Islam, and Medicine in Northern Cameroon*, Boulder: Westview Press.
Robinson, C.J. (1983) *Black Marxism*, London: Zed Press.
Schiebinger, L. (2013 [1993]) *Nature's Body: Gender in the Making of Modern Science*, New Brunswick: Rutgers University Press.
Sepúlveda, J.G.D. (1941 [1547]) *Tratado sobre las Justas Causas de la Guerra contra los Indios*, Translated by M. Menendez y Pelayo and M. Garcia-Pelayo, Mexico, DF: Fondo de Cultura Económica.
Smellie, W. (1790) *The Philosophy of Natural History*, Vol. I, Edinburgh: Printed for the Heirs of Charles Elliot, etc.
Snorton, C.R. (2017) *Black on Both Sides: A Racial History of Trans Identity*, Minneapolis: University of Minnesota Press.
Sow, A.I. (1966) *La Femme, la vache, la foi: Écrivains et poètes du Foûta-Djalon*, Paris: Julliard.
Spillers, H. (1987) 'Mama's Baby, Papa's Maybe: An American Grammar Book', *Diacritics*, 17(2): 64–81.
Stelder, M. (2021) 'The Colonial Difference in Hugo Grotius: Rational Man, Slavery and Indigenous Dispossession', *Postcolonial Studies*, 1–20. DOI: https://doi.org/10.1080/13688790.2021.1979297
Vattel, E.D. (1916 [1758]) *The Law of Nations or Principles of the Law of Nature Applied to the Conduct of Nations and Sovereigns*, Vol. I-II, Translated by C.G. Fenwick, Washington, DC: Carnegie Institution of Washington.
Villeneuve, R.-C.G.D. (1814) *L'Afrique, ou histoire, mœurs, usages et coutumes des Africains*, Vol. III, Paris: Nepveu.
Voltaire, F.M.A.D. (1876–83) *Oeuvres Complètes*, Vol. XVIII and XXI, Paris: Garnier.
Weheliye, A.G. (2014) *Habeas Viscus: Racializing Assemblages, Biopolitics, and Black Feminist Theories of the Human*, Durham: Duke University Press.
Wolff, C. (2017 [1749]) *The Law of Nations Treated According to the Scientific Method*, Translated by J.C. Drake, Carmel: Liberty Fund.
Wynter, S. (2006) 'On How We Mistook the Map for the Territory, and Reimprisoned Ourselves in Our Unbearable Wrongness of Being, of *Desêtre*: Black Studies

Toward the Human Project', in L.R. Gordon and J.A. Gordon (eds) *Not Only the Master's Tools: African-American Studies in Theory and Practice*, Boulder: Paradigm Publishers, 107–69.

Wynter, S. (2015) 'The Ceremony Found: Towards the Autopoetic Turn/Overturn, Its Autonomy of Human Agency and Extraterritoriality of (Self-)Cognition', in J.R. Ambroise and S. Broeck (eds) *Black Knowledges/Black Struggles: Essays in Critical Epistemology*, Liverpool: Liverpool University Press, 184–252.

Wynter, S. and K. McKittrick (2015) 'Unparalleled Catastrophe for Our Species? Or, to Give Humanness a Different Future: Conversations', in K. McKittrick (ed) *Sylvia Wynter: On Being Human as Praxis*, Durham: Duke University Press, 9–89.

Yusoff, K. (2018) *A Billion Black Anthropocenes or None*, Minneapolis: University of Minnesota Press.

PART 3

The Environment and the Nonhuman

8

TERRAQUEOUS FEMINISMS AND THE INTERNATIONAL LAW OF THE SEA

Gina Heathcote

This chapter is structured through the examination of three objects, the map, the ship and the robot, that span the nonhuman, the material and technology to envisage human–nonhuman relationships with the ocean while developing a posthuman feminist analysis of international law. I am interested in what an embodied human encounter with the ocean produces in terms of frames of knowledge, understandings of matter and ethical commitments and what that means for the international law of the sea. Important scholarship within international law on materiality and reproduction highlights the potential of objects and things, matter, to matter. This scholarship demonstrates how objects offer entry points to epistemologies and ethical transformation of the discipline away from, or to undo, the reproduction of the status quo through law (Hohman and Joyce 2018). This is recognition that:

> international law (which) has, in fact, been engaged, over the course of some five centuries of emergence and consolidation, in reproducing a very particular mode of human self-organisation, which is based on a historically and geographically extremely specific understanding and organising the relationship between individual human beings, human communities and the non-human world.
>
> *(Parfitt 2019: 8)*

The map, the container ship and the automated military vessel as ocean robotic: each of these objects is examined in this chapter to unmoor humanist epistemologies and their stranglehold on the production of knowledge within international law – in particular, the international law of the sea and the land-based jurisprudence that oceanic governance commences from.

DOI: 10.4324/9781032658032-12

As a posthuman feminist analysis, the chapter engages an international law of objects and the knowledge histories of the global order to move beyond feminist concerns that loop between resistance and compliance, within gender law reform strategies (Kouvo and Pearson 2007), toward theorizing of a terraqueous international legal subjectivity. My posthuman feminist approach follows Braidotti's account of the nexus between posthuman theories and feminist theories, as well as the twofold critique of humanism when posthuman and feminist theories are read together (2019). In holding a space for feminist approaches within my account of posthumanism the ways in which humanist frames have never completely unraveled their centering of a specific (male, European, white, Christian, heteronormative, able-bodied) subject that masters nature is exposed. Posthuman feminisms thus engage the Anthropocene and the vectors of identity that have privileged some humans within the humanist project. The international law of the sea, my site of inquiry in this chapter, inherits and reproduces the privilege of masculine, European power (Perera 2013): the casting of Aboriginal peoples as flora and fauna via the creation of the nation-state of Australia being an explicit example where difference is juxtaposed, feminized and legally rendered Other to European whiteness. For Perera, 'the seemingly timeless flow of oceans becomes enmeshed with the terrestrial – that is to say with the (geo)political and historical' (2013: 62) and the white, male, European explorer casts his gaze over the ocean and new territories alike: feminizing, taming, Othering. At the same time I incorporate technology and the posthuman proclivities of military capital in the development of nonhuman technologies at sea. This serves as an important reminder of the spectrum of posthuman encounters and the necessity of feminist interrogations of posthuman possibilities.

Alert to the international law of the sea as a masked history of privilege and empire (Ranganathan 2021), as a space of ongoing violent encounters (Barad 2019), facilitator of the global flow of capital (Campling and Colas 2021), and environmental carelessness (Johnson and VanderZwaag 2000), I offer an important lens for highlighting the risks and possibilities a turn to law, and/or the ocean, holds for posthuman feminisms. While international law is premised on the nation-state as the primary legal subject, defined through the control of land territories, I examine the expanding jurisdiction of states into the ocean, via the international law of the sea, and argue for an international law of the sea unmoored from land co-ordinates, baselines, ports, longitudes, and latitudes and, importantly, the state. I deploy terraqueous frames as a space of continuity with Indigenous knowledge frames and, equally, with the flows of military-capital that depend upon up land-based jurisprudence to submerge the histories and status quo of violent anthropocentric and humanist greed. I argue for the international law of the sea as providing a starting point for imagining legal subjectivity differently while acknowledging a different, non-state, nonhuman subjectivity demands an alternative conception of ontological and epistemological, and ultimately ethical, relations.

The chapter proceeds as follows. In section two, 'map', following an introduction to the international law of the sea, I examine the possibilities for a terraqueous map of the world. Drawing on Roberts' (2021) account of the expansions of state territorial and sovereign rights into the ocean, I examine the alternative map of ocean encapsulated by a map of the Pacific derived from the drawings of the arioi priest, Tupaia (Salmond 2005: 170; also see: Salmond 2012). Salmond (2005: 170) describes the Pacific arioi as 'orators, priests, navigators, travelling performers, warriors and famed lovers, distinguished by their tattoos and red barkcloth garments'. Tupaia encountered the Englishman Captain James Cook in 1767 and subsequently joined Cook's fleet in mapping the Pacific. Credited with considerable ingenuity and important contributions to the subsequent English exploration of the Pacific, Tupaia's map has, over time, been understood as simplified, incomprehensible and, more recently, as an important record of the intersection of two different knowledge frames: presenting European and Pacific worldviews in overlap (Jolly 2007: 510–11, also see: Eckstein and Schwarz 2019).

Drawing on Roberts' account of the contemporary law of the seas as always already terraqueous and Tupaia's alternative epistemology for knowing terraqueous encounters, I argue for a terraqueous frame to guide how feminist posthumanisms speak to the international law of the sea. I use the map as a mechanism to see existing onto-epistemologies that govern oceanic relationships. In section three, 'ship', I contrast the maps of the world produced by shipping containers and the colonial routes they retrace and inscribe onto international law with Indigenous maps of the Pacific to demonstrate the need within feminist legal writing for, following Barad, a simultaneous ethical, ontological and epistemological shift (2019: 110). I argue feminist legal theories and the space between resistance and compliance benefit from a posthuman feminist approach that dislodges mainstream legal histories. The shipping container and trade routes demonstrate the interplay between ethical and ontological frames, where the map or the ship is never absent from commitment to a specific terraqueous encounter. In section four, 'robot', I further examine the interplay of nature, technology, matter and nonhuman animals that speaks to the persistence of military security and the flow of capital as shaping international legal forms. The potential romance and allure of a posthuman feminist turn to terraqueous thinking must simultaneously pay attention to existing posthuman encounters on the ocean that reinscribe violence through the untethered flow of military objects and capital. The chapter concludes with reflections on human-technologies and terraqueous worldviews as a means to think through both feminist posthumanisms and international law. Drawing from the analysis of the map, ship and robot,

I argue for the conceptualization of the sea as posthuman legal subject and thus the international law of the sea as an important frame for future posthuman feminist encounters that unmoor the posthuman from the humanist, patriarchal and Anthropocenic instrumentalization it currently risks.

Map

The relationship of international law to land territories informs the mapping of the physical and political world, leading toward the formation of nationalisms that dictate much of contemporary international legal relations. This centers human relationships to land as dictating the conditions and metrics for the organization of international law. That which is beyond national jurisdiction emerges in the gaps and spaces beyond land: the oceans (UNCLOS 1982), the deep seabed (UNCLOS 1982: Part XI; Implementation Agreement 1993), outer space (OST 1967) and arctic regions (Byers 2013). Framed as global commons, these areas are understood and regulated by international law as special regimes but often, in reality, collapse back into directives for states in the absence of any alternative legal regime for areas beyond national jurisdiction. The international law of the sea, governed by customary international law and the UN Convention on the Law of the Sea (UNCLOS 1982), frames responsibilities for states as extending from coastlines (or baselines) into the ocean. Coastal states accrue changing rights and responsibilities over maritime regions under the international law of the sea regime according to the location on oceanic maps that start with the land territory of states. States enjoy full sovereign rights up to 12 nautical miles from the baseline in their territorial waters (UNCLOS 1982: Article 3). The UNCLOS further permits states the capacity to enforce territorial jurisdiction in a contingent zone which may extend a further 12 nautical miles beyond the territorial sea (UNCLOS 1982: Article 33). Beyond this, states have the rights to the control (access, extraction, exploitation, protection) of natural resources for up to 200 nautical miles from the coastal states' baseline in a maritime region created via UNCLOS and named as the Exclusive Economic Zone (UNCLOS 1982: Part V). This simple legal map of jurisdiction extending from the baseline of a coastal state is then complicated by the geography of the coastline, the proximity of neighboring states and the shape of the continental shelf, which may further extend a state's right to natural resources up to 350 nautical miles from the baseline (UNCLOS 1982: Article 76). Furthermore, rights of transit passage, innocent passage and the rights of military vessels further allocates rights to ocean vessels and which, through the continued operation of flag state jurisdiction at sea, allocates the jurisdiction on board vessels back to the state where the vessel is registered (UNCLOS 1982: Article 91). Terraqueous encounters help illustrate the knowledge systems and structures that inform cartographic practices, which tend to replicate the construction of the ocean as 'a land-based perspective that emerges from an understanding of the planet as subdivided into political rather than ecoglobalist categories' (Blum 2015: 25). The sea is mapped within international law as ungoverned through that which is beyond the reach of state jurisdictions and simultaneously defined by the enclosure and encounters of states at sea.

Roberts' argues that the legal creation of the Exclusive Economic Zone under UNCLOS forms a terraqueous ocean that already permits privilege to expand from the land into the sea (2021: 10). Roberts' in speaking to the existence of the US's Exclusive Economic Zone, which not only extends from the baseline of the US but from the many US territories, shows how a map of land-based jurisdiction with the Exclusive Economic Zones included allows a vision of the existing terraqueous legal map of the world to emerge. This terraqueous (legal) map refuses the ocean as an empty space and indicates the privilege of specific states, such as the US, through control of ocean jurisdictions. A feminist posthumanism must navigate the known legal and political maps of jurisdiction and these ominous lines and borders on the ocean that are yet to be drawn on standard maps of the world. However, in both a terraqueous and the more standard land-based map of the ocean, the sea is always the site for mastery by humans and not a space where an embodied human experience of the nonhuman might shape ways of knowing, seeing, thinking or of justice. A feminist posthuman account of oceanic governance, interested in ocean and nonhuman subjectivities, might first inquire into alternative ways of mapping the ocean to expose the political and legal geographies that confine the ocean to that which is not land.

The legal map of the ocean is, in its casting of privileges, rights and jurisdiction, not neutral and is both informed by and informs basic perceptions of being and living on earth. This legal map of the ocean privileges states, as the key beneficiaries of rights on/to/in/across the ocean. This is illustrated by the poverty of enforcement and protection of human rights at sea (Treves 2010), which simultaneously encodes the history of capital and military, of extraction mindsets and the deep misery of slavery, within the legal map of the ocean. The privileging of states further determines the privileging of human over nonhuman lives on the ocean and works to reproduce a humanist vision of human lives where racialized, classed, gendered and sexual logics inform the humans that benefit from Anthropocene greed. The description of maritime zones as legal jurisdictions is a map of the ocean that holds a historical and future way of knowing the world and which underscores an ethical commitment to the status quo. To engage the ocean as a posthuman subject, posthuman feminisms must rethink their maps of the ocean, to dislodge the state, as well as human(ist) and land-based jurisprudence.

Tupaia's map is one of multiple alternative ocean framings that exist. Aboriginal and Torres Strait Island peoples in the Northern regions of the territory otherwise known as Australia, identify themselves as saltwater people and perceive the land/ocean relation as integrated rather than a form of border, or boundary (Sharp 2010). Indonesian concepts of tanah-air think through the interface between ocean and land outside of humanist frames (Alverdian 2022). Marshallese wave riders, also known as ri-meto, navigate the Pacific through a recognition of the contours of the ocean, and the motion of waves, as a mechanism for knowing human-ocean relations and navigation without reference to land (Genz 2018: 4). These frames of knowledge are integral to thought and being, matter and justice, across these communities and undermine the self-referential framing of European knowledge histories within international law. Similarly, Steinberg's reflections on the possibility of oceanic studies that commence with the ocean (rather than land) as providing the starting point for engagement describes an ontology aligned with Lagrangian oceanography that works to 'abandon attempts at finding stable metrics that can fix and organize spaces and the activities that transpire within and instead turn their attention to the processes that are continually constructing spatial patterns, social institutions, and socio-natural hybrids' (2013: 162). Steinberg imagines an ocean that is understood without fixed grids, drawing in the work of Lagrangian oceanographers, and offers one possibility for a reimagined legal subjectivity. This would be a form of subjectivity that does not start with the human and does not center the human, with all its ordering and Othering, that emerges in existing and dominant cartographies. For international lawyers, the state as legal subject that projects outward from land to accommodate the ocean through the fixed borders of land territories must at once be seen as already terraqueous. Furthermore, the international law of the sea remains circumscribed by the ontology of European cartographic forms, and the epistemology of seeing the world through the human, the state, property, hierarchies of belonging and binarized thinking.

If sovereign states and legal jurisdictions that extend from land provide the fixed points for mapping the ocean of European knowledge histories, a post-human ocean is not only a wet form of subjectivity but one that is untethered and instead preoccupied with an ontology of motion, patterns and movement. Barad's identification of virtual spaces, touching with infinite possibilities unfolds a similar posthuman dynamic to argue, '[e]ach bit of matter, each moment of spacetimemattering, is shot through with an infinite set of im/possibilities for materially reconfiguring worlds and pastfuturespresents; surely these matters are nothing less than matters of justice' (2019: 110). This heralds the possibility of the ocean as subject that understands matter as meaning and matter and meaning as integral to justice. In this inquiry, in this chapter, this gives rise to legal arrangements and their infinite futures, their complex pasts found already in the lives of saltwater people, tanah-air and wave riders, or, Tupaia's map which swirls in response to his movement and the movement of the ocean around him.

In contrast to legal maps of the ocean, Tupaia's map is today understood as placing Tupaia within, rather than outside, of the ocean; a direct contrast to the aerial view of cartography otherwise. Tupaia's map, a map drawn – and copied – to assist the English explorer Captain James Cook to navigate, and map, the Pacific in the eighteenth century remains, in copy, in the British Library today (see Figure 8.1). In the map, the Pacific Ocean, its islands and atolls, swirl around and are understood in relation to the map's creator, Tupaia. Once perceived as a primitive, childlike attempt at map making, Tupaia's map is now understood as an important account of two knowledge frames, European and Pacific, in dialogue and thus permitting European navigation of the Pacific under Tupaia's tutelage. Today those islands, and atolls, are increasingly enclosed by the rising ocean and acidification caused by climate change that 'threatens the physical, biological, and human elements necessary for Pacific Island cultures to sustain their co-existence and evolving relationship with a defined place and to maintain their unique set of customs, beliefs, language, traditional knowledge, objects, and built environment' (Keener *et al* 2012: 5). As the site on which the Anthropocene harm has arrived most acutely, changing ocean and land relations, the Pacific Ocean offers not only an urgent human concern (Rayfuse 2013: 5) but also an alternative conception of terraqueous encounters that exists in contrast to the legal and political maps of the ocean, drawn from land (McLeod *et al* 2019).

Tupaia's map offers itself as an object that holds Barad's conception of ontologies and frameworks of knowing and epistemologies as understood through matter and its flux (2007: 93). Following posthumanist critiques of both humanism and anthropocentrism, I engage the nonhuman matter of the map while holding prescient the contributions of feminist and queer understandings of subjectivity (Braidotti 2021: 198). The scholarship of blue humanities scholars emerges as a mechanisms for understanding and theorizing the relationship between watery lifeforms and human–nonhuman encounters, shifting the humanist perceptions of academic traditions that center human knowledge as distinct from nature and uses both water and the ocean as a mechanism for upending dominant intellectual maps of the world. The emergence of a specifically watery imagination of posthuman relations recalls water as human, humans as watery, the earth as watery and retells the humanities through liquid frames and the trans-species dependencies that are never contained to land. For Probyn (2018), this is understood through human–nonhuman digestion and the ocean's expulsion of human excess. For Neimanis (2017), this is a phenomenology of bodies of water, bodies as water, water as body that reframes the human reader's anticipated encounter with the self to find herself not so distinct from water, such that water is human matter. Elsewhere Neimanis – like Braidotti – explores the convergence of the Anthropocene and race, classed, gendered bodies to consider a

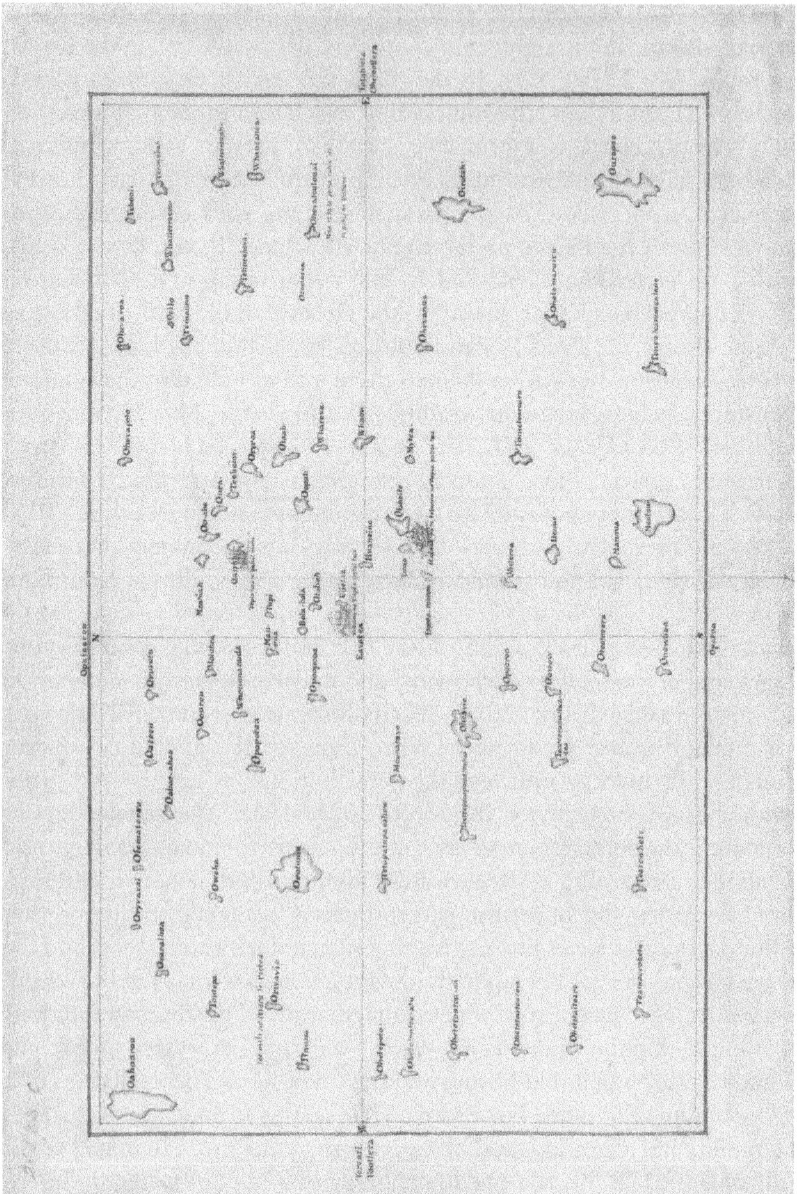

FIGURE 8.1 Tupaia's Map, 1770, British Library, London, © British Library Board BL Add MS 21593.C.

need for posthuman feminisms that examine how whiteness is drawn into the maintenance of the nature–culture dualism (2019). The complex nature/culture imaginaries that emerge understand the mechanisms through which humans are always in the ocean and the ocean in humans, in terms of biological dependencies, creative frames, philosophical and human–nonhuman encounters while holding present the violence of slavery that the ocean holds in the, following Sharpe, wake (2016: 40). Braverman and Johnson collate the specific crossovers between blue humanities and legal scholarship and describe the need for acknowledging:

> [O]cean governance is not a managerial or technical problem to be solved through the acquisition of more or better knowledge or through an expansion of existing legal regimes. The unique material and symbolic dynamics of the sea and its inhabitants thus force us to de- and uncenter our systems of governance and our modes regulation. Put differently, recognizing the fluidity of land and sea requires a reconsideration of the existing institutions, temporal frameworks, and categories with which we engage the oceans, illuminating our responsibilities toward these spaces and to what lies and lives within them.
>
> *(Braverman and Johnson 2019: 19)*

These posthuman feminist texts offer a way of seeing and arriving at the ocean that is no longer premised on *terra firma* as starting point, or ocean as outside the human sphere of reference, such that the blue spaces on political and legal maps are not voids to be filled but known through human–nonhuman encounters. This raises a challenge to legal subjectivity that, first, places humans on land and, second, constructs a normative universe that considers the ocean as ulterior, a second thought and Other. If the ocean was our legal subject where would humans be placed? Would humans be outside her domain or the ocean within us, the human as ocean, three quarters always, as the earth? Lagrangian oceanographers might suggest that this quest for fixed points to map a subject, in this case the ocean, is part of the same land-based jurisprudence that Tupaia's map discards. Tupaia's map provides unique evidence of the relational nature of European and Pacific knowledge frames, as well as a terraqueous encounter that undoes the liberal subject of Enlightenment through the integration of human dependencies and relations with the nonhuman, a way of seeing the world where the human is immersed within the ocean and the land is no longer the border of the ocean.

Ship

The underwater cable – fiber optic, dragging Netflix, and perhaps this text, under the ocean and to your screens – does not land on the ocean seabed in a random crisscrossing of watery networks. The tentacles of underwater cables, rather, map colonial and contemporary trade routes anew – forging the lifestyle and accessibility of port cities globally. Likewise, container ships and their routes remap colonial ocean routes, retelling a legacy of slavery, inequalities and indentured labor through an economic dependency on the ocean and the container ship. Both underwater cables and container ships trace colonial and slave misery whilst delivering goods and communications to the world's cities, centering property and continuing a history of human-ocean dependencies that also entrench privilege through control of technologies at sea (Thorat 2019; Mahmud 2010). The work of property, commerce and labor in the production of the map is noted by Jolly, when she identifies the distinct understanding of the ship encountered by Tupaia:

> his vision was likely a rather differently 'situated knowledge'. I suspect it located the observer not soaring high above the islands, powerfully riding on the confident coordinates of longitude and latitude, plotting a changing global position relative to east and west, north and south, but rather lying low in a canoe, looking up at the heavens, scanning the horizon for signs of land, and navigating the powerful seas with the embodied visual, aural, olfactory, and kinesthetic knowledge passed down through generations of Pacific navigators.
>
> *(Jolly 2007: 509)*

Jolly contrasts the crew on Cook's ship, laborers, earners, and embedded in a hierarchy of power that extends from the King in England to the organization and control of the ship. The knowledge framework that informs the ship constructs and lays beneath the map of the ocean. A legal map of the ocean, with jurisdictions neatly contained in nautical miles extending from the coastline, equally holds a way of knowing the world and holds not only the history of people as property but a contemporary frame of capital accumulation, labor exploitation and free markets in its wake.

From a feminist perspective, the turn to law inscribes the risk of reappropriation by legal and political institutions of the ethical commitment, be it to women's lives, gender equality or ecological protection. The ship's trajectory across the ocean might then suggest that the corrective of law reform is a limited approach to challenging a system that neither sees its own histories of violence nor the violence enacted through the remapping of the tentacles of capital over oceans. A feminist posthumanism in starting with the legal subject, and in a turn to the ocean, must then consider what different oceanic subjectivities might feel like.

The ship in this iteration thus interjects into the troubling repetitions within feminist legal reforms that have been described as caught (or contained) within a dynamic of resistance and compliance, reinscribing liberal forms on political and legal maps (Kouvo and Pearson 2007; Charlesworth *et al* 2019). A terraqueous knowledge frame gives aperture to non-Western knowledge histories and invokes the frames through which land–ocean cartographies embody human–nonhuman knowledge histories and carry dynamic, alternative knowledge structures. The Lagrangian oceanographer pursues a means to see, to feel and trace

> the ocean [a]s a space of circulation because it is constituted through its very geophysical mobility. As in Lagrangian fluid dynamics, movement is not something that happens between places, connecting discrete points on a 'rim'. Rather, movement emerges as the very essence of the ocean region, including the aqueous mass at its center.
>
> *(Steinberg 2013: 165)*

The consequence, Steinberg argues, is a focus on 'exchange over production or emphasizing the hybrid nature of cultural identities' (2013: 165). A feminist posthuman encounter with the international law of the sea might, similarly, unmoor its expectations from the fixity of sovereign territories to trace the flows and motions of human and nonhuman worlds, where ideas recycle as matter might and where justice need not be tied to the history of property and its movement across the ocean. The Lagrangian model permits the interplay of ethico-onto-epistem-ologies (Barad 2007: 185) to be detached from a specific origins story, of colonial expansion, slavery and trade routes, to trace how alternative maps of the world were/are already spoken and shaping thought, human and nonhuman lives, matter and matterings.

The international law of the sea in this posthuman feminist structure is no longer articulated through the needs of states – including the economic gains that are traded through intersecting lines on the ocean and, increasingly, its soil and subsoil (see Jones *et al* 2023). The ocean as subject is also an affective pool of remembering of humans cast overboard because of the hierarchies of humanness normalized in the traditions of European law (Sharp 2016; Neimanis 2019). The ocean as subject is dynamic and changeable such that justice cannot only engage the human–nonhuman binary but interrogates different earth stories, stargazing, wave ridings and weavings of matter and technologies for survival (Hamilton-Faris 2022). In this posthuman feminist voicing the starting point is terraqueous, wet and earthy, fluid and ancient, suffocating and drowning. The terraqueous thus exposes the existing flows of capital and extraction, over the Exclusive Economic Zone or into the Area – as defined and maintained via UNCLOS – and via the shipping container and the underwater cable and the deadly histories they lay again and again and again. And yet the ship's hull, resplendent with barnacles and other ocean critters, and the underwater cable, interlocking with seabed dwelling organisms and at risk from sandwaves and other geohazards, do not need human lives (or memory) to establish entanglements of matter.

Not all ships use the ocean in the same way. Mermaids (Hodson 2019) and shepherds (Alberro 2021) thus signal already framed logistics of flow and movement where the co-ordinates of action are driven by different human perspectives. I am thinking of activist encounters in terraqueous worlds, that unravel land-based jurisdiction and play with the freedom of the high seas to undo the excesses of Enlightenment man and the Anthropocene (Nagtzaam 2013–14); abortion providers and refugee rescuers, whale protectors and all those that bear witness at sea (Urbina 2019).

For feminist posthumanist thinkers, Tupaia's map juxtaposed with shipping routes, that always invoke the colonial and contemporary trajectories of trade and capital, brings to the fore ways of knowing, ways of seeing and ways of mattering that are at once troubled and troubling for a law reform model that is tethered to land. As such, Roberts' borderwaters are extended, not just through recognition of how the Exclusive Economic Zone or the potential mining of the Area advances jurisdiction into the ocean but the shipping lanes of global capital equally reinscribing privilege and the reallocation of resources from the Global South to the Global North. The ocean as a space of global reproduction of the status quo thus facilitates a posthuman account of human–nonhuman entanglements and figurations.

Contemporary feminist analysis of international law and the various sites of gender law reform have identified a flux between resistance and compliance. This analysis sees the mechanisms through which law appropriates feminist forms and resurfaces them within the fixity of legal forms that then, in turn, reproduce a faux feminist law that fails to undo dominant understandings of gender and sexuality. In this scholarship the state, as international legal subject, is rarely interrogated and an unlikely candidate for removal (Bird 2022; Charlesworth 1997). The land-based geographies of knowledge that dominant feminist legal theories script their analysis of international law from is ungirded if an oceanic turn is felt to offer a different frame. Feminist posthumanism and wet global governance must then first acknowledge the maps of capital and colonialism through surfacing trade and technologies that already know the ocean, and a terraqueous law is imagined as not new but also not a singular frame. In these entanglements the technologies of oceanographers, technology in the ocean and the maps of oceanic violence, commerce and knowledge are imbued into a means for gently rocking away from the fixed points of land. Ultimately, reading with Yusoff, the dynamism of geology might, in this telling, also surface and unsettle (2019: 104). I want to frame the unseen accounts of (in)justice and knowledge that are already present in the international law of the sea and to think outside of those fixed frames. The siren song of posthumanism calling humans out of the Anthropocene must also be conscious of further, existing, posthuman encounters that enact human–nonhuman subjects within the ocean. The ship or the underwater cable or, as I think through in the following section, the cartographies of knowledge enacted through marine technologies controlled by forms that reinscribe a commitment to extraction and harm.

Robot

Military technology at sea draws attention to the creation of the US Ghost Fleet, a fleet of autonomous naval vessels. While the term ghost fleet has been used in the past to refer to abandoned maritime objects/vessels, the US embarked on a project to build a Ghost Fleet composed of a ten-vessel fleet of automated marine vessels (Grome 2018). The vessels, originally scheduled for production between 2019 and 2024, included capacity for vertical landing pads, an important adjunct capacity of the vessels, given the parallel development of aerial automated vehicles with capacity to land and take off vertically. At the time of writing, in addition to the smaller Sea Hunter and Sea Hawk, the US Navy had invested in two further, larger 'overlord' ships, named Nomad and Ranger; all four vessels were deployed as part of the 2022 RIMPAC multinational maritime exercise in the Pacific. These larger vessels operate with a crew onboard, responsible for navigation in ports and transit passages and undertaking additional tasks when the vessels move through the High Seas while being controlled from California, despite being built with capacity for a fully autonomous mode. The legal definition of a warship (UNCLOS, Article 29), which requires a crew, may in part influence current operational decisions to maintain crews on the two overlord ships, giving each legal status – and the corresponding rights – of a warship as a result. These developments are an excellent harbinger of the risks of engaging in an account of human–nonhuman futures within a feminist frame without attention to the terraqueous technologies that already map the ocean. Through identifying the ongoing development of autonomous naval vehicles and the various hybrid arrangements already deployed by the US Navy, the capacity for both the ocean and technology to enhance the status quo of militarized thinking and its entwinning with the flow of capital is signaled.

Through turning my attention to marine robots, I identify existing nonhuman operatives that move through the ocean, in particular the development of automated military vessels, to think about the potential of posthuman futures to reinscribe the preoccupations of Anthropocene and humanist versions of the global. I place the automated marine vessel in a history of maritime encounters including oceanic nuclear histories and military encounters on the oceans. I juxtapose this with posthuman feminist engagements with technologies as a site of human–nonhuman dependencies and argue for attention to the mechanisms through which existing Anthropocene and humanist knowledge frames shape technologies. Automated vessels are not a particularly new maritime object but the scale and function of those envisaged as part of the US Navy's Ghost Fleet are significant shifts from the prior use of small wave-motion surveillance devices, or wave-glider, such as the one 'captured' by the Chinese navy in 2016 and the Saildrones deployed in the Persian Gulf. In line with my approach across the chapter in centering an object, the robot, an unfolding of ethico-onto-epistem-olgical (Barad 2019: 381) concerns surface that interlock rather than confront different or discrete concerns.

Legal understanding of the use of aquatic robots returns to the UNCLOS and examines their legality through the maritime jurisdictions as they progress from land across territorial waters, the Exclusive Economic Zones and into the High Seas. The preoccupation of legal scholars' centers largely on the regulation (and freedoms) for military vessels, although autonomous shipping vessels are also in development. In these iterations the jurisdictions mapped from land, via UNCLOS, shape the nature of inquiries into the legality, or otherwise, of autonomous vessels in maritime environments. Unlike my preceding analysis, where changing understandings of human–nonhuman dependencies are perceived as unlocking ways of seeing different knowledge frames and reconceiving of justice, here the assertion of the existing legal regime as sufficient to contain new technologies underpins the long history of military-capital dictating the ways in which human encounters with the ocean are mediated. This, however, is not just a set of freedoms bestowed on naval powers and multinational enterprise but also a re-invoking of troubling frames of knowledge about the Other, both non-Western and the environment.

Within the discourse, scholarly and media, the identification of the threat that China poses at sea, and the South China Sea in particular, repeats an orientalist frame that permits a two-tier mode of access to the ocean. The US's Ghost Fleet has been likened to the arms race during the Cold War, such that Grome writes:

> Already, both China and Russia-the United States' greatest geopolitical rivals-are steadily advancing their own autonomous vehicles and weaponry programs, demonstrating the current unfolding of a relatively quiet arms race. Seizing upon the mantra of 'Peace through Strength', the hope is to utilize the technologically-advanced Ghost Fleet to maintain and perpetuate peaceful relations through the demonstration of military superiority.
>
> *(Grome 2018: 34–5)*

The invoking of Cold War histories is not only contained in the politics of deterrence. The Cold War acts of nuclear testing in the Pacific further underscore the terraqueous maps of military endeavors that have long been anchored outside the constraints of land-based jurisdiction to subject both human and nonhuman others to the excesses of humanist logic. Genz writes of the circumnavigation of the Pacific by Marshallese ri-meto, Captain Korent and a small crew of Marshallese survivors, as a process of breaking from the 'primary identity as nuclear refugees to begin recovering their most intimate connections to the sea' (Genz 2018: 5). The violence enacted during the Cold War, in the name of nuclear deterrence, on both the environment and the peoples, crossing human–nonhuman vulnerabilities, returns as the Ghost Fleet enacts new spaces of imagined danger, contained through deterrence and military power. The ship-as-robot traces both military and trade routes that have always been terraqueous and prepared to refuse the logics of territorial jurisdiction through the othering of ways of knowing, the ways that Tupaia knew, and that Marshallese poet Kathy Jetñil-Kijiner in poetic dialogue with Aka Niviâna speaks of as 'ocean and sand' (Jetñil-Kijiner and Aka Niviâna 2019). The nuclear testing in the Pacific and its intergenerational displacement, deaths and destruction encapsulate the mantra of peace through strength that the myth of military superiority depends upon. For a feminist posthumanism to know the sea as subject then she must also know another way of holding the injustice of the objects of capital and the knowledge frames both embraced and displaced.

The US–Marshallese agreement that maintains the relationship between the Marshallese and the United States also maintains US access to the jurisdiction of the Exclusive Economic Zone of the Marshallese territory. Jetnil-Kijliner describes the Marshall Islands as 'a country more sea than land' (Jetñil-Kijiner and Aka Niviâna 2019: 00.43 seconds). Recalling Roberts' account of the Exclusive Economic Zone, created through UNCLOS, as an expansion of territorial claims by powerful states, such as the US, heralds the importance of land territories that expand maritime boundaries in profoundly unsettling ways (2021). The terraqueous map of the US presents an alternative knowledge encounter and, juxtaposed alongside the fear of Chinese claims into the South China Seas, exposes the failures of not seeing the existing legal and political maps of terraqueous knowledge. The robot at sea embeds within this a vision of how a very specific mode of justice is realized through both terraqueous and human–nonhuman frames. Returning to Barad (2019), the posthuman feminist account of the ocean, as legal subject, must therefore engage an ethico-onto-epistem-ological frame for unknowing military capital while rendering it visible as partial, harmful and particularized.

Terraqueous Unmoored

This chapter has argued that the ocean is not waiting to be 'discovered' as the alternative to land-based jurisdiction in a feminist posthuman account of the law of the sea. Rather the terraqueous map of Exclusive Economic Zones, Tupaia's map, military maneuvers at sea and container ship logistics transpose existing terraqueous worldviews that arc over geographies and temporalities. A feminist posthuman encounter with the international law of the sea surfaces human and nonhuman worlds. These worlds have significant capacity to dislodge anthropocentric law and linear histories of the unencumbered subject (human and state) of Enlightenment philosophies through finding a Lagrangian law unmoored from land but capable of knowing land–sea relations in dynamism. Following Parfitt (2019), the reproduction of the nation-state traditionally framed as circumscribed by land and of the ocean as untamed by human political and legal geographies is rethought as simultaneously permitting and obscuring very specific worldviews. A posthuman feminist encounter with the law of the sea must, in contrast, avoid the allure of a romanticized ocean geography that risks the binary of resistance and compliance associated with existing feminist law reform. In acknowledging the military and economic livelihoods that already construct technologies to map and know the ocean there chimes loudly a reminder of the capacity of capital to at once pivot through the individual (state, human, corporation) as legal subject while infiltrating and appropriating technologies and knowledge into the language of legal liberalism. At the same time Tupaia's map provides a place holder for the mechanisms of knowledge traditions both intertwined and discrete from Western Enlightenment frames, as does the Marshallese wave-rider or ri-meto, saltwater people or tanah-air or even Lagrangian thinking.

Within these unmoorings the international law of the sea floats as a curious terraqueous frame. On the one hand, land directs from the shoreline the shape and form of a legal map of the sea. Cartographies reproduce this, over lines of longitude and latitude, with the ocean and its maritime zones demarcated by shades of blue and otherwise understood in relation to the rim of land. Yet, on the other hand, capital already knows a different, terraqueous map, where the Exclusive Economic Zone enshrined in UNCLOS expands the reach of states. This reach enables some states to command access to nonhuman resources while the unregulated freedoms of the High Seas equally disguise capital and military excess; an excess of destruction, an excess of extraction, an excess of pollution and an excess of objects that mete out harm to humans and nonhumans in equal measure.

Knowledge flows in unexpected directions, such that, feminist posthumanism raises the possibility of oceanic knowledge in a different register, asking questions of the international law of the sea just as the international law of the sea and a turn to the oceans asks questions of feminist posthumanism. Tupaia's map pivots and locates humans in relation to the ocean while integrating multiple, complex ways of learning, neither rejecting Cook's worldview nor discarding oceanic understandings of the Pacific. Feminist posthumanism might also encounter the ocean as a pivot between worldviews and as a reflection for the already submerged technologies of capital and militarism that make the most of nonhuman encounters to support the status quo of capital and Anthropocene greed. In unmooring, the dynamic encounter of the wave-rider is instructive and 'the embodied knowledge of the sea is indispensable' (Genz 2018: 4).

Bibliography

Primary Sources

Treaty on Principles Governing the Activities of States in the Exploration and Use of Outer Space, including the Moon and Other Celestial Bodies (OST) (opened for signature January 1967, entered into force October 1967).

United Nations Convention on the Law of the Sea (UNCLOS) (opened for signature 10 December 1982, entered into force on 16 November 1994).

Secondary Sources

Alberro, H. (2021) 'In and Against Eco-Apocalypse: On the Terrestrial Ecotopianism of Radical Environmental Activists', *Utopian Studies*, 32(1): 36–55.

Alverdian, I. (2022) 'The Tanah-Air Concept and Indonesia's Maritime Nation Aspiration', *Journal of Maritime Studies and National Integration*, 5(2): 64–80.

Barad, K. (2007) *Meeting the Universe Halfway: Quantum Physics and the Entanglement of Matter and Meaning*, New York: Duke University Press.

Barad, K. (2019) 'After the End of the World: Entangled Nuclear Colonialisations, Matters of Force and the Material Force of Justice', *Theory & Event*, 22: 524–50.

Bird, F. (2022) 'ISIL in Iraq: A Critical Analysis of the UN Security Council's Gendered Personification of (Non)States', *Laws*, 11(5): 1–21. DOI: https://doi.org/10.3390/laws11010005

Blum, H. (2015) 'Terraqueous Planet', in A.J. Elias and C. Moraru (eds) *The Planetary Turn: Relationality and Geoaesthetics in the Twenty-First Century*, Evanston: Northwestern University Press.

Blum, H., F. Buehler, M. Calway-Fagen, M. Eyring, I. Liang and B.R. Roberts (2019) 'Archipelagos, Oceans, and American Visuality', *Journal of Transnational American Studies*, 10(1): 5–21. DOI: https://doi.org/10.5070/T8101044020

Braidotti, R. (2019) *Posthuman Knowledge*, Cambridge: Polity Press.

Braidotti, R. (2021) *Posthuman Feminism*, Cambridge: Polity Press.

Braverman, I. and E.R. Johnson (2019) *Blue Legalities*, Durham: Duke University Press.

Byers, M. (2013) *International Law and the Arctic*, Cambridge: Cambridge University Press.

Campling, L. and A. Colas (2021) *Capitalism and the Sea*, London: Verso Publishing.

Charlesworth, H. (1997) 'The Sex of the State in International Law', in N. Naffine and R. Owens (eds) *Sexing the Subject of Law*, Sydney: Law Books Company.

Charlesworth, H., G. Heathcote and E. Jones (2019) 'Feminist Scholarship on International Law in the 1990s and Today: An Inter-Generational Conversation', *Feminist Legal Studies*, 27: 79–93. DOI: https://doi.org/10.1007/s10691-018-9384-1

Eckstein, L. and A. Schwarz (2019) 'The Making of Tupaia's Map: A Story of the Extent and Mastery of Polynesian Navigation, Competing Systems of Wayfinding on James Cook's *Endeavour*, and the Invention of an Ingenious Cartographic System', *The Journal of Pacific History*, 54(1): 1–95.

Genz, J.H. (2016) 'Resolving Ambivalence in Marshallese Navigation: Relearning, Reinterpreting, and Reviving the "Stick Chart" Wave Models', *Structure and Dynamics*, 9(1): 8–40.

Genz, J.H. (2018) *Breaking the Shell: Voyaging from Nuclear Refugees to People of the Sea in the Marshall Islands*, Honolulu: University of Hawai'i Press.

Grome, E.D. (2018) 'Spectres of the Sea: The United States Navy's Autonomous Ghost Fleet, Its Capabilities and Impacts, and the Legal Ethical Issues That Surround', *Journal of Maritime Law and Commerce*, 49(1): 31–70.

Hamilton-Faris, J. (2022) 'Ocean Weaves: Reconfiguration of Climate Justice in Oceania', *Feminist Review*, 130: 5–25.

Hodson, L. (2019) 'Mermaids and Utopias: The High Seas as Feminist Space?', in I. Papanicolopulu (ed) *Gender and the Law of the Sea*, Leiden: Brill Publishing.

Hohmann, J. and D. Joyce (eds) (2018) *International Law's Objects*, Oxford: Oxford University Press.

Jetñil-Kijiner, K. and A. Niviâna (2019) 'Rise: From One Island to Another', poem video. www.kathyjetnilkijiner.com/; for text https://350.org/rise-from-one-island-to-another/#poemonline (Accessed: February 2022).

Johnson, D.M. and D.L. VanderZwaag (2000) 'The Ocean and International Environmental Law: Swimming, Sinking, and Treading Water at the Millennium', *Ocean & Coastal Management*, 43(2–3): 141–61.

Jolly, M. (2007) 'Imagining Oceania: Indigenous and Foreign Representations of a Sea of Islands', *The Contemporary Pacific*, 19(2): 508–45.

Jones, E., C. van Eijk and G. Heathcote (2023) 'The Common Heritage of Kin-Kind', in M. Arvidsson and E. Jones (eds) *International Law and Posthuman Theory*, Abingdon: Routledge.

Keener, V.W., J.J. Marra, M.L. Finucane, D. Spooner, M.H. Smith and Pacific Islands Regional Climate Assessment (2012) *Climate Change and Pacific Islands: Indicators and Impacts: Report for the 2012 Pacific Islands Regional Climate Assessment (PIRCA)*, Washington, DC: Island Press.

Kouvo, S. and R. Pearson (eds) (2007) *Feminist Perspectives on Contemporary International Law: Resistance and Compliance*, Cambridge: Cambridge University Press.

Mahmud, T. (2010) 'Law of Geography and the Geography of Law: A Post-Colonial Mapping', *Washington University Jurisprudence Review*, 3(1): 64–106.

Mainwaring, S. and R.J. Aldrich (2021) 'The Secret Empire of Signals Intelligence: GCHQ and the Persistence of the Colonial Presence', *The International History Review*, 43(1): 54–71.

McLeod, E., M. Bruton-Adams, J. Förster, C. Franco, G. Gaines, B. Gorong, R. James, G. Posing-Kulwaum, M. Tara and E. Terk (2019) 'Lessons from the Pacific Islands – Adapting to Climate Change by Supporting Social and Ecological Resilience', *Frontiers in Marine Science*, 6: 289. DOI: https://doi.org/10.3389/fmars.2019.00289

Nagtzaam, G. (2013–2014) 'Gaia's Navy: The Sea Shepherd Conservation Society's Battle to Stay Afloat and International Law', *William & Mary Environmental Law & Policy Review*, 38(3): 613–94.

Neimanis, A. (2017) *Bodies of Water: Posthuman Feminist Phenomenology*, New York: Bloomsbury Publishing.

Neimanis, A. (2019) 'The Weather Underwater: Blackness, White Feminism, and the Breathless Sea', *Australian Feminist Studies*, 34(102): 490–508. DOI: https://doi.org/10.1080/08164649.2019.1697178

Nurse, L.A., R.F. McLean, J. Agard, L.P. Briguglio, V. Duvat-Magnan, N. Pelesikoti, E. Tompkins, and A. Webb (2014) 'Small Islands', in V.R. Barros, C.B. Field, D.J. Dokken, M.D. Mastrandrea, K.J. Mach, T.E. Bilir, M. Chatterjee, K.L. Ebi, Y.O. Estrada, R.C. Genova, B. Girma, E.S. Kissel, A.N. Levy, S. MacCracken, P.R. Mastrandrea and L.L. White (eds) *Climate Change 2014: Impacts, Adaptation, and Vulnerability. Part B: Regional Aspects. Contribution of Working Group II to the Fifth Assessment Report of the Intergovernmental Panel on Climate Change*, Cambridge: Cambridge University Press, 1613–54.

Parfitt, R. (2019) *The Process of International Legal Reproduction: Inequality, Historiography, Resistance*, Cambridge: Cambridge University Press.

Perera, S. (2013) 'Oceanic Corpo-Graphies, Refugee Bodies and the Making and Unmaking of Waters', *Feminist Review*, 103(1): 58–79. DOI: https://doi.org/10.1057/fr.2012.26

Probyn, E. (2018) 'The Ocean Returns: Mapping a Mercurial Anthropocean', *Social Science Information*, 57(3): 386–402. DOI: https://doi.org/10.1177/0539018418792402

Ranganathan, S. (2021) 'Decolonization and International Law: Putting the Ocean in the Map', *Journal of the History of International Law*, 23: 161–83. DOI: https://doi.org/10.1163/15718050-12340168

Rayfuse, R.G. (2013) 'Sea Level Rise and Maritime Zones: Preserving the Maritime Entitlements of "Disappearing" States', in M.B. Gerrard and G.E. Wannier (eds) *Threatened Island Nations: Legal Implications of Rising Seas and a Changing Climate*, New York: Cambridge University Press, 167–91.

Roberts, B.R. (2021) *Borderwaters: Amid the Archipelagic States of America*, Durham: Duke University Press.

Roberts, B.R. and M.A. Stephens (2017) *Archipelagic American Studies*, Durham: Duke University Press.

Salmond, A. (2005) 'Their Body Is Different, Our Body Is Different: European and Tahitian Navigators in the 18th Century', *History and Anthropology*, 16(2): 167–86.

Salmond, A. (2012) 'Tupaia, the Navigator-Priest', in S. Mallon, K. Māhina-Tuai and D. Salesa (eds) *Tangata o le Moana: New Zealand and the People of the Pacific*, Wellington: Te Papa Press, 57–76.

Sharp, N. (2010) *Saltwater People: The Waves of Memory*, Sydney: Allen and Unwin.

Sharpe, C. (2016) *In the Wake: On Blackness and Being*, Durham: Duke University Press.

Steinberg, P.E. (2013) 'Of Other Seas: Metaphors and Materialities in Maritime Regions', *Atlantic Studies*, 10(2): 156–69.

Thorat, D. (2019) 'Colonial Topographies of Internet Infrastructure: The Sedimented and Linked Networks of the Telegraph and Submarine Fiber Optic Internet', *South Asian Review*, 40(3): 252–67.

Treves, T. (2010) 'Human Rights and the Law of the Sea', *Berkeley Journal of International Law*, 28(1): 1–14.

Urbina, I. (2019) *The Outlaw Ocean: Crime and Survival in the Last Untamed Frontier*, New York: Knopf.

Yusoff, K. (2019) *A Billion Black Anthropocenes or None*, Minneapolis: University of Minnesota Press.

9

BECOMING COMMON – ECOLOGICAL RESISTANCE, REFUSAL, REPARATION

Marie Petersmann

Introduction

In this chapter, I focus on the *lago bullicante* – literally the 'lake that boils and gets agitated' – in the Prenestino neighborhood of Rome, Italy. It is a case set in the 'local', yet its particular subjective, spatial and temporal dynamics inform modalities of collective action that are common to practices of ecological resistance, refusal and reparation across different jurisdictions and geographies.

Three reasons make the *lago bullicante* stand out for me when thinking about posthumanist approaches to (international) law against the backdrop of ecological concerns. First, the collective action – as I will elaborate next – was triggered by water that sprung from the underground due to illegal human activities. In this case, water was the driving force that ordered the political and legal actions that have since emerged, together with the vegetations and animals that live from and with it. The *lago bullicante* – also known as the 'insurgent lake' – is therefore a striking example of a collective action enacted from continuously evolving human–nonhuman relations, organized out of and in terms of the agency of water and its generative force across the soils, plants and animal species it sustains. Second, and by way of consequence, these political and legal actions speak directly to the theme of posthumanism, as they are neither confined to nor address merely a collective composed of active human subjects that represent or speak on behalf of passive nonhuman objects. Rather, the action is ignited by a more-than- *and* less-than-human collective that displaces at once the human in relation to the nonhuman, but also the individual in relation to the collective. Finally, and consequently, these political and legal actions are embedded in practices

DOI: 10.4324/9781032658032-13

of what I call 'posthumanist commoning'. This is a practice that is part of a longer lineage of collective actions around the commons – *beni comuni* – in Italy, itself embedded within a context of global rise of commoning movements (Grear and Bollier 2020; Weston and Bollier 2013). This practice of commoning, which bears transversal and transnational dimensions through alliances built within a network of resisting collectives across different jurisdictions and geographies, is notably different from the 'commons' that have played a central (and perhaps reinvigorated) role today in international legal and governmental discourses committed to better protect, manage and control 'common pool resources' (Ostrom 2008) from ecological degradations (Jones *et al* 2023). In this chapter, I argue that it is *after* the human, *after* the individual, *after* the commons and, perhaps, even *after* the state, that relevant insights for a posthumanist theory for international law are fully revealed.

Using the example of the *lago bullicante*, the overall aim of this chapter is to reflect on the modalities of posthumanist collectives that act beyond or without the liberal 'human' subject, showing how their transversal and transnational collective actions can help refuse and reconfigure given categories of international law such as property, the subject and the common good. The objective is to let the case of the *lago bullicante* in Rome inform posthumanist approaches to international *law*, and reveal important limitations that critical posthuman theory entails when rethinking *international* law.

The chapter is divided in three sections. The first section introduces the case of the 'insurgent lake' in Rome as a practice of ecological resistance. The second reflects on the non-, more- and in-human features of the collective action at hand, and how it gives rise to an ecological refusal of the 'human' as a meaningful category of thought and of practice. The third and final section engages with 'posthumanist commoning' as a transnational mode of ecological reparation. My use of 'posthumanist' can here be understood as aligned with the 'posthuman' that is 'generated by the intersecting critiques of humanism and of anthropocentrism' (Braidotti 2019: 34). Whereas Braidotti and other feminist scholars like Jones (2023) and Arvidsson (2023a, 2023b) use the term 'posthuman' to refer to this dual and simultaneous move of *de*-humanism and *de*-anthropocentrism (Jones and Arvidsson 2023), I prefer the notion of 'posthumanism' to clearly emphasize the refusal and rejection of other invocations of a post/trans/meta-human that rely on modernist aspirations to improve the human as such. Moving beyond the liberal category of the 'human', I conclude by exploring how these posthumanist modalities of transversal and transnational ecological resistance, refusal and reparation speak to international law. To this end, I draw out the conceptual and material tools that a critical posthumanist theory can offer when (re)thinking collective action against the backdrop of ecological collapse, while also pointing out important blind spots and limitations, especially in relation to international legal forms and actions.

The Ecological Resistance of the 'Insurgent Lake' of Rome

More than a hundred years have passed since the chemical-textile company *Società Generale Italiana della Viscosa* opened its doors to 2500 workers – of whom 60 percent were women – in the area of Prenestino, Rome, in 1922. The plant, which produced artificial silk, used highly toxic carbon disulfide to manufacture rayon (Tola 2019: 195). The artificial silk factory was built on a swamp, on top of the paleo-ditch of *Acqua Bullicante* where a groundwater stream known as *Fosso della Marranella* runs (Procesi *et al* 2022: 6). One hundred years later, this area of east Rome has developed into a densely populated, highly urbanized and gentrifying neighborhood, which counts the lowest number of green areas in the city (Battisti *et al* 2017: 180). Water played a major role in this process, by both enabling this particular development and disenabling others. Indeed, the *Viscosa* factory established itself on the site of the *Aqua Bullicante* in 1922 as the presence of the subterranean aquifer enabled it to use water essential for the production of artificial silk (Fiocca 2022: 54). Yet, it is this same aquifer that, in 1992, prevented the planned construction on the site of what was supposed to become the largest shopping mall of its time in Rome. 'Matterphorically' – denoting here the articulation of meaning in relation to matter (Gandorfer and Ayub 2021) – the water resisted against the construction on site of the planned mall.

The *Viscosa* factory operated from 1923 until 1954. Of the 15 hectares of property, half were built for the workers' housing and other service facilities. A small pine forest was also planted on the site. When the factory closed in 1954, the area was abandoned, leaving time and space for fauna and flora to reappropriate the site. In 1968, to protect the landscape features of the pine forest, the hill area was expropriated by the municipality (*Decreto Ministeriale del 23 marzo 1968 ex L. 1497/1939 per preservare le "bellezze naturali"*") based on an Italian law adopted in 1939 for the 'Protection of Natural Beauty' (*Legge 29 giugno 1939, n. 1497 "Protezione delle bellezze naturali"*) and established as a public garden (Vecchiotti 2019: 107). In 1969, the industrial plant and surrounding land were purchased first by the *SNIA Viscosa* company and later, in 1990, by the *Società Pinciana* (commonly referred to as the Ex-SNIA company). The objective of the Ex-SINA' purchase was to convert the former factory into Rome's largest shopping mall. The project, however, was immediately opposed by the local community, which sought to protect one of the rare public gardens in the city (Engel 2022). The protection of the pine forest as a public garden by local activists testifies that protests and mobilizations existed on-site already before the emergence of the *lago bullicante*, which this chapter builds on. When in 1992, the Ex-SNIA company started digging the ground with a falsified permit to illegally build the parking lot of the planned shopping mall, it inadvertently hit the aquifer of *Acqua Bullicante*, thereby creating a leakage of water that proved impossible to divert to sewers. The construction site and its nearby area were soon flooded, giving rise to a 1-hectare by 5-meter deep lake. The *Lago Ex-SNIA* – later renamed *lago bullicante* – emerged from the underground, and with it a collective came into being to fight for the maintenance of the lake and its ecosystem.

At first, an unorganized form of civic resistance took hold of the site and its newly constituted lake. In 1993, the CSOA Ex-SNIA (which stands for *Centro Sociale Occupato Autogestito*) occupied and self-managed the remaining industrial building to prevent the Ex-SNIA company from pursuing its illegal construction plans. It took years before the abruptly interrupted excavation pit filled with water, drowning debris and construction materials, finally turned into an ecosystem (Tola 2019: 208). Once the water level stabilized, fauna and flora slowly accustomed, turning the site into one of the few green areas of the Prenestino neighborhood just below the pine garden (Battisti *et al* 2017: 180; see Figures 9.1 and 9.2). In 1997, the Italian Ministry of Cultural and Environmental Goods eventually recognized this green area as a site of cultural and environmental interest (*Decreto del Ministero dei Beni Culturali ed Ambientali*) and inaugurated the public park *Parco Prenestino* – later renamed *Parco delle Energie* – of approximately 6.5 hectares (Vecchiotti 2019: 110; see also Figure 9.2).

FIGURE 9.1 The *lago bullicante*, Rome © Pierre Kattar 2021.

FIGURE 9.2 An overview plan of the *lago bullicante* © Francesco Pasta 2020.

For the next close to ten years, however, the site would remain closed to the public (Ex-SNIA Archive).[1] According to Italian law, when the state expropriates a private property 'for the common good', that property must be effectively used for such purpose within ten years, or the prior owner can reclaim it. The inaction from the part of the state to open the site to the public constituted a real threat for the site and its ecosystem, as the former owner of the Ex-SNIA company would regain its private property rights over the land, which now included the *lago bullicante*. Massive public protests were therefore held over the years to pressure the municipality to intervene on the site. Days before the ten-year deadline in 2007, the municipality sent workers to 'open a breach' (the *breccia di Portonaccio*) in the factory's perimetral brick wall, finally creating a public access gate to the park (Pasta 2020).

1 The Forum Parco delle Energie established an important archive to collect documents found in the abandoned factory and sustain a process of remembrance about the struggles of the site. On the history and role of this archive and its political project of remembrance that weaves together the past of the factory and the present of the lake, both industrial and natural history, see (Tola 2019).

Following years of resistance against real estate speculation and plans to construct a residential complex in the area, the *Parco delle Energie* was finally recognized as a public park opened to everyone, the communal management of which was granted to the *Forum Parco delle Energie* in 2008. In 2011, a meeting space for the collective was inaugurated (*La Casa del Parco*). It consists of a polyfunctional indoor and outdoor space (Vecchiotti 2019: 112). Ever since then, the Forum has been fighting for the lake to be recognized as a 'natural monument' (*monumento naturale*). Under Italian law, 'natural monuments' are areas characterized by a 'natural' feature, such as a rich biodiversity, that is particularly emphasized due to its specific aesthetic quality that grants them a high 'cultural' and symbolic significance (*Legge quadro 394 del 6 dicembre 1991*).[2] In Italy, the state delegates the protection and selection of protected areas – including 'natural monuments' – to the regions. On 30 June 2020, the Lazio region finally recognized the *lago bullicante* as *monumento naturale* (*Decreto del Presidente della Regione Lazio n. T00108 (B.U.R. 2/7/2020 n. 83)*). At the time of writing, in 2023, the area is thus divided into three sectors: the public *Parco delle Energie*, the state-owned *lago bullicante* recognized as a 'natural monument', and the privately owned ruins of the Ex-SNIA factory (see Figure 9.2).

Ultimately, the *lago bullicante* emerged from a series of 'unplanned stochastic events': from the illegal development of a construction site to the inadvertent leakage of an aquifer, thereby turning an abandoned and degraded industrial site into an ecosystem worthy of conservation with 'about 300 plant species, 11 plant communities, 3 EU priority habitats, 62 bird species including 3 taxa of conservation concern at continental scale' (Battisti *et al* 2017: 179). As Battisti *et al* observed: '[t]he case of ex SNIA Viscosa is a serendipitous example of unintended restoration where no financial resources have been used' (ibid: 183). While it is arguably the general absence of humans that enabled this wild urban restoration process of ecological reparation, the latter was only possible due to the presence of particular humans engaged to defend this ecosystem. The spark that ignited the collective action was the accidental hitting of the water vein – the paleo-ditch of *Acqua Bullicante* and the groundwater stream known as *Fosso della Marranella* – but only the slowness of urban city development and transformation in Rome, the decades of inaction by the Roman municipality and the relentless resistance against further urban developing plans by the local community, allowed the lake to transform into a flourishing ecosystem (Pasta 2020). The continuous

2 According to the glossary of the European Environment Agency, a 'natural monument' is a 'natural/cultural feature which is of outstanding or unique value because of its inherent rarity, representative of aesthetic qualities or cultural significance', at www.eea.europa.eu/help/glossary/eea-glossary/natural-monument.

transformations that the site underwent, most recently by being recognized as a 'natural monument' – a hybrid, both human and nonhuman, natural and cultural, Anthropocene-like legal creature – resulted from the tireless resistance of a collective ready to *act with* the lake. It is to this collective and its actions I now turn.

An Ecological Refusal of the 'Human' – Becoming More- and Less-Than-Human

This second section reflects on the dynamics of collective action that the *lago bullicante* illuminates. The collective that today cares for the site, the lake and its ecosystem did not exist prior to the appearance of water over ground. While immediate protests took place to re-act against the construction plans of the shopping mall before 1992, it was the sudden creation of the flooded area that led to an ongoing mobilization to care for the maintenance and protection of the site. The collective that acts today, in other words, emerged from and through those humans and nonhumans who were interpellated by the sudden spring of water from the underground. It is, as such, the intra-actions between humans and nonhumans with differential, asymmetrical yet mutually constitutive agencies that enacted this ecosystem, the existence of which cannot be disentangled from the humans and nonhumans that constitute and hold it together. This ecosystem, as a relata, emerged from relations between humans and nonhumans. As Barad puts it indeed: 'relata do not pre-exist relations' (Barad 2007: 33). Relata, in other words, have no individual, exclusive or separate agency prior to the relations that constitute them. This, of course, is not to say that the inhabitants of the area and the underground water of the aquifer had no agency prior to the digging of the latter in 1992, but that following the enactment of the lake, its becoming was contingent upon the entangled agencies of the humans and nonhumans who mutually constitute its being. The power of the water, in this case, can neither be disentangled from the illegal digging exerted by the Ex-SNIA company against the land, nor can it be disentangled from the mobilization of the inhabitants of the Prenestino area of Rome, who cared for its maintenance as well as all the species – whether the plants, vegetations, insects or animals, but also the concrete skeleton of the factory that is still engulfed in the water – and who today form part of the restored ecosystem.

Each action taken by the collective, and each new legal form that the site and its ecosystem were transformed into – from a private property, later partly expropriated into a public garden, and the lake now recognized as a 'natural monument', hosting three EU priority habitats as special areas of conservation in danger of disappearing (Battisti *et al* 2017: 179) – were thus enactments of differentiated/entangled agencies between humans and nonhumans with 'boundary-making practices that produce "objects" and "subjects" and other differences out of, and in terms of, a changing relationality' (Barad 2007: 93). These differences matter since an entangled agency does not mean that everything is connected to everything or that everything becomes one. Instead, each action both joins and disjoins those within and without the collective that acts, without 'producing (absolute) separation' (Barad 2019: 265). The differential degree of agencies and the differences between humans and nonhumans they produce are therefore key when it comes to understanding the collective action at stake. As Ferreira da Silva puts it, it is a process of 'differentiation without separability' (Ferreira da Silva 2016: 64–5). Equally important here are the 'boundary-making practices [of differentiated/entangled agencies] that produce "objects" and "subjects"', where the inverted commas serve to highlight a departure or rupture from traditional understandings of both objects and subjects. Indeed, throughout modernity and especially within Western epistemological frameworks, objects and subjects were defined as opposing poles within a dichotomy and seen as mutually exclusive. While the category of the subject was crafted on the basis of an ideal-type figure of a free, self-possessed and autonomous White human being, in contrast, objects referred to what could be owned, appropriated and exploited – not only nonhuman animals, plants, minerals and land, but also inhuman chattel slaves, Native and Aboriginal peoples (Wynter 1975: 10–11). Such dehumanized objects were amenable to human subjects' control and deprived of their own agency or power to act. When revisiting these categories, the point is then not to get rid of the distinction between subjects and objects but to rethink their intra-relations and emergence as 'subjects' and 'objects', where one comes into being as such only and always in its relation to the other. A reconfiguration of subjects and objects through such a prism inevitably leads to a displacement and a refusal of conventional liberal understandings of 'subjects' and 'objects'.

Indeed, rethinking collective action through differential yet entangled agency between humans and nonhumans disrupts therefore an absolute separation between subjects and objects within the collective that acts. The collective is inherently of a *more-than*-'human' nature, since it displaces at once the modern centering of the 'human subject' as sole agent of (legal and political) action, and re-centers the 'nonhuman other' into the frame of analysis and of action (Tschakert 2020). This is evident in the case of the *lago bullicante*, where the human collective acts not for but with nonhumans, and its composition and agency change on the basis of the evolution of its state of (well-)being. But the collective can also be of a *less-than*-'human' nature. The displacement of the 'human subject' in Indigenous, Black and decolonial works, as well as by feminist activists engaged in refusing the patriarchal figure of the White 'Man' against which being 'Human' is positioned (Odysseos 2023; Jackson 2020; Weheliye 2014; Wynter 2003), have recovered the notion of the 'inhuman' to attend to the blurring in Blackness between dehumanized humans and nonhumans. Historically, the liberal understanding of the 'human' subject originally placed Black beings outside of this category, and into that of nonhuman objects as chattel slaves (Walcott 2021: 16). In addition to this 'thingification', Black humans objectified as nonhumans were also bestialized as abject animals – as *sub*-humans and hence '*in*-human' (Jackson 2020: 18; Bennett 2020). As Wynter noted: '[t]he indigenous, the unchosen, was to be transformed from the human subject of his own culture into the inhuman object of the European culture' (Wynter 1975: 10). While the category of the 'inhuman' is today used in different ways by different authors – with Barad, for example, using it to refer to 'the indeterminate non/being non/becoming of mattering and not mattering . . . which holds open the space of the liveliness of indeterminacies that bleed through the cuts and inhabit the between of particular entanglements' (Barad 2012: 222) – I use it here to refer to the simultaneous dehumanization of the human (the human turned into nonhuman) and the structural subjugation of the nonhuman (the nonhuman turned into the inhuman) (Yusoff 2021: 667). The 'inhuman', then, refers to being both *sub*- and *supra*-human *at once* – not as being more *or* less human but 'more *and* less' than human (Harney and Moten 2021: 140).

For Yusoff, speaking of the 'inhuman' is therefore a way to 'understand Blackness as a historically constituted and intentionally enacted deformation in the formation of subjectivity, a deformation that presses an inhuman categorization and the inhuman earth into intimacy' (Yusoff 2019: 11). 'In the forced alliances with the inhuman', Yusoff contends, 'a different mode of subjective relation is forged, where Blackness is a name for nonnormative subjectivity' (ibid: 28). This understanding of an inhuman 'nonnormative subjectivity' desediments the Whiteness of being (a human subject), which remains posited as the norm against which all other modes of being and becoming are measured. While scholars like Margaret Davies are working to pluralize 'normativities' by recognizing those of nonhumans, thereby de-centering the normativity of humans and reckoning with 'the existence of multiple normative worlds' (Davies 2022: 21),[3] 'inhuman normativities' is doing something else or rather something more. In addition to breaking with the sole attention granted to the normative subjectivity of the 'human' and reckoning with nonhuman normativities – thereby advancing a form of *more-than-human* normativity – it also breaks with a 'human' normativity as such by refusing to think with the ideal-type figure of the 'Human' and foreground the lived experience and potentiality of the 'inhuman' instead – thereby advancing a form of *less-than-human* normativity. To paraphrase

3 For Davies, this demands to 'position law and normativity in general as ontologically prior to the designation of subjects and objects: everything becomes subject and object within plural normative relationships' (Davies 2022: 1).

Yusoff, then, the 'inhuman' enacts 'a refusal of the white overburden of [being human] that has secreted its excess into every pore of the Earth' (Yusoff 2019: 108). If working with the 'inhuman' simultaneously engages a way of being more- and less-than-'human', this dual refusal of the 'human' and its normativity – including its normative mode of legally ordering the world as we know it – transpires as essential to de-humanize normativity and re-humanize it otherwise.

If this twofold reconfiguration might register more as an academic endeavor than a legal and political strategy, the collective actions with and for the *lago bullicante* show traces of such processes. While the *more-than-human* dimension is evident, the *less-than-human* one may not be apparent at first sight. This might not come as a surprise, since many forms of ecological resistance practiced in Europe today have been denounced for articulating their struggles in anti-capitalist rather than broader anti-colonial terms. As Gay noted in relation to the ZAD (*zone à défendre*) of Notre-Dame-des-Landes in France – whose struggle echoes that of the *lago bullicante* in Rome – these ecological movements are often practiced as 'white utopias' with no reckoning with the White privileges of the human activists involved (Gay 2020). Siva, from the British Black and People of Colour collective *Land in Our Names* (LION), also stressed the need to reckon with the interconnectedness between ecological repair, healing and concrete reparations for damages done to people and nonhumans through colonialism and extractivism while emphasizing the centrality of racism to these enterprises and their persistent inheritances in the present (Siva 2023: 161).

As it stands, many European ecological resistance struggles keep falling short of embedding their insurgencies into a 'decolonial ecology' that bridges the divide between environmentalism and decolonization (Ferdinand 2022). Yet, a 'decolonial ecology' is imperative to challenge the 'double fracture' of modernity – an environmental fracture on the one hand, driven by a technocratic and capitalist mode of inhabiting the earth leading to its ecological devastation, and a colonial fracture on the other hand, instilled by Western colonialism and imperialism that resulted in racial slavery and the annihilation of Native, Indigenous and Aboriginal modes of inhabiting the earth otherwise (ibid: 1). In a similar vein, in this volume Hohmann and Schwöbel-Patel caution against new materialist theories and practices that are decoupled from broader historical materialist traditions that bring to the fore the racial foundations of the global capitalist order (Hohmann and Schwöbel-Patel 2023).[4]

4 As Arvidsson cautions as well, however: 'the "new" of new materialism is not a reference to a materialism that is "new" in relation to historical materialism or Marxism . . . the case is rather that new materialism(s) primarily builds on matter and materiality such as it has been

But the less-than-'human' is not limited to a displacement of the 'human' through the 'inhuman'. Indeed, central to the figure of the liberal 'human' being displaced lies also an ideal of humanist individualism – of a self-possessed, free and autonomous mode of being 'human'. The sociality that is performed in works that recover the 'inhuman', instead, rejects the individual in favor of the collective. At the heart of this in- or less-than-human understanding lies therefore also a process of de-individualization. The collective agency does not lie with a bundle of preexisting individually constituted agents, but with the collective that emerges from its intra-relating human and nonhuman constituents. Relata, as noted above, do not preexist relations. Drawing on Berlant's reworking of individuality, it is a 'nonsovereign relationality' that is 'the foundational quality of being in common' – 'a genre carved from within dynamics of relation rather than a state prior to it or distinct from it' (Berlant 2016: 394). It is this understanding of the less-than-'human' as necessarily collective or common – as a process of becoming common – that one can retrieve in practices of ecological resistance that refuse the liberal, individualistic, 'human' figure. As argued earlier – with Gay, Siva and Ferdinand – not every form of de-individualized becoming common inherently reflects an inhuman nonnormative subjectivity (or Black sociality), but traces of a de-individualized sociality necessarily underpin any relationally composed practice of commoning. As Harney and Moten note, this 'rejection of interpersonal [or interindividual] relations, and therefore of the person as an independent, strategic agent' marks the difference between 'common life' – or a life shared in common – and 'undercommon living' (Harney and Moten 2021: 122; see also Harney and Moten 2013). It is in the undercommons that 'the condition of possibility of becoming-common' lies, or perhaps more precisely 'of being-in-(the)-commons' (Moten 2018: 24), where the only mode of being is becoming.[5] Returning to the case of the *lago bullicante* in Rome in the next and final section, it is in this more- and less-than-'human' ecological practice of resistance and refusal that we find a case of 'posthumanist commoning'. This practice of 'posthumanist commoning' speaks to both the *more-than-human* by centering nonhuman water, vegetation and all animals affected, and the *less-than-human* by recovering

considered in physics . . . philosophy of science, and philosophy broadly conceived . . . [in] the Spinozian philosophical tradition, especially as popularized and interpreted by Gilles Deleuze and Felix Guattari'. As such: '[t]he materialism in relation to which "new" materialism is new is thus not historical materialism or Marxism, but the much broader and "older" field of physics and the philosophical question of matter as it is considered in e.g., Aristotle, Spinoza, Nietzsche, Freud and not the least by the said Deleuze and Guattari' (Arvidsson 2023b).

5 This 'being-in-the-common(s)' resonates also with Jean-Luc Nancy's understanding of 'being-in-common' as a 'being-with', whereby '[t]he meaning of being is not common', and hence 'existence *is* only in being partitioned and shared'. Against this backdrop, 'the question should be the community of being, and not the being of community. Or if you prefer: the community of existence, and not the essence of community' (Nancy 1991: 1–2, 4–5).

the inhuman, collective and anti-liberal understanding of the practice of commoning.

'Posthumanist Commoning' as Ecological Reparation

In Italy, the practice of posthumanist commoning can be viewed as pertaining to a longer lineage that traces back to autonomist movements committed to occupy and de-commodify social centers in the 1960s and 1970s, driven by principles of self-management and self-organization by the collective (Ghelfi 2023; Gray 2017; Montagna 2006). Such collective actions were primarily situated in urban settings and centered on social struggles (Paolini 2020). As noted by Nelson and Braun, the disengagement of the Italian *Autonomia* movement from environmental politics was 'undeniably conditioned by the political context of the 1970s', where 'in contrast to environmental movements elsewhere in Europe, for the Italian Greens "ecologism was born *against* the class struggles of the 1970s"' (Nelson and Braun 2017: 230, quoting Virno 1996: 253). The progressive intersectional convergence of the social and ecological struggles brought about alliances between social and ecological commoning. While keeping a distinction between 'social commons' (such as culture, knowledge or digital information) that do not operate under a logic of scarcity, and 'natural commons' (such as forests, rivers or the atmosphere) that do operate under a logic of scarcity, Hardt and Negri famously called for a general 'ecology of the common' (Hardt and Negri 2009: 139, 171).

The 2011 water referendum that overturned the privatization of water supplies in Italy (Mattei 2012) enabled a broadening of the understanding of 'common goods' (*beni comuni*) not as 'common pool resources' but as ecological relations that ensure and sustain livable conditions (Capra and Mattei 2015). The commons, here, are then best described as an activity or as a practice – as a verb, rather than as a noun (Linebaugh 2009: 279). Replacing the noun 'commons' with the verb 'commoning' serves 'to denote the continuous making and remaking of the commons through shared practice', where the commons is not a static community that exists *a priori* or a society to come *a posteriori* but something that is only ever constituted through acting and doing in common (Bresnihan 2015: 96).

Relations, rather than relata. *Becoming*, rather than being. *Commoning*, rather than the commons. The ongoing and unfolding nature of the collective action also implies that the dynamics of inclusion and exclusion depend on how an entity relates to and actively participates in the commoning practice, rather than seeing the 'commons' as 'being a discrete right vested in a person' (Bresnihan 2015: 97). Such 'resistant acts of ecological reparation' (Papadopoulos *et al* 2023) resemble what Papadopoulos coined as 'more-than-social movements' for ecological repair that create 'alterontological' forms of living (Ghelfi and Papadopoulos 2021, 2022; Ghelfi *et al* 2021). This emphasis on the more-than-social coincides with a posthumanist approach, as it rethinks social relations beyond human collectives and brings nonhumans and their agency to the foreground.

Much has already been written about commoning and posthumanism (Weber 2018). Thinking with the notions of more-and less-than-'human' collective action that I elaborated on earlier – where both nonhuman and inhuman normativities enter the frame of analysis – what I wish to bring to the attention of the reader are not only the reconfigured subjectivities at stake but also the specific spatio-temporal dynamics of posthumanist commoning. Indeed, if the example of the *lago bullicante* has shown how the collective that acts is not merely composed of 'human' subjects, little has so far been said about the spatiality and temporality of this collective that acts. These spatio-temporal dynamics will serve as important markers when turning to the (international) legal implications of posthumanist commoning in the conclusion.

The spatiality of the actions of the posthumanist commoning practice around the *lago bullicante* reaches both under and over ground, from the aquifer to the soil and its living ecology. The materiality of the space is both liquid and solid, from the water to the concrete infrastructure of the abandoned factory and all the vegetation and animals that today inhabit this space. The infrastructure is here 'no longer an effect but a cause' for the living, both human and nonhuman (Barua 2021: 1468). What is more, the space is delineated into different sites, the protection of which is secured through distinct legal forms – the privately owned ruins of the Ex-SNIA factory, which cannot be destroyed due to their industrial archaeological relevance; the state-owned lake recognized as a 'natural monument' (*demanio*); and the public park overseen by the collective *Forum Parco delle Energie*. Fundamentally, however, the spatiality of the collective that acts is not bounded by or to these local sites. Indeed, the ecological practice of posthumanist commoning reaches beyond the area of Prenestino, beyond the city of Rome, and beyond the state of Italy. On 17 September 2022, a transnational action took place with another posthumanist collective acting with an artificial/natural lake, located in Forest, Brussels, Belgium. Similar to the *lago bullicante*, the Belgian *marais Wiels* emerged in 2007 from the construction site of the former Wielemans-Ceuppens brewery abandoned in 1980, where there, too, an aquifer was accidentally pierced (Ranzato 2023; Bousenna 2022). On the day of the 'twinning' of the two anthropogenic lakes-turned-biodiversity-rich-ecosystems in the heart of urban metropolises, it was declared that '[t]his twinning symbolizes the new European struggle for a livable and regenerative city for all, humans and nonhumans' (MaraisWiels 2022).[6] Indeed, such transnational collaborative ecological actions can help strategize for further establishments and maintenance of experimental socio-ecological

6 The original text, in French, reads as follows: *Ce jumelage symbolise la lutte nouvelle européenne pour une ville vivable et régénérative pour tous et toutes, humains et non-humains.* (My translation).

regenerations through practices of posthumanist commoning (Papadopoulos 2018). The question of maintenance is key, here, since the violence and attacks faced by many of such collectives often leads to their dismantling.

Finally, the temporality and politics of time of such practices of posthumanist commoning can therefore best be described as imminent, fragile and continuously ongoing. As established earlier, these collectives did not exist as such prior to their actions but emerged through them. Whereas a spark can ignite action – in this case, the water springing from the underground – ecological reparation, as a slowly unfolding event, takes time. Whereas the temporality of ecological (re)generations is slow, the temporality of the collective that acts must be fast yet steady at once. Fast to act, steady to organize. A steady organizing is key to secure resistance – a resistance against anthropogenic ecological harms through an ecological refusal of anthropocentric, individualistic and exploitative modes of relating to nonhumans. This is the time of resistance. Time is resistance. Time as resistance. The ecological reparation must attend to the nonhumans and their temporalities of (re)generation, and to the humans in all their differential intra-relating – those present to act with the posthumanist commoning practice, and those acting against. The dismantling of infrastructures of resistance – as recently observed with the agreement from the part of the French state not to build the airport in Nantes, thereby enforcing the dismantling of the occupying *ZAD* – testify to the temporal conflicts or conflicts of time that resistant acts of ecological reparation can face, being forced into an end, while 'commoning' as an activity, a verb, a doing, is always ongoing and unfolding. What is, then, the end of posthumanist commoning? In the form of a conclusion, let me draw some possible answers to this question by reflecting on the end(s) of posthumanist commoning in relation to international law.

Conclusion

What would it mean, and what would it imply, for international law/yers to think with posthumanist commoning? Which insights can be drawn from posthumanist commoning – as practices of ecological resistance, refusal and reparation – for international law, and how can the case of the *lago bullicante* be helpful in this endeavor? Many scholars already pointed out the problematic nature of 'environmental' protection in international law, rooted in neo/colonial understandings of 'nature' as a resource amenable to economic exploitation, the externalities of which must be regulated (Natarajan and Khoday 2014; Natarajan and Dehm 2022; Petersmann 2022: 17–55; Jones 2023: 110–27). Many also linked this problem to the principle of state sovereignty when it comes to regulating environmental pollution, as well as the lack of enforcement of international environmental laws due to jurisdictional constraints. These constraints entail standing and admissibility issues before supra-national judicial mechanisms, as well as issues related to extra-territorial state responsibility (Petersmann 2021). Much has also been written about the need to rethink the notion(s) of 'property' and 'possession' – especially in relation to 'land' and 'territory' – as the kernels of (international) law (Davies 2012; Porras 2014; Mattei *et al* 2019; Cotula 2021). These questions are all directly related to what counts or what registers as the 'common good' or the 'public interest' in international law (Petersmann 2022: 113–29), with issues such as the protection of the 'environment', access to 'land' and the use of 'natural resources' all being paramount in such debates. Discussions about the protection of the 'commons' have therefore come to the forefront to (re)configure what counts as such, by expanding or rethinking doctrines of 'common heritage', 'common concern' or the 'global commons' (Brunnée 2007; Ranganathan 2016; Feichtner and Ranganathan 2019). In recent years, attention for the 'commons' particularly increased in relation to ecological concerns. It is against the backdrop of this resurgence of the 'commons' that the related yet distinct practice of 'commoning' developed.

As I argued in this chapter, however, the complexities of 'commoning' and the challenges that these practices pose to law cut deeper. As Gutwirth and Stengers put it:

> [A]n embracing of the commons by jurists is not a small challenge, since it requires them to reconsider nothing less than the 'rule of law'. If the law is yielded by the process of commoning, if it has become a commons, its 'role' has obviously taken over from its 'rule'. Thinking the 'role of law' for the commons is a difficult test for jurists.
>
> (Gutwirth and Stengers 2016: 11)

If the 'role' of law needs to be reconfigured in relations to practices of 'commoning' – or put the other way around, if practices of 'commoning' necessarily reconfigure the 'role' of law, since the certainty of its 'rule' is challenged by the imminent, ongoing and continuously emerging nature of the activity – this reconfiguration presents additional challenges when it comes to *international* law. Indeed, practice of 'commoning' applied to ecological concerns reconfigure at once the subjectivity, spatiality and temporality of international law.

In terms of subjectivity, there is not only a move away from the liberal figure of the 'human subject' that one can observe in transversal practices of posthumanist commoning – with a broadening of the frame of analysis and of action from 'humans' to more- *and* less-than-'humans' – but also a displacement of the state as key interlocutor. The heterogeneity of participants in posthumanist collective actions is further complicated by the diverging and at times conflicting terms of their commitments (Bulle 2022: 48). For some, the goal might be to better implement or to reform the (international) legal order and its key doctrines – by overcoming, for example, divides between private and public property, or by advocating for a recognition of 'rights' granted to particular ecosystems. For others, the goal might instead be to break free from the (international) legal order and from the state more generally, thereby embedding the struggles into an abolitionist and anarchist approach. As exemplified with the *lago bullicante*, such approaches are also organized supra-nationally, where the nation-state loses its primordial anchor as geographical legal *order*, and practices of *ordering* (which are not necessarily 'legal' as such, since both the state and hence the law lose their relevance) emerge through forms of collaboration, cooperation and solidarity across more-than-social movements. And not the least, as the 'boiling' and 'agitated' *lago bullicante* shows, both order and ordering can emerge through 'insurgent' water, waterflows and related element agents agnostic to national, international and transnational jurisdictions. But the diverging and conflicting sensitivities and commitments of practices of posthumanist commoning will also determine the nature and form of the collective actions at stake. While reformist approaches to (international) law or the legal order might engage with the state and the law as such to demand an inclusion and recognition of the collective and its actions – as instantiated with the *lago bullicante* by the municipal expropriation of private property to establish a public garden, and the recent recognition of the lake as a 'natural monument' by the region – anarchist approaches to law and abolitionist practices of posthumanist commoning can enact refusals and rejections of the legal order that rest on occupying, (re)ordering and inhabiting a site otherwise, not with but against the law. While reformist approaches to the legal order can attract and cultivate sporadic collective actions of support and calls for change on a site, practices of posthumanist commoning, as forms of (legal) (re)ordering, demand enduring enactments of alternative living. As aptly put by Berlant: commoning transpires here as an act 'not to possess but to be possessed, to submit to being dispossessed of property in the self' (Berlant 2016: 400).

In terms of spatiality too, the transversal practices of posthumanist commoning enable to shift attention from a register of protection of the environment to a terrestrialization of the living (Petersmann 2023a). Important insights apply here to international law, especially its relation to and understanding of territoriality. Practices of posthumanist commoning displace the territoriality of struggles for a *terrestrializing* of (geo)politics. Such a *terrestrializing* can help attending to and engaging with 'critical zones' where the adjective 'critical' itself gets a new meaning: instead of trying to indicate a distance from the situations that require judgment, it points to the effort of gaining a critical proximity with the situations that we have to live in (Latour and Weibel 2020: 9). In contrast to territoriality, terrestrial perspectives 'modify the very definition of the land on which politics take place', and require 'another placement for science, another definition of law and sovereignty, another understanding of how entities overlap' (ibid: 8, 227). The living ecology of the terrestrial space – from the subterranean to the atmosphere – shifts the focus of analysis and of action by trans-forming and queering boundaries and binaries: territorial versus extra-territorial concerns, private versus public property, humans versus non-/in-humans, state versus non-state (legal) orders.

Finally, in terms of temporality, practices of posthumanist commoning are also relevant to (re)think the time(s) and temporality of international law. Much has already been written about the limitations of the *ex post* nature of environmental protection before courts, and the weak implementation of international laws that seek to protect the environment *ex ante* (Hilson 2019; Dehm 2022). The increasing invocation of granting 'rights' to nonhumans – whether animals or broader ecosystems – will face the same challenges due to the contradictory temporalities of law (Petersmann 2023a). In contrast, practices of posthumanist commoning enact forms of ecological resistance, refusal and reparation with distinct – and at times also conflicting – temporalities of action, from sporadic interventions to enduring occupations. In this chapter, and following posthuman feminist scholar Emily Jones, I tried to reckon with the tensions and paradoxes that emerge when thinking with and against international law, by 'noting that, through working within the system and seeking to improve it, one risks legitimizing the system itself' (Jones 2023: 155). In trying to navigate these complexities and complicities, I found inspiration in practices of posthumanist commoning that reveal emancipatory modes of ecological resistance, refusal and reparation that experiment with forms of cooperation (Harcourt 2023) and co-existence beyond, beneath or against a state's (re)actions for the living.

To conclude, if practices of posthumanist commoning gain their meaning and relevance *after* the human, *after* the individual, *after* the commons and, arguably, also *after* the state, this 'after' must not be misunderstood as implying an abandonment of human and state-based duties and responsibilities, but as a necessity to re-collectivize them otherwise. What is at stake here are distinct ways of thinking and acting in relation to such duties and response-abilities by broadening the analytical lens to include non- and in-human interests and agencies (with all their differential vulnerabilities and asymmetrical power imbalances) to enact forms of ecological resistance, refusal and reparation that can account for them (Petersmann 2023b). As such, the situated example of the *lago bullicante* served to reflect upon and attend to the polysemic nature of this 'after' – not as an absolute overcoming of the 'human', the 'individual' or the 'state' legal order, but as their radical reconfigurations in favor of the more- and less-than-'human', the collective and the (legal) ordering. It is here that novel modalities of 'becoming common' – inspired by and unfolding from Indigenous, Native and Black practices of survival and fugitive socialities – can shed light on the imperative to revisit and refuse liberal categories of international law that keep organizing, structuring and maintaining enduring socio-ecological catastrophes.

Acknowledgments

This research was supported by the Dutch NWO 'Veni' Grant (VI. Veni.211R.026) on 'Anthropocene Legalities: Reconfiguring Legal Relations within More-than-Human Worlds'. The research was carried out during a ten-month residential fellowship at the Istituto Svizzero di Roma (ISR) as part of the 'Transdisciplinary *Roma Calling*' programme (2022–2023). I am grateful to Matilda Arvidsson and Emily Jones for their constructive comments on an earlier draft, and to the participants of the transdisciplinary event 'Becoming Common – Ecological Resistance, Refusal, Reparation' I hosted at the ISR on 17–18 May 2023, at <www.istitutosvizzero.it/tavola-rotonda/becoming-common>.

References

Arvidsson, M. (2023a [Forthcoming]) 'On Gardens of the Anthropocene: Gendered Violence, Colonial Legal Enclosures, and Feminist Posthuman Kinship', in A. Grear and D. Kwek (eds) *New Materialist Tangles in and for the Anthropocene*, Bristol: Bristol University Press.

Arvidsson, M. (2023b) 'Posthuman Feminism as a Theoretical and Methodological Approach to International Law', in M. Arvidsson and E. Jones (eds) *International Law and Posthuman Theory*, Abingdon: Routledge (this volume).

Barad, K. (2007) *Meeting the Universe Halfway: Quantum Physics and the Entanglement of Matter and Meaning*, Durham: Duke University Press.

Barad, K. (2012) 'On Touching – The Inhuman That Therefore I Am', *Differences: A Journal of Feminist Cultural Studies*, 23(3): 206–23.

Barad, K. (2019) 'Quantum Entanglements and Hauntological Relations of Inheritance: Dis/continuities, SpaceTime Enfoldings, and Justice-to-Come', *Derrida Today*, 3: 240–68.

Barua, M. (2021) 'Infrastructure and Non-Human Life: A Wider Ontology', *Progress in Human Geography*, 45(6): 1467–89.

Battisti, C. *et al* (2017) 'Paradoxical Environmental Conservation: Failure of an Unplanned Urban Development as a Driver of Passive Ecological Restoration', *Environmental Development*, 24: 179–86.

Bennett, J. (2020) *Being Property Once Myself: Blackness and the End of Man*, Boston: Harvard University Press.

Berlant, B. (2016) 'The Commons: Infrastructures for Troubling Times', *Environment and Planning D: Society and Space*, 34(3): 393–419.

Bousenna, Y. (2022) 'L'insurrection des ruines – Le Lago Bullicante', *Socialter*, 166–73.

Braidotti, R. (2019) 'A Theoretical Framework for the Critical Posthumanities', *Theory, Culture & Society*, 36(6): 31–61.

Bresnihan, P. (2015) 'The More-than-Human Commons: From Commons to Commoning', in S. Kirwan, L. Dawney and J. Brigstocke (eds) *Space, Power and the Commons: The Struggle for Alternative Futures*, Abingdon: Routledge, 92–112.

Brunnée, J. (2007) 'Common Areas, Common Heritage, and Common Concern', in J. Brunnée, D. Bodansky and E. Hey (eds) *The Oxford Handbook of International Environmental Law*, Oxford: Oxford University Press, 551–72.

Bulle, S. (2022) 'How the Non-Human Turn Challenges the Social Sciences: The Case of Environmental Struggles at Notre-Dame-des-Landes, France', in A. Mubi Brighenti and M. Kärrholm (eds) *Territories, Environments, Politics: Explorations in Territoriology*, Abingdon: Routledge.

Capra, F., and U. Mattei (2015) *The Ecology of Law: Toward a Legal System in Tune with Nature and Community*. Berrett-Koehler Publishers.

Cotula, L. (2021) 'The Shifting Contours of Property "Social Function" in the Neoliberal Era', *Transformative Private Law Blog*. www.transformativeprivatelaw.com/the-shifting-contours-of-property-social-function-in-the-neoliberal-era/

Davies, M. (2012) 'Persons, Property, and Community', *Feminists@Law*, 2(2).

Davies, M. (2022) *EcoLaw: Legality, Life, and the Normativity of Nature*, Abingdon: Routledge.

Dehm, J. (2022) 'The Temporalities of Environmental Human Rights', in K. McNeilly and B. Warwick (eds) *The Times and Temporalities of International Human Rights Law*, London: Bloomsbury.

Engel, M. (2022) 'The Ecological Potential of Rome's Urban Wilderness', *Common Edge*. https://commonedge.org/the-ecological-potential-of-romes-urban-wilderness/

Feichtner, I. and S. Ranganathan (eds) (2019) 'Symposium: International Law and Economic Exploitation in the Global Commons', *European Journal of International Law*, 30: 541.

Ferdinand, M. (2022) *Decolonial Ecology: Thinking from the Caribbean World*, Translated by A.P. Smith, Cambridge: Polity Press.

Ferreira da Silva, D. (2016) 'On Difference Without Separability'. https://biennial.com/files/pdfs/7879/d-ferreira-da-silva-on-difference-without-separability.pdf

Fiocca, G. (2022) 'Dove la natura si riprende i suoi diritti: Lago Bullicante Ex Snia – Roma', *Crítica Urbana*, 54–8.

Gandorfer, D. and Z. Ayub (2021) 'Introduction: Matterphorical', *Theory & Event*, 24(1): 2–13.

Gay, A. (2020) 'La crise d'une utopie blanche?', in J. Lindgaard (ed) *Éloge des Mauvaises Herbes: Ce que nous devons à la ZAD*, Paris: Les Liens qui Libèrent, 157–67.

Ghelfi, A. (2021) 'Farming in the Ecological Condition'. https://newalphabetschool.hkw.de/farming-in-the-ecological-condition

Ghelfi, A. (2023) 'New Peasantries in Italy: Eco-Commons, Agroecology and Food Communities', in D. Papadopoulos, M. Puig de la Bellacasa and M. Tacchetti (eds) *Ecological Reparation: Repair, Remediation and Resurgence in Social and Environmental Conflict*, Bristol: Bristol University Press, 194–207.

Ghelfi, A. and D. Papadopoulos (2021) 'Ungovernable Earth: Resurgence, Translocal Infrastructures, and More-Than-Social Movements', *Environmental Values*, 30(6): 681–9.

Ghelfi, A. and D. Papadopoulos (2022) 'More-Than-Social Movements: Politics of Matter, Autonomy, Alterontologies', in L. Pellizzoni, E. Leonardi and V. Asara (eds) *Handbook of Critical Environmental Politics*, London: Edward Elgar, 505–27.

Ghelfi, A., D. Papadopoulos, L. Pellizzoni and R. Raffaetà (2021) 'When Experimental Practice Comes First', *Technscienza: Italian Journal of Science & Technology Studies*, 12(1): 63–97.

Gray, N. (2017) 'Beyond the Right to the City: Territorial Autogestion and the Take Over the City Movement in 1970s', *Antipode*, 50(2).

Grear, A. and D. Bollier (eds) (2020) *The Great Awakening: New Modes of Life Amidst Capitalist Ruins*, Santa Barbara: Punctum Books.

Gutwirth, S. and I. Stengers (2016) 'The Law and the Commons', Presentation at 3d Global Thematic IASC-Conference on the Knowledge Commons) [on file with author].

Harcourt, B.E. (2023) *Cooperation: A Political, Economic, and Social Theory*, New York: Columbia University Press.

Hardt, M. and A. Negri (2009) *Commonwealth*, Cambridge: Harvard University Press.

Harney, S. and F. Moten (2013) *The Undercommons: Fugitive Planning & Black Study*, Wivenhoe: Minor Compositions.

Harney, S. and F. Moten (2021) *All Incomplete*, Wivenhoe: Minor Compositions.

Hilson, C. (2019) 'Framing Time in Climate Change Litigation', *Oñati Socio-Legal Series*, 9(3): 361–79.

Hohmann, J. and C. Schwöbel-Patel (2023) 'A Monument to E. G. Wakefield – New and Historical Materialist Dialogues for a Posthuman International Law', in M. Arvidsson and E. Jones (eds) *International Law and Posthuman Theory*, Abingdon: Routledge (this volume).

Jackson, Z.I. (2020) *Becoming Human: Matter and Meaning in an Antiblack World*, New York: New York University Press.

Jones, E. (2023) *Feminist Theory and International Law: Posthuman Perspectives*, Abingdon: Routledge.

Jones, E. and M. Arvidsson (2023) 'Introduction to Posthuman Theory and International Law', in M. Arvidsson and E. Jones (eds) *International Law and Posthuman Theory*, Abingdon: Routledge (this volume).

Jones, E., C. van Eijk and G. Heathcote (2023) 'The Common Heritage of Kin-Kind', in M. Arvidsson and E. Jones (eds) *International Law and Posthuman Theory*, Abingdon: Routledge (this volume).

Latour, B. and P. Weibel (eds) (2020) *Critical Zones: The Science and Politics of Landing on Earth*, Cambridge: MIT Press.

Linebaugh, P. (2009) *The Magna Carta Manifesto: Liberties and Commons for All*, Berkeley: University of California Press.

MaraisWiels (2022) 'Jumelage'. www.facebook.com/MaraisWiels/photos/pcb.202136212249842/202135862249877

Mattei, U. (2012) *Beni Comuni: Un Manifesto*, Roma: Editori Laterza.

Mattei, U. *et al* (2019) 'Commons as Possessions – the Path to Protection of the Commons in the ECHR System', *European Law Journal*, 25(3): 230–50.

Montagna, N. (2006) 'The De-Commodification of Urban Space and the Occupied Social Centres in Italy', *City: Analysis of Urban Trends, Culture, Theory, Policy, Action*, 10(3): 295–304.

Moten, F. (2018) *The Universal Machine (Consent Not to Be a Single Being)*, Durham: Duke University Press.

Nancy, J.-L. (1991) 'Of Being-in-Common', in Miami Theory Collective (ed) J. Creech (trans) *Community at Loose Ends*, Minneapolis: University of Minnesota Press, 1–12.

Natarajan, U. and J. Dehm (eds) (2022) *Locating Nature: Making and Unmaking International Law*, Cambridge: Cambridge University Press.

Natarajan, U. and K. Khoday (2014) 'Locating Nature: Making and Unmaking International Law', *Leiden Journal of International Law*, 27(3): 573–93.

Nelson, S. and B. Braun (2017) 'Autonomia in the Anthropocene: New Challenges to Radical Politics', *South Atlantic Quarterly*, 116(2): 223–35.

Odysseos, L. (2023) 'After Rights, After Man?Sylvia Wynter, Sociopoetic Struggle and the "Undared Shape"', *The International Journal of Human Rights*.

Ostrom, E. (2008) *Governing the Commons: The Evolution of Institutions for Collective Action*, Cambridge: Cambridge University Press.

Paolini, F. (2020) *Environment and Urbanization in Modern Italy*, Pittsburgh: University of Pittsburgh Press.

Papadopoulos, D. (2018) *Experimental Practice: Technoscience, Alterontologies, and More-than-Social Movements*, Durham: Duke University Press.

Papadopoulos, D., M. Puig de la Bellacasa and M. Tacchetti (eds) (2023) *Ecological Reparation: Repair, Remediation and Resurgence in Social and Environmental Conflict*, Bristol: Bristol University Press.

Pasta, F. (2020) 'A Construction Mistake in Rome That Created a Lake and United a Neighbourhood', *Failed Architecture.* https://failedarchitecture.com/a-construction-mistake-in-rome-that-created-a-lake-and-united-a-neighborhood/

Petersmann, M.-C. (2021) 'Response-abilities of Care in More-Than-Human Worlds', *Journal of Human Rights and the Environment*, 12(1): 102–24.

Petersmann, M.-C. (2022) *When Environmental Protection and Human Rights Collide: The Politics of Conflict Management by Regional Courts*, Cambridge: Cambridge University Press.

Petersmann, M.-C. (2023a) 'Life Beyond the Law – from the "Living Constitution" to the "Constitution of the Living"', *ZaöRV/Heidelberg Journal of International Law*, 82(4): 769–97.

Petersmann, M.-C. (2023b) 'In the Break (of Rights and Representation): Sociality Beyond the Non/Human Subject', *The International Journal of Human Rights* https://www.tandfonline.com/doi/full/10.1080/13642987.2023.2227124.

Porras, I. (2014) 'Appropriating Nature: Commerce, Property, and the Commodification of Nature in the Law of Nations', *Leiden Journal of International Law*, 27(3): 641–60.

Procesi, M. *et al* (2022) 'Science and Citizen Collaboration as Good Example of Geoethics for Recovering a Natural Site in the Urban Area of Rome (Italy)', *Sustainability*, 14(4429): 1–15.

Ranganathan, S. (2016) 'Global Commons', *European Journal of International Law*, 27(3): 693–717.

Ranzato, M. (2023) 'Lago Bullicante e Marais Wiels, inselvatichimento vs speculazione', *Il Giornale Dell'Architettura.* https://ilgiornaledellarchitettura.com/2023/01/10/bullicantea-e-marais-wiels-traiettorie-di-presente-e-futuro

Siva, S. (2023) 'Land in Our Names: Building an Anti-Racist Food Movement', in D. Papadopoulos, M. Puig de la Bellacasa and M. Tacchetti (eds) *Ecological Reparation: Repair, Remediation and Resurgence in Social and Environmental Conflict*, Bristol University Press, 161–3.

Tola, M. (2019) 'The Archive and the Lake: Labor, Toxicity, and the Making of Cosmopolitical Commons in Rome, Italy', *Environmental Humanities*, 11(1): 194–215.

Tschakert, P. (2020) 'More-Than-Human Solidarity and Multispecies Justice in the Climate Crisis', *Environmental Politics* 31(1):, 1–21.

Vecchiotti, A. (2019) 'Scenari di trasformazione per l'area Ex Snia di Roma – Un approccio di Sviluppo Urbano Integrato Collaborativo fondato sull'esperienza berlinese', Master Thesis, Politecnico di Torino. https://webthesis.biblio.polito.it/11768

Virno, P. (1996) 'Do You Remember Counterrevolution?', in P. Virno and M. Hardt (eds) *Radical Thought in Italy: A Potential Politics*, Iowa: University of Minnesota Press, 241–60.

Walcott, R. (2021) *The Long Emancipation: Moving Toward Black Freedom*, Durham: Duke University Press.

Weber, L.G. (2018) 'The Commons', in R. Braidotti and M. Hlavajova (eds) *Posthuman Glossary*, London: Bloomsbury, 83–6.

Weheliye, A. (2014) *Habeas Viscus: Racializing Assemblages, Biopolitics, and Black Feminist Theories of the Human*, Durham: Duke University Press.

Weston, B.H. and D. Bollier (2013) *Green Governance: Ecological Survival, Human Rights and the Law of the Commons*, Cambridge: Cambridge University Press.

Wynter, S. (1975) 'Black Metamorphosis: New Natives in a New World', New York Public Library, Schomburg Center for Research in Black Culture, Unpublished.

Wynter, S. (2003) 'Unsettling the Coloniality of Being/Power/Truth/Freedom: Towards the Human, After Man, Its Overrepresentation – an Argument', *CR: The New Centennial Review*, 3(3): 257–337.

Yusoff, K. (2019) *A Billion Black Anthropocenes or None*, Iowa: University of Minnesota Press.

Yusoff, K. (2021) 'The Inhumanities', *Annals of the American Association of Geographers*, 111(3): 663–76.

10

THE WAR ON DRUGS AS THE WAR ON THE NONHUMAN

Kojo Koram and Oscar Guardiola-Rivera

Introduction

International law's claim to universality rests on its self-appointed position as one of the markers of relations between humans. As a result, it seeks to cohere itself upon a defined category of what qualifies as the human. However, the writings of scholars such as Anthony Anghie, Ntina Tzouvala or Peter Fitzpatrick point to an alternative source for coherence for the law, arguing that the law, unable to provide a fixed image of the human, binds itself together through an opposition to an imagined negation of the human. Far from being a neutral instrument of statecraft, the law is heavily indebted to *Europeanized notions of humanity, which read 'certain physical characteristics, usually skin colour' as not merely physiognomic differences but indications of varying intellectual, moral and even spiritual capacity between populations* (Fitzpatrick 1992: 65). The imposition of enlightenment thought upon the world, with international law being one of the tools in this imposition, determined new hierarchies of categorization, governing the lives of both humanity and nature. While this was true of the colonial past, it is also true of the so-called post-colonial present. While the majority of formerly colonized states are now formally independent, as Tzouvala notes, the logic of race still permeates international law today, being tied to narratives of civilization and progress (Tzouvala 2020).

Donna Haraway's work captures how the demarcation between human and nonhuman negates the common heritage of kin (Haraway 2016). Whereas Haraway argues for a 'multispecies togetherness' that pushes us beyond the patriarchal model of communities of care being formed around the heteronormative family, normative thought remains tethered

DOI: 10.4324/9781032658032-14

to the frame of genetic blood ties separating humans from each other and, by extension, the natural world at large, breaking human–nonhuman kinship. This fundamental human–nonhuman cut in the theorization of life upon earth has had a devastating impact in a number of different fields, from climate to deforestation to species conservation (Jones 2023). A growing literature that looks at international law from a posthuman perspective highlights how the anthropocentric model of law relegates categories such as water, land, animals, plants and racial others out of the category of legal subjectivity and into the position of objects (Jones 2021; Petersmann 2021).

In this context, this chapter will discuss a specific international and legal project that emerged in the mid-twentieth century, exacerbating the climate crises through an organized policy of eviscerating some of the most biodiverse areas in the world. The establishment of the United Nations following the Second World War provided an institutional international forum for a previously unimaginable project of global drug control and eradication. The result was the three United Nations treaties that, at present, define the illegality of drugs in international law: The Single Convention on Narcotic Drugs, 1961; The Convention on Psychotropic Substances, 1971; and The Convention Against Illicit Traffic in Narcotic Drugs and Psychotropic Substances, 1988. The Single Convention required signatories to make illegal the 'cultivation, production, manufacture, extraction, preparation, possession, offering, offering for sale, distribution, purchase, sale, delivery on any terms whatsoever, brokerage, dispatch, dispatch in transit, transport, importation and exportation of drugs contrary to the provisions of this Convention' (Article 36, *Single Convention*). This is the apotheosis of a trajectory of increasing prohibition of drugs in international law since the 1909 Conference of Shanghai Opium Commission. For the past 50 years, this trajectory has realized itself in a project that has been better known as the so-called war on drugs. In terms of extraction and exploitation, the war on drugs is the only area where a cluster of national, transnational and international law regulates biodiversity and has declared an explicit War of destruction and eradication – that destruction and eradication being upon drugs themselves in terms of plant life.

The War on Drugs

Over the course of the twentieth century, a legal narrative around drugs emerged that arbitrarily discriminated them for being the primary conduit in facilitating movement between different states of consciousness and being, thereby transposing the consumers of drugs from the realm of the human to the nonhuman. In the international law context, this is evident in the development of the *International Opium Convention of 1912*, through which international trade in opium was brought under international legal regulation, to the present international legal regulation extended to more drugs. Many aspects of our current framework are arbitrary and ethically untenable (Daniels *et al* 2021).

The Opium Convention of 1912 was an outcome of the 1909 Conference of Shanghai Opium Commission. It was an effort by the main colonial powers of its time to control manage, and secure continued revenues from the international trade in opium – also as it limited the ways and means for which opium was to be produced, traded and used to primarily pharmaceutical. The 1909 Conference and the 1912 Convention followed on a period of extensive international trade in opium. The UK, through its large-scale opium production in its British India crown colony, had secured substantial trade revenues from and political power in China – as UK and other colonial powers had created and expanded trade- and consumer-markets of opium-usage reaching previously unprecedented levels. The problem for China was not only that of an exponential rise in opium-usage with the social, cultural and political implications that followed suit, but primarily that of an ever-expanding imperial political and economic influence of Western powers within its sovereign territories. In response, China had sought to outlaw the opium trade within its territories. These developments preceded the two so-called Opium wars between Western colonial powers and China, in 1839–1842 and 1856–1860. China failed in its efforts, suffering major losses in the wars. In addition to forcing China into a series of humiliating so-called unequal treaties, presenting the Western colonial powers with trading rights and sovereign and economic benefits at Chinese harbors and trading hubs, the trade in opium was securely legalized under international law: first freely for the winning Western powers and later, after the 1912 Convention, primarily tradeable toward pharmaceutical purposes.

A few years later, in 1925, the control of the international trade in drugs was extended to include hashish and its derivates in the *International Convention Relating to Dangerous Drugs of 1925*. At that time an international body was also established – the Permanent Central Opium Board (PCOB) – to oversee the control of the international trade in drugs. By this the international drug control was brought under the auspice of the League of Nations, and later transferred to the UN and the World Health Organization (WHO) after World War II. The presence of this international legal history is made to materially matter in international drug control in contemporary practices: WHO, for example, still draws on drug assessments of hemp made under the 1912 and 1925 Conventions (Riboulet-Zemouli *et al* 2022). At present, the international control on drugs is carried out by WHO and the International Narcotics Control Board (INCB), as well as the UN Office on Drugs and Crime.

The historical and significant shifts in opium trade follows a narrative present in the history of international law: from the use of international law to secure free trade and massive revenues for Western and colonial powers; to the seizing of control over the very same trade by the same powers under international law and its institutions, limiting the purposes of trade and use (mainly pharmaceutical); to an extended ban, in 1961, on trade and use of drugs outside of Western pharmaceutical business models – legally secured by transnational patent laws enabling the transformation of plants like the poppy and hemp to extractable value exclusively for patent owners. The ban and, somewhat later also the formalization of the extraction business model through transnational patent law, coincided with the nominal withdrawal of colonial powers from its former colonies, and the transformation of international law from an explicit vehicle of colonization to an international law that had 'overcome' its colonial past (Arvidsson and Bak-McKenna 2020).

The narrative in international law around drugs as the primary conduit in facilitating movement between different states of being, transposing drug users from the realm of the human to the nonhuman, thus follows a broader trajectory in international law (Tzouvala 2020). From the colonial era of drugs as a means for Western colonial powers to balance international trade and to gain sovereign power in the Global South and East, to the era of so-called post-colonial independence in which the control over the profitable trades in drugs are 'lost' to the newly independent international legal subjects *if* the use of, and such trade in drugs, were allowed to exist outside of pharmaceutical business models supported by transnational patent laws, and international trade laws. To eradicate that which will not be controlled thus became the focus of the war on drugs. The war meant subjugating both 'post-colonial' subjects – the newly established states emerging as formally and nominally 'equal' international legal subject, as well as its continuously racialized subaltern populations – and the potent plants the regulation of which so much international legal effort had already been invested.

As a result, the twentieth century turns in the drugs war provide us with an instantiation of the relationship between colonial and environmental violence that scholars like Shela Sheik illuminate, showing how a shared discursive terrain connects the contemporary wars against plant life with the wars against the bodies of racially subaltern subjects (Sheikh 2017: 98). Through policies developed and disseminated through INCB, as well as the UN Office on Drugs and Crime, policies of crop eradication, aerial fumigation and pesticide spraying became the centerpiece of both drug prohibition and counterinsurgency policies in countries like Colombia and Afghanistan. During the same century – and intensified in the aftermath of the Vietnam war – the international legal framework of war – International Humanitarian Law (IHL) – from which the war on drugs draws many of its political and legal imaginaries, as well as the international environmental legal protection during warfare, have seen a development toward outlawing the use of crop eradication, ariel fumigation and pesticide spraying as part of warfare practices. This all emerged at the same time as the development of IHL was advocating for the outlawing precisely the practices of these forms of violence within formal warfare (Arvidsson and Sjöstedt 2023).

Furthermore, the drug war has exacerbated the climate crises through an organized policy of eviscerating some of the most biodiverse areas in the world. As Hannah Martin has argued 'the coca plant that has been pushed into the realm of the outlaw' (Meszaros Martin 2018: 232). The war on drugs has turned a particular category of plant life from an object to a subject, an active agent imbued with the power to consume the human, rather than the other way round (Taussig 2004). As Martin argues, this narrative becomes the prelude for a war against this supposedly monstrous, malignant manifestation of the threat of the nonhuman 'as outlawed species and ecologies become subject to legalized destruction, we begin to see how the law continuously intervenes in and reformulates the environment' (Meszaros Martin 2018: 232).

In this chapter, and drawing on posthuman, decolonial and critical plant scholarship of authors such as Michael Taussig, Matilda Arvidsson and Denise Ferreira da Silva, we show just how indebted the fear of drug's 'transgressive' nature is to racialized conceptions of 'nonhumanity', with drugs being deemed the conduit between ideal and denigrated states of humanity. Posthuman theory challenges received ideas of what it means to be human and offers a lens through which we can perceive the continuity between what we categorize as human and what we categorize as nature to allow for the concept of subjectivity, even legal personality, to transcend traditional bodily boundaries. We will examine the full scale of the application of the category of the nonhuman by illustrating how the racially and geographically subaltern populations, in the international legal 'post-colonial' order of the war on drugs, is taken as the embodiment of nonhumanity in association with the transgressive plant life collectively termed as 'drugs'. We thereby argue that the war on drugs is deeply embedded within categorizations and narratives of the human and the nonhuman. This narrative that permeates the war on drugs is subsequently, in this chapter, brought into discussion with alternative worldviews on the relationship between the human and the nonhuman, including Indigenous onto-epistemologies which illustrate the paucity between the categories of the human and the nonhuman. In this context, we thereby argue that, if drug policy reform is to ensure that the current violence of the war on drugs is not repeated in a new form, a mere change in the law will not be enough. Based on the history of the war on and through the international legal regulation of drugs, more or 'better' laws risk becoming yet another 'turn' in a history of colonial oppression and extractivist global order. Rather, there will be a need for a wider reconfiguration of the way international law categorizes subjects as human or nonhuman, both in terms of racialized subjects and naturalized subjects, to ensure that the violence continually perpetuated against these subjects comes to an end.

Colombia and COP26

In 2021, one of the authors of this chapter sat at a table for a panel sponsored by the *New York Times* in preparation for COP26 – the United Nations Climate Change Conference that took place in Glasgow in 2021. The adults sitting at the table were ready to perform their familiar theatrics of mastery, to use their fancy words in fancy-sounding treaties, their techno-solutionism, miming mimetic beings in wonderlands of what until yesterday was pure make-believe, all to persuade the other adults in the audience with their percentages and numbers. These numbers would outline the millions spent in the fight against drugs, a fight that has devastated the Andes and the Amazon, condemning these countries to underdevelopment. However, before these adults could speak, a brave, young activist stood up from the audience and spoke. 'Indigenous peoples', she stated, 'are treated like children'. 'However', she continued:

> they are custodians of most of the rainforests that are the lungs of our planet. They suffer the most by your wars and feigned diplomacy. Not only that, they may also have the solutions for the climate crisis. And yet, they're not sitting at the table.
>
> *(Dunbar-Johnson* et al *2021)*

This young Scottish activist was right. She pulled the handbrake. She pressed pause and gave us time to think – time to think about the fact that what one eats when sitting with others at the table is not the other's food and substance but their *position* and *perspective*.

What the young Scottish activist said reminds us of the Kogi people of the Sierra Nevada de Santa Marta, in the Caribbean coast of Colombia, where one of the authors of this chapter comes from. There, the people would sit for a long time around a fire with their *poporos*, curvaceous containers shaped like an hourglass (tourists often describe them as Coca-Cola bottles) which contain lime made from crushed seashells that is added to toasted coca leaves. When used with a stick rotated around the spout of the *poporo* to put gobs of lime in their mouths while chewing the coca leaves, it looks as if they were writing their thoughts in the curves and dashes of a peculiar geometry.

The speed and rhythm of the rotating movements and the sounds correspond to the movement of speech and thought, which the Kogi call *kunsamunu*. This term refers to the fact that, for the Kogi, words are tactile or vegetable like threads of fibers and therefore edible. Thus, to dialogue is to eat each other's words spiced, cooked and stitched together with the lime, the spit and the psychoactive alkaloid that activates the mix of scribbles and sounds. Materially and corporeally, the same as breathing or thinking. This is how they create a common space. A breathing space, in kinship and spirit.

The Spit + Coca matter is the very opposite of gold and the gold of standards that in Western economics and law define what has value and what does not have value, acts unequivocally like poison, or is 'evil': Coca leaves are considered illegal under the 1961 *Convention*, and placed by the INCB on its list of narcotic drugs and banned substances. This is so insofar as the Spit + Coca matter, like all matter, including our breathing and thinking bodies, is injurable and 'vulnerable to both time and good taste'. Which is to say, not what missionaries, conquistadors, transnational patent law, pharmaceutical business models and modern financiers would consider 'valuable' and 'culture' in accordance with their conventional perspective and frames of mind in which what is time-bound is less valuable than the timeless.

In other words, these are transgressive substances and materials underpinning philosophies and aesthetics not of form but of material substance and force, which can be affected just as much as they can affect us when we eat them or otherwise put them in our bodies. Like words, which are also edible. But what do these words ('position' and 'perspective'), mean in the Indigenous thought that the young Scottish activist invoked in all its concreteness?

Nature's Agents

To begin, we could say that every position in a structure or ecosystem is political, at least in the sense that everything is relational and related. Not relative, but mimetically related. Consider nature, for example, which creates resemblances and similarities. It can be said that the highest capacity for producing similarities is Man's. Granted, the human gift for seeing similarities, mimicry and resemblances might be but a drum rudiment of a powerful compulsion, present since earlier times, to become and behave like something else. But, if so, we must take stock of the real impact of time as suggested by the consideration of nature's mimetic faculty of which human mimesis and *inventio* is part of.

We can do so in at least two ways. First, by reminding ourselves that as nature's agents we invent and animate structures that did not exist before, the 'vibrant matter' in the words of Jane Bennett (2009). But once they are brought into being they become stable and acquire objective properties. From that point onwards, they affect us as well as their existing environs. This kind of temporal naturalism entails that we are ethical agents in the sense that we are ethical flesh (we are vulnerable, injurable, perishable in time) and this flesh is thoroughly historical (Allen & Mendieta 2021; Cornell 2017; Braidotti 2013). Thus, we all suffer in our flesh but do so in different forms in accordance with the affordance of material circumstances and the environment we live in. The latter affects us just as we affect it, which means that inventio, the mimetic faculty of bringing other things into being and becoming like other things – a mode of appearance, so to speak – is prior to any structured, framed or constituted 'mode of being'.

Second, and following from the preceding, this points to a broader sense of reciprocity and responsibility for the structures that hold together a material world (needless to say, a sense wholly different than that of contemporary international law, or the one pursued in the war on drugs). These reciprocities are an implication of the reality of time and the mimetic faculty an extension of a concept of medium and media (as in *medio ambiente* or environment, but also *medios* as means or media of sensing and sense-making) that does not alienate signs and symbolic forms from their materials or abstractions. We have learned from Indigenous peoples in the Americas how their technologies of memorialization (such as knotted *khipus*, pictographic storytelling and law-drawing, the creation of biocultural sites, or domains of coca leaf- and word-munching etc.) are conceptually entwined with their tactility, edibility and transformability, and then built into those sign systems and symbolic forms is a relational circuit between 'a design and its physical twining' (Garcia 2020: 195 ('which is to say [a relational circuitry] between structure and material iteration'); Allen 1998: 22 (defining the Quechua word 'pacha' as 'a specific configuration of matter, activity, and moral relationship – a state of experience . . . a world moment'); see also Taussig 1980: 161).

In this distinct combination between temporal naturalism, ethical materialism and animated structuralism, reciprocity is not a matter of simple exchange between individuals and cannot be reduced to either contractualist exchange-ism or circulation. It is a mutual interpenetration, entangled, mimetic, creative, of individual or collective actions and the structure of the world threading into a tight fabric what would be incorrectly distinguished as a binary culture/nature opposition according to the conventions of perspective built into mainstream, crude stories of 'state of nature', sexual or social contract such as those blindly repeated in jurisprudence, anthropology and philosophy courses, and which underpin much of our current restricted diplomacy and state-legal practice (Alaimo 2010).

However, over the long haul of Western history, especially in modern times, the mimetic faculty, although still an active presence among young people and, perhaps also in ritual practices and magic, has been largely eclipsed from rational consciousness. Or repressed, as Michael Taussig astutely observes (Taussig 2020; citing Benjamin 1978: 335–6; Marques 2015: 298).

As Taussig explains, taking stock of all the things we have learned through decades of accompanying our Indigenous *maestros* and teachers, the wordsmith *palabreros* of Las Pavas and the Afro-Amerindians of the Cauca region in Colombia, it is not so much that the role of mimetic relations has really been eclipsed. Rather, like a damned river or the damned of the earth, these relations have found alternative routes. When things are not intrinsically connected, relational and related, there's always the possibility of establishing non-sensuous correspondences that 'provide mimetic links between things and activities not obviously mimetically related'. Symbols and language can be thought of in this way too. If so, it could be said that when we sit at the dinner table, we eat each other's words too (Taussig 2018: 29).

Dehumanizing Necropolitics

Indigenous systems have often taken more care to encode the legal rights of the nonhuman into their models of mutual recognition, phenomenal self, and flourishing. Drawing on these systems and their complex conceptions of the rights of nature, we can begin to reframe the theoretical relationship between humans and the specter of deviant and transformative nature, that is, drugs. The imposition to expel this malignant form of plant life (existing outside of regulatory forms of unequal powers and of value extraction) from the face of the earth – through the war on drugs, as embedded in and accommodated through formal and informal international law – has accelerated deforestation, community displacement, crop mutations and permanent damage to arable land as aerial fumigation campaigns rain pesticides upon nature (del Olmo 1998). The war on drugs as both a political and colonial project draws on moral justifications for militarized security projects, and ethically untenable policies carried into wars for humanitarian intervention, through a vision of an evisceration of the earth. Yet these demonized drugs continue to be grown, cultivated and traded, emerging through hidden production sites in the tropical Andes or the deepest corners of the Amazon Jungle. Like rose through concrete, the relentless human craving for psychoactive plant substances – for transformation through the plant – continues to emerge regardless of the environmental devastation that counter-dugs international law and policy visits upon the earth. This renders the project to eliminate drugs a futile attack on the natural world, one that attacks without ever being close to producing its desired impact.

This contradiction goes right to the core of the paradox that is international law's universalist claim. While international law claims to do one thing (here, to be eradicating drugs), in reality, this supposedly global, universal policy has little impact on its intended bull's-eye (which, over the history of international law has changed substantially from engendering international trade in drugs, to regulating it for very specific purposes of pharma-business value extraction). Rather, it's core impact is the destruction of ecosystems. The crop eradication and aerial fumigation policies advanced by the UN Office on Drugs and Crime run counter to the organization's commitments to environmental sustainability and to protect biodiversity in the context of escalating climate change. It is also in explicit contradiction to international environmental law. And, as mentioned earlier, it runs counter to the commitments to environmental protection during warfare under IHL – the difference being that the 'war on drugs' is not formally a war in terms of international law, but a de-humanizing, de-relational necropolitics. The turning of warfare into the reserve weapon of a (Europeanized) universal humanity has fueled the environmental devastation visited upon nature as conceptualized in a dichotomy of either resources for extraction or threats to be eradicated. Moreover, the requirement that the 1961 Convention on Narcotic Drugs placed upon producing countries to centralize and then eradicate drug cultivation, production and consumption ensured that they would be carrying the heaviest burden when it came to realizing the Treaty's aims. These countries are, in many cases, the former colonies where colonial powers expedited the transformation of local plant life and cultures of plant use into commercial models for colonial revenues in the international trade of drugs. The national, transnational and international legal structure of drugs prohibition enforcement has guaranteed that the force of international law falls heaviest on those countries where organic, plant-based drugs are produced, upon Indigenous peoples whose subjectivity is, to them, discursively intertwined with these transgressive substances, and upon racially subaltern communities who are traditionally excluded from the 'legitimate' economic sphere and thereby can find themselves enveloped into this illegitimate counter-side of global trade. The war on drugs is yet another example of how international law, while nominally having overcome its colonial past, is continuing colonial dehumanizing practices and politics.

However, the intervention (or intrusion) of the Indigenous subject into the anesthetized space of international law can open up new possibilities for conceiving of this relationship. A symbolic moment in the shift away from the war on drugs came in March 2009, at the 52nd session of the UN Commission on Narcotic Drugs (CND). Then Bolivian President, Evo Morales, traveled to the diplomatic meeting in Vienna to petition for the removal of the raw coca leaf from schedule 1 of the drugs that are prohibited by the Single Convention (Ferreira da Silva 2009). In the midst of his speech, where he called for support for Bolivia's initiative, Morales pulled out a coca leaf. Holding it up for the audience to verify, he then placed the prohibited substance into his mouth. He continued with this speech while chewing the coca leaf, critiquing 'the socio-cultural projections' that resulted in the suppression of the chewing of coca in international law. Placing the blame firmly at the door of the law, Morales condemned the 1961 Convention as 'an attack on the rights of indigenous peoples'. He also decried the international drug treaty for contradicting the new Bolivian Constitution, which enshrined that 'the State protects the native and ancestral coca as cultural patrimony, as a renewable natural resource of the biodiversity of Bolivia, and as a factor of social unity' (Constitution of Bolivia, Article 384). Furthermore, Morales declared that UN Office of Drugs and Crime Executive Director Antonio Maria Costa, seated in the audience, should, by law, take him to jail for what he is doing in an attempt to render visible the violent absurdity of the drug laws: 'I am a producer of the coca leaf', he cried out, 'I am a consumer of the coca leaf. The coca leaf represents the culture of the people of the Andean region' (*Speech at the High-Level Segment of the 52nd Session of the Commission on Narcotic Drugs* 2009).[1]

Following the failure to win support in 2009, Morales' Bolivia exerted further pressure on the international community by withdrawing from 1961 Convention in 2011, only agreeing to re-adhere to it once a new reservation allowing for the traditional uses of the coca leaf was implemented in 2013 (Russo 2014: 10–11). Bolivia's ability to unilaterally withdraw from the 1961 Convention and then re-enter as a party on its own terms shook the foundations of international drug policy, built as they were on the idea of compulsory adherence. Morales not only intervened at the CND as a Head of State but he also embraced the subject position of the racial subaltern subject. As the first Indigenous Amerindian President of his country, Morales represents a global/historical political figure that cannot be comprehended outside of a consideration of 'raciality and indigeneity' and the significance of his election has been taken to form a challenge to the persistent coloniality of world ordering (Ferreira da Silva 2009: 38). For Denise Ferreira de Silva, Morales functions as

> an indigenous, racial, peasant . . . [who] . . . refigures past and present deployments of physical and symbolic violence that now configure the globe as a political space. That is, he exemplifies the radical political subject and the global subaltern (indigenous/racial) entity, which have been assembled by the threads of previous global/historical (colonial, national) moments.
>
> *(ibid)*

In this chapter, we have argued that the war on drugs can be read as deeply embedded within the wider global sacrifice, both in international law and more generally, of the negated sub-human as embodied by the racial subaltern subject. Morales' performance carries weight as a return of the Amerindian, the victim of the divide between inclusive and exclusion that was made at the birth of international law (this being primarily attributed to Vittoria), back into the realm of the universal on its own terms. The twenty-first century intervention of an Amerindian president at the CND challenged not only the 1961 Convention but also the geo-temporality presumed within international law. For Morales to interject his raciality and Amerindian

1 Authors' translation. Original Spanish: 'Yo soy productor de esta hoja de coca. No por productor soy narcotraficante. Yo soy consumidor de esta hoja de coca. . .. Esta [hoja de coca] representa la cultura de pueblos de la Región Andina', *Chewing Coca at the UN* (2009). Vienna: Drug Reporter. https://drogriporter.hu/en/chewing-coca-at-the-un/ (Accessed: 22 March 2023).

indigeneity into the domain of the universal was to enter into transformation and become recognizable to international law on his own terms, as well as to challenge the stunted universalism that has been acclaimed by a 'sacrificial' international law. As Oscar Guardiola-Rivera tells us:

> Following Evo's election, indigenous and peasant memory and knowledge has become a political force to be reckoned with, regionally and worldwide. It is as if, five hundred years after the genocide that took place in the Americas, we have all been given a second chance. Perhaps now, when the Indians of the Andes and the Amazon speak, we will listen.
>
> *(Guardiola-Rivera 2010: 425–6)*

In subsequent years, Bolivia has been able to experiment with novel models of socializing the production of coca, allowing traditional coca farmers to grow and cultivate the plant with a legally defined geographic area for the interest of the state.

Conclusion

In this chapter, we have argued that the war on drugs has caused untold damage to the natural world. As the history of international law's commitment to regulate the trade in and use of plant life known as 'drugs' for specific extractionist, revenue and power purposes tells us, and as a half century project of legitimized violence created by three UN treaties still in force today show – specifically the 1961 Convention's call to eradicate the recreational use of three forms of organic plant life (cannabis, coca, opium) – international law has overridden the rights of the nonhuman in defense of a narrow, Western conception of morality and ideal social behavior. Overall, it is clear that a reformed relationship with drugs, drawing on Indigenous cosmologies, can help address the crisis we see in relation to human relationships with our natural habitats. Furthermore, such a perspective can be used to correct the decline in biodiversity and environmental sustainability across the globe that drug policies have wrought. However, law is now increasingly being uncovered as a facilitator of, rather than a mitigator against, the racial hierarchization and the demonization of the nonhuman world in normative thought. In contradistinction to the sphere of legal recognition between those who recognize each other's sovereignty – as is the formal recognition of the nominal equality between states in the 'post-colonial' international legal order – the rights of the racial subaltern and natural world have their legal standing eroded, leaving us to unpack how racialization and environmental damage has been constitutive of the category of 'the human' and learn how the breaking of race will require an exploding of the boundaries of the human. Despite an acclaimed equality amongst all peoples as its foundation, international law in the twentieth and twenty-first centuries continued to be anchored in a universalizing notion of humanity that is based upon a conceptualization of the nonhuman as its enemy. With sub-humanity still encapsulating ideas regarding race and geography, even in this 'post-colonial' world, the bodies of particular peoples continue to signify this enemy, including racialized subjects and those who use drugs. The potential for drug prohibition in international law, as a legal project directed against the 'evil' of sub-humanity, to impact asymmetrically upon the bodies of racial subaltern subjects was always already present within international law. If national, transnational and international drug policy reform aims to ensure that the current violence of the war on drugs is not repeated in a new form, it will require not only a change in international law but also a wider reconfiguration of the relation between international law's use of violence and nonhuman subjectivity, both racialized and naturalized, who are subjects of that violence.

References

Alaimo, S. (2010) *Bodily Natures: Science, Environment, and the Material Self*, Bloomington: Indiana University Press. www.jstor.org/stable/j.ctt16gzmvh (Accessed: 22 March 2023).

Allen, C.J. (1998) 'When Utensils Revolt: Mind, Matter, and Modes of Being in the Pre-Columbian Andes', *Res: Anthropology and Aesthetics*, 33: 18–27. DOI: https://doi.org/10.1086/RESv33n1ms20166999

Allen A. & Mendieta E. (2021) 'Introduction', *Decolonizing Ethics. The Critical Theory of Enrique Dussel*, ed. by A. Allen & E. Mendieta, 1–21, University Park: The Pennsylvania State University Press.

Arvidsson, M. and M. Bak-McKenna (2020) 'The Turn to History in International Law and the Sources Doctrine: Critical Approaches and Methodological Imaginaries', *Leiden Journal of International Law*, 33(1): 37–56. DOI: https://doi.org/10.1017/S0922156519000542

Arvidsson, M. and B. Sjöstedt (2023) 'Ordering Human-Other Relationships: International Humanitarian Law and Ecologies of Armed Conflicts in the Anthropocene', in V. Chapaux, F. Mégret and U. Natarajan (eds) *The Routledge Handbook of International Law and Anthropocentrism*, London: Routledge.

Benjamin, W. (1978) 'On the Mimetic Faculty', in E.F.N. Jephcott and P. Demetz (eds) *Reflections: Essays, Aphorisms, Autobiographical Writings*, 1st ed., New York: Harcourt Brace Jovanovich.

Bennett, J. (2009) *Vibrant Matter: A Political Ecology of Things*, Durham: Duke University Press.

Braidotti, R. (2013) *The Posthuman*, London: Polity.

Cornell, D. (2017) 'Derrida's Negotiations as Techniques of Liberation', Discourse. Journal for Theoretical Studies in Media and Culture, 39.2: 195–215, Detroit: Wayne State University Press.

Daniels, C. *et al* (2021) 'Decolonizing Drug Policy', *Harm Reduction Journal*, 18(1): 120. DOI: https://doi.org/10.1186/s12954-021-00564-7

del Olmo, R. (1998) 'The Ecological Impact of Illicit Drug Cultivation and Crop Eradication Programs in Latin America', *Theoretical Criminology*, 2(2): 269–78. DOI: https://doi.org/10.1177/1362480698002002007

Dunbar-Johnson, S., L. Bilimoria and A. Watson (2021) 'The NYT Debate: Journeys Towards COP26', YouTube video. www.youtube.com/watch?v=rr-wxCkukcU (Accessed: 22 March 2023).

Ferreira da Silva, D. (2009) 'An Outline of a Global Political Subject: Reading Evo Morales's Election as a (Post-)Colonial Event', *Seattle Journal for Social Justice*, 8(1): 25–49.

Fitzpatrick, P. (1992) *The Mythology of Modern Law*, London: Routledge. DOI: https://doi.org/10.4324/9780203162125

Garcia, E. (2020) *Signs of the Americas: A Poetics of Pictography, Hieroglyphs, and Khipu*, Chicago: University of Chicago Press.

Guardiola-Rivera, O. (2010) *What If Latin America Ruled the World? How the South Will Take the North into the 22nd Century*, New York City: Bloomsbury.

Haraway, D.J. (2016) *Staying with the Trouble: Making Kin in the Chthulucene*, Durham: Duke University Press.

Jones, E. (2021) 'Posthuman International Law and the Rights of Nature', *Journal of Human Rights and the Environment*, 12(2): 76–101. DOI: https://doi.org/10.4337/jhre.2021.00.04

Jones, E. (2023) *Feminist Theory and International Law: Posthuman Perspectives*, Abingdon: Routledge. DOI: https://doi.org/10.4324/9781003363798

Marques, P.N. (2015) 'Introduction', in *The Forest and the School/Where to Sit at the Dinner Table?* Berlin Köln: Archive Books.

Meszaros Martin, H. (2018) '"Defoliating the World"', *Third Text*, 32(2): 230–53. DOI: https://doi.org/10.1080/09528822.2018.1486526

Petersmann, M.-C. (2021) '"I Wish There Was a Treaty We Could Sign": An Inquiry into the Making of the Global Pact for the Environment', *Indiana Journal of Global Legal Studies*, 28(2): 7–80. DOI: https://doi.org/10/gm2w3c

Riboulet-Zemouli, K., F. Ghehioueche and M.A. Krawitz (2022) 'Cannabis Amnesia – Indian Hemp Parley at the Office International d'Hygiène Publique in 1935', *Authorea*. DOI: https://doi.org/10.22541/au.165237542.24089054/v1

Russo, M. (2014) 'The Coca Plant and Bolivian Identity', *International Research-Scape Journal*, 2(1): 1–14. DOI: https://doi.org/10.25035/irj.02.01.03

Sheikh, S. (2017) *Translating Geontologies*, Edited by J. Graham, New York: Columbia Books on Architecture and the City, 165–84. https://cup.columbia.edu/book/and-now/9781941332313 (Accessed: 22 March 2023).

Speech at the High-Level Segment of the 52nd Session of the Commission on Narcotic Drugs (2009). Vienna: UN. www.youtube.com/watch?v=FzuL5vHLMPA (Accessed: 22 March 2023).

Taussig, M. (1980) *The Devil and Commodity Fetishism in South America*, Chapel Hill: University of North Carolina Press.

Taussig, M. (2004) *My Cocaine Museum*, Chicago: University of Chicago Press (Carpenter Lectures).

Taussig, M. (2018) *Palma Africana*, Chicago: University of Chicago Press.

Taussig, M. (2020) *Mastery of Non-Mastery in the Age of Meltdown*, Chicago: University of Chicago Press.

Tzouvala, N. (2020) *Capitalism as Civilisation: A History of International Law*, Cambridge: Cambridge University Press.

11

SUPPLANTING ANTHROPOCENTRIC LEGALITIES

Can the Rule of Law Tolerate Intensive Animal Agriculture?

Maneesha Deckha

The rule of law is a concept in motion. Whether adopted as foundational to the constitutional backdrop of nation-states or circulating as a higher-order international law general principle of law, the now-transnational concept defies a fixed meaning and has been subject to multiple interpretations. Its open-endedness permits it to attend to pressing social problems and matters of justice heretofore unseen or undertheorized and which exceed its normal liberal legal parameters and colonial formation. In this contribution, I suggest that the rule of law is deployable against the planetary scourge of animal-based food systems (ABFS) and the more-than-human violence ABFS occasion.[1] Drawing on posthuman feminist theory, the chapter contributes to the growing field of global animal law that explores animal law issues through international law and transnational law frameworks (Blattner 2019; Cao *et al* 2016; Peters 2020, 2017, 2016: 3–4; Stucki 2017), by highlighting the potential of the rule of law to challenge the legitimacy of at least some forms or portion of ABFS.

The magnitude of present-day ABFS' environmental imprint, their role in producing zoonotic pandemics, and their violence and exploitation of nonhuman animals has produced an emergent public discourse – despite industry influence and resistance from the general public who still favor animal-based consumption – calling for a food systems re-orientation toward veganism and plant-based foods (Sanford *et al* 2021: 3–4). This is a call emanating from some nongovernmental and academic sectors for a global transformation

1 I adopt the term ABFS from Krithika Srinivasan's recent work in this area (Srinivasan 2021: 2). My use incorporates land and aquatic animals.

DOI: 10.4324/9781032658032-15

(Almiron and Fernández 2021: 141–3). The high-profile 2019 Intergovernmental Panel on Climate Change's *Special Report on Climate Change and Land* reviewed and affirmed the existing evidence for a wide-ranging planetary systems rethink, including of the food and agricultural sector. It did not make any dietary recommendations, but some notable authors of the Special Report commented on the benefits for emissions reductions if a plant-based shift occurred in at least countries with high levels of animal consumption (Sanford *et al* 2021: 10, 14, discussing Shukla *et al* 2020). Other United Nations (United Nations Food and Agricultural Organization, United Nations Environmental Program) bodies have released global overview reports documenting the environmental evidence against consuming meat and other animal products (UN Environment Programme 2021: 54, 2019: 42; UN Food and Agricultural Organization 2018: 8, 16–19, 52, 2006: 270–5). And the European Regional Office of the World Health Organization (2021: 7), while not authoring or endorsing any bold policy position recommending a largely plant-based diet for the world, has produced a regional fact sheet in its European Office discussing the benefits of a plant-based diet.

Thus far, however, no national governments have adopted a policy or legislative platform to shift their food systems away from ABFS toward plant-forward systems. We can observe multiple reasons for governmental silence. Perhaps most obviously is the political unwillingness to contest the human cultural normalization of eating animals or their by-products, most pronounced in Western countries, but also present among the global elite influenced by Western diets and status symbols. The staggering scale of violence against animals in present-day ABFSs simply doesn't register against this entrenched normalization,[2] or, if it does, animal suffering is denied, dismissed, minimized or defended (Buttlar and Walther 2022: 2; Milfont *et al* 2021: 2–3).

Another source of political recalcitrance to name such violence, or even highlight the harm to humans the planet that killing animals at present unprecedented levels causes, is the mythical and romantic narratives that have long attached to ABFS and immunize farmers from government oversight. As a result, farmers are legally given free rein in many countries as to how they raise 'their' animals and also enjoy strong lobbying influence directed at minimizing government regulation and maximizing government protection of otherwise non-viable industries. It is a situation of 'regulatory capture' that legally yields a race to the bottom in terms of animal agricultural, aquacultural and fishing practices with sobering outcomes for animals, people and the planet (Goodfellow 2016: 196–9; Sankoff 2019: 302–3).

2 Even critical social science disciplines otherwise concerned with foregrounding 'nature' can invisibilize 'food' or farmed animals (Arcari *et al* 2021: 942–3).

Due to structural limitations as well as systemic anthropocentrism, it would be optimistic to expect that voluntary industry transformation in the agricultural, aquacultural, or commercial fishing sectors will occur. While there may be some appetite for reform, it will very likely not be at a pace or scale required to avoid further environmental disaster or reduce harms to animals or marginalized humans working in or affected by the negative externalities of animal agriculture. To the contrary, these industries are expected to grow globally (Milfont *et al* 2021: 1).

Despite the seemingly colossal and intractable nature of the global problems presented by ABFS, a handful of domestic legislators have come forward in recent years to propose laws aimed at stemming the growth of large factory farms and altering the dietary preferences of national populations through imposing taxes on animal products. At the international law level, no such legal effort has yet materialized even in the form of support in principle for domestic market regulation. What has emerged at this level are soft law instruments, notably the IPCC's *Special Report on Climate Change and Land*, suggesting that nations consider regulatory instruments such as reversing current subsidies for high-intensive emissions food, subjecting their agricultural sector to carbon pricing and exchange trading regimes as they do the fossil fuel industries, and other policy instruments that may produce behavioral change 'to consume less meat' (Hurlbert *et al* 2019: 697, 702, 722). In this chapter, I suggest that elected representatives or other legally minded decision-makers at the national or international level should not view such initiatives or measures as simply a matter of politics, and thus properly made irrelevant if they do not win majority support and get legally enacted through classic democratic channels. Instead, such legally minded decision-makers should view such proposals as implicating a higher order national constitutional and international law principle: the rule of law. Specifically, I argue that the rule of law *connects to and is promoted by* emergent legislative proposals in a handful of jurisdictions around the world to curtail intensive ABFS.[3] Indeed, as I discuss later, a recent proposal spurred by the COVID-19 global pandemic from the American Bar Association, calling for an International Convention for the Protection of Animals, establishes such a connection.

Why does making this connection, and theorizing the rule of law in this substantive way, matter? For all its multiple connotations and the divergent

3 I focus on intensive agriculture because the little legislative action that has come forward has focused on this form of food production. The focus is not meant to minimize the devastation caused by commercial fishing or intensive aquaculture to animals, people and the planet or the harm caused to animals and ecosystems by noncommercial iterations of these industries. I leave the analysis, however, connecting the rule of law to commercial fishing and aquaculture as well as noncommercial iterations of these industries for future research.

meanings ascribed to it, the rule of law – in its domestic and international iterations – champions the principle of legality and the promotion of justice (Humphreys 2010: 1–2, 6). Liberal legal scholars laud the concept as the grounding of any viable national legal system (Bingham 2010; Raz 1990; Humphreys 2010: 1–2). The concept is less authoritative than treaties in the international legal sphere and less prominent at the international legal level generally, yet the concept is nonetheless salient within international law (Humphreys 2010: 7–9), with emergent scholarship on an 'international rule of law' seeing it as general principle of law that can be used to supplement regulatory gaps or to interpret treaties for the benefit of individuals vis-à-vis their state governments (ibid: 6–7). Despite its uneven and perhaps dwindling purchase in some parts of the world, and its inefficacy in alleviating the global problems many believed its adoption in nation-states would such as poverty and violence (ibid: 1), the concept that rose to global prominence through British imperialism remains an influential legal rhetorical device. Notwithstanding its open-endedness, the concept enjoys widespread regard in global decision-making circles and amongst a considerable sector of the general public in the Global South (Lino 2018; Humphreys 2010: 1). Global scales exist to measure the presence of the rule of law in countries, shaping donor fund allocations and development project investments (LexisNexis 2022). Additionally, media and social influencers also deploy the concept to criticize government excess (Arvay and Wu 2020; Zouev 2020).

The rule of law, then, as it is typically conceived across domestic and international jurisdictions (of which I say more later), has enormous potential to apply broadly and, as this chapter argues, is relevant to and promoted by intensive ABFS-curbing legislative measures. The hoped-for effect of the present argument is to help generate a legal and political culture, and supporting policy and legislation, that mandates as a matter of *legality* and *justice*, and not simply political will tolerant of government abdication and industry self-regulation, government action at national and international levels to dismantle ABFS. Government action is needed to support nascent but growing plant-forward cultural change emanating in order to stimulate the radical change in food systems that multiple nongovernmental transnational actors have identified as necessary for planetary health and the well-being of all beings (Kristiansen *et al* 2021: 154, 163; Ndlela and Murcott 2021: 28; Willett *et al* 2019: 447, 478–80, 484).

The analysis begins in the first section by situating the thesis – namely, how the globally resonant and the international law-relevant concept of the rule of law as a baseline for a society that is characterized by legality and justice is boosted by national legislative action to rein in intensive agriculture – in relevant theoretical frameworks. This part considers the benefits of applying feminist posthumanist theory to counter romanticized representations of ABFS but also the limits of posthumanist scholarship in calling for an end to animal agricultural practices. The second section provides an overview of the emergence of recent legislative proposals in some countries of the Global North that have called for reducing the scope of intensive ABFS. The third section then discusses the pliability of the rule of law to serve as an agent of social change in the realm of intensive ABFS. This section first explains how the rule of law can be a persuasive discursive legal tool in supporting legal regulation to address social problems and support progressive social values. It then explains why the intensive ABFS-curbing initiatives discussed in the second section regarding the present-day food system should be seen as initiatives that promote the rule of law, emphasizing the iterative connection between the rule of law and social justice.

Nothing in this chapter is meant to suggest that the rule of law, rightly seen by many as a foundational 'handmaiden' to imperialism (May 2021: 2354), is a universally benign, non-imperial or effective guarantor of justice today (ibid: 2356, 2359). As Christopher May has commented, 'the rule of law and imperialism remain intertwined' (ibid). Nor does the analysis dispute that continued investments in the rule of law and a liberal legal order in its typical Western legal and thus anthropocentric framing also prop up capitalism and the exploitation it entails (ibid: 2354; Goodale 2005: 554–5, 562). But even as its critics have noted, the idea of the rule of law can denote a more plural vision, once that is thicker and more substantive than how the concept is typically imagined, and which contests the traditional bounds of Western liberal legality from which it is derived (May 2021: 2353, 2355). This is arguably what would occur if the rule of law was invoked in favor of animals. Animals are legal non-subjects and intensely vulnerable in the liberal legal tradition (Deckha 2021: 85, 2015: 55, 64, 2013: 800–4; Eisen 2017: 941, 943–4), due to the very property rights that the empire-building version of the rule of law exalted and current economically oriented accounts view as critical for a nation to thrive (May 2021: 2353, 2355–6). If the rule of law were to be rhetorically marshalled in legal strategies to help foment a plant-forward food system, as I argue it has the potential to do so here, such strategies would be a deployment of the rule of law that *counters* the norms of private property and thus imperialism and liberalism by *de-propertizing* billions of animals. It is thus a legal strategy worth considering further, especially given the regulatory capture the animal agricultural industry enjoys despite the colossal suffering it requires, a legal phenomenon partly explained by the romanticized narratives that still surround ABFS.

Countering Bucolic Visions: The Promise and Limits of Posthuman Theory

Mythologizing Farming and Agriculture as Inherently Virtuous

In a criminal trial defending a woman charged with public mischief for giving water to thirsty pigs on a transport truck en route to slaughter, her defense lawyers deliberately avoided referring to the place where the pigs had been raised as a 'farm' (Animal Liberation Currents 2017: para 33). The defense lawyers knew that changing the narrative around farming was important to their case (and something which their submissions deliberately strove for at every turn).[4] The term 'farming' and even 'agriculture' gives rise to naturalized and romanticized agrarian connotations and corresponding narratives and cultural scripts (such as 'the successful farmer is hard-working, self-reliant and religious, living and working in harmony with nature to preserve the land for future generations of farmers, that is, for the family and community' (Walter 1997: 49)) that justify intensive animal agriculture (Vanclay and Enticott 2011: 257, 259; Pilgrim 2019: 75–7). These connotations, narratives and cultural scripts about 'farming' support farm subsidies and otherwise shape public policy (Sutherland 2020: 1156), as well as conceal the brutalities that intensive animal agriculture inflicts on animals (Stucki 2017: 278–9; Khazaal and Almiron 2016: 374–5). They also facilitate deceptive imaging such as happy cows or chickens on packaging and in marketing (Stucki 2017: 278–9; Khazaal and Almiron 2016: 385; Silver 2019; Gillespie 2018). They also bolster the arguments for industry self-governance.

Reappraising Animal Farming and Agriculture From an Animal-Centered Frame

The favorable social construction of farming and agriculture as still 'natural' and 'traditional' and of farmers as the 'original conservationists' (Vanclay and Enticott 2011: 264) also obscures the extreme technologically mediated nature of the breeding and raising of animals for human consumption. Most readers will be aware of the breathtaking re-drawing of American animal agriculture from more local, small-scale operations in the mid-twentieth century to the current intensive farming regime (Wadiwel 2014: 538–9), a model that has been exported and adopted around the globe (Mazac and Tuomisto 2020: 2; Walter 1997: 49). Many further realize the overwhelmingly industrialization of ABFS, that is, how animals are housed and how they are 'processed' during their lives once born (e.g. automated breeding, feeding, watering, milking, artificial daylight, assembly line castration and debeaking (Cassuto and Dibenedetto 2020: 5156)), in slaughter (e.g. mechanized slaughter chutes, stun bolts, blades, gassing, shredding, etc. (Cassuto 2012: 226)) and after death (e.g. defeathering, deskinning, boiling, rendering and further 'product' processing (Gillespie 2018)). What may be less transparent is how technologically mediated animals' *bodies* are from conception

4 The trial judge (who, not incidentally, grew up on a farm and said so) rejected the defense's terminology asserting the term 'farm' would be used in the trial going forward (James Silver, Guest Lecture in my Animals, Culture and the Law class, Faculty of Law, University of Victoria, 9 October 2017). The defense was ultimately successful in the case, but not for animal rights reasons. For further analysis, see Deckha 2018: 74–5, 77–8.

onward. Farmed animals have been subject to an unprecedented level of genetic breeding for specific traits and are also exposed to subsequent bodily interventions once born (Weisberg 2015: 40; Holloway *et al* 2009: 394–5).

Posthumanist scholarship, particularly feminist new materialist scholarship that binds the present collection together, helps reveal farmed animals as corporate biotechnological inventions and illuminate the routine spillover across and porosity between bodies and species in general (Banerjee 2016: 400–2; Braidotti 2013; Braidotti 2009: 526–8). Such intellectual work can help to dispel the romanticized visions of farming and agriculture that persist despite overwhelming industrialization and conglomeration. As such, feminist new materialism and the larger version of posthumanism in which it is housed can help make space for plant-based interventions into cultural foodscapes heavily dominated by animal-based eating (Muhlhauser *et al* 2021: 2–3).

However, a limit of feminist new materialism and posthumanist scholarship in general, is their typical disinclination to oppose the human instrumentalization of animals (Giraud 2019: 20; Leth-Espensen and Svensson 2020: 554). Although rigorously critical of anthropocentrism and human exceptionalism, posthumanists do not necessarily accept, and thereby resist, claims about nonhuman species integrity and corresponding moral or legal rights to life and bodily integrity for animals (Weisberg 2015: 49–50; Lindgren and Öhman 2019: 1205–6). The relational partnerships of 'co-mingling' and 'entanglements' of humans with animals and non-animals that feminist new materialists and posthumanists emphasize and exalt at a molecular and intimate bodily level is an important counter-narrative to human exceptionalism. Yet, such hallmark feminist new materialist concepts are also paradoxically invoked to implicitly endorse or even explicitly celebrate animal uses in industries where human workers are seen to be intimately involved in caring for 'agential' animals (Twine 2013: 143, 157–8; Hollin *et al* 2017: 934–5; Weisberg 2009: 35–7). Those who adopt these positions defend these endorsements through Donna Haraway's influential ideas of mutual co-constitution, kinship, 'naturecultures' or 'becoming-with' (Heath and Meneley 2010: 433–42),[5] and her larger instruction that our ethical obligation is not to stop killing animals, which she sees as an impossible but also unnecessary goal, but to ensure that animals live and die well (Twine 2013: 139–40; Giraud 2013: 104).

In short, the 'care' that many influential posthumanist feminists proffer as a better model than industrial alternatives embeds ethical exclusions that are still a type of violence (Hollin *et al* 2017: 935–7; Timeto 2021: 325–6; Bruckner *et al* 2019: 45–6; Gillespie 2011: 103, 121; Stanescu 2019: 1123). Thus, while feminist new materialist and posthumanist accounts alert us to the

5 For how Haraway's positions have shifted over the years away from posthumanist dismissal of animal rights, see Timeto 2021: 315–16.

highly naturalized and thus deceptive narratives that underpin ABFS today, and some scholars immersed in this theoretical model do highlight animal abuse and the suffering animals experience in animal-use industries (Sands 2019), feminist new materialist and posthumanist scholarship is largely not aimed at dismantling ABFS and can even help romanticize so-called humane or ethical versions of farming or agriculture due to the human-animal relations in them. A more animal-centered theoretical framework, one that is attuned to the violence of power asymmetries even in 'better' farms, zoos, or research labs such as that available in feminist animal care ethics, ecofeminism and critical animal studies (Deckha 2021: 16–20; Adams and Gruen 2021), is required to press posthumanist theory toward an anti-exploitation orientation (Timeto 2021: 323–4; Bruckner *et al* 2019: 39n2). The remainder of the chapter adopts these latter theories' anti-exploitation ethics as theoretical frames for the legal analysis.

Emerging Legislative Animal Farming Reduction Models

Restricting Concentrated Animal Feeding Operations

But, there is some resistance emerging in legislative corridors. Perhaps most prominent is US Senator Cory Booker's proposed federal legislation, the *Farm System Reform Act*.[6] If passed, the bill would prohibit new concentrated animal feeding operations (CAFOs) as well as prevent existing ones from increasing in size, and phase out existing CAFOs that have in excess of 1000 cows/calves, 82,000 laying hens and 125,000 non-laying hens by 2040 (Baise 2020; Case 2020).[7] The bill's effect, if passed, would be dramatic. As one industry trade publication put it, '(w)hat Sen. Booker wants to do is end CAFO operations which raise over 99% of our poultry, 99% of turkeys, 98% of hogs, and 70% of dairy cows' (Baise 2020). In addition to the *Farm System Reform Act* bill, there have been a few initiatives at the state level to target the scope of intensive farming; these bills, if passed, would stop new construction or expansion of 'confinement feeding operations'[8] and prevent new mega-dairies.[9] One-year moratoria against large CAFOs have succeeded at the municipal level in South Dakota and Wisconsin.[10]

6 Farm System Reform Act US Bill S 3221 (2019–116th Cong) s 102.
7 Note that Senator Booker has co-sponsored bills that would support intensive agriculture on smaller scales. See, for example, Justice for Black Farmers Act US Bill S 300 (2021–117th Cong) and Climate Stewardship Act US Bill S 1072 (2021–117th Cong).
8 US, HF 440, 89th Gen Assem, Reg Sess, IA, 2021.
9 US, SB 583, 81st Gen Assem, Reg Sess, OR, 2021.
10 For more on one county in South Dakota that has taken up this work see Faulk County Record 2019: 10. Three counties in Wisconsin passed such moratoria (Polk County Resolutions 2019; Kaeding 2019; Now Media Group 2016).

Outside of the United States, there has been some action to restrict CAFOs in countries with animal-centered diets but no current proposed legislation. In Switzerland, a then-newly elected Green party member brought forth a petition that launched a nationwide vote in 2019 on factory farming that failed to win majority approval (Totally Vegan Buzz 2019). In the United Kingdom, the newly announced Action Plan for Animal Welfare ('Plan') is, as its name suggests, aimed at improving animal welfare; it does not seek to circumscribe intensive or other animal agriculture (Harvey 2021). In terms of secondary industries that support intensive agriculture, however, it is notable that the Plan includes proposed legislation to ban live animal transport (ibid). Animals will also be legally recognized as sentient beings in one of the three legislative pillars of the Plan – the Animal Sentience Bill – which is arguably a symbolic move that may lead to future change (Sebo and Shann 2021). Though this symbolism and corresponding welfare measures in the Animal Sentience Bill are significant, there is nothing in the Plan that presently aims to restrict the scope of domestic intensive agriculture (ibid).[11]

Circumscribing Animal Consumption – Taxation and Divestment

Legislation has also been introduced to scale down consumption of animal products at an individual level. Proposals to tax animal consumption have come forward in Denmark, Germany, and Sweden, though none of these bills passed (Withnall 2016; BBC News 2012; Schulz 2020; Relman 2019; Charlton 2019; Sverige Radio 2013). More localized initiatives to restructure choice, and without stigmatizing animal-eating preferences as socially undesirable and thus deserving of special taxation, appear to have been more successful. Most recently at the municipal level the city of Berkeley, California, has asked the state's public pension fund to divest from intensive agriculture and redirect investment to plant-based opportunities (Gor 2021b). And Berkeley and larger municipalities are leading action on adjusting the animal to plant-based ratio of foods the cities purchase in their delivery of services (Gor 2021a).

Common Theme Across Initiatives: Reducing Scope of Intensive ABFS

The preceding proposals that restrict CAFOs and tax animal consumption or seek to divest from it are not identical. Notably, in addition to different details and legislative routes, the former are production-side oriented while

11 Currently, in the United Kingdom, the not-for-profit Humane Being is planning to mount a legal challenge against the British government to have it stop intensive animal farming (Hamlett 2021).

the latter target consumption. However, legislative proposals to eliminate further intensification in ABFS in terms of operational size and proposals to amplify consumer taxes on animal flesh, or have pension funds and purchasing menus divest from intensive farming however, are not categorically different. None are classic welfarist ones aimed at improving animal welfare through, for example, eliminating the most egregious practices of animal confinement, but are directed at abating the growth of intensive ABFS. The former is a direct effort to reduce the scope of the industry, while the latter constitute indirect efforts to achieve the same goal. They thus share the common theme of targeting behaviors that exploit animals. We may classify all of them as 'intensive ABFS-curbing' measures.

Despite the multiple merits of phasing out intensive ABFS, it is clear that the legislative initiatives above the municipal level have not been met with majority support from state or national lawmakers to pass into law or attracted the attention of the international law community. Would a concerted strategy linking such initiatives to the rule of law make a difference for those unswayed by the multitude of reasons to support intensive ABFS-curbing proposals? It is not clear. But creating such a narrative is worth considering as it underscores not simply the social undesirability of the practices at issue but also the principled *legal* basis for governments to respond and the international law community to take notice.

A Plant-Forward Legality: Thickening the Rule of Law Beyond the Human

Where can such responsibility come from in countries with no constitutional provision to possibly be mined for its animal-protective principles? As I argue in this section, one answer is the unwritten constitutional principle of the rule of law that formally permeates legal cultures in Western societies, has emerged as an international law concept (Wohlwend 2021: 2–3), and also circulates through a global rule of law vision through a legal and professional elite (Rijpkema 2013: 196). More specifically, the acknowledgment that the rule of law requires that justice-oriented social mores translate into legal requirements can be tapped to develop an argument in favor of farmed animal protection.

Typical, Narrow Iteration

A wide array of scholars, despite their ultimate divergent delineations of the scope of the rule of law, identify the following governance features inherited from the British originary version as a baseline for the concept: the formulation of clear and transparent laws accessible to the public (accessibility), government fairness and accountability in public law decision-making (order not arbitrariness), the operation of administrative regimes pursuant to legal authority (legality versus illegality) where government actors are not themselves above the law (formal equality), and judicial independence and the availability of judicial review of executive and administrative action (judicial supremacy) (Liston 2005: 147–52; May 2021: 2351–2). This baseline for the rule of law envisions the rule of law as safeguard against government excess through the existence of a set of rules communicated in advance to the (human) public subject to the laws that are predictable and universally applied (Liston 2011: 40–1; Gordon 2010). It also envisions it as unrelated to morality (Craig 2017: 95–6). In both veins, the baseline is a narrow or 'thin' vision of the rule of law, and the more classic iteration adopted by Western governments (Peerenboom 2004: 2–5), as well as the international law community (Wohlwend 2021: 13).

Proactive Rule of Law

However, there are more substantive visions of the rule of law and as May has noted, 'many states (and many other global actors), for much of the time, do seem to accept some version of the (thicker) rule of law' (May 2021: 2353). Thicker visions of the rule of law allow for morality to shape what the rule of law means (ibid; Tremblay 1997). They acknowledge that normative values are legitimate and even necessary in the legal arena and allow the law to shift to better reflect changing social values. Historically, this account of the rule of law assumes individual citizens have moral rights and duties with respect to one another and political rights against the state, broadly speaking (Dworkin 1986: 11–12). It also insists that those rights be recognized in positive law so they may be enforced (ibid). A binary distinction is not drawn between the rule of law and substantive justice. Rather, this view requires the rule of law to encapsulate and enforce moral rights (ibid). This view often rejects a strict dichotomy between form and substance (Craig 2017: 107; May 2021: 2351).

In some versions, the rule of law plays a catalyzing force, prompting governments to act rather than simply refrain from acting and enforcing certain rights protections, and can even mediate private relationships (Gordon 2010). This more 'proactive' rule of law version believes that the rule of law can be a tool that *compels* government action, and not just arrests it, typically in the service of realizing a more just society. Professing such a vision is to believe in larger social norms and a state duty to actively bring them into reality (Dworkin 1986). International law visions of the rule of law frequently endorse this generative role for nation-states to bring into effect new protections to guard against vulnerabilities in their populations, rather than simply maintain existing allocation of protections, helping to model typically a robust sense of an inclusive liberal democracy (Zimmermann 2017: 9;

Krygier 2014: 53). To the extent that '(i)nternational law can be understood as a value-based system', the meaning of the 'rule of law' in international law is similarly infused with social justice orientations despite the contestation over meaning amongst international law lawyers, and differences from the domestic national understandings (Krieger *et al* 2019: 12).

Some point out that a substantive rule of law, such as this, is really just an endorsement of a particular ideology of law (ibid: 109). Yet, thin, legal positivist conceptions of the rule of law are not immune from this critique – they are based on substantive liberal legal foundations, principally moral autonomy and respect for the individual (ibid). In that sense, a thin conception of the rule of law can also be seen as endorsing a particular theory of law and, itself, rests on particular understandings of human liberty, equality and dignity (Allan 2014: 155–8). In the context of the common law, these substantive foundations and values are critical tools for articulating formal legal rules and principles (ibid: 111). Ultimately, the debate surrounding whether minimalist of maximalist version of the rule of are to be preferred is not this chapter's focus. Rather, the present purpose is to point to the availability of a proactive vision to activate government response to animal vulnerability.

Connecting the Rule of Law to the Harms of ABFS

A substantive, proactive vision of the rule of law has brought about considerable recent social change in terms of civil liberties and human rights in many countries around the world where judges, legislatures and populations have embraced this vision. What is its potential to apply to 'animal rights' issues such as intensive ABFS through serving as a legal basis for the measures discussed earlier in the second section? On the one hand, the potential seems minimal as the common law legal system in which the concept is rooted is an anthropocentric one (Deckha 2013: 784, 801, 810), and judicial cases and scholars promoting a thick version of the rule of law have done so in the context of considering *human* rights claims (Coen 2018). It is not simple to integrate animal interests into constitutional cultures premised on the dignity of the human above all others (Eisen 2017). Even a thin version of the rule of law is rarely connected to animal interests.[12]

On the other hand, the rule of law is a capacious, open-ended, and oft-contested concept amenable to a variety of legal and political meanings and there is no precedent in common law jurisdictions that *explicitly* restricts the norm-generating potential of the concept to human interests. It is a

12 An exception to this occurred in the dissenting judgment of the Chief Justice of the Alberta Court of Appeal in *Reece v Edmonton (City)* 2011 ABCA 238. For discussion of the groundbreaking nature of this dissent, please see Deckha 2013.

foundational concept that does not bring to mind an image of a 'human'; inspected from this angle, the rule of law is less tethered to humans and human claims than the concept of personhood arguably is (Deckha 2021: 87–96). The rule of law can thus conceivably promote other-than-human interests alongside and independently of human interests. Ideas of core constitutional national values and new international law norms can transcend the human subject even though such readings of constitutionalism or international law are not traditional or mainstream, particularly where the nonhuman subjects dwell in an intensely vulnerable legal state (Eisen 2017: 910).

This outlook about the rule of law's potential to ameliorate animals' socio-legal predicament is reflected in a recent resolution from the American Bar Association,

> urg(ing) all nations to negotiate an international convention for the protection of animals that establishes standards for the proper care and treatment of all animals to protect public health, the environment, and animal wellbeing.
>
> *(American Bar Association 2021)*

The resolution calls for an International Convention for the Protection of Animals (ICPA) and also 'encourage(s) the U.S. State Department to initiate and take a leadership role in such negotiations' (ibid). The resolution came about in the midst of the COVID-19 pandemic and cites the pandemic and its devastating fallout as an urgent 'wake-up call' for governments to act to restrict and regulate certain human–animal practices to avoid future potential of zoonotic disease (ibid: 11).[13] Most notably for present purposes, part of the rationale the ABA gives for the resolution invokes the rule of law. Specifically, it is stated in an appended report that the resolution promotes one of the goals of the ABA, namely 'to "advance the rule of law" by "work[ing] for just laws"' (ibid: 2 citing ABA Mission and Goals). The report supporting the resolution identifies the lack of minimal international standardized protection for animals as relevant to the urgent global social problems presented by zoonoses, environmental devastation and animals' status as sentient beings (American Bar Association 2021: 2, 6–9). The report also cites the 'ethical imperative to treat animals with proper care and respect' as a further reason that the international convention it envisions for animals would be 'just' (ibid: 2fn14).

The ABA's ICPA is not directed at restricting ABFS but only 'the capturing or hunting of high-risk wildlife' and some 'sale and use of wild animals

13 The Resolution also notes the earlier work by Professor David Favre and the Global Animal Law Association in calling for similar measures (ibid: 3, citing Favre 2012).

for commercial, culinary, or medical purposes'; it is also directed at *regulating* 'high-risk wildlife management', and the trade, use and transporting of wild animals (ibid: 4). It is consequently topically different and also primarily a welfarist measure and thus differently oriented than the intensive animal agricultural measures discussed earlier. However, these qualities do not preclude the rule of law rationale the resolution's supporting report highlights from applying to other instances of human-animal relations.

The reasons the ABA's supporting report gives for the rule of law basis for the ICPA resolution – promotion of public health, environmental reasons, animal well-being and ethical obligations – also relate to the problem of ABFS, as we have seen. The absence of legal protection is also part of the rule of law argument the ABA crafts in its report, an absence that is equally pertinent in many national jurisdictions regarding lack of protection for intensively farmed animals (Blattner 2019: 347–54; Sankoff 2019: 7–10; Cassuto 2012: 226, 236). But the rule of law rationale for regulation or restriction can even be invoked in those regions where there is considerably more regulation in favor of farmed animals (such as at the European Union level) than elsewhere globally. Improving regulation in favor of animals as the ICPA resolution envisions, but also restricting certain practices or industries altogether, aids animal well-being and makes inroads into other social goals such as public health and environmental issues as already referenced. It is thus reasonable to transpose the rule of law rationale that the ABA assembles as a partial basis for the legal need for an ICPA to provide a legal basis for the measures discussed earlier. In other words, we can view the rule of law as connected to and in favor of the ABFS-curbing measures discussed earlier.

Conclusion

Bucolic myths about ABFS help shield intensive animal agriculture from government regulation, public scrutiny and much-needed social redirection toward plant-based societies. Feminist new materialism and posthumanist feminist scholarship aids in exposing these myths about what is 'natural' and thus normative, but it is necessary to turn to more animal-centered theories that impugn the industries that exploit animals to theorize legal strategies that can curb these industries. It is possible to then apply this anti-animal exploitation outlook to work within anthropocentric legal systems that treat animals as property and deploy existing legal principles in unconventional ways to help abolish intensive agricultural farming and its multiple adverse effects.

One such foundational principle is the rule of law. The idea of the rule of law as a higher-order legality concept translates across almost every nation-state and at the international level. Existing widespread respect for this concept amongst jurists as well as jurisprudential precedent in favor of a thicker vision of the rule of law can be tapped in favor of animal-friendly legislation. A proactive rule of law recognizes the inseparability of ethical values, rights and legal theory from the form and content of the rule of law, and demands our lawmaking institutions recognize these substantive elements in positive law need not be anthropocentric in design our outlook. This social-justice oriented version of the rule of law can provide a legal tool to help persuade recalcitrant lawmakers to support legislative initiatives targeting intensive animal farming. Whether such invocation makes pragmatic and ethical sense is a question for further research that this chapter has shown is worth exploring. The present analysis illuminates that such legislative initiatives implicate the rule of law as understood by legal jurists at a national level, and at an international understanding of the global rule of law. It is a legal strategy that can assist in not only highlighting ABFS as a grave social problem in need of a remedy, but also in connecting this problem to the foundational and exalted principles of legality and social justice and thus spotlighting the legal urgency by which governments and the international law community must act to provide a remedy.

References

Adams, C. and L. Gruen (2021) *Ecofeminism: Feminist Intersections with Other Animals and the Earth*, New York: Bloomsbury.

Allan, T.R.S. (2014) 'Freedom, Equality, Legality', in J.R. Silkenat, J.E. Hickey Jr. and P.D. Barenboim (eds) *The Legal Doctrines of the Rule of Law and the Legal State (Rechtsstaat)*, Cham: Springer International Publishing, 155–69.

Almiron, N. and L. Fernández (2021) 'Including the Animal Standpoint in Critical Public Relations Research', *Public Relations Inquiry*, 10(2): 139–61.

American Bar Association (2021) 'Resolution 101C', *American Bar Association, Adopted by the House of Delegates*, 22 February. www.americanbar.org/content/dam/aba/directories/policy/midyear-2021/101c-midyear-2021.pdf (Accessed: 12 March 2022).

American Bar Association. 'ABA Mission and Goals', *About the American Bar Association.* www.americanbar.org/about_the_aba/aba-mission-goals/ (Accessed: 12 March 2022).

Animal Liberation Currents (2017) 'R v. Krajnc – Trial Documents (Defence Submissions)', *Animal Liberation Currents*, 5 May. https://animalliberationcurrents.com/r-vs-krajnc-trial-documents/ (Accessed: 13 March 2022).

Arcari, P., F. Probyn-Rapsey and H. Singer (2021) 'Where Species Don't Meet: Invisibilized Animals, Urban Nature and City Limits', *Environment and Planning E, Nature and Space*, 4(3): 940–65.

Arvay, J. and D. Wu (2020) 'As Civil Liberties Erode, Canada Must Not Allow COVID-19 Outbreak to Infect the Rule of Law', *CBC News*, 26 March. www.cbc.ca/news/opinion/opinion-charter-rights-freedoms-covid-1.5508222 (Accessed: 12 March 2022).

Baise, G. (2020) 'Vegan Senator Declares War on Big Livestock Farms', *Western Farm Press*, 28 January. www.farmprogress.com/commentary/vegan-senator-declares-war-big-livestock-farms (Accessed: 12 March 2022).

Banerjee, B. (2016) 'Kinship Between "Companion Species": A Posthuman Refiguration of the Immigrant Condition in Shaun Tan's the Arrival', *Journal of Postcolonial Writing*, 52(4): 399–414.
BBC News (2012) 'Denmark to Abolish Tax on High-Fat Foods', *BBC News*, 10 November. www.bbc.com/news/world-europe-20280863 (Accessed: 12 March 2022).
Bingham, H. (2010) *The Rule of Law*, New York: Allen Lane.
Blattner, C. (2019) *Protecting Animals Within and Across Borders*, Cambridge: Cambridge University Press.
Braidotti, R. (2009) 'Animals, Anomalies and Inorganic Others', *PMLA: Publications of the Modern Language Association of America*, 124(2): 526–32.
Braidotti, R. (2013) *The Posthuman*, Cambridge: Polity Press.
Bruckner, H.K., A. Colombino and U. Ermann (2019) 'Naturecultures and the Affective (Dis)entanglements of Happy Meat', *Agriculture and Human Values*, 36: 35–47.
Buttlar, B. and E. Walther (2022) 'Escaping from the Meat Paradox: How Morality and Disgust Affect Meat-Related Ambivalence', *Appetite*, 168: 105721.
Cao, D., S. White and D. Bilchitz (2016) *Animal Law and Welfare – International Perspectives*, Cham: Springer.
Case, S. (2020) 'The Case Against Factory Farming: On This Issue, Senator Cory Booker Is Correct', *National Review*, 19 March. www.nationalreview.com/magazine/2020/04/06/senator-booker-is-right-about-factory-farming/ (Accessed: 12 March 2022).
Cassuto, D.N. (2012) 'Meat Animals, Humane Standards and Other Legal Fictions', *Law, Culture and the Humanities*, 10: 225–36.
Cassuto, D.N. and T. DiBenedetto (2020) 'Suffering Matters: NEPA, Animals, and the Duty to Disclose', *University of Hawaii Law Review*, 42: 41.
Charlton, E. (2019) 'This Is Why Denmark, Sweden and Germany Are Considering a Meat Tax', *World Economic Forum*, 28 August. www.weforum.org/agenda/2019/08/this-is-why-denmark-sweden-and-germany-are-considering-a-meat-tax/ (Accessed: 12 March 2022).
Climate Stewardship Act US Bill S 1072 (2021-117th Cong).
Coen, A. (2018) 'International Order, the Rule of Law, and US Departures from Refugee Protection', *The International Journal of Human Rights*, 22: 1269–84.
Craig, P. (2017) 'Formal and Substantive Conceptions of the Rule of Law: An Analytical Framework', in R. Bellamy (ed) *The Rule of Law and the Separation of Powers*, London: Routledge, 95–115.
Deckha, M. (2013) 'Initiating a Non-Anthropocentric Jurisprudence: The Rule of Law and Animal Vulnerability Under a Property Paradigm', *Alberta Law Review*, 50(4): 783–814.
Deckha, M. (2015) 'Vulnerability, Equality, and Animals', *Canadian Journal of Women and the Law*, 27: 47–70.
Deckha, M. (2018) 'The "Pig Trial" Decision: The Save Movement, Legal Mischief, and the Legal Invisibilization of Farmed Animal Suffering', *Ottawa Law Review*, 50: 65–98.
Deckha, M. (2021) *Animals as Legal Beings: Contesting Anthropocentric Legal Order*, Toronto: University of Toronto Press.
Dworkin, R. (1986) *Law's Empire*, Cambridge: Belknap Press of Harvard University Press.

Eisen, J. (2017) 'Animals in the Constitutional State', *International Journal of Constitutional Law*, 15: 909–54.
Farm System Reform Act US Bill S 3221 (2019-116th Cong).
Faulk County Record (2019) 'Concentrated Animal Feeding Operations in Faulk County', *Faulk Country Record On-Line*, 137(2), 9 January. www.faulkcountyrecord.com/wp-content/uploads/2019/01/FCR-01-09-2019.pdf (Accessed: 13 March 2022).
Favre, D.S. (2012) 'An International Treaty for Animal Welfare', *Animal Law*, 18: 237–80.
Gillespie, K. (2011) 'How Happy Is Your Meat? (Dis)connectedness in the "Alternative" Meat Industry', *The Brock Review*, 12: 100–28.
Gillespie, K. (2018) *The Cow with Ear Tag #1389*, Chicago: Chicago University Press.
Giraud, E.H. (2013) '"Beasts of Burden": Productive Tensions Between Haraway and Radical Animal Rights Activism', *Culture, Theory and Critique*, 54: 102–20.
Giraud, E.H. (2019) *What Comes After Entanglement? Activism, Anthropocentrism, and an Ethics of Exclusion*, Durham: Duke University Press.
Goodale, M. (2005) 'Empires of Law: Discipline and Resistance Within the Transnational System', *Social & Legal Studies*, 14: 553–83.
Goodfellow, J. (2016) 'Regulatory Capture and the Welfare of Farm Animals in Australia', in D. Cao and S. White (eds) *Animal Law and Welfare – International Perspectives*, Cham: Springer International Publishing, 195–235.
Gor, N. (2021a) 'How One Small City in California is Going Plant-Based', *Sentient Media*, 5 April. https://sentientmedia.org/how-one-small-city-in-california-is-going-plant-based/#:~:text=On%20March%209%2C%202021%2C%20Berkeley,community%20health%2C%20and%20animal%20rights (Accessed: 13 March 2022).
Gor, N. (2021b) 'Why California Cities Should Divest from Factory Farms', *Sentient Media*, 5 May. https://sentientmedia.org/why-california-cities-should-divest-from-factory-farms/ (Accessed: 13 March 2022).
Gordon, R. (2010) 'The Role of Lawyers in Producing the Rule of Law: Some Critical Reflections', *Theoretical Inquiries in Law*, 11(1): 441–68.
Hamlett, C. (2021) 'The People Fighting the UK's Factory Farm Expansion', *Byline Times*, 3 March. https://bylinetimes.com/2021/03/03/people-fighting-uk-factory-farm-expansion/ (Accessed: 13 March 2022).
Harvey, F. (2021) 'Animals to Be Formally Recognised as Sentient Beings in UK Law; Set of Government Measures Will Include Halting Most Live Animal Exports and a Ban on Hunting Trophy Imports', *The Guardian (London, England)*, 12 May. www.theguardian.com/world/2021/may/12/animals-to-be-formally-recognised-as-sentient-beings-in-uk-law (Accessed: 13 March 2022).
Heath, D. and A. Meneley (2010) 'The Naturecultures of Foie Gras', *Food, Culture & Society*, 13: 421–52.
Hollin, G., I. Forsyth, E. Giraud and T. Potts (2017) '(Dis)entangling Barad: Materialisms and Ethics', *Social Studies of Science*, 47: 918–41.
Holloway, L., C. Morris, B. Gilna and D. Gibbs (2009) 'Biopower, Genetics and Livestock Breeding: (Re)constituting Animal Populations and Heterogeneous Biosocial Collectivities', *Transactions of the Institute of British Geographers*, 34: 394–407.
Humphreys, S. (2010) *Theatre of the Rule of Law: Transnational Legal Intervention in Theory and Practice*, Cambridge: Cambridge University Press.

Hurlbert, M., J. Krishnaswamy, E. Davin, F.X. Johnson, C.F. Mena, J. Morton, S. Myeong, D. Viner, K. Warner, A. Wreford, S. Zakieldeen and Z. Zommers (2019) '2019: Risk Management and Decision making in Relation to Sustainable Development', in P.R. Shukla, J. Skea, E. Calvo Buendia, V. Masson-Delmotte, H.O. Pörtner, D.C. Roberts, P. Zhai, R. Slade, S. Connors, R. van Diemen, M. Ferrat, E. Haughey, S. Luz, S. Neogi, M. Pathak, J. Petzold, J. Portugal Pereira, P. Vyas, E. Huntley, K. Kissick, M. Belkacemi and J. Malley (eds) *Climate Change and Land: An IPCC Special Report on Climate Change, Desertification, Land Degradation, Sustainable Land Management, Food Security, and Greenhouse Gas Fluxes in Terrestrial Ecosystems*. Geneva: IPCC. DOI: https://doi.org/10.1017/9781009157988.001

Justice for Black Farmers Act US Bill S 300 (2021-117th Cong).

Kaeding, D. (2019) 'Burnett County Passes 1-Year Moratorium on Large-Scale Farms', *Wisconsin Public Radio*, 2 August. www.wpr.org/burnett-county-passes-1-year-moratorium-large-scale-farms (Accessed: 13 March 2022).

Khazaal, N. and N. Almiron (2016) 'An Angry Cow Is Not a Good Eating Experience', *Journalism Studies*, 17: 374–91.

Krieger, H., G. Nolte and A. Zimmermann (2019) *The International Rule of Law: Rise or Decline? Foundational Challenges*, Oxford: Oxford University Press.

Kristiansen, S., J. Painter and M. Shea (2021) 'Animal Agriculture and Climate Change in the US and UK Elite Media: Volume, Responsibilities, Causes and Solutions', *Environmental Communication*, 15: 153–72.

Krygier, M. (2014) 'Rule of Law (and Rechtsstaat)', in J.R. Silkenat, J.E. Hickey Jr. and P.D. Barenboim (eds) *The Legal Doctrines of the Rule of Law and the Legal State (Rechtsstaat)*, Cham: Springer International Publishing, 45–59.

Leth-Espensen, M. and M. Svensson (2020) 'Beyond Law's Anthropocentrism: A Sociolegal Reflection on Animal Law and the More-Than-Human Turn', *Animal Studies Journal*, 67: 35–50.

LexisNexis (2022) 'Measuring the Rule of Law', *LexisNexis Rule of Law Foundation*. www.lexisnexisrolfoundation.org/tools.aspx?p=tools (Accessed: 13 March 2022).

Lindgren, N. and J. Öhman (2019) 'A Posthuman Approach to Human-Animal Relationships: Advocating Critical Pluralism', *Environmental Education Research*, 25: 1200–15.

Lino, D. (2018) 'The Rule of Law and the Rule of Empire: A.V. Dicey in Imperial Context', *The Modern Law Review*, 81: 739–64.

Liston, M. (2005) 'Administering the Canadian Rule of Law', in L. Sossin and C. Flood (eds) *Administrative Law in Context*, 3rd ed., Toronto: Emond Montgomery, 139–81.

Liston, M. (2011) 'Governments in Miniature: The Rule of Law in the Administrative State', *SSRN*. www.ssrn.com/abstract=1808278 (Accessed: 13 March 2022).

May, C. (2021) 'Rule of Law and Imperialism', in I. Ness and Z. Cope (eds) *The Palgrave Encyclopedia of Imperialism and Anti-Imperialism*, Cham: Springer International Publishing, 2350–60.

Mazac, R. and H.L. Tuomisto (2020) 'The Post-Anthropocene Diet: Navigating Future Diets for Sustainable Food Systems', *Sustainability*, 12: 1–15.

Milfont, T.L., N. Satherley, D. Osborne, M.S. Wilson and C.G. Sibley (2021) 'To Meat, or Not to Meat: A Longitudinal Investigation of Transitioning to and from Plant-Based Diets', *Appetite*, 166: 105584.

Muhlhauser, P., M. Drews and R. Reitz (2021) 'Grilling Meataphors: Impossible™ Foods and Posthumanism in the Meat Aisle', *Humanities*, 10(1): 49.

Ndlela, T. and M. Murcott (2021) 'Innovative Regulation of Meat Consumption in South Africa: An Environmental Rights Perspective', *Potchefstroom Electronic Law Journal*, 24: 1–47.

Now Media Group (2016) 'Bayfield County Approves CAFO Ordinance', *Wisconsin State Farmer*, 29 January. www.wisfarmer.com/story/life/state/2016/01/29/bayfield-county-approves-cafo-ordinance/87279912/ (Accessed: 13 March 2022).

Peerenboom, R. (2004) *Asian Discourses of Rule of Law*, Abingdon: Taylor & Francis Group.

Peters, A. (2016) 'Global Animal Law: What It Is and Why We Need It', *Transnational Environmental Law*, 5(1): 9–23.

Peters, A. (2017) 'Introduction to Symposium on Global Animal Law (Part I): Animals Matter in International Law and International Law Matters for Animals', *AJIL Unbound*, 111: 252–6.

Peters, A. (2020) *Studies in Global Animal* Law, Berlin: Springer.

Pilgrim, K. (2019) 'Beyond the Story of Sustainable Meat', *Society & Animals*, 27(1): 75–91.

Polk County Resolutions (2019) 'Polk County Resolution No. 33–19 2019, Resolution Creating Polk County Ordinance Regarding Temporary Moratorium on Livestock Facilities', 15 October. www.co.polk.wi.us/vertical/Sites/%7BA1D2EAAA-7A29-46D6-BF1A-12B71F23A6E1%7D/uploads/Res2019_33-19_Creating_Ordinance_RE_Temp_Moratorium_on_Livestock_Facilities.pdf (Accessed: 13 March 2022).

Raz, J. (1990) 'The Politics of the Rule of Law', *Ratio Juris*, 3(3): 331–9.

Reece v. Edmonton (City) (2011) ABCA 238.

Relman, E. (2019) 'Germany's Considering a New Tax on Meat – But It Might Not Be a Model for Democrats Who Want Americans to Eat Fewer Hamburgers', *Business Insider*, 15 September. www.businessinsider.com/germany-considering-meat-tax-fight-climate-change-2019-9 (Accessed: 13 March 2022).

Rijpkema, P. (2013) 'The Concept of a Global Rule of Law', *Transnational Legal Theory*, 4: 167–96.

Sands, D. (2019) *Animal Writing: Storytelling, Selfhood and the Limits of Empathy*, Edinburgh: Edinburgh University Press.

Sanford, M., I. Painter, T. Yasseri and J. Lorimer (2021) 'Controversy Around Climate Change Reports: A Case Study of Twitter Responses to the 2019 IPCC Report on Land', *Climatic Change*, 167(3–4): 59.

Sankoff, P. (2019) 'Canada's Experiment with Industry Self-Regulation in Agriculture: Radical Innovation or Means of Insulation?' *Canadian Journal of Comparative & Contemporary Law*, 5(1): 299–348.

Schultz, F. (2020) 'Could Germany Impose a Tax on Meat?', *Euractiv*, 10 January. www.euractiv.com/section/agriculture-food/news/could-germany-impose-a-tax-on-meat/ (Accessed: 13 March 2022).

Sebo, J. and A. Shann (2021) 'The UK Animal Sentience Bill Is Good, but Animals Deserve Better', *Sentient Media*, 18 May. https://sentientmedia.org/the-uk-animal-sentience-bill-is-good-but-animals-deserve-better/ (Accessed: 13 March 2022).

Shukla, P.R., J. Skea, E. Calvo Buendia, V. Masson-Delmotte, H.O. Pörtner, D.C. Roberts, P. Zhai, R. Slade, S. Connors, R. van Diemen, M. Ferrat, E. Haughey,

S. Luz, S. Neogi, M. Pathak, J. Petzold, J. Portugal Pereira, P. Vyas, E. Huntley, K. Kissick, M. Belkacemi and J. Malley (eds) (2020) 'IPCC, 2019: Summary for Policymakers', in *Climate Change and Land: An IPCC Special Report on Climate Change, Desertification, Land Degradation, Sustainable Land Management, Food Security, and Greenhouse Gas Fluxes in Terrestrial Ecosystems*. Geneva: IPCC. DOI: https://doi.org/10.1017/9781009157988.001

Silver, J. (2019) 'Effective Legal Advocacy, Inside & Outside', Canadian Animal Law Conference, Dalhousie, Nova Scotia, 5 October.

Srinivasan, K. (2021) 'Debating Animal Agriculture in Contemporary India: Ethics, Politics, Ecologies', *Environment and Planning E: Nature and Space*. DOI: https://doi.org/10.1177/25148486211045477

Stanescu, V. (2019) 'Selling Eden: Environmentalism, Local Meat, and the Postcommodity Fetish', *American Behavioral Scientist*, 63: 1120–36.

Stucki, S. (2017) '(Certified) Humane Violence? Animal Welfare Labels, the Ambivalence of Humanizing the Inhumane, and What International Humanitarian Law Has to Do with It', *AJIL Unbound*, 111: 277–81.

Sutherland, L.A. (2020) 'Virtualizing the "Good Life": Reworking Narratives of Agrarianism and the Rural Idyll in a Computer Game', *Agriculture and Human Values*, 37: 1155–73.

Sverige Radio (2013) 'Borg Says "No" to Meat Tax', 22 January. https://sverigesradio.se/artikel/5417214 (Accessed: 13 March 2022).

Timeto, F. (2021) 'Becoming-with in a Compost Society – Haraway Beyond Posthumanism', *International Journal of Sociology and Social Policy*, 41: 315–30.

Totally Vegan Buzz (2019) 'Swiss Politician Battles to Outlaw Factory Farming', 23 October. www.totallyveganbuzz.com/news/swiss-politician-battles-to-outlaw-factory-farming/ (Accessed: 13 March 2022).

Tremblay, L.B. (1997) *Rule of Law, Justice, and Interpretation*, Montreal: McGill-Queen's University Press.

Twine, R. (2013) 'Is Biotechnology Deconstructing Animal Domestication? Movements Toward Liberation', *Configurations*, 21: 135–58.

United Nations Environment Programme (2019) 'Global Environment Outlook GEO-6: Healthy Planet, Healthy People', in *Global Environment Outlook 6*, Cambridge University Press, 4 March. www.unep.org/resources/global-environment-outlook-6 (Accessed: 13 March 2022).

United Nations Environment Programme (2021) 'The Heat Is on: A World of Climate Promises Not Yet Delivered', *Emissions Gap Report 2021*, 26 October. www.unep.org/resources/emissions-gap-report-2021 (Accessed: 13 March 2022).

United Nations Food and Agricultural Organization (2006) *Livestock's Long Shadow: Environmental Issues and Options*, Rome: Food and Agriculture Organisation of the United Nations.

United Nations Food and Agricultural Organization (2018) *The Future of Food and Agriculture: Alternative Pathways to 2050*, Rome: Food and Agriculture Organisation of the United Nations.

US, HF 440, 89th Gen Assem, Reg Sess, IA (2021) www.legis.iowa.gov/legislation/BillBook?ga=89&ba=HF440 (Accessed: 13 March 2022).

US, SB 583, 81st Gen Assem, Reg Sess, OR (2021) https://olis.oregonlegislature.gov/liz/2021R1/Downloads/MeasureDocument/SB0583/Introduced (Accessed: 13 March 2022).

Vanclay, F. and G. Enticott (2011) 'The Role and Functioning of Cultural Scripts in Farming and Agriculture', *Sociologia Ruralis*, 51: 256–71.

Wadiwel, D. (2014) 'Chicken Harvesting Machine: Animal Labor, Resistance, and the Time of Production', *The South Atlantic Quarterly*, 117: 527–49.

Walter, G. (1997) 'Images of Success: How Illinois Farmers Define the Successful Farmer', *Rural Sociology*, 62: 48–68.

Weisberg, Z. (2009) 'The Broken Promises of Monsters: Haraway, Animals and the Humanist Legacy', *Journal for Critical Animal Studies*, 7: 21–61.

Weisberg, Z. (2015) 'Biotechnology as End Game: Ontological and Ethical Collapse in the "Biotech Century"', *NanoEthics*, 9: 39–54.

Willett, W., J. Rockstrom, B. Loken, M. Springmann, T. Lang, S. Vermeulen, T. Garnett, D. Tilman, F. Declerck, A. Wood, M. Jonell, M. Clark, L.J. Gordon, J. Fanzo, C. Hawkes, R. Zurayk, J.A. Rivera, W. De Vries, L. Majele Sibanda, A. Afshin, A. Chaudhary, M. Herrero, R. Agustina, F. Branca, A. Lartey, S. Fan, B. Crona, E. Fox, V. Bignet, M. Troell, T. Lindahl, S. Singh, S.E. Cornell, K. Srinath Reddy, S. Narain, S. Nishtar and C.J.L. Murray (2019) 'Food in the Anthropocene: The EAT-Lancet Commission on Healthy Diets from Sustainable Food Systems', *Lancet*, 393: 447–92.

Withnall, A. (2016) 'Denmark Ethics Council Calls for Tax on Red Meat to Fight "Ethical Problem" of Climate Change', *The Independent*, 27 April. www.independent.co.uk/climate-change/news/denmark-ethics-council-calls-for-tax-on-red-meat-to-fight-ethical-problem-of-climate-change-a7003061.html(Accessed:13March 2022).

Wohlwend, D. (2021) *The International Rule of Law: Scope, Subjects, Requirements*, Northampton: Edward Elgar.

World Health Organization, European Regional Office (2021) 'Healthy and Sustainable Diets: Key Workstreams in the WHO European Region (2021)', *WHO*. www.euro.who.int/en/media-centre/sections/fact-sheets/2021/factsheet-healthy-and-sustainable-diets.-key-workstreams-in-the-who-european-region-2021 (Accessed: 13 March 2022).

Zimmermann, L. (2017) 'Introduction: Between Global Norms and Local Translation', in *Global Norms with a Local Face: Rule-of-Law Promotion and Norm Translation*, Cambridge: Cambridge University Press, 1–22.

Zouev, A. (2020) 'COVID and the Rule of Law: A Dangerous Balancing Act', *United Nations*. www.un.org/en/coronavirus/covid-and-rule-law-dangerous-balancing-act (Accessed: 13 March 2022).

12

WILL HUMAN RIGHTS SAVE THE *ANTHROPOS* FROM THE ANTHROPOCENE? RIGHTS-BASED ENVIRONMENTAL PROTECTION STRATEGIES AND POSTHUMAN THEORY

Jasmijn Leeuwenkamp

Introduction

In the context of the anthropogenic climate crisis, human rights are considered as both part of the problem and as part of a promising response to this problem. On the one hand, human rights in the form of international law are increasingly seen as a powerful weapon against the manifold injustices that are effectuated or exacerbated by climate change.[1] As several scholars have pointed out, climate change poses serious threats to many different human rights under international law (Boyle and Anderson 1996: 3; Kotzé 2014: 257; Adelman and Lewis 2018: 11; Atapattu and Schapper 2019: 4–5; Fraser and Henderson 2022: 4), such as the right to life, health, livelihood, food, water (Westra 2010), privacy, and property of both present and future (Shue 2014a; Johnston 2016; Lawrence and Köhler 2018) generations. This insight has placed international human rights law at the heart of recent climate litigation cases (Savaresi and Auz 2019; Fraser and Henderson 2022), with cases being brought forth for present and future generations at both domestic and international levels (see, for example: *Urgenda v. The Netherlands*; *Milieudefensie et al v. Shell*; *Athabaskan Petition to the IACHR*; *Cité Soleil Petition to the IACHR*; *Future Generations v. Ministry of*

1 There is a bulk of literature on climate change as a human rights issue. See for example: Nickel 1993; Boyle and Anderson 1996; Hiskes 2009; Humphreys 2010; Leib 2011; Shue 2014a; 2014b; Knox 2014; UNEP 2015; Grear and Kotzé 2015; Bos and Düwell 2016; Skillington 2017; Oksanen *et al* 2017; Knox and Pejan 2018; Boyle 2018; Atapattu and Schapper 2019; Townsend 2020; Phelan 2020; GNHRE, *Declaration on Human Rights and Climate Change*. For an overview of literature on this topic see https://gnhre.org/research-repository/.

DOI: 10.4324/9781032658032-16

the Environment and Others; *PSB et al v. Brazil*; *La Rose v. Her Majesty the Queen*; *Neubauer v. Germany*; *Greenpeace et al v. Spain*. For an overview of human rights-based climate litigation cases, see: Savaresi and Setzer 2021).

On the other hand, international human rights law is problematically grounded in an outdated humanist framework of exclusive human mastery and control over 'nature' that has presumably resulted in the destructive relation to all beings traditionally regarded or treated as 'objects'. The international human rights law tradition has been vehemently criticized for being Eurocentric/Western, colonial, inherently exclusionary, and othering those on the 'darker side' of modernity by defining universal 'Man' in rational, civilizing and exclusionist (white, male, Western) terms (Spivak 2005; Kapur 2006; Douzinas 2007; Mignolo 2009; Maldonado-Torres 2017), but more recently also for being inherently anthropocentric (Westra and Wenz 1995: x; Boyle and Anderson 1996: 3; Grear 2011, 2018; Jones 2021). Posthumanist, decolonial and other critical theorists have successfully rejected the dominant humanist epistemologies underlying international human rights law by refuting and destabilizing its central dichotomies – nature/culture, subject/object, man/woman, Western/non-Western, civilized/uncivilized, human/animal, human/nonhuman, human/machine, etc. – in favor of frameworks that aim to move beyond these traditional hierarchies: posthumanism, network theory, tentacular thinking, string theory (Latour 2004, 2017; Haraway 2008, 2016; Braidotti 2013; Grear 2015a; Tsing 2015).

The term 'human rights' is thus 'fraught with ambiguities', as Grear & Kotzé write, as

> critiques of human rights are legion – and compelling – and yet despite this, human rights-based arguments and claim-making practices seem to play an increasingly important role in the protection not only of human environmental interests but also (though most often indirectly) of the interests of the environment.
>
> *(2015: 1)*

Considering this ambiguity, how should we evaluate the limitations of human rights–based climate litigation that arise from these critiques?

Although much scholarly work has linked human rights to climate justice (Caney 2014; Shue 2014b; Skillington 2017), atmospheric justice (Vanderheiden 2008), a green future (Hiskes 2009; Düwell *et al* 2018) and a healthy (Knox and Pejan 2018; Townsend 2020) or safe (Nickel 1993) environment, there has not been enough attention paid to the interconnections between the genealogy of human rights, the histories of imperialism and fossil fuel capitalism, modern science and (liberal) humanism. The two main lines of critique of human rights – its anthropocentrism (seeing humans apart from and hierarchically above 'nature') and its (colonial/Eurocentric) humanism – now exist relatively apart, and as such must be brought together in order to meaningfully address the different types of 'anthropo'-centrism that underlie human rights. I say different types because different conceptions of the type of 'human' or 'anthropos' seem to be centralized. In the contested notion 'Anthropocene' the 'anthropos' refers to a biological species-human (as a geological force), whereas the 'anthropos' in 'anthropocentrism' seems to refer to human 'culture' as opposed to 'nature' (as a metaphysical ordering), and the 'anthropos' that has traditionally been opposed to Western 'Humanity' refers to colonized, subaltern Others that traditionally formed the object of anthropology and sociology (Douzinas 2013, 54). As I argue below, it is the *anthropos* in this latter sense that might not be 'saved' by the discourse of the Anthropocene.

Although the frameworks discussed above relate to one another, the debates on anthropocentrism and posthumanism have traditionally focused on separate issues:

> whereas critiques of anthropocentrism denounce the species hierarchy that culminates in human exceptionalism and privilege, posthumanism more specifically engages a critique of the humanist ideal of 'Man', and the political and philosophical programs of progressive Enlightenment (or 'civilization') that rest upon this ideal.
>
> *(Braidotti and Bignall 2019: 4)*

Instead of focusing solely on the anthropocentrism of human rights, posthuman theory exemplifies the need for a more critical perspective that rejects the hierarchical logic inherent in the humanist understanding of what it means to be human in relation to other humans *and* the nonhuman world.

By understanding anthropocentrism through Braidotti's posthumanist approach (Braidotti 2013, 2022) and Wynter's analysis of Western colonial humanism (Wynter 2003), I show how both 'inter-' and 'intra-species' hierarchies are founded on the same 'hierarchy of being' (Grear 2015a: 229) that has resulted in what Wynter calls the 'over-representation of Man' (Wynter 2003). I apply this perspective to the Dutch *Urgenda* case – which is a domestic case, but one that draws on international human rights law and which is regarded as an important precedent for international climate change litigation (Krommendijk 2022: 60; Wewerinke-Singh and McCoach 2021: 275; Burgers and Staal 2019: 813; Leijten 2019). I do so to illustrate that the reframing of the climate crisis as an international human rights law issue has at least two important limitations.

First, by referring to anthropocentric human rights, climate litigation cases only focus on the preservation of *human* life (and property), thereby disregarding all nonhuman life and the interconnections and interdependencies that obtain between both forms of life. Second, as posthuman and decolonial theories have shown, the anthropocentrism of human rights is conceptually and historically grounded on a hierarchical logic that defines the 'human' in teleological terms – the overrepresentation of Man in Wynter's terms – and which is only conceptually possible through the externalization of the human and nonhuman 'Others'. The universal 'human' of human rights (the rights of 'Man') and the notion of a universal 'anthropos' in 'Anthropocene' mask these exclusions and the related inequalities in power, responsibility and vulnerability that characterize the climate crisis.

In the following, I first outline the way human rights were instrumentalized in the *Urgenda* case. I then put forward the two limitations that characterize the reliance on human rights in such climate litigation cases in the second and third section respectively. Reflecting on these limitations, I propose that the exclusionary logic underlying the notion of 'human' that is the subject of international human rights law affects the legal imaginary that lies behind human rights–based climate litigation, and should therefore be reassessed in light of this critique. I conclude that a critical analysis of the genealogy of (international) human rights shows that taking up a human rights strategy as a response to climate change seriously limits a more radical re-evaluation of how to legally protect both human and non-human life in an entangled and unequal world.

Human Rights in the *Urgenda* Case

In December 2019 the Dutch climate foundation Urgenda won a historic court case against the Dutch state, demanding that the Dutch government had to reduce its emissions significantly by the end of 2020 to fulfill its international human rights law obligations – a goal that the state eventually also reached (coincidentally according to critics, due to mitigating circumstances related to the COVID pandemic).[2] The ruling showed that climate action by states (and recently also by fossil fuel corporations in the Shell case)[3] can be successfully enforced through human rights–based litigation, an outcome that made the *Urgenda* case, according to the *New York Times*, 'the "strongest" climate ruling yet' (Schwartz 2019). Legal scholars enthusiastically framed the ruling in favor of Urgenda as a boost to the argument that 'climate change is a human rights issue' (Minnerop 2019; Burgers and Staal

2 NOS (2022) 'Klimaatdoel in Urgenda-vonnis definitief gehaald', *NOS Nieuws*. https://nos.nl/artikel/2416400-klimaatdoel-in-urgenda-vonnis-definitief-gehaald (Accessed: 23 June 2022).

3 Luttikhuis, P. and E. van der Walle (2021) 'Deze uitspraak over Shell laat zien: het klimaat is een mensenrechtenkwestie', *NRC*, 21 May. www.nrc.nl/nieuws/2021/05/26/uitspraak-over-shell-laat-zien-het-klimaat-is-mensenrechtenkwestie-a4045058 (Accessed: 19 September 2021).

2019; Nollkaemper and Burgers 2020, 812). In the more recent *Milieudefensie et al v. Shell* case, the Dutch NGO Milieudefensie referred to the same international human rights law articles in building their case for demanding emission reduction by oil company Shell (Hösli 2021). While these cases are both domestic cases under Dutch law, they both refer to obligations under international human rights law. The cases' significance thus transcends the Dutch context, by creating promising precedents for future climate litigation cases.

Urgenda is a foundation that strives for a 'sustainable society'.[4] In 2013 it accused the Dutch government of failing to protect its citizens' lives and well-being, demanding that the Dutch government reduce its greenhouse gas emissions by at least 25 percent, compared to 1990, by 2020. Urgenda eventually won the case by referring, amongst other legal documents, to article 2, the 'right to life', and article 8, the 'right to respect for private and family life' of the European Convention on Human Rights (ECHR). Both these rights 'include the positive international legal obligation to take concrete actions to prevent a future violation of these interests (a duty of care)' (Leijten 2019: 114). By referring to the hazardous effects of climate change as outlined by climate scientists, the case was made that the Dutch government had to reduce its emissions in order to prevent these dangers from infringing on the international human rights of its own citizens in the future.

Notwithstanding the importance of reducing carbon emissions, this case shows just how ambivalent international human rights law can be in relation to climate change, not only because the lives and livelihoods of those that are most affected by climate change are, for the most part, not located in Europe but in countries in the Global South (Gonzalez 2015; Williams 2021), but also because it raises questions regarding the effectivity and even viability of preexisting international legal institutional frameworks for addressing the climate crisis. In what follows, I will take the *Urgenda* case as an example, to illustrate how the framing of the legislation illuminates two main, interconnected limitations of international human rights law in climate litigation. First, I argue that referring to human rights, which are anthropocentric, implicitly prioritizes human life at the expense of nonhuman life. Second, as posthuman and postcolonial theories have shown, the anthropocentrism of human rights is conceptually and historically grounded on a hierarchical logic that defines the 'human' in teleological terms and externalizes this human's 'Others'.

4 Missie en werkwijze (n.d.) *Urgenda*. www.urgenda.nl/over-urgenda/missie-en-werkwijze/ (Accessed: 20 April 2022).

Anthropo-centered Human Rights

One of the reasons why strategies relying on international human rights might not be the most suitable for overturning destructive relations to the climate, is that the human rights framework is inherently anthropocentric (Grear 2011; Kotzé 2014). In the instance of the Urgenda case, this is illustrated by the fact that here courts only recognized humans' right to life and their right to home and family life. This relatively limited framing of the climate crisis mistakenly views it as a solely human issue that threatens a particular human way of life (although, as we will see, human vulnerability is itself differentiated along geolocation, colonial history, race, gender and class). More specifically, international human rights–based arguments are conceptually founded on the normative distinction between humans and nonhumans, thereby foreclosing the possibility of recognizing nonhuman life as worthy of protection.

International human rights derive from a exclusionist conception of the 'human'. They are grounded upon essential traits that are thought to define what it means to be human: rationality, action and morality. This conceptualization stems from the Modern idea that only human beings can and should distinguish themselves from 'nature' – presented as the realm of passive 'objective facts', 'dead nature' (Merchant 1989), the body, and all non-rational beings (including women) – and achieve the 'nobler' state of science, civilization and progress. Crucially, this led to a relation with nature in which the latter became devalued, appropriated and instrumentalized as raw material for extractivism and labor, and as an object for knowledge, experimentation and control. As such, international human rights are conceptually grounded in a Baconian 'epistemology of mastery' (Adelman 2015) and a misguided Cartesian dichotomy of mind/matter-nature/culture.

Scholars such as Latour (1993, 2017), Haraway (1991, 2016), Moore (2017), Braidotti (2013, 2022), Tsing (2017) and Barad (2007) have opposed the Nature/Culture divide, exemplifying how human–nonhuman relations are in fact characterized by complex, entangled and interdependent relations that cannot be reduced to agents on the one hand and objects or the 'environment' on the other. According to Latour, our inability to respond adequately to the present ecological crisis stems from the 'cloak of axiological neutrality' with which 'nature' has been covered by what he refers to as the 'Moderns' (Latour 2017: 22). As the Moderns (the theorists and scientists of the discourse of Modernity) ontologized 'nature' as passive objectivity, it has become impossible to fully recognize the way nature (re)acts. In Latour's view, to say that we can ultimately distinguish the natural world (Nature) from the human world (Culture), is nothing more than to say that 'an arbitrary portion of the actors will be *stripped of all action* and that another portion, equally arbitrary, will be *endowed with souls* (or consciousness)' (ibid: 58). What Latour shows is that to think of humans as separate from nature – or to think of norms, rights and actions in strict opposition to 'dead objective facts' – is itself a normative gesture. These norm-making processes cast the former as ('free') agents and the latter as inert objects that 'wait' for human observation, classification, intervention, cultivation and civilization. Understanding humans rather as part of nature, as 'bounded to the earth' (Latour) or 'terra' (Haraway), in 'companionship with other species', is thus regarded as the first step in dealing with this 'trouble' (Haraway 2016).

This Modern or humanist framework forms the philosophical and legal backbone of international human rights law. The universal promise of international human rights law stems directly from the egalitarian and liberal principles of the Enlightenment. These principles are philosophically grounded in the capability of rational reflection (Rorty 1998: 171) and the related idea that the essence of being human lies in the capacity to *transcend nature*. A good illustration of the idea that rationality defines what it means to be human is Kant's view that 'the vocation of the human being and the characteristic of his formation' is to be 'destined by his reason to live in a society with human beings and in it to *cultivate* himself, to *civilize* himself, and to *moralize* himself by means of the arts and sciences' (Kant 2007: 470 [7: 324]). For Kant, one of the main sources of inspiration for universal human rights and duties, 'reason itself does not operate instinctively, but rather needs attempts, practice and instruction in order gradually to progress from one stage of insight to another' (Kant 2007: 109 [8:18–19]). In other words, within this tradition of thought humans are regarded as having dignity and rights only insofar as they are (made) capable to leave the *state of nature* and become 'civilized'. In political liberalism 'nature' thus became the realm of 'servitude, violence and brutality' to defend an 'anthropocentric and political order based on the rule of law' (Braidotti 2022: 71), which became the sign of moral 'progress'.

Grear explains that these 'dualistic assumptions' (Nature/Culture divisions) 'saturate the anthropocentrism of human rights and, significantly, of human rights *as law*' (2018: 133). In other words, the anthropocentrism of international human rights law is expressed most forcefully in its commitment to an individualistic, rationalistic and disembodied archetype which became the dominant subject of law (Grear 2015a). However, these dualistic assumptions cannot be reduced to a simple binary schema, such as human/nature. As posthumanist, feminist and critical race theorists have shown, this hierarchy is sustained and legitimized through the workings of interrelated ideas about human/sub-human border cases intersecting with the human/nature dichotomy, such as femininity, irrationality, infantility or animality. This is a crucial point because it enables one to understand how the nature/culture distinction and anthropocentrism function as constitutive parts of a broader scientific and capitalist discourse of civilization and Progress in which 'nature' serves as a normative category, signifying that which should be controlled, cultivated and appropriated. Moreover, a generalizing approach toward the human-nature dyad risks overlooking the particular context from which destructive practices that contributed to the climate crisis emerged (and as such the unequal responsibility for climate change).

Related to this issue is the way that nature has been recast as an external factor – the 'environment'. In this guise, the effects of climate change are understood as unfortunate phenomena whose source and cause originate from outside 'the human'. As Jones points out, international environmental law 'reproduces a problematic subject/object binary for which humans are the central subject of the law and "the environment" is mere object' (Jones 2021: 82). In the Urgenda case, this externalization of nature is illustrated by the fact that the case only focuses on the human right to life and the right to home and family life, which are regarded as under threat due to the (future) effects of the abstract notion of 'climate change'. In this sense, nature is recast as a dangerous external problem affecting innocent citizens' way of life. This way of framing the issue hides the interconnection between the mostly Western way of life, the capitalist system that sustains it, and ecological disasters (which mostly happen outside the view of the Global North). By seeing human life as inherently separate from 'nature' (the nature-culture distinction), the phenomenon of 'climate change' becomes externalized, treated as an unwelcome disorder by nature that must be governed and controlled by human political decisions and the rule of law.

For a similar reason Malm and Hornborg (2014) criticize the notion 'Anthropocene': it generalizes humankind as one species-being that is responsible for the ecological destruction, masking the major role that modern fossil-fuel technologies play in effectuating destructive climate change (64). They rightly oppose Chakrabarty's claim that in case of the climate crisis, 'unlike in the crises of capitalism, there are no lifeboats here for the rich and the privileged' (Chakrabarty 2021: 45), emphasizing that there *will* be lifeboats for the rich and privileged (Malm and Hornborg 2014: 66). The Global North can use its money, power and other resources gained from centuries of imperialism and fossil fuel capitalism to look after the economic needs of its own elites and to protect its way of living through technological 'solutions'. Similarly, rejecting the racial violence that is implicit in the White universalizing discourse of 'the Anthropocene', Yusoff (2018) argues that we can only speak of 'a billion Black Anthropocenes or none'. She points out that geology as a practice and science has never been neutral, but rather has always inscribed property relations of matter (as slaves) and value (as gold) into Black bodies (6, 71). As such, the Anthropocene narrative in her view 'replicates the political and racial divisions of matter' (80). In Yusoff's words: 'As the Anthropocene proclaims the language of species life –*anthropos* – through a universalist geologic commons, it neatly erases histories of racism that were incubated through the regulatory structure of geologic relations' (2).

By claiming that the climate crisis affects everyone equally ('*the* Anthropocene'), and that the West must heroically 'take the lead' in fighting climate change (through 'historic' climate litigation cases like *Urgenda*), Western states occlude the overwhelming role they have played (and still do) in causing climate change. Powerful Western states disregard the fact that precisely those areas that are and have been subject to appropriation, extractivism and domination are now disproportionally vulnerable to harm by climate change, and they repeat the old narrative of 'discovering' and bringing enlightenment in the form of human rights law and climate technology, by turning climate change into a post-political technical or legal problem, of mainly 'future generations' (Catney and Doyle 2011: 179; Swyngedouw 2010).

The problem of implying a universal 'anthropos' in the Anthropocene discourse should therefore not be seen apart from implying a universal 'human' in the international legal human rights discourse. As the longer-standing debate on the (non-)universality of human rights shows, which I will discuss in the next section, the notion of 'human' implied in international human rights law is founded on the same system or hierarchy of being as the overrepresented Man of humanism.

The 'Human' of Human Rights is Still an Overrepresentation of 'Man'

Regarding the human species as one universal *anthropos* that must be decentered risks misrecognizing the social and political dimensions of anthropocentrism that are tied to its patriarchal, racial and colonial past. Over the past decades, ecofeminists have emphasized the link between the domination of nature and the oppression of women and other Others. They have pointed out that being assigned to the realm of 'nature' has not only been a way of science to construct nonhumans as passive 'objects', but it has also been a 'cover for a naturalization of inequalities' (Braidotti 2022: 70). Plumwood describes this naturalization as follows:

> The category of nature is a field of multiple exclusion and control, not only of non-humans, but of various groups of humans and aspects of human life which are cast as nature. Thus racism, colonialism and sexism have drawn their conceptual strength from casting sexual, racial and ethnic difference as closer to the animal and the body construed as a sphere of inferiority, as a lesser form of humanity lacking the full measure of rationality or culture. [. . .] To be defined as 'nature' in this context is to be defined as passive, as non-agent and non-subject, as the 'environment' or invisible background conditions against which the 'foreground' achievements of reason or culture (provided typically by the white, western, male expert or entrepreneur) take place. It is to be defined as a *terra nullius*, a resource empty of its own purposes or meanings, and hence available to be annexed for the purposes of those supposedly identified

> with reason or intellect, and to be conceived and moulded in relation to these purposes.
>
> *(Plumwood 1993: 4)*

Plumwood hereby rightly points out that anthropocentrism is intrinsically connected to androcentrism, eurocentrism, extractivism, coloniality and whiteness, but also to the humanistic idea of civilization, development and Progress, in which human rights have come to play a vital role.

Wynter's notion of the 'over-representation of Man' connects these multiple axes of domination, although it is less centered on the exclusion of nonhumans. In her analysis of the connections between humanism and colonialism, Wynter shows, in line with posthuman theorists (Jansen *et al* 2021), how today's multiple crises and forms of oppression overlap and intersect, by relating them to the overrepresentation of a certain mode of being human: 'Man'. In Wynter's view, the climate struggle should not be seen apart from struggles with respect to race, class, gender, sexual orientation and the unequal distribution of the earth's resources (Wynter 2003: 260), as these according to her are 'all differing facets of the central ethnoclass Man vs. human struggle (261)'. With this she means the overrepresented conception of the human, 'Man', on the one hand, and the human species itself, on the other (260). Her point is that the present (climate) asymmetries are an effect of colonial history and a particular mode of Being/Power/Truth/Freedom that is grounded in Modern humanism, and that this mode of being lies at the root of our ecological problems. Moreover, it is in Wynter's view precisely due to this overrepresentation that notions of being human in relation to nature that are different from the Modernist nature/culture distinction have been misrecognized and devalued.

The 'Man' that is the subject of the Rights of Man has precisely the characteristics of this overrepresented mode of being: it is a humanist ideal of human superiority, grounded in theories on the domination of nature (from Bacon and Descartes to Locke and Kant) and in the universalizing and imperializing project of Enlightenment. International human rights law is problematically entangled with this discourse and the imperial and capitalist projects that inspired it, and as such has been criticized for being Eurocentric and colonial (Spivak 2005; Kapur 2006; Mignolo 2009; Douzinas 2013; Maldonado-Torres 2017), and undemocratic (Spivak 2005; Tully 2014). In what follows I will briefly reconsider some of these points of critique, as a critical analysis of the notion of 'human' that underlies international human rights law in my view shows that it is founded on a hierarchical logic that should not be seen apart from the global asymmetries and injustices that make up the current climate crisis.

The humanist idea of Man as a teleological notion that follows a hierarchical logic (the 'Great Chain of Being'), can already be found in Mirandola's

Oration on the Dignity of Man. In this 'manifesto of humanism' (*Oration*: xiii), Mirandola asks what in human nature makes 'man' such a miraculous, admirable, and eminent creature (3), and asserts that 'God bestowed seeds pregnant with all possibilities, the germs of every form of life. [. . .] If vegetative, he will become a plant; if sensual, he will become brutish; if rational, he will reveal himself a heavenly being' (8–9). The humanist conception of man thus invokes a higher form of humanness, or *humanitas*, embodied in the Vitruvin Man of Leonardo da Vinci, the *homo universalis*, which signified a human being ('Man') that had developed all potential talents and (intellectual) faculties to perfection, and, as such, positioned *him*self away from the lower (mere 'natural') beings and more closely to the divine. Thus, in humanism the essence of Man is linked to the potential to become a different degree of being (human) through its rational capabilities (its *telos*), which became a civilizational ideal in Europe's imperial context (Braidotti 2013: 13–15).

The liberal and egalitarian Enlightenment discourse of the "Rights of Man" must be understood as emerging from two interrelated contexts, that together explain why "Man" emerged as an unmarked category, referring implicitly to white, bourgeois, male humans whose default subject position represented a universal prototype for humanity and the essence and "dignity' of which was believed to be grounded in its ability to reason. The first is the humanist construction of "Man" that emerged during the Renaissance, and the second is the broader context of European imperialism (Arendt 1994). As Hunt points out, the rights of Man from the outset proved to be too general for political purposes and rather served the humanist purpose of defining 'what distinguished humans from the divine on one end of the scale and from animals on the other' (Hunt 2007: 23). This latter distinction obviously makes human rights inherently speciesist: it serves to rank human animals above all nonhuman animals and legitimizes their oppression and instrumentalization (Kymlicka 2018: 764).

The idea that the essence and dignity of man should be defined in terms of rational capacities could thus only be constructed by contrasting it with forms of being regarded as subhuman/irrational. As we already saw in the ecofeminist critique, this relation with otherness is not merely coincidental but structural. It is not the case that there historically have been different ways of being in the world of which one has simply been the most valued, accidentally presented as universal. Rather, the invention of Man as the only essence of Being/Power/Truth/Freedom inherently demanded a 'physical referent of the idea of the irrational/subrational Human Other' (Wynter 2003: 266). Wynter describes the constitutive relation of this non-being to being aptly: 'All other modes of being human would instead have to be seen not as the alternative modes of being human that they are "out there," but adaptively, as the lack of the West's ontologically absolute self-description' (282).

In legitimizing colonial and imperial domination, this Western concept of the human poses a 'colonial or color-line that makes it possible to distinguish humans from non-humans and to think of humanity in terms of degrees – that one can be more or less human' (Maldonado-Torres 2017: 122). Jackson underscores this point by showing how 'the African' functioned as the borderline case in this hierarchical logic, dividing humans from animals: 'African peoples qualify as human but only tentatively so, given their purported physical or mental similarity to nonhuman animals and vice versa' (Jackson 2020: 22).

As this subhuman-ness is not contingent but constitutive, we should not aim to merely *include* women, non-white people and nonhumans into the Western liberal paradigm of recognition. It is not sufficient to 'humanize' those regarded as sub-human by 'giving' them recognition, inclusion or rights, as this leaves the very notion of 'humanity' that created the status of 'Other' unscrutinized. This is why 'feminism is in its essence a transformative project, not just a reparative one' (Braidotti 2022: 29), and why the 'recognition of personhood and humanity does not annul the animalization of blackness' (Jackson 2020: 17–18). Humanization and dehumanization are two sides of the same coin. 'Empowering' those who have been dehumanized by 'recognizing', after all, their humanness, or human-likeness, simply upholds the dominant way of being human (Man) and the universalizing discourse of rights connected to it.

The hierarchical logic and system of idealized humanness characterized the subject of law in general from the outset (Grear 2015a). Grear therefore argues that the exclusionist genealogy of law's subject is characterized by othering patterns that can never be overcome by recognition alone because 'the subject-object relations at the heart of the European rationalist project *impede* the full *juridical recognition* of the "others" to the paradigmatic master-subject (*anthropos*) of law: these [. . .] still only truly feature in law as *other-to-the-central-master-subject*' (Grear 2015a: 236). This master-subject was cloaked as universal but has in fact always been characterized, implicitly or explicitly, as a male, white, disembodied, rational 'knower', whose ultimately 'impossible disembodiment of rationality and its presumed subject/object relations sweep a set of intimately co-related, feminized "others" into the spectrum of "objects" and/or object-like entities and systems made subject to the knowing gaze of the *anthtropos*' (235). In other words, the humanist and Enlightenment ideas about the 'human' of human rights co-emerged with the disembodied rational subject that was understood as the 'bearer' of natural rights, within the context of European colonial expansionism and the scientific narrative of Progress.

As the emergence of the notions 'Man' and 'human' 'went hand in hand with the emergence of the concept of "rights"' (Mignolo 2009: 7–8), the humanists, by inventing both, also defined the 'locus of enunciation' (8), which means that they 'felt authorized to speak for man and the human' (9), hereby making themselves the neutral point of reference without reflecting on the privileged position of this declaring subject. The control of the concept 'human' by Western imperial knowledge meant to have control over who was deemed 'rational' enough to 'bear' the responsibility of having rights. As Mignolo writes: 'Roman legac[ies] of *humanitas* and *civitas* were rehearsed when European men and citizens appointed themselves to carry civilization to the *anthropos* of the planet' (15). Spivak makes a similar point when she states that human rights 'is not only about having or claiming a right or a set of rights; it is also about righting wrongs, about being the dispenser of these rights' (Spivak 2005: 132). She emphasizes how the privileged position of being the dispenser of rights 'enables' some to violate, to legitimize (right) violations (wrongs). This ambivalence of humanism, which Braidotti describes as 'complicitous with genocides and crimes on the one hand, supportive of enormous hopes and aspirations to freedom on the other', for her emphasizes the 'importance of where one is actually speaking from' (Braidotti 2013: 16). As we will see, the importance of location becomes especially relevant in times of ecological disaster.

The point is that by conceptualizing the human being as an empty potentiality, the intellectual and moral progress that is regarded as its 'higher destiny' become a political and historical condition that legitimizes the aim to 'govern' and 'civilize' the parts of the world that are deemed as 'underdeveloped'. The teleological model in which 'humanity is marked as an achievement and teleology' (Jackson 2020: 22), in which the axes of gender, sexualization, racialization, animalization and the contempt of matter and the body, intersect in the ontological construction of human- and subhuman-ness, functions as a tool for legitimating the political exploitation and domination of these (sub)human and nonhuman Others. The humanist invention of 'Man' that also became the universal 'human' of the human rights tradition should therefore not be understood apart from the colonial project of 'large-scale accumulation of unpaid land, unpaid labor, and overall wealth expropriated by Western Europe from non-European peoples' (Wynter 2003: 291). As the world became geographically 'discovered' and thereupon divided between more Enlightened and civilized ('developed') nations on the one hand, and more primitive and barbarous ('underdeveloped') peoples (because still in the realm of 'nature') on the other, humans became divided between 'Man' and not-fully-humans, so that the expansionist projects could be legitimized by regarding them as the 'burdensome' task of 'bringing' Christianity/Enlightenment/development to the not-yet-humans (and nonhumans) and to 'cultivate' the so-called *terra nullius*.

Critics emphasize the instrumental role that human rights played in this history of imperial expansion, driven by the capitalist logic of primitive accumulation, making these rights anything but neutral or universal. In this regard, Azoulay describes human rights as 'imperial devices' that 'facilitated the plunder and appropriation of material wealth, culture, resources, and documents, and generated the establishment of state institutions to preserve looted objects and produce a bygone past' (2019: 41).

As we have seen, this instrumental role is also reflected in the way the subject of law is constructed. As Grear writes: 'It is no coincidence that this "subject" reflects precisely the rationalistic, hierarchical scales of value decisive to the expansion of European capitalist ambition across the globe in the form of appropriative industrial expansionism' (Grear 2015a: 231) as it enabled granting 'naturalised civilisational priority and publicly sanctioned dominance to white (rational) property-owning European males "at home" and legitimating "the dispossession of indigenous people" through the "classist, racist hierarchies expressed by Western property-territorialism" abroad' (232). Taking these conceptual interlinkages seriously, the question is how this genealogy affects the role human rights play today in the context of climate change.

The Importance of Location

One aspect of international human rights law where the described genealogy seems to work through in the present, is in the formulation of the 'human right to development'. It reflects a capitalist impetus that also informed the formulation of international human rights (mostly in the form of property rights). The Declaration on the Right to Development, Gearty points out, awkwardly shows the limitation of such declarations in a time of climate crisis (Gearty 2010: 9–10), as it reads that the right to development entitles all (and only) humans 'to participate in, contribute to, and enjoy economic, social, cultural and political development' (Article 1.1) and 'implies the full realization of the right of peoples to self-determination, which includes [. . .] the exercise of their inalienable right to full sovereignty over all their natural wealth and resources' (Article 1.2). Such an idea of development, still widespread today, shows how the (universal) idea of political and moral progress (through the fulfillment of human rights) is ultimately connected to the economic development of a capitalist exploitative system that treats all nonhumans as mere resources, and climate threats as mere hindrances to this 'development'. The promise of development masks the fact that the capitalist way of living necessarily means 'living well at others' expense' (Lessenich 2019), including nonhuman others and communities that uphold other, non-exploitative relationships with those nonhumans.

It is now well-known that there is a great asymmetry between those who have contributed most to the emissions causing climate change – the 'developed' Western countries that have also benefited considerably from the imperial mode of living (Brand and Wissen 2021) and fossil fuel capitalist projects – and those who have experienced the most harm from climate change – 'developing' countries that have the least means to deal with the damaging effects (Catney and Doyle 2011: 176; Malm and Hornborg 2014; Humphreys 2014; Grear 2015b: 94; Klein 2016; Pulido 2018: 116; Sealey-Huggins 2018;

Malm and Zetkin Collective 2021: 320–1; Williams 2021). In short: the (right to) 'development' of some has resulted in the increased vulnerability of others.

This makes the instrumentalization of the 'Master's tool' in the form of international human rights law for countering the process that this very same framework of Progress inspired and legitimized somewhat bittersweet for the countries that are called 'developing' (as 'lack of the West's ontologically absolute self-description' of 'development'), but have largely been colonized, controlled and exploited, and are now extremely vulnerable to the climate effects resulting from this very same exploitative system. In Spivak's terms one might ask: are some more entitled to right the wrongs of climate injustice? Considering earlier mentioned strategies to construct a universal human right to a healthy environment or green future and liberal climate justice principles which are mainly located in Western-oriented philosophical and legal traditions, focusing on average emission rates, seriously debating any individual moral responsibility in relation to climate change (e.g. Sinnott-Armstrong 2010) and theorizing the 'just' distributions of burdens (meaning financial costs) from an ideal (meaning ahistorical) perspective, this might be the case.

Notwithstanding the fact that the asymmetry with regard to vulnerability and culpability are increasingly recognized in international environmental law treaties, such as the United Nations Framework Convention on Climate Change (UNFCCC) – the so-called Common but Differentiated Responsibilities and Respective Capabilities principle – these treaties are still focused on the 'sustainable development' (Article 3.4) of states that still have 'the *sovereign right to exploit* their own resources pursuant to their own environmental and developmental policies' (emphasis added), while also having 'the responsibility to ensure that activities within their jurisdiction or control do not cause damage to the environment of other States or of areas beyond the limits of national jurisdiction' (UNFCCC). Leaving the impossibility of the latter requirement in the light of the nature of climate change on the side for the moment, such documents do not only show the anthropocentrism of international environmental law but also raise important questions about what type of 'common future' is envisioned here. It keeps intact a discourse that focuses on liberal autonomous (human) individuals that must be protected from 'harm' by the unhealthy emissions of others, and on sovereign states that must govern the influence of its economic development on the external 'environment' within the limits of 'sustaining' the present mode of living for future generations. It must be clear that such a future can never be 'common'.

The Urgenda case is relevant here because it shows a certain ambivalence connected to human rights. On the one hand, the ruling impressively urged the Dutch state to take up its (minimal) responsibility of emission reduction to which the state committed in the Paris Agreement of 2015, by pointing towards the direct harm posed to its citizens when the state will not lower its emissions. On the other hand, however, as Wewerinke-Singh and McCoach (2021) have shown, the Supreme Court only recognized the rights of Dutch citizens residing in the Netherlands in holding the Dutch State accountable to protect its citizens' international *human* rights. The authors highlight how the Court follows an interpretation of Article 2 of the UNFCCC that shows a privileged and outdated perspective on the dangers of climate change, by phrasing that the 'ultimate objective' of the Convention is to '*prevent* dangerous anthropogenic interference with the climate system' (UNFCCC, Article 2., emphasis added).

They point out that the Court hereby assumes that the hazardous consequences already happening right now

> do not qualify as manifestations of dangerous climate change, maintaining instead that 'dangerous climate change' will likely only occur if over 1.5°C or 2°C of global temperature rise occurs [and] even go as far as referring to warming of up to 1.5°C as 'safe'.
>
> *(Wewerinke-Singh and McCoach 2021: 280)*

Similarly, many climate justice and environmental ethics scholars argue for demanding climate action on the basis that it threatens *future* generations. Boyle even writes: 'the fundamental challenge posed by climate change is not so much to human rights here and now, but to future generations and humanity itself' (Boyle 2018: 760).

This line of arguing stands in stark contrast with lived reality of the Global South, which can be illustrated by slogans such as '1.5°C to stay alive' (Sealy-Huggins 2017), and 'two degrees is suicide' (Pulido 2018: 120). According to Leon Sealy-Huggins (2017), we can only explain the misrecognition of the immense vulnerability of people living in the Caribbean, and by extension those living in the Global South, if we take into account the relations of colonialism and imperialism. He explains how the average temperature that was agreed upon in the Paris agreement mainly reflects the interests of the Global North:

> Part of how climate change politics operates is via the representation of the particular interests of a subsection of the global elite as being universally applicable to all human societies. The idea of a single average temperature target beyond which warming is 'dangerous' is an example of this kind of technocratic universalism.
>
> *(Sealy-Huggins 2017: 2445)*

According to Sealy-Huggins (2018) and others (Klein 2016; Yusoff 2018; Pulido 2018: 121; Malm and Zetkin Collective 2021: 318), we can only explain this technocratic universalism by seeing it as part of a general attitude of indifference and disregard of the powerful (Western) elites for lives in the Global South that we, in their view, can rightly call racist, as it reflects the assumption that white lives should be valued higher than Black and brown lives. It also explains why governments agreed to a temperature increase of two degrees Celsius during the 2009 UN climate summit in Copenhagen, even though it was by then 'fully understood that two degrees would eliminate some island states and be absolutely disastrous for much of Africa' (Pulido 2018: 120). As Klein puts it very aptly:

> [The] refusal to lower emissions [. . .] would have been functionally impossible without institutional racism, even if only latent. It would have been impossible without Orientalism, without all the potent tools on offer that allow the powerful to discount the lives of the less powerful. These tools – of ranking the relative value of humans – are what allow the writing off of entire nations and ancient cultures. And they are what allowed for the digging up of all that carbon to begin with.
>
> *(Klein 2016)*

This is also reflected, as some authors have pointed out, in the environmental racism of treating Black and brown lives as less valuable by treating their lands and neighborhoods as sites of 'waste', thereby making them more vulnerable to pollution and toxic environments (Westra and Wenz 1995; Resnick 2021).

Opening Up to Other Ways of Being Human

One could argue, however, that if climate change has an inherently racist dimension, human rights are certainly more needed than ever. Despite their troubled genealogy, international human rights have become a powerful political tool. However, as we have seen, international human rights are also problematically entangled with the racist and colonial origins of climate change. As technocratic universalism has served the interests of Global North in climate negotiations, regarding two degrees of temperature increase as 'save' indicates a continuation of the aforementioned human rights tradition that started in the Enlightenment period, in which a particular humanistic (male, white, rational) mode of being was regarded as universal.

In a similar vein, the fact that many 'less developed' countries cannot afford to think about future generations is not recognized by many scholars, because they approach climate change in a universal manner. When we fight climate change by referring to international human rights and its laws, we risk preserving a particular form of human life and mode of living, which has historically predominantly meant white and Western human life and an imperial mode of living (Brand and Wissen 2021; Jansen and Leeuwenkamp 2023), overlooking the interconnections of this way of life with the ecological exhaustion ultimately causing climate change. The *relation* between 'Man' and underrepresented humans and nonhumans is not altered: it leaves the very notion of 'human' and its correlated matrix of Being/Power/Truth/Freedom, with its racialized hierarchy, intact (Jackson 2020: 15).

This means potentially overlooking and misrecognizing the narratives and discourses that display different 'genres of the human', which are especially important in discussions of the Anthropocene, as Davis and Todd (2017) have argued. 'Systems that', as Klein describes,

> insist that humans must think seven generations in the future; must be not only good citizens but also good ancestors; must take no more than they need and give back to the land in order to protect and augment the cycles of regeneration. These systems existed and still exist, but they are erased every time we say that the climate crisis is a crisis of 'human nature' and that we are living in the 'age of man'.
>
> *(Klein 2016)*

In the context of international human rights law, it means that we should not just decenter the *anthropos* in anthropocentrism as a category left untouched but decenter the system that privileges 'Man' and the connected culture over and over again.

In other words, calling our era after a universal *anthropos* that is equally responsible for the destruction of the environment can be seen as continuing an imperial tradition of projecting Western human–nonhuman relations onto an abstract, universal humanity, crucially masking the unequal culpability in causing climate change and overlooking different (often Indigenous) systems of envisioning human–nonhuman relations. As Braidotti writes: 'Neither "Man" as the universal humanistic measure of all things, nor Anthropos as the emblem of an exceptional species', has 'the power to stop the climate change triggered by reckless overdevelopment' (Braidotti 2022: 69). Thus, taking up a posthumanist approach to international human rights law means rejecting on the one hand the particular humanism of human rights, in the form of the hierarchical (teleological) ontological conceptualization of the human and the mode of Being/Truth/Power/Freedom that accompanies it, and its correlated tendencies of humanization, civilization and Progress – and, on the other hand, the anthropocentrism of human rights, as this limits (re)valuing nonhuman ways of (co)living.

In the view of Braidotti and Bignall, we must not aim to combine the critiques of anthropocentrism and the critique of the humanist ideal of 'Man' into one coherent view, but rather preserve the divergences between them as this gives us a more nuanced perspective (Braidotti and Bignall 2019: 4).

Such a perspective entails opening up to different modes of being human in nondestructive relations to nonhumans, being aware of the differences in location, and without molding these perspectives into a coherent view of climate justice or monolithic environmental ethic. It means holding states accountable, not for neglecting *our* individual rights as rational beings, but for failing to take and promote the responsibility of care for the different forms of human and nonhuman life that are entangled to its real, material way of living.

Conclusion: A Posthuman Perspective on the Human Rights Turn in Climate Law

In this chapter I have problematized the relation between international human rights law and climate change by pointing out that the asymmetry between those responsible for and those mostly affected by climate change may be explained by the system that prioritizes a certain (white) mode of being over other ones – a mode of being in which human rights are problematically grounded. I challenge the idea that we should understand climate change primarily as an existential threat to 'our' *universal* human right to life and the right to preserve 'our' family life, as was done in the Dutch *Urgenda* case, as this implicitly prioritizes white, human lives and a capitalist mode of living that sees the 'environment' as background and external problem. International human rights are grounded in a humanist and anthropocentric framework that upholds Modern dichotomies and systems of valuing, which are criticized for having led to many of our present struggles, including the climate struggle.

The problem with invoking a universal idea of 'Man' or 'anthropos' as homogenously facing the climate crisis (calling our age the Anthropocene) by referring to self-evident international human rights thus has two major limitations. First, it falsely suggests that humans can be distinguished from 'nature' (the nature-culture distinction) by their moral potentiality which grants them certain 'rights'. International human rights and their laws are inherently anthropocentric, grounded on the idea(l) of humanness as the capability to transcend the realm of 'nature', represented as a set of dead objects, through rational reflection. This feature of human rights necessarily narrows the focus of climate litigation to the right to life of humans and recasts the 'environment' as an external factor imposing a threat to the human right to family life.

Second, as ecofeminist, decolonial and posthuman critics have shown, naturalization went hand in hand with dehumanization in constructing the human (Man) that had the right to colonize, exploit, govern and control Others deemed as more approximate to (the state of) nature. This created a normative distinction between 'developed' and 'developing/underdeveloped', taking 'civilization' or Progress as the ultimate aim of 'humanity', and legitimizing not just the capitalist system of ecological destruction that led to the extreme vulnerability of the 'underdeveloped', but which also legitimizes holding on to the anthropocentric liberal framework of 'justly' distributing among sovereign states the 'costs' of the unwelcome limitations posed by the demand of 'sustainable development'.

This narrow focus thus has two important implications. On the one hand, focusing solely on the human rights of national citizens forecloses the possibility to recognize that humans are very differently affected by the present crisis (the importance of location). Both the causes and effects are distributed asymmetrically, creating the most severe damage for those that have contributed the least to climate change. This is masked by suggesting that 'we' in the 'Anthropocene' are equally in this together and that there are no lifeboats. The *Urgenda* case illustrated that even on a domestic level, overseas (former colonial) territories of the Netherlands were excluded from the Court's ruling, implying that the existing legal institutional framework does not necessarily benefit the most vulnerable, even when the case is largely based on international human rights articles.

On the other hand, the variety of ways in which people have understood being human in relation to nature is misrecognized and devalued when this relation is understood in universal terms, whereas we urgently need other systems of organizing life and different genres of being human in order to create a livable future for *all* humans and nonhumans. The focus on the anthropocentric and humanist inspired international human rights law discourse forecloses the possibility to recognize long-standing value systems that do not so radically divide nature from culture and emphasize the entanglements of different forms of life, stressing the importance of being good ancestors. Alternatively, a post-anthropocentric posthumanist approach that emphasizes responsibilities of care that emerge from human–nonhuman entanglements would provide a more fruitful direction for future legal climate strategies.

References

Adelman, S. (2015) 'Epistemologies of Mastery', in A. Grear and L. Kotzé (eds) *Research Handbook on Human Rights and the Environment*, Cheltenham: Edward Elgar, 9–27. DOI: https://doi.org/10.4337/9781782544432

Adelman, S. and B. Lewis (2018) 'Symposium Foreword: Rights-Based Approaches to Climate Change', *Transnational Environmental Law*, 7(1): 9–15. DOI: https://doi.org/10.1017/S2047102518000067

Arendt, H. (1994) *The Origins of Totalitarianism*, reprint ed., Bostin: Houghton Mifflin Harcourt.

Atapattu, S.A. and A. Schapper (2019) *Human Eights and the Environment: Key Issues*, Abingdon: Routledge.

Azoulay, A.A. (2019) *Potential History: Unlearning Imperialism*, London: Verso.

Barad, K. (2007) *Meeting the Universe Halfway: Quantum Physics and the Entanglement of Matter and Meaning*, Durham: Duke University Press.

Bos, G. and M. Düwell (eds) (2016) *Human Rights and Sustainability: Moral Responsibilities for the Future. Routledge Studies in Sustainability*, London; New York: Routledge.

Boyle, A.E. (2018) 'Climate Change, the Paris Agreement and Human Rights', *International and Comparative Law Quarterly*, 67(4): 759–77. DOI: https://doi.org/10.1017/S0020589318000222

Boyle, A.E. and M.R. Anderson (eds) (1996) *Human Rights Approaches to Environmental Protection*, Oxford and New York: Clarendon Press, Oxford University Press.

Braidotti, R. (2013) *The Posthuman*, Cambridge: Polity Press.

Braidotti, R. (2022) *Posthuman Feminism*, Cambridge: Polity Press.

Braidotti, R. and S. Bignall (eds) (2019) *Posthuman Ecologies: Complexity and Process After Deleuze*, New York and London: Rowman & Littlefield International.

Brand, U. and M. Wissen (2021) *The Imperial Mode of Living; Everyday Life and the Ecological Crisis of Capitalism*, New York and London: Verso.

Burgers, L. and T. Staal (2019) 'Climate Action as Positive Human Rights Obligation: The Appeals Judgment in Urgenda v. the Netherlands', in J.E. Nijman and W.G. Werner (eds) *Netherlands Yearbook of International Law 2018*, The Hague: T.M.C. Asser Press, 223–44. DOI: https://doi.org/10.1007/978-94-6265-331-3_10

Caney, S. (2014) 'Two Kinds of Climate Justice: Avoiding Harm and Sharing Burdens: Two Kinds of Climate Justice', *Journal of Political Philosophy*, 22(2): 125–49. DOI: https://doi.org/10.1111/jopp.12030

Catney, P. and T. Doyle (2011) 'The Welfare of Now and the Green (Post) Politics of the Future', *Critical Social Policy*, 31(2): 174–93. DOI: https://doi.org/10.1177/0261018310395921

Chakrabarty, D. (2021) *The Climate of History in a Planetary Age*, Chicago: The University of Chicago Press.

Davis, H. and Z. Todd (2017) 'On the Importance of a Date, or Decolonizing the Anthropocene', *ACME: An International Journal for Critical Geographies*, 16(4): 761–80.

Douzinas, C. (2007) *Human Rights and Empire: The Political Philosophy of Cosmopolitanism*, London: Routledge-Cavendish.

Douzinas, C. (2013) 'The Paradoxes of Human Rights', *Constellations*, 20(1): 51–67. https://doi.org/10.1111/cons.12021

Düwell, M., G. Bos and N. van Steenbergen (eds) (2018) *Towards the Ethics of a Green Future: The Theory and Practice of Human Rights for Future People*, London: Routledge.

Fraser, J. and L. Henderson (2022) 'The Human Rights Turn in Climate Change Litigation and Responsibilities of Legal Professionals', *Netherlands Quarterly of Human Rights*, 40(1): 3–11. DOI: https://doi.org/10.1177/09240519221085342

Gearty, C. (2010) 'Do Human Rights Help or Hinder Environmental Protection?', *Journal of Human Rights and the Environment*, 1(1): 7–22. DOI: https://doi.org/10.4337/jhre.2010.01.01

GNHRE (n.d.) 'Declaration on Human Rights and Climate Change'. https://gnhre.org/declaration-human-rights-climate-change/ (Accessed: 29 October 2021).

Gonzalez, C.G. (2015) 'Human Rights, Environmental Justice, and the North-South Divide', in A. Grear and L. Kotzé (eds) *Research Handbook on Human Rights and the Environment*, Cheltenham: Edward Elgar Publishing. DOI: https://doi.org/10.4337/9781782544432

Grear, A. (2011) 'The Vulnerable Living Order: Human Rights and the Environment in a Critical and Philosophical Perspective', *Journal of Human Rights and the Environment*, 2(1): 23–44.

Grear, A. (2015a) 'Deconstructing Anthropos: A Critical Legal Reflection on "Anthropocentric" Law and Anthropocene "Humanity" ', *Law and Critique*, 26(3): 225–49. DOI: https://doi.org/10.1007/s10978-015-9161-0

Grear, A. (2015b) 'The Closures of Legal Subjectivity', in A. Grear and L. Kotzé (eds) *Research Handbook on Human Rights and the Environment*, Cheltenham: Edward Elgar, 79–101. DOI: https://doi.org/10.4337/9781782544432

Grear, A. (2018) 'Human Rights and New Horizons? Thoughts Toward a New Juridical Ontology', *Science, Technology, & Human Values*, 43(1): 129–45. DOI: https://doi.org/10.1177/0162243917736140

Grear, A. and L. Kotzé (eds) (2015) *Research Handbook on Human Rights and the Environment*, Cheltenham: Edward Elgar Publishing. DOI: https://doi.org/10.4337/9781782544432

Haraway, D.J. (1991) 'A Cyborg Manifesto: Science, Technology, and Socialist-Feminism in the Late Twentieth Century', in *Simians, Cyborgs, and Women: The Reinvention of Nature*, New York: Routledge, 149–82.

Haraway, D.J. (2008) *When Species Meet*, Minneapolis: University of Minnesota Press (Posthumanities, 3).

Haraway, D.J. (2016) *Staying with the Trouble: Making Kin in the Chthulucene*, Durham: Duke University Press.

Hiskes, R.P. (2009) *The Human Right to a Green Future: Environmental Rights and Intergenerational Justice*, Cambridge: Cambridge University Press.

Hösli, A. (2021) 'Milieudefensie *et al* v. Shell: A Tipping Point in Climate Change Litigation Against Corporations?', *Climate Law*, 11(2): 195–209. DOI: https://doi.org/10.1163/18786561-11020005

Humphreys, S. (ed) (2010) *Human Rights and Climate Change*, Cambridge and New York: Cambridge University Press.

Humphreys, S. (2014) 'Climate Justice: The Claim of the Past', *Journal of Human Rights and the Environment*, 5: 134–48. DOI: https://doi.org/10.4337/jhre.2014.02.09

Hunt, L. (2007) *Inventing Human Rights: A History*, 1st ed., New York: W.W. Norton & Co.

Jackson, Z.I. (2020) *Becoming Human: Matter and Meaning in an Antiblack World*, New York: New York University Press.

Jansen, Y. and J. Leeuwenkamp (2023) 'The Pull to the Right of the Right, Religion, and the Ecological Crisis: Evaluating a Religio-Secular Perspective through a Reading of Bruno Latour's Late Work', In A. Omer, and J. Lupo (eds) *Religion, Populism, and Modernity: Confronting White Christian Nationalism and Racism* (Contending Modernities). University of Notre Dame Press, 182–222.

Jansen, Y., J. Leeuwenkamp and I. Urricelqui (2021) 'Posthumanism and the "Posterizing Impulse" ', in H. Paul and A. van Veldhuizen (eds) *Post-Everything: An*

Intellectual History of Post-Concepts, Manchester: Manchester University Press, 215–33. DOI: https://doi.org/10.7765/9781526148179.00020

Johnston, R. (2016) 'Lacking Rights and Justice in a Burning World: The Case for Granting Standing to Future Generations in Climate Change Litigation', *Tilburg Law Review*, 21(1), 31–51. DOI: https://doi.org/10.1163/22112596-02101002

Jones, E. (2021) 'Posthuman International Law and the Rights of Nature', *Journal of Human Rights and the Environment*, 12: 76–101. DOI: https://doi.org/10.1163/22112596-02101002

Kant, I. (2007) *Anthropology, History, and Education*, Edited by Robert B. Louden and Günter Zöller, Cambridge: Cambridge University Press.

Kapur, R. (2006) 'Human Rights in the 21st Century: Take a Walk on the Dark Side', *Sydney Law Review*, 28(4): 665–88.

Klein, N. (2016) 'Let Them Drown', *London Review of Books*, 1 June. www.lrb.co.uk/the-paper/v38/n11/naomi-klein/let-them-drown (Accessed: 3 November 2021).

Knox, J.H. (2014) 'Climate Ethics and Human Rights', *Journal of Human Rights and the Environment*, 5: 22–34.

Knox, J.H. and R. Pejan (eds) (2018) *The Human Right to a Healthy Environment*, 1st ed., Cambridge: Cambridge University Press. DOI: https://doi.org/10.1017/9781108367530

Kotzé, L.J. (2014) 'Human Rights and the Environment in the Anthropocene', *The Anthropocene Review*, 1(3): 252–75. DOI: https://doi.org/10.1177/2053019614547741

Krommendijk, J. (2022) 'Beyond *Urgenda* : The Role of the ECHR and Judgments of the ECtHR in Dutch Environmental and Climate Litigation', *Review of European, Comparative & International Environmental Law*, 31(1), 60–74. DOI: https://doi.org/10.1111/reel.12405

Kymlicka, W. (2018) 'Human Rights Without Human Supremacism', *Canadian Journal of Philosophy*, 48(6): 763–92. DOI: https://doi.org/10.1080/00455091.2017.1386481

Latour, B. (1993) *We Have Never Been Modern*, Cambridge: Harvard University Press.

Latour, B. (2004) *Politics of Nature: How to Bring the Sciences into Democracy*, Cambridge: Harvard University Press.

Latour, B. (2017) *Facing Gaia: Eight Lectures on the New Climatic Regime*, Cambridge: Polity.

Lawrence, P. and L. Köhler (2018) 'Representation of Future Generations Through International Climate Litigation: A Normative Framework', *German Yearbook of International Law*, 60(1): 639–66. DOI: https://doi.org/10.3790/gyil.60.1.639

Leib, L.H. (2011) *Human Rights and the Environment: Philosophical, Theoretical, and Legal Perspectives*, Leiden: Martinus Nijhoff Publishers.

Leijten, I. (2019) 'Human Rights v. Insufficient Climate Action: The *Urgenda* Case', *Netherlands Quarterly of Human Rights*, 37(2): 112–18. DOI: https://doi.org/10.1177/0924051919844375

Lessenich, S. (2019) *Living Well at Others' Expense: The Hidden Costs of Western Prosperity*, Medford: Polity.

Maldonado-Torres, N. (2017) 'On the Coloniality of Human Rights', *Revista Crítica de Ciências Sociais*, 114: 117–36. DOI: https://doi.org/10.4000/rccs.6793

Malm, A. and A. Hornborg (2014) 'The Geology of Mankind? A Critique of the Anthropocene Narrative', *The Anthropocene Review*, 1(1): 62–9. DOI: https://doi.org/10.1177/2053019613516291

Malm, A. and Zetkin Collective (2021) *White Skin, Black Fuel: On the Danger of Fossil Fascism*, London: Verso.

Merchant, C. (1989) *The Death of Nature: Women, Ecology, and the Scientific Revolution*, San Fransisco: HarperOne.

Mignolo, W.D. (2009) 'Who Speaks for the "Human" in Human Rights?', *Hispanic Issues Series*, 5(1): 7–24.

Minnerop, P. (2019) 'Integrating the "Duty of Care" Under the European Convention on Human Rights and the Science and Law of Climate Change: The Decision of The Hague Court of Appeal in the Urgenda Case', *Journal of Energy & Natural Resources Law*, 37(2): 149–79. DOI: https://doi.org/10.1080/02646811.2019.1584441

Moore, J.W. (2017) 'The Capitalocene, Part I: On the Nature and Origins of Our Eological Crisis', *The Journal of Peasant Studies*, 44(3): 594–630. DOI: https://doi.org/10.1080/03066150.2016.1235036

Nickel, J.W. (1993) 'The Human Right to a Safe Environment: Philosophical Perspectives on Its Scope and Justification Symposium: Earth Rights and Responsibilities: Human Rights and Environmental Protection', *Yale Journal of International Law*, 18(1): 281–96.

Nollkaemper, A. and L. Burgers (2020) 'The State of the Netherlands v. Urgenda (Neth. Sup. Ct.)', *International Legal Materials*, 59(5): 811–48. DOI: https://doi.org/10.1017/ilm.2020.39

Oksanen, M., A. Dodsworth and S. O'Doherty (eds) (2017) *Environmental Human Rights: A Political Theory Perspective*, 1st ed., Abingdon: Routledge. DOI: https://doi.org/10.4324/9781315188249

Phelan, A.L. (2020) 'The Environment, a Changing Climate, and Planetary Health', in A.L. Phelan (ed) *Foundations of Global Health & Human Rights*, Oxford: Oxford University Press, 417–38. DOI: https://doi.org/10.1093/oso/9780197528297.003.0020

Plumwood, V. (1993) *Feminism and the Mastery of Nature*, New York: Routledge.

Pulido, L. (2018) 'Racism and the Anthropocene', in G. Mitman, M. Armiero and R. Emmett (eds) *Future Remains: A Cabinet of Curiosities for the Anthropocene*, Chicago: University of Chicago Press, 116–28.

Resnick, E. (2021) 'The Limits of Resilience: Managing Waste in the Racialized Anthropocene', *American Anthropologist*, 123(2): 222–36. DOI: https://doi.org/10.1111/aman.13542

Rorty, R. (1998) 'Human Rights, Rationality, and Sentimentality', in *Truth and Progress: Philosophical Papers*, Cambridge: Cambridge University Press, 167–85. DOI: https://doi.org/10.1017/CBO9780511625404.010

Savaresi, A. and J. Auz (2019) 'Climate Change Litigation and Human Rights: Pushing the Boundaries', *Climate Law*, 9(3): 244–62. DOI: https://doi.org/10.1163/18786561-00903006

Savaresi, A. and J. Setzer (2021) 'Mapping the Whole of the Moon: An Analysis of the Role of Human Rights in Climate Litigation', *SSRN Electronic Journal* [Preprint]. DOI: https://doi.org/10.2139/ssrn.3787963

Schwartz, J. (2019) 'In "Strongest" Climate Ruling Yet, Dutch Court Orders Leaders to Take Action', *The New York Times*, 20 December. www.nytimes.com/2019/12/20/climate/netherlands-climate-lawsuit.html (Accessed: 23 June 2022).

Sealey-Huggins, L. (2017) '"1.5°C to Stay Alive": Climate Change, Imperialism and Justice for the Caribbean', *Third World Quarterly*, 38(11): 2444–63. DOI: https://doi.org/10.1080/01436597.2017.1368013

Sealey-Huggins, L. (2018) *The Climate Crisis Is a Racist Crisis: Structural Racism, Inequality and Climate Change*, Edited by A. Johnson, R. Joseph-Salisbury and B. Kamunge, London, UK: Zed Books, 99–113. www.worldcat.org/oclc/1061285873

Shue, H. (2014a) 'Changing Images of Climate Change: Human Rights and Future Generations', *Journal of Human Rights and the Environment*, 5: 50–64. DOI: https://doi.org/10.4337/jhre.2014.02.06

Shue, H. (2014b) *Climate Justice: Vulnerability and Protection*, 1st ed., Oxford: Oxford University Press.

Sinnott-Armstrong, W. (2010) 'It's Not My Fault: Global Warming and Individual Moral Obligations', in W. Sinnott-Armstrong (ed) *Climate Ethics*, Oxford: Oxford University Press. DOI: https://doi.org/10.1093/oso/9780195399622.003.0029

Skillington, T. (2017) *Climate Justice and Human Rights*, New York: Palgrave Macmillan. DOI: https://doi.org/10.1057/978-1-137-02281-3

Spivak, G.C. (2005) 'Use and Abuse of Human Rights', *Boundary* 2, 32(1): 131–89. DOI: https://doi.org/10.1215/01903659-32-1-131

Swyngedouw, E. (2010) 'Apocalypse Forever?', *Theory, Culture & Society*, 27(2–3): 213–32. DOI: https://doi.org/10.1177/0263276409358728

Townsend, D. (2020) *Human Dignity and the Adjudication of Environmental Rights*, Cheltenham: Edward Elgar Publishing. DOI: https://doi.org/10.4337/9781789905946

Tsing, A.L. (2015) *The Mushroom at the End of the World: On the Possibility of Life in Capitalist Ruins*, Princeton and Oxford: Princeton University Press.

Tully, J. (2014) 'Two Traditions of Human Rights', in M. Lutz-Bachmann and A. Nascimento (eds) *Human Rights, Human Dignity, and Cosmopolitan Ideals: Essays on Critical Theory and Human Rights*, London: Ashgate Publishing Limited, 139–57.

United Nations Environment Programme (UNEP) (2015) 'Climate Change and Human Rights'. www.unep.org/resources/report/climate-change-and-human-rights

United Nations Framework Convention on Climate Change. 'United Nations'. https://unfccc.int/resource/docs/convkp/conveng.pdf

Vanderheiden, S. (2008) *Atmospheric Justice: A Political Theory of Climate Change*, Oxford: Oxford University Press.

Westra, L. (2010) 'Climate Change and the Human Right to Water', *Journal of Human Rights and the Environment*, 1(2): 161–88.

Westra, L. and P.S. Wenz (eds) (1995) *Faces of Environmental Racism: Confronting Issues of Global Justice*, Lanham, MD: Rowman & Littlefield.

Wewerinke-Singh, M. and A. McCoach (2021) 'The State of the Netherlands v. Urgenda Foundation: Distilling Best Practice and Lessons Learnt for Future Rights-Based Climate Litigation', *Review of European, Comparative & International Environmental Law*, 30(2): 275–83. DOI: https://doi.org/10.1111/reel.12388

Williams, J. (2021) *Climate Change is Racist: Race, Privilege and the Struggle for Climate Justice*, London: Icon Books.
Wynter, S. (2003) 'Unsettling the Coloniality of Being/Power/Truth/Freedom: Towards the Human, After Man, Its Overrepresentation – An Argument', *CR: The New Centennial Review*, 3(3): 257–337. DOI: https://doi.org/10.1353/ncr.2004.0015
Yusoff, K. (2018) *A Billion Black Anthropocenes or None*, Minneapolis: University of Minnesota Press.

INDEX

Note: Page numbers in *italic* indicate a figure on the corresponding page.

For Product Safety Concerns and Information please contact our EU representative GPSR@taylorandfrancis.com
Taylor & Francis Verlag GmbH, Kaufingerstraße 24, 80331 München, Germany

www.ingramcontent.com/pod-product-compliance
Ingram Content Group UK Ltd.
Pitfield, Milton Keynes, MK11 3LW, UK
UKHW020154200926
475702UK00016B/2696
* 9 7 8 1 0 3 2 0 4 4 0 4 0 *